CHARLES TAYLOR AND LIBERIA

ABOUT THE AUTHOR

Colin Waugh grew up in Scotland and was educated in the UK, before pursuing a career which has ranged across post-conflict work, investment management, politics, writing and publishing. He has lived and worked in several African countries over the past twenty years while visiting many others and his assignments, both public and private, have increasingly included projects with a bearing on Africa.

CHARLES TAYLOR AND LIBERIA

AMBITION AND ATROCITY IN AFRICA'S LONE STAR STATE

COLIN M. WAUGH

Zed Books
LONDON | NEW YORK

To Cynthia

Charles Taylor and Liberia: Ambition and Atrocity in Africa's Lone Star State
was first published in 2011 by
Zed Books Ltd, 7 Cynthia Street, London N1 9JF, UK
and Room 400, 175 Fifth Avenue, New York, NY 10010, USA

www.zedbooks.co.uk

Copyright © Colin M. Waugh 2011

Photo credits: cover image, pp. 128, 137 © Pascal Guyot/AFP/Getty Images; pp. 14, 62 © AFP/Getty Images; pp. 38, 41, 185 © Colin M. Waugh; pp. 79, 87 © Larry C. Price; p. 95 © Keystone-France/Gamma-Keystone via Getty Images; p. 102 © Plymouth House of Corrections; p. 166 © Peter Strandberg; pp. 171, 175 © Christophe Simon/AFP/Getty Images; p. 183 © Getty Images; pp. 216, 263 © Issouf Sanogo/AFP/Getty Images; p. 246 © Patrick Bernard/AFP/Getty Images; p. 320 © Ato Kwamena Dadzie/AFP/Getty Images; p. 339 Guido Benschop/AFP/Getty Images.

The right of Colin M. Waugh to be identified as the author of this work has been asserted by him in accordance with the Copyright, Designs and Patents Act, 1988

Designed and typeset in Monotype Bulmer
by illuminati, Grosmont
Index by John Barker
Cover designed by Alice Marwick
Maps designed by Phil Green
Printed and bound by CPI Group (UK) Ltd,
Croydon, CRO 4YY

Distributed in the USA exclusively by Palgrave Macmillan, a division of St Martin's Press, LLC, 175 Fifth Avenue, New York, NY 10010, USA

All rights reserved. No part of this publication may be reproduced, stored in a retrieval system or transmitted in any form or by any means, electronic, mechanical, photocopying or otherwise, without the prior permission of Zed Books Ltd.

A catalogue record for this book is available from the British Library
Library of Congress Cataloging in Publication Data available

ISBN 978 1 84813 848 3 hb
ISBN 978 1 84813 847 6 pb

CONTENTS

ABBREVIATIONS	vii
ACKNOWLEDGEMENTS	ix
Introduction	1

PART ONE The land of the freed

ONE	Foundations of a settlement	13
TWO	The spirit of Liberia	35
THREE	Confronting the old order	56

PART TWO From dictatorship to anarchy

FOUR	Sergeant-in-charge: Samuel Doe's presidency	85
FIVE	Doe's decline, Taylor's travels	106
SIX	Charles Taylor's war	123
SEVEN	The pantomime of peace	153

PART THREE	Power in Greater Liberia	
EIGHT	Greater Liberia: prospering and assimilating	181
NINE	Sierra Leone: Liberia's sister revolution	202
TEN	Election victory and the Taylor presidency	228
PART FOUR	Fallout from a revolution	
ELEVEN	A government embattled	259
TWELVE	Relations with the United States	287
THIRTEEN	Liberian legacy	310
FOURTEEN	Justice à la carte	334
	NOTES	351
	BIBLIOGRAPHY	360
	INDEX	364

ABBREVIATIONS

ACDL	Association for Constitutional Democracy in Liberia
ACS	American Colonization Society
AFL	Armed Forces of Liberia
AFRC	Armed Forces Revolutionary Council (Sierra Leone)
ATU	Anti Terrorist Unit
AU	African Union
BTC	Barclay Training Centre
CRC	Central Revolutionary Command, 1994 breakaway faction of NPFL
ECOMOG	Economic Community of West African States Monitoring Group
ECOWAS	Economic Community of West African States
ICC	International Criminal Court
IGNU	Interim Government of National Unity
INPFL	Independent National Patriotic Front of Liberia
LNTG	Liberian National Transitional Government
LPC	Liberian Peace Council
LUDF	Liberian United Defence Force
LURD	Liberians United for Reconciliation and Democracy
MDM	Movement for the Redemption of Liberian Muslims
MOJA	Movement for Justice in Africa
NPFL	National Patriotic Front of Liberia
NPP	National Patriotic Party

NPRAG	National Patriotic Reconstruction Assembly Government
OAU	Organization of African Unity
PAE	Pacific Architects and Engineers, US private security firm
PAL	Progressive Alliance of Liberia
PRC	People's Redemption Council
RUF	Revolutionary United Front (Sierra Leone)
SCSL	Special Court for Sierra Leone
TRC	Truth and Reconciliation Commission of Liberia
TWP	True Whig Party
ULAA	Union of Liberian Associations in the Americas
ULIMO	United Liberation Movement for Democracy in Liberia
ULIMO-K	ULIMO-Alhaji Kromah, post-1994 ULIMO splinter
ULIMO-J	ULIMO- Roosevelt Johnson, post-1994 ULIMO splinter
UN	United Nations
UNAMSIL	United Nations Mission in Sierra Leone
UNMIL	United Nations Mission in Liberia (previously UNOMIL)
UNOMIL	United Nations Observer Mission in Liberia
UP	Unity Party

ACKNOWLEDGEMENTS

While much of the research for this book was carried out between early 2009 and late 2010, the experiences and contacts which provided the inspiration to undertake the project date from the mid-1990s. Across that span of time I received ideas and information from a wide range of Liberians and other West Africans, both professionals and ordinary people, living and working in their home countries, in the United States, the United Kingdom and elsewhere. Those who were in the region during the period of the Liberian Civil War and the Charles Taylor presidency provided particularly useful contemporary accounts, commentary and insights.

During recent visits to Liberia for research I have been grateful for the support of Joseph Varney in planning and logistics, which ensured smooth movement around the countryside; in the United States, past and current members of the ULAA provided background, contacts and guidance, while some of Charles Taylor's former administration and family as well as peers cooperated with interviews. The International Committee of the Red Cross and the US embassy in Liberia also lent assistance.

In Ghana the comments and critique provided by Akyaaba Addai-Sebo greatly improved the quality and accuracy of the manuscript, while other friends there kept an active interest in the progress of the work and provided helpful material.

From the international community Steve McLaughlin was an early supporter of this project in both Monrovia and Washington DC, giving helpful contacts in the United States over a sustained period of time, while Maddie Klugman's research into international media sources added valuable inputs. Two productive writing spells were spent in Mozambique with the encouragement and companionship of Ana Paula Santos.

The meticulous editing work of Katharine Mann helped to refine the structure of the book and polish the final product; Phillip Green's long hours spent in map design and production resulted in some excellent illustrations of the often complex political geography of the region and Liberia's military campaigns; and last but not least I express my appreciation to publishers Zed Books, and for the support of Ken Barlow in particular, which allowed this challenging project to get under way and to reach successful publication.

INTRODUCTION

This is a story about Liberia during the times of the man who, for people outside that country, has become its best known former president, Charles McArthur Ghankay Taylor. It is equally the story of how Charles Taylor first served, then used and abused his country. It is a story of intrigue, of escape and of survival in times of war. It is about the quest for power and enrichment for the few, among whom Taylor was the master. But it is only the beginning of the story of the many ordinary Liberians, whose suffering and sacrifice started before Taylor came to power and did not end after his departure. For a brief moment he represented hope for many of them, but for a much longer time he represented a pain and anguish much greater than those they had known before.

As a visitor spending many months working and travelling in the late 1990s and early 2000s in three of Liberia's neighbours, Sierra Leone, Côte d'Ivoire and Ghana, the impact of the country's conflict was all too visible. The presence of large Liberian refugee populations in the cities and inside the borders of these countries helped demonstrate why their governments' concern for bringing the conflict under control was so urgent. That was an issue of interest for those in my host countries but not an immediate involvement for me. Why a book about Liberia in the time of Charles Taylor, when in fact of all the countries affected Liberia was, until then, the one that I had set foot in the least?

I gained an interest in the story of Charles Taylor and Liberia at first through a personal relationship, and through contact over several years with young Liberians, during extended working assignments in both Ghana and Sierra Leone. Living in exile among their peers, these young refugees had fled by land, by sea and occasionally by air to a handful of neighbouring countries, part of a whole segment of society dispersed across the region during the civil war years of the 1990s and again during the renewed warfare and violence at the close of the Taylor era in 2002–03. Some who fled Liberia at first for Sierra Leone were forced to move again as the war in that country erupted and re-erupted, displacing them to Guinea, Côte d'Ivoire, Ghana or further afield.

The Taylor enigma

When working in the region in 1997 I was fascinated by the apparent willing acceptance, if not overwhelming embrace, by those recent exiles and the Liberian electorate at home of the candidacy of Charles Ghankay Taylor for president. As informed as any, initially at least, the expatriate Liberians welcomed his rule in the full knowledge that he was largely responsible for their plight and the suffering of many others who had stayed at home.

Charles Taylor was an ambitious and intelligent Liberian from a modest background who succeeded in gaining an overseas education and used it to enter politics. He started well, and had a natural charm and a determination which produced results and gained him a following. But he had a ruthless side to his character and an appetite for strong-arm tactics; in the context of Samuel Doe's Liberia where democratic methods were suppressed, this quickly translated into violence, and the ability to deploy violence translated into power.

Despite promising beginnings in his career Charles Taylor finished badly, and his failure as a leader had tragic consequences for Liberia. His early efforts to bring about change in his homeland were soon eclipsed by ambition for material gain, with scant regard for the development of Liberia and the welfare of the majority of Liberian people. He was a shrewd and effective political campaigner but when elected president he proved to be a poor manager both of his deputies and of his country. Soon after he assumed the presidency, those whom he had antagonized on his path to power conspired against him and, with the help of the most powerful international allies, closed in on Charles Taylor's Liberia.

Taylor was a revolutionary, a freedom fighter who went on to become the head of a gangster government. At a time when only gangsters held power in his country, he was the strongest and most successful among them. The forces he commanded were responsible for many despicable acts against society and humanity, and for their acts Taylor is ultimately accountable. He was a patriot who in the end became an international pariah, when he was singled out by a selective application of international justice to stand trial for his role in wartime Sierra Leone.

The Taylor story puzzled me as an intriguing phenomenon, a political enigma. But also, as the young Liberians displaced abroad went about their new lives, I was impressed by their universal refusal to be downtrodden and dispirited by the conditions in which they found themselves. The other side of that positive impression was the observation of their frequent unwillingness to show either gratitude or deference to the inhabitants of their host countries, to whom after all they owed their survival. That was perplexing to me at first – but again it prompted an exploration into a different aspect of the background to the conflict, one which drew on the history of Liberia and its wider position in the economics and society of the West African region.

A further, more pleasurable, stimulus for this project was the usually enjoyable opportunity to interact with Liberians at work, socially or in the course of random encounters around the region. It was hard not to be drawn to the friendly, boisterous nature of Liberians at play and to marvel at their embrace of the opportunity for the special kind of decadence afforded by refugee life, as well as straining to follow their bantering usage of Liberian English, which to the outsider of the mother tongue is at first an almost incomprehensible form of speech. For a linguistic challenge, give me Amharic, Kinyarwanda or Shangana any time. Nevertheless, many of its users proudly referred to it as 'Standard English' rather than what is in fact Liberia's very own variant of coastal West African pidgin, a corrupted hybrid dish of raw Atlantic African English with a thick Krio base, with just a hint of French garnish on the side.

Context of the war and definitions

The years between the initial attack by Charles Taylor's rebel forces, the National Patriotic Front of Liberia (NPFL), in late 1989 and the formal ending of hostilities with the staging of democratic elections in July 1997 are what is most usually referred to as the period of the Liberian Civil War. However, widespread civil conflict in Liberia began well before 1989, with the launching of the Samuel Doe regime's ethnically motivated massacres of its own population to some degree before the elections of 1985 but unquestionably thereafter.

For many living in the country at the time, the true beginning of Liberia's civil conflict was the unsuccessful post-election coup led by Thomas Quiwonkpa, who more than anyone can be considered the 'father' of the NPFL before the movement became so overwhelmingly dominated by Charles Taylor after mid-1990. From 1985 onwards, the Samuel Doe administration effectively began a systematic purge of targeted non-Krahn actors in government and society, while giving its army free rein to kill Nimba County citizens and loot their properties in periodic flare-ups of persecution. It also signalled the end of any pretence that Doe's 1980 'revolution' had been the beginning of a period of opportunity for all Liberians and the end of ethnically biased government in Monrovia.

The reality of the overthrow of a century and a half of settler-dominated rule in Liberia was that a repressive and elitist group represented by the True Whig Party (TWP) had been replaced by an even more ethnically motivated, more violent and more tyrannical regime, whose foreign backers, the United States, were willing to turn a blind eye to almost every atrocity that its African puppet committed.

INTRODUCTION 5

Equally, when war came to a temporary halt in late 1990, although there were to be over a dozen broken or ignored ceasefires and peace agreements during the following five years, there were also long stretches between hostilities when fighting ceased totally. Even when the battles raged, the fighting was mostly confined either to relatively limited regions of the countryside, or to assaults on the capital, Monrovia. Much of the 1990–94 conflict period was characterized by a stalemate regarding control of the capital, while other regions remained under the relatively stable occupation of the NPFL, and latterly also by regional West African peacekeeping forces and the other armed factions in the struggle. Thus, to characterize the period as one of seven years of constant fighting in Liberia would not give an accurate portrayal of events.

Liberia's civil conflict flared again, however, between 1999 and 2003, this time while Charles Taylor was president of the country and it was he who was defending the capital against mostly Guinean-backed rebels of the Liberians United for Reconciliation and Democracy (LURD) in an increasingly desperate struggle to remain in power. When Liberians talk of the various 'Battles of Monrovia', they refer to the first battle as the 1990 assault on the capital, followed by Taylor's 'Operation Octopus' in October 1992 and then the Easter 1996 uprising sparked by the attempted arrest of the prominent factional leader and Taylor rival, Roosevelt Johnson. Again, Liberians often make references to 'World War Three' when referring to the battles which took place in and around the capital during the final assaults by LURD in June 2003.

In colloquial speech Monrovians are often given to dark humour and deep irony when lamenting aspects of their plight, using phrases such as the 'Imported Government of No Use' to describe the puppet regime (Interim Government of National Unity – IGNU) foisted upon Monrovians from 1990 to 1994, or the phrase 'Every Car or Moving Object Gone' when talking about the troops of the Economic Community of West African States Monitoring Group (ECOMOG), the peacekeeping-cum-looting force imposed upon them by Nigeria and other regional neighbours during the same period.

The Liberian Civil War in its popular, narrower definition was started by Charles Taylor and a group of his close supporters at the head of the NPFL; as such he can rightly be held responsible for the death, trauma and destruction which followed. But from another point of view and certainly in the minds of those Liberians who were already being persecuted over a period of years, the actions of the NPFL in 1989 were seen as an intervention on their behalf to prevent a creeping genocide being carried out by the Liberian government against a significant segment of its own population.

In this sense, there were similarities at the outset between the intervention of the NPFL in Liberia in 1989 and other African resistance movements which succeeded against oppressive dictatorships. Yoweri Museveni's National Resistance Movement in Uganda blossomed against the backdrop of Milton Obote's rigged elections and ethnically based brutality. The invasion of Rwanda by Paul Kagame's Revolutionary Patriotic Front during the Rwandan genocide of 1994 overcame a regime bent on ethnic slaughter in an even more extreme set of circumstances.[1] However, in Liberia, despite early similarities with these conflicts, once the nature and methods of Charles Taylor's fighting forces became evident to the world, and once he proved unable to win the lightening military victory over the people's oppressor which Paul Kagame did in Rwanda in mid-1994, the similarity quickly ended.

The assertion was often made by the NPFL leader in the early days that the sole objective of his campaign was (he hoped) a short, sharp, effective war leading to the removal of a murderous tyrant, after which the Liberian people could choose their own leader. Initially, this seemed credible enough, although it was also clear to many from Taylor's actions and utterances in his early years that winning the presidency of Liberia for himself was his true goal. Whatever Taylor's ultimate aim, his objective of waging a brief and decisive campaign, followed by the restoration of civilian order, turned out to be far from the reality.

That is the first major difference from the 1994 Rwandan Civil War, which lasted little more than a hundred days and after which there was a clear victor and a fresh start for the country, no matter how bitter the fallout for the losers and the survivors. In Liberia, intermittent conflict and temporary administrative arrangements in lieu of elected government were the lot of the Liberian people for a further seven years following Charles Taylor's armed return. But even after Taylor's election, and even to no small extent after his departure from office, the Liberian people continued to suffer under a political elite more bent on personal power and enrichment than willing to learn from the mistakes of the past and work for their country's future.

The other major difference in the Liberian conflict was that, with the exception of the defending troops of Samuel Doe, the Armed Forces of Liberia (AFL), throughout the period, the struggle was not between conventional armies, but for the most part between informal brigades of untrained fighters, many of them teenagers or children and only a minority of whom had any exposure to professional military training. After the initial period of rapid territorial gains in 1990, with the exception of the breakaway Independent National Patriotic Front of Liberia (INPFL), almost none of the combatant groups displayed any discipline or respect for humanity in their treatment of civilian populations. None was paid wages, instead being given 'looting rights' by their leaders, an aspect which in itself helped contribute to prolonging the conflict. In Rwanda, by contrast, while there were massive wartime atrocities on both sides, the conquering RPF army maintained a degree of internal order and discipline throughout, which was never in evidence among any of the major warring parties, government or rebel, during Liberia's war.

The United States and its foreign policy play a prominent part in this story. First, because the USA was at the heart of Liberia's creation and remained intrinsically involved with it for the first century and a half of the country's existence; second, because of geopolitics, when Liberia came to be the strongest African ally of the USA during the Cold War years; third, because Charles Taylor was so in awe of America and spent the bulk of his young adult years there in education, work and activism, only returning to play a role in his own country's political affairs for the first time after the age of 30; fourth, because, when the country was plunged into a decade and a half of conflict, and when most Liberians as well as many foreigners expected the USA to intervene directly, it stood on the sidelines offering only occasional half-hearted covert initiatives and humanitarian assistance; and lastly because, when Taylor had finally overcome all the obstacles to taking power in his own right, legally and democratically as well as militarily, it was the USA that ultimately ensured that he would not be allowed to remain in that office. Nor would he be allowed to remain at liberty, because his transgressions were deemed to have become too great for his country and the world to bear.

In the Samuel Doe era, with an abundance of ignorance, alternative priorities and an abject lack of interest in the plight of its orphaned African grandchild, the USA first ignored Liberia, then condoned and ultimately financed its tyrant's takeover, later leading to humanitarian catastrophe in the continent's oldest republic. The geopolitical priorities of the United States and the need for loyal African proxies to help stem the spread of communism on the continent were the imperatives of the dramatically changing Liberian political environment in which Taylor came to maturity – and through which he planned to manoeuvre himself towards power. Ronald Reagan and Assistant Secretary of State for Africa Chester Crocker became the main supporting actors in an unfolding drama in which Charles Taylor already planned to write himself a leading role.

A country destroyed and a region torn

The story of Liberia is unique, as is the story of its former president who is the subject of this book. Liberians both believed in him and then despised him for who he was and what he did to their country. He brought it inspiration and powerful leadership; he consistently charmed his people and first seduced them into following him, then turned their lives into a living hell. With Taylor's impact on Liberia and West Africa, the country's story has acquired a new and compelling aspect that has to be told; but even before his time and without his huge importance, Liberia itself is worthy of the many books that have been written about it, just because of its special position in Western as well as African history.

Liberia is special for its role as a resettlement homeland in the ending of slavery; it is special for its role in American social history and in the history of the black race; it is special for its unique and complex indigenous life and customs, described briefly in this book although only superficially understood in the telling; and now, most recently, it is special for its role in the evolution of international justice, as a pioneering legal forum deliberates on the guilt or innocence of an elected head of state for crimes allegedly committed against a neighbouring state, in violation of international laws.

The most recent events narrated in this work relate to the trial proceedings in the Special Court for Sierra Leone, and are the main focus of Chapter 14. During Taylor's testimony as well as through his responses under cross-examination, new light was shed on lesser-known aspects of his career, and material from the trial transcripts has been included as appropriate throughout the text. Taylor denied the charges brought against him and rejected many of the prosecution's allegations. Many of the exchanges between Taylor and the prosecution became heated, and the reader should recognize that many of his statements made in the course of the proceedings remain unsubstantiated, as well as being contradicted by others both inside and outside the court.

Although I am not a Liberian and have not spent extensive time in the country, this project has nevertheless always been a compelling one for me. I am reminded of the reflections of the Nigerian statesman Nnamde Azikiwe as he was drawn to learn about Liberia in the early twentieth century, also having never visited the land. Fascinated with the land as a young writer and aspiring public servant, he said: 'Therefore I vowed to study Liberian diplomacy and history, to understand them in such detail, without ever stepping on the shores of Liberia, that Liberians themselves would marvel at this feat!'

Whether or not Liberians will marvel at the account contained in these pages I leave up to them; and my handful of visits to their land over the past decade have only served to strengthen my interest

CHARLES TAYLOR AND LIBERIA

in their story as well as caused me to ponder more deeply what the final end game of Charles Taylor in their nation's fate might be. Whatever that role and however the current issues of accountability, legality, diplomacy and reconstruction resolve themselves, for me as a writer the allure of their land as a compelling topic for literature can never be diminished.

PART ONE

THE LAND OF THE FREED

ONE

FOUNDATIONS OF A SETTLEMENT

> To those who speak of a Pan-African Union, I ask:
> What are we supposed to share? Each other's poverty?
>
> Félix Houphouët-Boigny, president of Côte d'Ivoire[1]

End of the Tubman era

In Harley Street's London Clinic, on 23 July 1971, Liberia's president William Vancarat Shadrach Tubman lay dead from a haemorrhage, the complication of a recent prostate operation. He had served as president for over twenty-seven years. His passing signalled the beginning of the end of a long period of single-party rule in the Republic of Liberia. Thanks to its extensive rubber plantations and mineral resources his small West African homeland had prospered handsomely, surpassed by few others in Africa for its economic growth rate. Days after Tubman's death, the reins of power were handed over to his deputy, William Tolbert, who had already served for over a decade as vice president of the tropical country of 3 million inhabitants, with an area the size of Tennessee, or a little more than Ireland and Wales combined. It appeared as a picture of stability in government, a smooth transition of power from ruler to deputy, unusual by the standards of an African continent where

PRESIDENT TUBMAN, NOVEMBER 1956, WEARING A LIBERIAN TRIBAL CHIEF'S COSTUME

the transition from one head of state to the next was increasingly brought about by armed coups rather than through a peaceful dynastic succession.

Already unique on the continent as Africa's oldest independent nation, since 1847 a self-governing republic, never colonized by any European power, Liberia was ruled for over a century by the representatives of a single political dynasty, the True Whig Party (TWP). The elite which governed Liberia was composed of the descendants of freed American slaves, known as the Americo-Liberians, who were resettled to Africa in the early nineteenth century with the political blessing and financial support of the US government.

Presidents Tubman and Tolbert were descendants of the settler stock of the nation's founding fathers, whose emigration to Africa had been organized by a body called the American Colonization Society (ACS). In July 1971, other African nations were completing their first decade of independence, still economically underdeveloped and politically immature. Some espoused pan-African idealism, while others experimented with socialist economics. Nearly all continued to depend on overseas assistance for survival – whether the support was from recently departed European colonial masters or from new partners in the East.

But Liberia was different. When William Tubman died, his successor just carried on the work of government and the running of the economy, whose official currency was the US dollar, and whose flagship economic enterprise, the Firestone rubber plantation, was the largest of its kind in the world, at the time encompassing a million acres under cultivation and employing over 10,000 hard-currency-earning Liberians just outside the country's capital, Monrovia. William Tubman's settler predecessors first arrived on West Africa's shores over 150 years earlier, as the result of an initiative of the United States government of the day. On 3 March 1819, the US Congress passed an act to enable the return to the African continent of any Africans recaptured from slaving vessels on the high seas by the American navy. The US government provided $100,000 in funding for the measure.

In February of the following year, a son of freed African slaves from Virginia named Elijah Johnson set sail from New York harbour with some ninety others, mostly African-American freemen, in a ship called the *Elizabeth*, bound for Sierra Leone on the west coast of West Africa, where there was a British colonial settlement. They hoped to find the land upon which to establish a colony for returnees of African origin from the United States. The only white people on the voyage were three ACS agents who accompanied them to handle the administrative and financial aspects of the expedition.

Freetown, Sierra Leone's principal trading port, was also populated by former slaves freed from European ships crossing the Atlantic Ocean, and the new arrivals hoped that their plans would meet with the local authorities' approval. Explaining their mission to their British hosts, the voyagers were not made welcome, however. The incumbent governor Charles McCarthy offered them neither hospitality nor encouragement.

On 8 March 1820, they left and sailed to Sherbro Island, along the coast to the south of Freetown. Here the crew was stricken by malaria, which killed all of the white agents as well as twenty-two of the African-American voyagers and they soon left, exhausted and landless, returning to Fourah Bay outside Freetown.[2]

Shotgun settlement in the palaver hut

The following year, the settlers who had arrived on the *Elizabeth* were still based outside Freetown, when a second ACS party arrived aboard a ship called the *Nautilus*, under the command of Captain R.F. Stockton.

The new settlers sailed to Cape Mount on the other side of the Mano river estuary and came ashore, meeting an African ruler, King Peter of the Dey tribe. Trading some goods in exchange for supplies, the white agents, on behalf of the settlers who remained on board ship, then explained their aspirations to found a settlement and negotiated for the purchase of land on which they might set up their new homeland. The freemen came with their high visions of a religious society carrying their Bibles and praying often along the way.

All that did not impress, nor did it entice, the king of the Dey, who was a big slave trader himself. Peter was interested in trade, but was not at all interested in the permanent presence of these anti-slavery religious pioneers from thousands of miles away. Indeed, at the time the Americans arrived he was in the process of negotiating for the sale of some of his own captive countrymen to a French frigate, also moored nearby.

King Peter and the local tribes were nothing unusual in that regard. Many of the tribes along the coast had for decades engaged in a brisk business in slavery with various different European traders and the sudden arrival of these 'free' former slaves could be highly disruptive to the business they had developed. King Peter sent the settlers on their way. They then sailed further south down the coast, coming next to Grand Bassa on 9 April. Here they encountered another native leader, King Jack Benn at Jumbotown, and once again traded with him, offered gifts, but received a similar reception to their proposal to settle.

Retracing his steps, Stockton sailed back and arranged a meeting with King Peter and the leaders of other tribes, the Mambe and the Bassa, in King Peter's village in Montserrado, on 15 December 1821. Pulling out their pistols and pointing them at King Peter's head, the pioneers gave their ultimatum to the King of the Dey at gunpoint: an agreement was finally struck. In exchange for about $300 worth of beads, tobacco, gunpowder and guns, the settlers received 130 acres of land on Cape Montserrado on which to found their colony.

On nearby Providence Island they finally raised the American flag, symbolically claiming a home. It was here that Elijah Johnson, leader of the first expedition that had left some twenty-two months earlier, uttered the immortal words: 'for two long years I have sought a home; here I have found one, here I remain.' That declaration by Johnson (one of whose sons went on to become the eleventh president of Liberia) is enshrined in Liberian history, and the words even became mandatory learning in the curriculum in Liberian schools.[3]

The Dey, still reluctant partners in their recent land deal with the settlers, soon launched an attack on the newcomers. The colonists, led by Elijah Johnson, marshalled superior firepower of their own and beat back the natives' attacks. Having outgunned the Dey and holding on to their outpost, they were at last able to establish a city in 1822, which they initially called Christopolis. Fighting against the natives continued, however, with the local tribes continuing to harass the new settlers as they tried to build their city on the cape. After months of skirmishing, the Dey launched an all-out attack on the colony in November 1822, which threatened to wipe out the settlers.

However, the British Navy was still patrolling the coast and landed some officers and sailors who succeeded in negotiating a truce between the Dey and the colonists. Still with no formal presence on the virgin shores to the east of Sierra Leone, the British also had an interest in the new territory, doubtless with a view to adding it to their expanding colonial empire in West Africa before the French laid claim to it. The American settlers, despite being desperate for help, however refused to submit to British rule, while nonetheless accepting the British protection in the meantime.

According to legend, the commander of a British gunboat initially approached Johnson offering to send for additional help if the new colony would agree to raise the British flag. Johnson famously replied: 'We want no flagstaff put up here that will cost more to take down again than it will to whip the natives.'[4]

Mythical Matilda Newport

An important date in the settlers' calendar, which dates back to their earliest skirmishes with the native population, was Matilda

Newport Day, 1 December, celebrated by Americo-Liberians right up until the 1970s, in an undisguised commemoration of supremacy over the native population of their own country. Until that time, the minority Americo-Liberian community still remembered a patriotic figure (who many native Liberians say was entirely fictitious), who, as the story goes, prevailed single-handedly over an attacking band of hundreds of indigenous Liberians almost two centuries ago.

The legend that was passed down in Americo-Liberian lore was that during the battle of Crown Hill between the colonists and an attacking throng of native Liberians in 1822, Matilda Newport, a formidable settler woman, went back to a cannon on the hilltop which her defending forces had just abandoned in retreat, and then, using all her cunning, turned the settlers' defeat into a historic victory. It is said that she fired the cannon at the natives using a coal from her pipe, annihilating a large number of the attackers and scattering the remainder, after which the battle was won.[5] Not surprisingly, native Liberian scholars dispute the story and some have even questioned the existence of Matilda Newport, let alone her incredible feat of bravery in battle.

In the only recorded history of the events of that time, written by Jehudi Ashmun, a white ACS pioneer who had been on board the *Elizabeth* in 1822 (the ship Matilda Newport is said to have arrived on) and who acted as the colony's governor from 1824 to 1828, there is no mention of a Matilda Newport or the heroic events of such a figure at that battle. And yet the story was often repeated, and indeed taught, in Liberian schools as part of the history of the country.[6]

The new settlement was soon renamed Monrovia after the US president who encouraged its creation, James Monroe, himself a founding father in his own still fledgling United States of America. Over the following century, as European powers rushed to colonize the surrounding territories, then struggled to control them and exploit them commercially, settler Liberia remained independent and relatively underdeveloped within a European-dominated coastline of commodity trading ports. With next to no administrative structure in its hinterland, Liberia was run like a large plantation on the west coast of Africa with a way of life largely modelled on that of the American South, from which most of the country's settlers had arrived. The neighbouring possessions had names like the Gold Coast, the Ivory Coast and the Slave Coast, while Liberia itself started life as the Pepper Coast, also known as the Grain Coast, as it became famous for the melegueta pepper, or the 'grain of paradise' to those who sought it.

For the first twenty-five years of its existence, the new settlement was administered by the agents of the ACS, temporarily seconded white men who supervised the growth of the territory without sharing any particular aspirations for its future. However, with the need to secure its commercial interests, raise taxes and negotiate with foreign states, particularly in competition with the British and French presences in the area, the settlements' leaders moved to transform Liberia into a sovereign republic.

In 1845, a constitution was drafted with the support of the ACS and in 1847 Liberia became the continent's first independent republic, some 110 years ahead of Ghana, the second country in sub-Saharan Africa to achieve self-rule. Liberia adopted its own constitution, based on that of the United States, together with a national seal, inscribed with the inspiring slogan 'The love of liberty brought us here'. The period of stewardship by the white agents came to an end and Joseph Jenkins Roberts became the republic's first president, serving from 1848 until 1855. A Liberian national flag was created. Today it contains a single white star on a blue background and eleven red and white stripes for the eleven original signatories of Liberia's independence; a blue canton symbolizing the continent of Africa and a white star representing the freedom of the former slaves who came to found the country.

President Roberts was the first non-white leader to represent the independent settler colony after a quarter of a century of white ACS governors, but, although a poor immigrant from Virginia, he was also hardly black, rather a mulatto or an 'octoroon' as he is referred to in historical accounts.

The second president of Liberia, Stephen Benson (1856–1864), was also mulatto, and for the next several decades there developed a struggle for supremacy in government between the black settlers

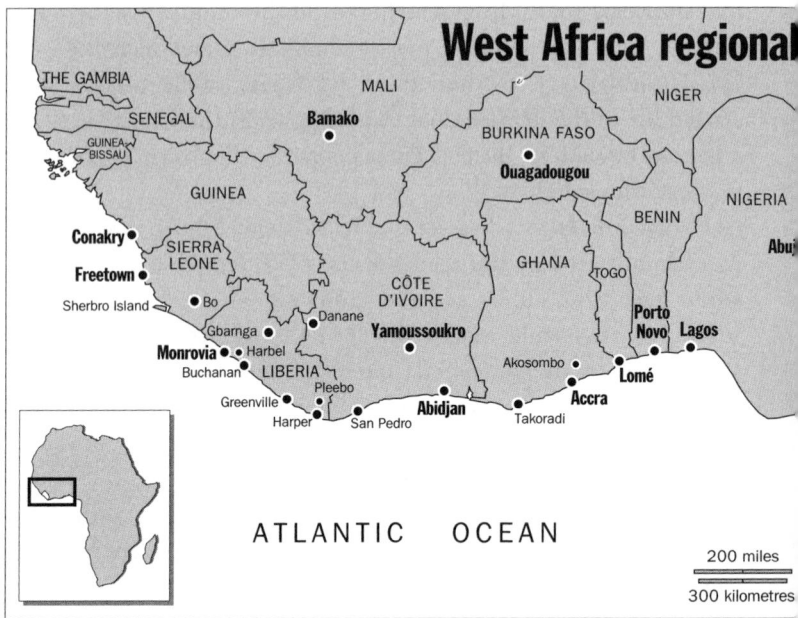

and the mulattoes. Following one such power struggle, resulting in the ousting, imprisonment on corruption charges and subsequent violent death of President E.J. Roye (the American-born descendant of Nigerian Ibo parents, regarded as Liberia's first truly 'black' president[7]) J.J. Roberts came back to power in the early 1870s to serve for another term.

A Western colony in all but name

Indeed, while historically much has been made of Liberia's status as the first independent republic in Africa, as run by blacks and not under the banner of a foreign master, in reality the Americo-Liberians who founded the settlement and launched it into nationhood were neither particularly black nor had anything at all in common with Africans, especially the ones they had chosen to share their new territory with. They were light in skin colour – as were a majority of freed slaves from the United States in the early nineteenth century – often the offspring of a white slave-owning father and a female slave mother. On the cotton plantations of the antebellum South, when a child was born to a female slave worker in this way the usual practice was to give the child its freedom, as it was after all also the progeny of the farmer. Aside from releasing the child from bondage it avoided embarrassing questions being asked around the plantation as well as the suspicions of a prying plantation owner's wife.

The story of Matilda Newport clearly illustrates the strong propensity of the settlers to emphasize their superiority over native Liberians in the early days, and there are many other such examples of how the leaders of the new Liberian colony dominated the indigenous people they encountered, whether by manipulation, trickery, superior technology or direct force. In tracing the origins of Liberia's recent bloody confrontations, those favouring a revisionist view of Liberian history have pointed to the fact that for the first twenty-five years of its existence the colony was run exclusively by white people, the ACS agents, and it was their repression and mistreatment of the people of the interior, not the conduct of the freed former slaves, which set the tone and the custom for future settler–native animosities.

According to this view, the black former slaves were not in accord with the violent and coercive methods of the white agents, but nevertheless assimilated their ways. This they did to such an extent that by the time of the founding of the republic in 1847, the country's new elite, the mulatto descendents of the American freemen, were fully inured to the exploitation of the natives and the establishment of an apartheid society.[8]

Liberia's new status, its lofty ideals, establishment of constitutional government and commitments to sovereignty, freedom and independence, were not only a new departure for the still immature and economically struggling settlement in West Africa, they were also somewhat in advance of what the mother country, the United States, was able to accept initially. While Britain, France and other powers soon recognized the embryonic Republic of Liberia, the United

States refused the country diplomatic relations for another fifteen years; in antebellum Washington DC the southern states refused to accept the presence of a black ambassador in the diplomatic corps, and recognition was denied. It was not until the presidency of Abraham Lincoln that Liberia was given full recognition by the country whose philanthropists and social engineers had conceived and financed it, as well as nurturing its early growth.

When European colonial navies patrolling off Liberia's coast in the 1820s sought clarification from the US government as to whether the territory was a US possession, the latter's reply confirmed that the United States was committed to the cause and the success of the settlement but that its defence and physical survival were nevertheless not the responsibility of the US government.[9]

As the settlement became established and more outsiders arrived, these Americo-Liberians quickly became known by the native population as 'Congo', a mistaken reference to the origin of the different group of arrivals who were set free from their continental European captors on the oceans off West Africa, at around the same time.

The latter group were newly captured slaves bound for the Americas, set free from their Portuguese, Spanish and French masters on the Atlantic by British (after the Slave Trade Act of 1807), and later also by US, naval anti-slavery interception. While many slave ships made their way to the Americas from Angola, Mozambique and even further afield in Africa, a large number came from the region of the Congo Basin, transported towards the ocean along the tributaries of Africa's second longest river. Thus, they were dubbed 'Congo' upon arrival in their new homeland, as were the other group, the Americo-Liberians, despite the latter having no recent African origins. Whether liberated by British frigates on the high seas of the Atlantic Ocean or emancipated thanks to liberal policies in North America, all non-native Liberians henceforth were soon given the same derogatory nickname by the native population.

In practice, relatively few true Congo so-called 'receptives' were settled in Liberia, and the majority of the settler population was made up of freed slaves returning from the United States. By contrast, in neighbouring Sierra Leone, the majority of the ancestors of today's

Krio settlers were of recaptive origin. For the Liberian arrivals of New World origin, many of them proud of their lighter pigmentation and privileged social status derived from the association with the United States, being dubbed with the crudely African nickname of 'Congo' was derogatory if not insulting.

By the late nineteenth century, Liberia's surrounding colonial powers, Britain and France, were in the final stages of carving up most of West Africa between themselves. Given their eagerness to establish the boundaries of their African territorial acquisitions, and to prevent simmering rivalries between France and Great Britain flaring into conflict, the Liberian government was forced to designate the limits of its territory officially.

In 1903, the British gained a concession of Liberian territory, which was transferred to Sierra Leone, thereby emphasizing the fragility of the country's sovereignty. The Liberian Frontier Force was established to protect the country's borders against further European imperial incursions. However, Liberia's finances were shaky. In an attempt to resolve its growing indebtedness to European creditors, a commission was appointed by President Theodore Roosevelt to help Liberia reorganize its finances.

In 1912 Washington helped to arrange a $1.7 million loan, extended by bankers Kuhn Loeb & Co. and including British, German and Dutch participation. One of the lenders' conditions was that Liberia should accept the appointment of the American Reid Page Clark as General Receiver of Customs. Clark was given control over a part of Liberia's public finances and had responsibility for payment for payment of the debt service, customs officials and the Liberia Frontier Force. Soon afterwards Liberia's secretary of the Treasury, John L. Morris, complained bitterly about Liberia's loss of sovereignty and Clark's dictatorial behaviour.[10]

This early dependence on outsiders in exchange for their dominance of the economy was a pattern which endured and which ultimately contributed to imbalances in the wider economy and society of Liberia. Referring to the situation in the early period, former interim government president Amos Sawyer said: 'The presence of foreign receivers was a major irritant to Liberian sensibilities, and violence was directed at Europeans and Americans in some parts of the country.'[11]

Entering the unknown Liberia

For decades, the Americo-Liberian settlers had scarcely entered the regions that lay inland of their coastal communities, let alone mapped their contours or attempted to control them administratively. The challenges of traversing the rough, malaria-infested terrain and dark, forbidding tropical rainforests, as well as the prospect of encountering unfriendly natives along the route, were a strong enough deterrent for most from exploring the hinterland.

The True Whig Party, founded in 1869, was the sole repository of political power in Liberia for over a century. Its leading members were without exception Christian fundamentalist, Americo-Liberian settler stock, conservative in their beliefs and relentless in their efforts to build and maintain the privileges that they had fought to establish in their segregated colony. The Liberian settler government, unlike its wealthier European counterparts, did not however have the resources at its disposal to establish an administration in the countryside and so it was forced to rely on a system of indirect rule over the lands that fell within its national boundaries. To this end, successive True Whig administrations in Monrovia relied on the native chiefs in each province to carry out the day-to-day functions of local government on their behalf.

The countryside was subdivided into districts within each of Liberia's three interior provinces (Western, Eastern and Central), each under the administration of a provincial commissioner and his district commissioners, directly dispatched from Monrovia. The commissioners in turn worked at local level with the native paramount chiefs, who were the real power in the communities, as the Americo-Liberian commissioners were in fact colonial representatives sent to enforce laws and supervise the collection of taxes.

Communal forced labour was a legal requirement of each community, to provide manpower for the construction of roads and other public works, while adult males could also be directed to provide porterage to passing travellers in their regions. These measures were directed by the government in Monrovia and enforced by the local chiefs, who were in exchange given the right to exercise power within their area and also received financial incentives from the central government. All of these measures were overseen by the district commissioners, backed up by a new rough-and-ready army called the Liberia Frontier Force, which became infamous among the rural populations for the brutality of its methods in enforcing Monrovia's fiscal measures. Delinquents were either imprisoned or alternatively tied down outdoors face up in the scorching sun, or forced to stand in water up to their knees for a day, among other forms of rudimentary torture.[12]

The government in Monrovia pursued a policy based on extraction, both of natural resources and fiscally through its imposition of taxes. The districts had no more than observer status in the national government, and prior consultation with local representatives regarding the launch of new mining or logging ventures was the exception rather than the rule.

When the Monrovia administration set out to generate direct revenues from its provinces, it levied taxes on the rural communities, notably a hut tax, which was again collected locally and from which the chief was allowed to keep 10 per cent as inducement. The extent to which the tax regime levied an uneven burden on the native population is illustrated by statistics from 1925, when over $300,000 was collected from the interior in hut taxes, while the main tax paid in Monrovia, a property tax, raised a total of only $4,688.[13]

Resentment by the native populations rarely erupted into large-scale organized revolt, with the exception of a major coastal insurrection by the Kru tribe in 1915. Their coastal region centred on Sinoe County had throughout early Liberian history been a bastion of native opposition to Americo-Liberian rule, and fighting against Monrovia's rule raged until Colonel Elwood Davis was dispatched to put down the revolt.

During the early development of the provinces, the Americo-Liberians used their institutions of Christianity and Freemasonry as a basis for the integration of the native populations who were allowed to gain access to education and thereby enter the Monrovia political system. Thus natives gaining an education would also assimilate the religion of their new institutional environment.

Closely related to the religious assimilation was the cultural inflection which was required of upwardly mobile native Liberians in order to enter the fringes of Americo-Liberian society, if not its corridors of power. In college in Monrovia or in the workplace, there was often a simultaneous display of pride in traditional culture accompanied by its negation in the execution of their administrative functions in the civil service or in business. The integration process established a paradoxical pattern of behaviour among the educated native population, whereby segments were drawn into the elite, while at the same time these newly empowered appointees became isolated from their cousins in the countryside.

This estrangement from their native roots generated second-degree resentment among the elders of the newly educated rural workers and their stay-at-home peers. Apparently for some the integration of their own young people into Monrovia had just brought the bad things from the capital closer to home. A rural elder interviewed in 1976 complained: 'even our children went and got educated and came back to rule us. They are now getting worse than those people who came here before. They make us even to be afraid of them now.'[14]

Nevertheless, by the 1970s, due to the advances being made by many native Liberians in reaching higher education and securing positions in academia, the civil service or business, the visible distinctions between Americo-Liberians and those of native origin tended to diminish or at least be masked, in a conscious effort by the latter group to gain acceptance and advancement. In the social structure of the times, there was clearly an advantage for the son of a native or mixed-parentage couple to conceal or at least downplay his tribal background, in order to progress more rapidly in a society dominated by the settler elite. Naturally lighter-skinned native Liberians could get on better in society than their darker pigmented brothers and sisters, often passing off as Americo-Liberians.

Some would change or modify their names when submitting job applications, or modify their accents in the workplace and social settings, just as aspirants from humble origins around the world strive to imitate social superiors to gain acceptance and integration into the upper echelons of their profession. Thus the assimilated minister of finance during William Tolbert's administration, Alvin Gow, de-emphasized his typically Krahn surname, demoting it to middle-initial status and re-emerging among his True Whig Party peers as Alvin G. Jones.

Another important factor in the tendency towards a blurring of boundaries stemmed from the improved access to education by adopted native children in Americo-Liberian families. Especially around Monrovia, it was common practice for a wealthy settler family to adopt a young boy or girl from the Bassa or other nearby native communities and bring the child up as part of its family. While native parents often welcomed the opportunity to send their children to grow up and work in an Americo-Liberian household, settler families also sometimes brought young Liberians from the hinterland against their will to serve on plantations or in their houses in Monrovia, even when their own parents needed them to work in their own family's farm or business.

Whatever the original route to assimilation, the result was that it often led to the chance for an education otherwise beyond the reach of a native adolescent, who would normally be at work in unskilled rural employment by his or her mid-teens. In such cases, a further route to assimilation into the slowly emerging new Liberian society could be achieved.

Paramount patronage

The system that existed in the countryside until the 1970s truly was one of patronage of the native chiefs by the central government in Monrovia in return for their maintenance of a subservient and passive population. An example of how this worked in practice was observed during an early 1970s' visit by a teaching group from the University of Monrovia to a school celebration in Bolahun, Lofa County. In his address to the local staff, the paramount chief of the Gbandi tribe, Tamba Kollie, reminded his audience: 'we happy with the place we got; the big big work like the president got is not for we'.¹⁵ Chief Kollie knew his place, or rather he knew his places; as well as being paramount chief in Lofa County, he was also the chairman of the Lofa True Whig Party – a classic example of assimilation-domination by the 'sell-out' representatives of native Liberia at work.

During this period the economic and administrative landscape of Liberia changed dramatically, giving a massive new financial lease of life to the central government in Monrovia. With the global economic boom and the arrival of the motor car in the industrialized world the demand for rubber was surging, and Liberia as a sovereign state had the power to license concessions to foreign enterprises to exploit the country's resources, in exchange for fees, taxes and royalties upon their production. While palm oil, timber, coffee, cocoa and later iron ore were also important natural resources available within Liberia, it was the establishment of the 1 million acre rubber plantation at Harbel, outside the capital, by the Firestone company in 1926 which more than anything else transformed the Liberian economy. Through the revenues that Firestone paid to the government, it also soon transformed the self-confidence of the country's rulers, allowing them more options in the manner in which they governed the hinterland territories.

The largest new rubber plantation was established at Mount Barclay outside Monrovia, soon renamed Harbel, after Harvey Firestone and his wife Idabelle; and a second was located at Pleebo, north of Cape Palmas. However, there was a growing need for a labour force to man the plantations, and once again the population of the hinterland was pressed into service. The continued use of large-scale forced labour in the facilities of an international company soon drew world attention to Liberia, however. Furthermore, under the administration of President Charles King (1920–30), the Liberian Frontier Force was used to compel native workers into service on the Spanish colony of Fernando Po.

These practices led to Liberia being condemned as a pariah state, and in 1929 the League of Nations conducted an inquiry into the country's continuing labour practices, which in effect amounted to slavery. The publication of their report in 1930 led to the eruption of a scandal, and impeachment proceedings against President King were instituted, leading to his resignation.

The modern commodity era begins

Despite these embarrassments, Liberia was producing what the booming 1920s world economy demanded and the revenues earned by the government on its commodity export businesses were substantial. Monrovia could now afford to establish more direct and effective control and administration of the native Liberian territory that lay beyond the small number of Americo-Liberian-run enclaves along the Atlantic Coast. The disgraced President King's successor, President Edwin Barclay (1930-44), was the first president to seriously begin the administration of the interior of Liberia.

The system of government that Barclay established and that was to endure for another half-century was founded firmly on patronage at every level, with the chiefs in the countryside kept sweet with their share of the spoils in exchange for keeping the rural population essentially subjugated and isolated from access to skilled jobs or education. A contemporary author summed up the essentials of the TWP oligarchy's character succinctly as being based upon 'Freemasonry, fundamentalist Christianity and Apartheid'.[16]

The historical, religious and economic relationships with the United States were soon reinforced by military cooperation. When native uprisings along the coast threatened Monrovia's supremacy in 1910, the US Navy sent warships to fight off attacks being staged by indigenous tribes against the central government's authority.

In the modern era, Liberia truly came into its own in terms of foreign relations with the United States. From the late 1950s, with the advent of the Cold War and superpower competition for influence in the Third World, Liberia's strategic position in Africa became a major regional asset to the United States. Liberia became a base for US surveillance of the region, as well as for support to covert activities against communist-leaning African states. In 1959, a security alliance was signed between the two countries, which gave the USA unrestricted access on twenty-four hours' notice to Robertsfield airport, a communications station used by Washington to maintain contact with its thirty-four embassies in Africa, and the Omega navigational station for coordinating and guiding transatlantic military and civilian air traffic. In addition the Voice of America radio station established its transmitter in Liberia, allowing daily broadcasts of the US view of the region and the world to reach millions of English-speaking Africans.

Because of the country's hard-currency economy, employment opportunities and stable government, people from around the region were drawn to Liberia. Many from less-well-off neighbouring countries seized the chance to work for US dollar wages and for the opportunity to share even in some small way in this booming outpost of African capitalism which next-door Ivorians referred to as *La Petite Amérique*.

The upper classes of *La Petite Amérique*, the Americo-Liberian settlers, had the lion's share of the spoils from the beginning. First with their purchases of rich agricultural land, bought from the natives in the mid-1800s, often for as little as 50 cents per acre, and then with their education and overseas connections to markets, education and technology, the Americo-Liberians quickly became the dominant economic and social caste of the Pepper Coast. By 1979 it was estimated that 4 per cent of Liberia's population owned over 60 per cent of the wealth, much of which was in the form of agricultural plantations, some of which extended to 10,000 or even 20,000 acres.

In the nineteenth century and well into the twentieth century in most countries rich or poor, black people never reached anything approaching political equality or the economic power of their white counterparts in the lands where they lived together, whether in the uneasy segregated society of the American South or the feudal colonial structures of the French, British and Portuguese possessions around the globe. Not only did the Americo-Liberians fare well by regional standards; in a century when Africans and descendants of Africans struggled for basic rights and often for simple survival, the self-governing black settlers of Liberia had it all.

Independent, incongruous, baptised in gunfire and founded by outcasts from a former colony whose own government repudiated colonization, Liberian society was indeed unique in so many ways. But in mineral-rich Liberia, in timber- and rubber-rich Liberia, the black man was in charge. Well, at least the Americo-Liberian black was. With no white bosses or racist neighbours to keep them out of the best jobs, houses and schools, with a government built on patronage and accommodation – but rarely communication – with the native hinterland, for them life in sweet Liberia earned its name many times over.

Helene Cooper, a Monrovian-born writer who later became diplomatic correspondent of the *New York Times*, described her good fortune at growing up in Liberia in the early 1970s:

> None of that American post-civil war/civil rights movement baggage to bog me down with any inferiority complex about whether I was as good as white people. No European garbage to have me wondering whether some British colonial master was somehow better than me. Who needs to struggle for equality? Let everybody else try to be equal to me.[17]

Indeed Americo-Liberian life from the 1960s onwards, which for the most part was life in Monrovia, was about good things, abundant food and electricity, air conditioning, an office job and a car for pa, a big house for ma and weekend sports, drive-in movies as well as time by the beach for the family. Fashionably American blue-jean-clad boys walked out with often bright-skinned girls, whose looks and distinctive language turned them into a stunning tribe all of their own, confident in manner and unique in appearance among all their peers on West Africa's colonial coast.

If the ruling classes of Liberia felt like and lived far more like Americans than Africans in the 1960s and 1970s, in some ways their social life and level of economic well-being was far better than their African-American peers, still in the early stages of their struggle for civil rights and economic equality on the other side of the Atlantic. Strong growth in a post-war economy led to boom times in the 1960s, and educated Americo-Liberians enjoyed the fruits of their country's economy. They lived the life of the well-to-do, dressing up for church on Sundays and entertaining in style on the verandas of their suburban mansions while their youngsters listened to Tamla Motown on the gramophone. In short they emulated a lifestyle more resembling that of their ancestors' former antebellum masters, than that of their own disadvantaged and disenfranchised African-American forebears.

The extravagance and the contrasts went well beyond the sartorial and the basic comforts of tropical life, however. President Tolbert had a town not far from Monrovia, formerly Bensonville, renamed in his honour. The family of the president, the descendants of freed slaves from South Carolina, owned many substantial properties around the town, which itself had originally been named after a mid-nineteenth-century Liberian president, Steven Allen Benson. In keeping with their prominent position in the country and the great material wealth at the disposal of the Tolberts, Bensonville appropriately became Bentol in the 1970s, and a zoo, an amusement park and artificial lake for water sports to entertain the Tolberts' guests were constructed on the site surrounded by and in full view of struggling country people from the surrounding area.[18]

Beginnings of dissent

As President Tubman's successor William Tolbert took office in July 1971, a 23-year old teacher and junior accountant was handing out leaflets on the campus of the University of Liberia, drawing attention to what he and other young activists felt were the political grievances of the underprivileged of his country and demanding action to change the wrongs in Liberian society.

Young Charles Taylor didn't come from quite the classic upper-class Liberian background, however, with his middle-class Americo-Liberian father and uneducated native Liberian mother. But as the third in a family of ten children, he spent his formative years in the household of a more privileged family, which effectively shaped his upbringing and outlook with regard to developments in the society around him.

Taylor grew up at the time when economic success, albeit for the few, and social reform, albeit limited, now permitted wider access to education for those from outside the upper classes of the coastal Americo-Liberian elite. Greater awareness of the opportunities among the indigenous Liberian students coming to Monrovia from the interior was slowly having an impact on attitudes and on society. By the early 1970s, the initially meagre reforms begun by President Tubman and continued by William Tolbert aimed at the wider representation of all Liberians in the running of their country were gaining momentum.

At around the same time another ambitious Liberian, Amos Sawyer, a native of Sinoe County, was entering a career in academia, also at the University of Liberia, and he was beginning to organize his fellow students to agitate for change.

After the indigenous tribes of Liberia were finally accorded legislative representation in 1964 under William Tubman, in the 1970s the administration of President Tolbert slowly set about promoting their members to positions in government. In a deeply conservative society even these measures met with disapproval from reactionary elements within the TWP oligarchy, while for others like young Charles Taylor it was clear that opportunities were being denied to the majority and the lip service to reform was not likely to offer much to his generation, irrespective of what the Tolbert government's long-term progressive vision was.

In its final years, the Tolbert cabinet split between the progressives and the conservatives. Progressives believed in gradual change, in elimination of the property requirement for voting eligibility, and in the establishment of legal opposition parties to contest democratic elections. Among the more liberal ministers were the minister of foreign affairs, Cecil Dennis; the minister of finance, James T. Phillips; and True Whig Party treasurer Clarence Parker. Aligned against them was an equally powerful faction of conservative hard-liners who felt that more change would lead to trouble and make it even harder to restore order. In addition to the president's brother Stephen Tolbert and party faithful like Reginald Townsend, the minister of mustice Joseph Chesson was one of those who argued in favour of maintaining Liberia's apartheid approach to government. Whether accommodation or repression would win the day was a debate which was eventually resolved by the tide of events, but it was already clear that for many ordinary Liberians the pace of change that Tolbert's progressives had in mind was too slow – impatience within Liberia was rising.

In the outside world, events were beginning to compound a situation of rising dissent at home. The oil crisis of the 1970s and a world economic downturn in commodity prices brought much of sweet Liberia's economic stability to a bitter close. Liberia's main exports – rubber, iron ore, timber, palm oil and other agricultural produce – were all experiencing declining prices. At the same time, voices for change were increasingly being raised at home: on the University of Liberia campus, in the newly connected hinterland counties, and among Liberians abroad, particularly in the United States – where young Charles Taylor arrived to continue his education in 1972.

TWO

THE SPIRIT OF LIBERIA

> The third harvest following the outbreak of the Hitler War was a momentous year for me. Something every young man in the Dewoin country looks forward to happened to me. I was initiated into the Zowolo, the highest Poro degree offered by the Dewoin tribe.
>
> Bai T. Moore, *Murder in the Cassava Patch*

Arthington journey: inauspicious early times

The journey to Arthington in Montserrado County seems long, although the town is less than 30 miles distant from the capital. The tarmac road that forms the start of the route towards Charles Taylor's childhood home leads north out of Monrovia along a paved road lined with small shops and stalls, zinc-roof structures and a steady flow of human traffic: Liberians rhythmically going about their business up and down the roadsides, by foot, just as they always have.

After the junction for Arthington at Buba Town, the road soon gives way to a level red clay and gravel highway with passing room enough for trucks and a barely serviceable surface for ordinary saloon car travellers. This in turn soon becomes a twisting mud track, soaring and diving through the undulating bush as it winds its way through Bakohn Town, Didum and a series of smaller villages and hamlets with neither infrastructure nor visible signs of commerce beyond the occasional roadside stall offering fruits and palm wine. The contours of its sharp potholes are baked solid into the surface in the dry season, before turning into suppurating impassable axle traps for much of the rainy season, from June to September, as major portions of the track are transformed into quagmires.

With neither signpost nor indicator of distance, the trip to Arthington in Liberia's dry season is as full of uncertainty for the navigator as it is uncomfortable for the passenger, but in a curious way perhaps a telling reminder of conditions in a country and the attitudes of its former president. During a few fading years of the twentieth century and barely into the twenty-first, Charles Taylor's brief period of rule left little in the way of improvement or infrastructure in Liberia's countryside, not even along the road to his own childhood family home.

Continuing the journey into Arthington village and forking off to the left by the palaver hut – the community's thatched-roof open-walled town hall where local issues could be aired and matters of concern decided – there is little to suggest that the former president's childhood family home is close by. The road gets worse and the knowledge of the local population as to the location of the 'Taylor House' seems increasingly vague; 'i' no far, you go so' an indifferent youth along the roadside advises, pointing up the yellow brush-topped hill towards nothing in particular, it seems, with still so many tortuous miles to go along the track. A time later, further directions to the house are given by a more eager passer-by: 'yeh, yeh, i' far small', spurring the expedition forward, still in a cloud of navigational opacity. But no, he was right, something is visible just as we push a little further through the village outskirts: the former Taylor family home is there.

Today the house is overgrown with weeds and the white plaster walls are riddled with bullet holes. However, even before rebels raked the childhood home of Liberia's twenty-second president with machine-gun fire, not much around the house or surrounding area was developed. The roads and infrastructure remained as basic as can be imagined. Unlike neighbours of a head of state or senior government ministers elsewhere in Africa, neither the surrounding residents nor remaining family members in the family community of the ex-president of Liberia ever received any particular advantages over their compatriots by way of facilities or infrastructure.

Born to poor parents of mixed settler and native backgrounds, Charles Taylor spent the first eight months of his life in Arthington, before moving to nearby Millsburg, where he spent the rest of his childhood.

Taylor's father, Nielsen Philip Taylor, was of Americo-Liberian descent, his grandparents having emigrated from the American South in the 1890s. Nielson received his education through the Lutheran Overseas Mission to Liberia in the 1940s, which brought with it his Scandinavian forename. He and his family started off farming cane sugar in a smallholding near Arthington, which at the time was a town of some 10,000 people. There they cut and cleaned sugar cane with a cutlass, as Liberians called it – basically a machete – and so as a youth Charles Taylor had to help in his father's fields, getting a taste of manual work on a subsistence farm. Nielsen later went on to become a teacher and moved to Zorzor in western Liberia's Lofa County for a time, before ultimately returning to Millsburg, serving an apprenticeship and qualifying as a judge, then working in the first circuit court of Monrovia.

Nielsen's wife, Louise Yassa Zoe Taylor, was from an altogether different background. She was a native Liberian from the Gola tribe, a group who traditionally inhabited a region in the centre of Liberia north of the capital. She came into service in the household of Charles Taylor's grandparents in Arthington with practically no education, beginning her schooling late and only managing to reach third grade by her late teens. She worked around the Taylor house as a servant girl, washing and cleaning. But Zoe had compensations, which didn't go unnoticed to Nielsen, the young man of the household, by then 21 years old. 'She was a very pretty lady, and, the story goes, some friskiness occurred in the house between them and my mother was impregnated', recalled Taylor.[1] Perhaps nothing out of the ordinary in the course of domestic life in any part of the world, although what was more unusual was that Nielson and Zoe went on to marry, rather than otherwise discreetly dealing with the unplanned birth to avoid family embarrassment, as might often occur elsewhere.

As it happens, Nielsen's parents, although educated Americo-Liberians, were also extremely religious, devout practising Baptists with strict views on marriage and family. They insisted that Nielsen marry Zoe, despite her lowly origins and also in spite of some other family members shunning the idea of Nielsen's union with a simple housemaid from the countryside. Zoe's side of the family thought differently – 'if she was good enough for him to touch, she was good enough to marry', they said – and so Nielsen and Zoe were soon wed, in the village of Arthington, where Charles was born shortly thereafter.

TAYLOR'S CHILDHOOD HOUSE IN ARTHINGTON

Humble origins and adoption

However, after a short time it seemed that a socially expedient solution was engineered after all. Before Charles had even reached his first birthday, he was adopted by a close friend of his grandmother, and taken in by her, to be raised in a quite established Americo-Liberian family, the Ciscos. Martha Anne Cisco, by then already a middle-aged woman, raised Charles from the age of eight months to almost 18, when she died. Not surprisingly, for practical purposes Charles spoke of her rather than Zoe as his real mother. Nevertheless, Taylor did not entirely leave his native heritage behind him. Years later, he would embrace his mother's culture by adopting a native middle name in place of the 'McArthur' he was given at birth, taking instead the Gola name Ghankay, or 'strong one', after he returned to Liberia in adulthood.

Receiving his pre-education at home, until aged 7, Charles began to attend Arthington Central School, which was a 45-minute walk from the house in Millsburg, a road he walked every day. Life was fairly tough all the same, in rural Montserrado County in the 1950s, and Taylor recalls that he didn't wear shoes until the age of 8 or 9. There was no running water or electricity. Charles described their access to amenities himself:

> No, no, no, no, you were lucky even to get a clean glass of water ... I was brought up in a mud house covered with something we called a tarpaulin. No, there was no running water. We went to the creek to draw our water. We took our baths in the same creek ... and did fishing in the same creek. No, there was no light and running water. That's maybe a different world, not for us.[2]

When he reached the age of 13, Charles moved to another school, a foreign missionary Baptist School called Ricks Institute, one of the most prestigious high schools in Liberia. He did well enough in Arthington to get a scholarship from a Lebanese-owned business group to pay the fees at Ricks, where most of the other students were from well-heeled Monrovian Americo-Liberian families.

But as a youth he began to prove as insolent as he was industrious in the classroom and soon got a bad name with the teaching staff. Already dedicating more time to girls than to books, in one incident he responded to a reprimand by baring his buttocks in the middle of class – and shortly afterwards urinating in the schoolyard well. It was not long before cheeky young Charlie was expelled from Ricks. One of his former teachers, Shadrick Cassell, still on the faculty at Ricks in the mid-1990s, remembered Taylor's behaviour and his expulsion from the institute: 'He was expelled for bad conduct and he's been a bad boy ever since: he was reckless and arrogant.'[3]

Nevertheless, through his own efforts Taylor managed to get onto a government-sponsored teacher training programme, at the Kakata Rural Teachers Training Institute, which allowed successful students to finish their high-school education while training as teachers at the same time. Finally qualifying at the age of 19, Charles Taylor set out to tackle his first job of adulthood, teaching science and maths in Bomi County, at the Charles E. Dewey Junior High School in Bomi Hills.

A trip to Bomi County

To reach the Bomi Hills area today from Monrovia you have to go westward along the so-called 'Babangida Highway', named after the former Nigerian president who was such a friend to Liberia's government in the 1980s. After clearing the congestion and lively roadside squalor of Monrovia's suburbs, what is one of the country's best paved roads soon leads into the beginning of the deep, humid Liberian rainforest only another 15 miles beyond. From the junction at the trading town of Klay, a right turn towards the city of Tubmanburg changes the scenery once more. From there the colour and cluttered confusion of peri-urban produce stalls and the ubiquitous vendors of car phone-chargers outside every vehicle window quickly give way to an altogether more rural scenario.

Suddenly out of the coastal metropolis with its melting pot of populations and diverse, ever adaptable trading patterns, everything changes: this is now rainforest equatorial Africa. The look and feel of the countryside beyond the edge of the tarmac road is the same as it could have appeared half a century ago. Deep lush green bush underlies spreading jungle with undergrowth vegetation fighting upwards for light and air amid the bulging, tentacled branches of overhanging trees. Along the roadside, diminutive, feeble wooden vending stalls are intermittently staffed by women selling two or three different vegetable items from their smallholdings. Other women pass by the roadside ambling with efficient gait, charcoal bundles big enough to fuel a home for a week's cooking effortlessly balanced on their heads.

Rubber plantations, medium-sized and small, deliver their crude output to Firestone collection stations every 10 or 20 miles, and miniature mosques surface from nowhere from time to time. These are interspersed with a smaller number of their counterpart Christian structures, whose signboards declare in cluttered lettering the details of the parish and of their Baptist, Presbyterian or Evangelical denomination.

For the motorist running short of fuel, at a few places he will be lucky enough to find it sold in gallon glass jars and personally siphoned at no extra charge by its vendor. Today, as the country approaches its second presidential election since Charles Taylor's departure from Liberia, the omnipresent white Toyotas and blue helmets are testament to the enduring UN presence deemed desirable by Liberia's new managers and masters, both national and international. Other than the rural security which their popular contingents offer, the Pakbatt and Banbatt outposts can be a rare source of Internet access available in an unwired countryside, while the UNMIL (United Nations Mission in Liberia) radio station's reliable transmissions deliver news, music, faith and conversation across Liberia's counties long after the signal from most Monrovia-based transmitters has faded.

WELCOME TO BOMI COUNTY SIGNBOARD

In 1967, when Charles Taylor came to take up his junior high teaching post, Bomi Hills was first and foremost an iron ore mining town, and many of his students there were not young teenagers but adult employees at the mine – which was then owned and run by the Bethlehem Steel Corporation out of Pittsburgh, Pennsylvania. In the Liberia of the times, people in the countryside involved in unskilled work might have next to no education and could only come into contact with schooling in adulthood. They discovered education as well as other amenities only when they arrived in the 'civilized' Liberia. Whether through domestic service, like Charles Taylor's mother, through offering their labour in mines or plantations, or through migration to the city in the hope of informal employment, this was the only route for many to go beyond the most basic childhood education. And so it could easily be that a fresh-out-of training teacher like Taylor could be teaching students more than ten years his senior. In Bomi Hills, Taylor also fathered his first child, Zoe, with a woman named Honerine Clarke, but when Charles moved on, both mother and daughter remained.

After his spell in Bomi, Taylor returned to teach in Arthington in 1968, because apparently the locals in his home town were resentful that one of their own had become so qualified then moved away to another part of the country to teach. So, to appease them, he returned to work in the same school where he had studied as a child, again teaching maths and science courses.

However, village life was too restrictive for the 20-year-old Charles, by now already eager for real advancement. So he moved to Monrovia and, while continuing to teach, enrolled in a US-based distance-learning programme, the La Salle Extension University programme, where he took a two-year correspondence course in accounting. In 1970 a part-time job also became available in President Tubman's Ministry of Finance, so the ambitious young self-educated teacher and aspiring accountant took that on too, working flat out to make ends meet. Soon, however, things began to move into a higher gear and new horizons opened up.

In 1971, following the death of President Tubman, the incoming President Tolbert appointed his brother Stephen as finance minister. Stephen Tolbert launched an initiative to improve standards at the ministry and instituted an open examination to recruit new talent. Taylor and another candidate scored well enough to be offered jobs and so Charles started as a full-time junior accountant in Tolbert's Ministry of Finance in Monrovia.

Then one of those life-changing moments occurred in the career of the ambitious young Liberian financial manager, an event which set Charles on a new path and probably altered the course of his life: he broke up with his steady girlfriend. Or, rather, he had a girlfriend taken away from him by a 'been-to', as the Americo-Liberians used to say. As Taylor tells it, one of his old friends from Ricks came back from the United States with a Master's degree and stole the girl away from him. 'This guy came back boasting he had a Master's ... and he comes and takes this girl from me', Taylor remembers. 'I said, oh my God, this is just too much for me. I have to go to school ... I'm just going to have to speed up the trip to America.'[4] That was difficult because of his work commitments in Liberia at the time, and in fact it would have been impossible for him to go to university right then. But Charles had a friend who put him in touch with a junior college in Boston and he soon started the college application process.

Society and economy

The uniqueness of Liberia as a historical and political phenomenon on the African continent is unquestionable: from its origins as a settlement populated by freed American slaves, who were encouraged to resettle by a government at home that saw them as a looming social problem in the pre-Civil War United States. Never a colony in the strict sense and an independent republic since 1847, Liberia was nevertheless ruled by non-native-born peoples of African descent for 133 years from its founding as a republic in 1847. To the country's political particularity was added an economic prominence in the middle of the twentieth century. Liberia began to grow rich, being endowed with the mineral and agricultural resources that the modern world demanded, leading many to think that the country represented an economic model for its African peers.

For the descendants of settler Liberians the land they lived in was an African jewel, what some thought of as a transplanted microcosm of the American economic dream. But politically it was a one-party autocracy which served the interests of a privileged minority population. The Americo-Liberians of Liberia enjoyed a material wealth not available to black people anywhere else on earth; but behind it all, less than 50 miles inland, what could be described as nirvana for the resettled Americans of colour was closer to a nightmare for the Liberian natives.

Monrovia symbolized Americo-Liberian life, and the city and its inhabitants never showed much respect for or interest in developing the countryside except as a reserve of natural resources and a supplier of manpower in peacetime or fighters in time of war. From the early years of the Republic of Liberia until the mid-twentieth century, the hinterland was ruled as a territory subjugated to the capital, with provincial and district commissioners dispatched from Monrovia to oversee the collection of taxes, and for the sourcing of labour for the rubber plantations and mines that provided the wealth of the country for its rulers and foreign exploiters.

Despite dominating the interior, the settlers and their ministers who profited from Liberia's great wealth neither understood nor were able to completely rule the territories beyond the coast. They spoke a pidgin English among themselves but for the most part could not understand any of Liberia's sixteen indigenous tribal tongues. Thus the need for rule by proxy took on considerable importance and Monrovia needed to ensure that the paramount chiefs of each community, town and territory (and, later on, county) were kept content with a share of the spoils in return for maintenance of local order and subjugation to the capital.

Although driven by the need to secure control of the resources that financed their way of life, there was much about the hinterland that discouraged the settlers from venturing far outside Monrovia and the other coastal settlements, and city dwellers remained largely ignorant of the customs and social forces that governed their uneducated rural compatriots. Resentment at the wealth of Monrovia was present in the countryside from the Liberian Republic's earliest times, coming to a violent head, for example, during the Kru uprising of 1915 and in other lesser revolts; although it was not until the last quarter of the twentieth century that the long-simmering frustration felt by native Liberians over the injustice of their exploitation by the settlers' descendants truly boiled over. The harsh actions of the Liberian Frontier Force, the hut tax, the practice of forced labour and the consequences of land appropriation had nevertheless always been a source of bitterness, however muted it may have seemed to the outside world or even to ordinary Monrovians.

Certainly, until the 1920s, for the people of the Liberian hinterland the rapidly evolving economy and society of their coastal neighbours, now compatriots, most of whom were living just one or two hundred miles away, was a world apart. Life in the interior could not have been more different from Americo-Liberian city life, and if it had not been for the arrival of Firestone and its increasing demands for a ready labour force, plus the diplomatic impositions on the Liberian government by outsiders to modernize and civilize, many more decades might have passed without meaningful contact between the tiny affluent coastal community of settlers and the much larger native population.

Liberty, fraternity, spirituality

If native Liberians knew little of the details of the lives of their settler cousins, their culture and society, and certainly did not share in the spoils of their economy, for their part the Americo-Liberians knew little and understood even less of the society and beliefs that underpinned the various communities of natives living in the interior of their adopted homeland. In particular, the social and political order in certain regions hinged strongly on the secret societies of the interior and their rituals, many of which often were often characterized as savage and abhorrent by the predominantly Christian urban settler community.

An appreciation of the spiritual-religious aspect of Liberian life in the hinterland is key to a fuller understanding of the nature and extent of much of the brutality which ensued for over two decades across Liberia. What has been passed off by some outside observers as the bizarre and barbarous practices of primitive tribes with neither culture nor humanity misses the mark. This deeper, less visible but equally powerful side to Liberian life warrants a brief exploration of the origins and purpose of the country's spiritual institutions and the relationship that indigenous Liberians had, and continue to have, with the supernatural.

Liberia's early settler community was staunchly fundamentalist Christian in its beliefs, for the most part mirroring the practices of the more conservative denominations typical of the Deep South and middle of America. Sunday was an occasion for mandatory church

Liberian ethnic and language groups

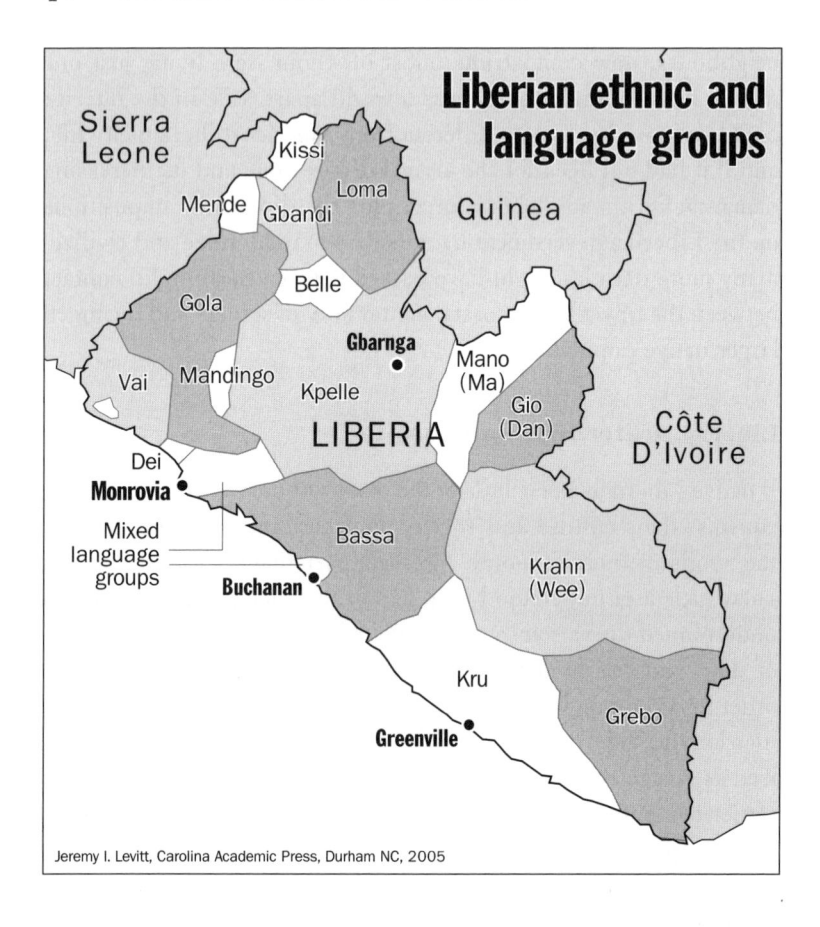

Jeremy I. Levitt, Carolina Academic Press, Durham NC, 2005

attendance dressed in full formal finery, as well as an important social forum to see and be seen in Monrovian society. Membership of a church was a requisite for social advancement, as was the practice of Freemasonry and membership for men in a Masonic lodge.

By the 1970s Liberia had seventeen Masonic lodges under the auspices of the Grand Lodge of Ancient Free and Accepted Masons of the Republic of Liberia, with a membership in excess of 1,000. Because of the secrecy, exclusivity and close association between Masonry and the True Whig Party, and because of their belief that

TRIBAL AFFILIATIONS OF LIBERIAN POPULATION, 1962 CENSUS

Tribe	Population
Kpelle	211,081
Bassa	165,856
Gio	83,208
Kru	80,813
Grebo	77,007
Mano	72,122
Lorma	53,891
Krahn	52,552
Gola	47,295
Gissi	33,914
Mandingo	29,750
Vai	28,898
Gbandi	28,599
Dey	5,396
Mende	4,974
No tribe (inc. Americo-Liberian)	23,478
Total	998,834

Source: 1962 Population Census of Liberia, Ministry of Planning and Economic Affairs, in Tuan Wreh. *The Love of Liberty* (London 1976).

decisions affecting the country were made by this esoteric group behind closed doors, the existence of the order grew to become an additional reason for resentment of the elite by the native population.

In the republic's earliest days, only light-skinned mulattoes were admitted to the Masonic lodges and darker-skinned Americo-Liberians were excluded. The first four presidents of Liberia were of light complexion, and it was not until Liberia's first dark settler president Edward J. Roye took office in 1870 that darker-toned Americo-Liberians were permitted access to the Masons, synonymous as they were with hegemony over political and business power in the country. It was much longer again, before Liberians of native origin would be allowed any kind of access to the world of Masonry, and even up until modern times its orders largely remained the exclusive preserve of the Americo-Liberian minority.

The Americo-Liberian hegemony over the Masonic orders continued right up until the time of President William Tolbert, who was the Grand Master of the Liberian Lodge. However, after the establishment of the country's first ever native-led administration in 1980, Freemasonry was banned in Liberia.

Poro practices and rituals

The secrecy which to this day surrounds aspects of membership in Masonic communities in Western societies is regularly a pretext for suspicion, ridicule and often resentment, sometimes leading to the propagation of conspiracy theories in response to the lack of hard information on Masons' beliefs and practices.

Native Liberians had for long had their own secret societies with cult practices and accompanying mysticism to more than match any of the rituals of the settlers' fraternal orders. In many communities in northern and western Liberia, the cornerstone institutions for traditional beliefs were the Poro societies (for men) and Sande societies (for women). In the south and east of the country, Poro societies have never existed, although in those regions there were parallel although less all-inclusive sodalities, such as the Kui in south-eastern Liberia.

The beliefs held by members of Liberia's secret societies, not surprisingly, focus on the relationship between humans and the land and natural world. The powers which rule their lives are thought to be those which exist all around them in nature, in the earth, the sky, in the forest and in its animals. And a key function of the elders or of the secret societies is their ability to contact, interpret and convey that natural spirituality from its sources to the people who inhabit the land.

In order to achieve and maintain this interaction with the spirits to protect the human community, various important rites are performed by the Poro and Sande, focusing on the initiation rituals undergone by young adults and the instruction received by them through their attendance in so-called 'bush schools'.

In the traditional Poro practice of initiation into adulthood, an elder of the society, fully disguised and known as a 'bush devil', selects youths to be taken into 'bush camps', sometimes for lengthy periods of ritual confinement, to undergo initiation into adulthood. Initiates swear never to disclose the details of their experiences in the bush schools to outsiders. Part of the mythology of the process reputedly involves the forcible abduction of youths for sacrifice and disembowelment, widely enough believed to spread fear among generations of Liberian children who believed the rumours that they might be taken away at night by a bush devil, never to be seen again.

A typical bush school in rural Liberia is located in a distant and inaccessible part of the forest, and may be recognizable from the outside by a clearing made through the surrounding trees being cut in a special pattern, within which palm branches are pleated together to form a type of concealed stockade in the bush.

During the period of adult initiation in the bush, lasting as little as two weeks or as much as several months, ceremonies are carried out where physical discipline is administered and pain is inflicted on adolescents. In addition to ritual flesh cutting or tattooing, circumcision may be part of the initiation, as well as the eating of the flesh and drinking the blood of a sacrificed animal. Symbolically, the process involves youths being eaten by wild spirits and re-emerging as adults, according to the secret societies' practitioners.[5]

Similar practices to those of northern Liberia's Poro also occur in western Côte d'Ivoire and in Sierra Leone, where the rainforest belt is contiguous with Liberia's and where related secret societies with similar rituals and beliefs have also existed historically. While the practices are shrouded in secrecy to this day, eyewitness accounts and anecdotal evidence can help to piece together aspects of secret-society life among the rainforest peoples.

Although there are accounts of the much more controversial ritual human sacrifice as well as cannibalism among rural Liberian communities, they do not appear to form part of strict Poro societal practice, which is not to say that members of Poro societies might not have engaged in such practices using the veil of secrecy provided by their societal affiliation to conceal their actions.

For the elders conducting initiations, ritual dress with the aim of total concealment of all parts of the human body is a crucial component of practice. It is believed that when acting in the capacity of priest or 'bush devil' – the English-language term most commonly used by modern Liberians – no part of the body should be visible; should a young inductee or outsider ever see the priest unfrocked or unmasked, he risks death or blindness.

The wearing of masks by the priests has a central function. Not only does it cover the head and face to preserve, in principle, the secrecy of the identity of the priest from his spiritual inductees, but in the Poro belief masks are also seen as a vehicle for harnessing the spirits of the bush and deploying their power among ordinary people. Thus it is not the mask itself which is believed to be endowed with such power and significance in secret society rituals; nor is it the status of the bush devil alone, whose secular identity in practice is known by most inductees. Rather, the supernatural force comes from the combination of wearing the bush devil costume and donning the mask, when acting in the capacity of priest in initiation ceremonies. It is at this point that the practitioner is then transformed into a spiritually powerful being, able to deploy supernatural strengths and to influence others in ways not possible when acting in his ordinary daytime role.

For the more mobile, recently urbanized populations who may have assimilated Christianity in adulthood, the practice of mainstream religion and membership of a secret society have by no means been mutually exclusive, and multiple affiliations with seemingly very different types of spiritual communities to this day are not seen by Liberians as a contradictory practice.

Thus, converts to Christianity from the interior might maintain membership in one or more secret societies, and, increasingly in modern times, people of mixed native and settler ancestry who have been brought up in the Christian faith have also become assimilated into rural secret societies and maintain active membership of both.

The important exception to the practice of simultaneous mainstream religious and secret societal affiliations is that membership of the latter by adherents of Islam is strictly forbidden.

Overall, Liberia's population in recent times has remained predominantly traditional in its spiritual beliefs, and today an estimated 75 per cent follow local religions as their primary faith, alongside the 15 per cent of the population who are Christians and roughly 10 per cent who are Muslims.

The Poro and Sande are believed to have existed for centuries, although their precise origins do not appear to be clearly recorded. Not unlike the Freemasons, the traditional societies have an important influence on the population's attitudes to power in the broad sense as well as extending to the specific importance of the attainment and maintenance of political power among and between the communities of the region.

Certainly those holding high office in both Monrovia and among rural communities have respected the importance of secret society membership, and many cabinet ministers as well as recent presidents of Liberia have held high positions in the traditional hierarchies. For example, President William Tolbert, although a staunch Freemason and chairman of the World Baptist Alliance, was also the 'Supreme Zo' – the highest ranking chief of the Poro Society – during his term of office.

President Samuel Doe, who came from the south-east of Liberia, where Poro societies do not exist, was nevertheless a member of a similar association, the Tarnue, while Charles Taylor and many of his top lieutenants held Poro Society membership.

The heart of the matter

During the modern Liberian civil conflict, there have been numerous documented accounts of human disembowelment and cannibalism, as well as references to the importance placed by fighters on consuming certain key organs of their victims, particularly the heart, as a means to neutralizing them spiritually and absorbing their power. These practices, while widespread during wartime, appear to fall more into the category of beliefs based on witchcraft and 'juju', or black magic, than having their origins in Liberia's secret societies.

Liberian lore as well as modern-day living accounts are punctuated with references to 'heartmen' and their threats to rural and suburban populations. In the mid-1930s, the British author Graham Greene took an assignment to travel through the Liberian interior. As documented in his book *Journey without Maps*, his experiences included encounters with communities where heartmen were believed to exist and where the fear of cannibals and belief in the existence of local leopard men and other forms of bush devil were widespread.[6]

Clearly the president of Liberia at the time of Greene's journey, Edwin Barclay (1933-44), took the existence of the leopard societies very seriously, sending informants into various regions to uncover the activities of groups suspected of being practising leopards. Frustrated that he was unable to make progress, in part because many of his spies apparently defected and joined the societies themselves, the president had an entire society rounded up, over 600 members in all, and brought to Monrovia for trial. The ringleaders were shot and the others given lengthy terms in prison.[7]

Whether or not such attacks by heartmen continue in modern Liberia in peacetime is a subject of speculation. What is clear from conversation with Liberians today, however, is that the phenomenon of heartmen is well established in their minds, testament to its enduring place in the traditional culture of the country.

Liberia's lightning societies are another example of the supernatural at work in the countryside. A pure application of man accessing nature's powers at will, whether to strike at a target or just to strike awe into the minds of onlookers, in the repertoire of initiates it is regarded as nothing out of the ordinary.

When Greene's Liberian sojourn brought him to Zigita, a town near the Guinean border, surrounded by forests and mountains on all sides, he came to appreciate the lightning societies and how they could harness the atmosphere's energy' which was so powerful and so frequently active in that vicinity. 'The use of lightning is little more than a postgraduate course to be taken when the ordinary initiations of the Bush School are over, just as the women may take poisoning as their graduate course', he wrote. *Journey without Maps* is not a science-fiction novel and Greene, no amateur traveller, was duly convinced.[8]

A century ago in the villages of rural Liberia, designated human instruments of leopard societies were believed to be involved in sacrificial abductions of victims, often children, inflicting nocturnal mutilations and carrying out brutal ritual murders to assuage the animal spirits by providing them with their necessary human offering.

An adult male of a village, living as a farmer or tradesman by day but as a leopard society member and clandestine leopard man by night, would steal off after dark and later return fully clad in his animal guise, then abduct a young child from his own or a neighbouring village into the bush for ritual tattooing, entailing the carving of symbols or marks into the skin of the victim with a knife, resulting in permanent scars, sexual mutilation or even their sacrifice.

Another early-twentieth-century foreign explorer, Lady Dorothy Mills, travelling in northern Liberia was frequently confronted with stories of ritual human leopard attacks and sacrificial abductions by bush devils. While she never personally witnessed an attack, the regularity of reference in ordinary conversation to the prevalence of occurrences, and the consistency of belief among the local population in their existence left Mills in little doubt that the existence of leopard men and their practices were still under way in numerous parts of the northern Liberian hinterland.[9]

There is a view that some of the more disturbing aspects of the style of combat in the Liberian civil struggle of the 1990s may have had their roots in the practices of the traditional societies and cannot simply be explained away as being a consequence of the fighters' intoxication or the desire of the combatants to spread terror among the enemy.

Indeed, the bizarre dress and gruesome wartime rituals, particularly of the young NPFL fighters, which observers noted from 1990 onwards, may have had real links with the traditional societal practices of native Liberia. Customs dating to early indigenous Liberian life such as the use of fearsome masks, the wearing of bizarre battle dress, disembowelment of victims and the display of slain enemies' skulls at prominent places inside captured territory, to name but a few practices, once again became commonplace in the early stages of the Liberian Civil War.

The battle dress and trademark barbarity displayed by Liberia's fighters of all factions also added to the sense of shock the civil war evoked among outside observers. During the Liberian conflict, the international media frequently portrayed the fighting practices and unspeakable atrocities of the different warring groups as savage, surreal and inexplicable.

Images of warriors in women's make up, decapitated bodies and skulls on sticks by roadside checkpoints, dismembered torsos, naked terrorists, heavily doped fighters going into battle in wedding gowns, multi-coloured wigs and extravagantly fearsome masks all served to deliver one broad message to the distant observer: something incomprehensible must have been happening in Liberia, something that we cannot relate to prior experience of war or to previous conceptions of what a 'normal' conflict should be like.

Traditional forces for contemporary power

It is apparent that historically a large proportion of Liberians believed in the importance of natural forces and spiritual power in their daily lives, in their wartime battles and in the attainment of temporal power. Equally, in the modern context, those with traditional beliefs strongly perceived the attainment and display of material power as a sign of spiritual strength, and therefore a reason for attributing respect and honour to its holder. This was a concept which the leaders of fighting factions in the Liberian Civil War all embraced to a greater or lesser degree as they sought to turn their military achievement into material gain. During the fighting, it was an important factor in gaining support in the countryside, in obtaining recruits, in holding territory and in running business operations once military success had been achieved.

Thus, to have been seen as all-conquering automatically was linked in the traditional mind as confirmation of holding natural powers. Modern-day warlords thus attempted to work their way into spiritual leadership as well as military and political positions, by assimilating the dress, titles, trappings and names of the people of the hinterland.[10] Charles Taylor, probably more than any of the aspirants to power, perceived this state of mind of native Liberians and worked to co-opt much of the spirituality of the natural world to reinforce as well as to reflect his great strengths in the eyes of the Liberian people.

THREE

CONFRONTING THE OLD ORDER

> When poor people become members of MOJA, they will learn how to put an end peacefully to 'monkey work baboon draw'[1] ... the power of the people to make other people better off will be used to make poor people better off.
>
> Togba-Nah Tipoteh, message to the people of Liberia,
> 23 December 2008

Tolbert's uncomfortable balancing act amid change

In 1970s' Liberia, William Tolbert tinkered with reform, recognizing the growing tensions between the economically empowered and the materially disenfranchised communities in his country. He attempted to bring more indigenous Liberians into government, and there was a steady increase in the numbers of native people attending university both at home and overseas during his term in office.

But education also brought activism, and in the spirit of the anti-colonialism of the times, the newly enlightened indigenous youth began to organize and pressurize the government for change. In less than a decade, it seemed as if Liberia had gone from being an oasis of African self-determination in a continent of colonies to a relic of oppression by a settler minority in a region which had by then thrown off its shackles of fealty to outside domination.

Tolbert's flaw was paradoxically what had somehow been his predecessor's strength: the 1950s and 1960s were the golden age of the True Whig Party and their economic strategy of wealth extraction from the interior. The order characterized by a fatherly President Tubman, holding sway in Monrovia and periodically touring the countryside to be received by the chiefs and elders of his loyal and subservient native population, was in those times somehow still a sustainable one. On his visits to rural areas, Tubman might personally donate the funds to build a new school or to construct a clinic, and his largesse would be warmly received.

But by the 1970s, with education, information and agitation becoming more widespread among native Liberians, Tolbert's openly autocratic image rubbed the wrong way with too many people. His style was entrepreneurial, but the transparency of his personal wealth and his inner circle's blatant exploitation of their position for material gain could no longer be countered by statesmanlike posturing, token displays of benevolence and promises of so-called 'indigenization' of national government.

President Tubman had built up, then reinforced, the foundations of the settler hegemony on the wealth of Liberia; but his rhetoric of a 'new deal for the hinterland' had created unfulfilled expectations which his successor then had to confront. President Tolbert was soon to learn the difficulties of engineering change in the same Americo-Liberian entitlement society – a rigid class system based on patronage and a rock-solid culture of exploitation.

In his time, William Tubman could claim the remoteness of the hinterland and poor communications as an excuse for underdevelopment of social infrastructure, but by the time his successor came into power the native populations were no longer satisfied with that explanation for their impoverishment.

An age of agitation

Around the world the spirit of revolution was sweeping through developed countries too – from student protests in Europe to civil rights activism, anti-Vietnam marches and the emergence of organizations like the Black Panthers in the United States. Liberia was no longer cut off from these influences and the awakening of its long-deprived indigenous people was propelled by those returning from college abroad or through those with access to progressive anti-establishment contacts within the region.

The left-wing Pan-Africanist Movement for Justice in Africa (MOJA) was founded on the University of Liberia campus in 1973 by Togba-Nah Tipoteh, a native Liberian from the Kru tribe. MOJA also had branches in Ghana and Gambia. Soon after, the All People's Freedom Alliance was also created, and in the late 1970s the Progressive Alliance of Liberia (PAL) entered the dissident fray in Monrovia. Founded in the United States in 1975 by Gabriel Baccus Matthews, PAL migrated back to Liberia in the late 1970s and soon became a fully fledged political movement, the People's Progressive Party (PPP). It gained recognition in 1978 as an official opposition party to the True Whig Party (TWP), and Baccus Matthews, a former Liberian diplomat in Washington DC, became a prominent agitator for change and lifelong standard-bearer for the progressive cause. In 1979, Amos Sawyer, a leading member of MOJA and a political science professor at the University of Liberia, put himself forward as opposition candidate for mayor of Monrovia. Sawyer was originally from Greenville, Sinoe County. His challenge to the TWP candidate, Edward Davis, who was a relation of the First Lady, Victoria Tolbert, caused a major controversy in the existing political order. Edward Davis eventually withdrew for the TWP in favour of Francis Horton.

Albert Porte, a dissident journalist and veteran advocate for social change, who had long been a critic of the Tolbert regime and its predecessors, took a major stand against the True Whig Party in 1974 when he published an attack on Stephen Tolbert, finance minister and brother of the president. Porte alleged that Tolbert had been comprehensively abusing his office for the benefit of his own business interests. Tolbert sued him for libel and won, in a much-publicized and highly acrimonious case, which nevertheless gained Albert Porte much sympathy and further helped to build resentment against Liberia's entrenched political elite.

Among Liberian students, a group called the SUP (the Student Unification Party for Free and Fair Elections), together with the Federation of Liberian Youth (FLY), was fast becoming a significant arm of the progressive movement. The pro-government side of the student community also found representation, with Americo-Liberian students represented by the All Student Alliance Party or ASAP, which retained its partisanship in lobbying for the interests of non-native Liberians of settler heritage. Although regarded by indigenous Liberians as the government opposition to the SUP, the ASAP also had representation among the expatriate student community in the United States.

Tolbert initially tried to engage with some members of the opposition and even appointed a handful to high office in his administration. Togba-Nah Tipoteh, then an economics professor at the University of Liberia, was elevated to the Tolbert cabinet and served as budget adviser to the Tolbert administration from 1971 to 1973 before founding MOJA.

For all Tolbert's desire for steady change in principle, circumstances were changing faster than he could manage. Faced with social unrest and the pressure of progressives on one side, he also had to confront conservative elements in his own party, who increasingly thought a clampdown rather than acquiescence was the answer to the rising tide of agitation.

But Tolbert also made errors of judgement, both at home and in foreign affairs. One of the domestic policies he employed to reduce unemployment (and therefore unrest) was to absorb the urban idle into the army to provide them with an occupation. But this also meant the introduction of a new, less dedicated and socially stable, and therefore unruly, element into the forces, which would have adverse consequences for the president when the situation deteriorated further. Within the army itself, advancement to the higher ranks was still reserved for Americo-Liberians, generating yet another discontented group, the talented, ambitious, non-commissioned officers of native upbringing.

In Liberia's strategic industries, there was pressure for reform too. Workers at the Liberia Mining Company (LMC) in Bomi Hills went on strike when they were laid off due to the mine's closure. The mine had steadily been running out of mineable iron ore over the past decade, and worker representatives had been lobbying for alternative employment when the inevitable day of closure came. In 1976 the LMC shut down the mine, offering workers one week's pay for every year of service and no guarantees of alternative work.

The labour force went on strike for two months pay per year of service, to the shock of the government, who had never been confronted before in this manner. The official National Union, in reality a puppet of the government, soon backed away from representing the miners' interests when they saw a showdown coming. Ultimately the dispute was resolved with the compromise of one month's pay per year of service, but importantly the principle of successful industrial action had been established. The following year, the government got a further surprise when workers at LAMCO (the Liberian American–Swedish Minerals Company) in Nimba County went on strike. The shock this time was that it was not for working conditions nor for more pay that LAMCO workers laid down tools, but for the right to elect their own representation, rather than having government-run 'unions' represent their interests in the workplace. Both the LMC dispute and the 1977 LAMCO strike demonstrated that in Liberia's lucrative industries as well as in its rural society, agitation for change had now well and truly surfaced.[2]

In attempts at business reform, Tolbert took on the Firestone Company, long the cash cow of Liberia, which had been left alone for decades to conduct its operations unhindered. The old order was shaken when the president directed that Firestone's accounts be audited for the first time in years, unearthing a raft of irregularities and unpaid taxes, which the government demanded in arrears.

By 1978, dissent was rising and opponents were becoming more openly confrontational. The ageing President Tolbert was losing his grip on the situation at home as well as failing to grasp the new realities of the wider world, some of which were very soon about to land on his doorstep.

Meanwhile, in international affairs, Tolbert's flirtations with a neutralist foreign policy to counterbalance the impact of the United

States, which had been a dangerous luxury in good times, were now becoming an outright path to political suicide as his regime needed all the outside support it could get. He opened diplomatic relations with Libya and Cuba, which displeased the United States.

Yet at the same time Tolbert announced the downsizing of key US intelligence installations, critical of US Cold War surveillance of regional adversaries such as Libya, and even cultivated contacts with Moscow and Beijing. Tolbert began to irritate Washington at a time when the United States was seeking new allies and bases across Africa to counteract the spread of revolutionary pan-Africanism and the threat of communism on the continent. Then in 1979, when the Carter administration in the USA sought bases around the globe for its Rapid Deployment Force to combat insurgencies in far-flung trouble spots, Tolbert refused the use of Robertsfield International Airport to the Americans. After this, the Pentagon and the CIA abandoned him as an ally.

The right to rice

In the climate of recession in the world economy in the 1970s, commodity-producing countries in particular were bearing the brunt of the downturn, and the price of rubber, Liberia's main cash crop, was depressed for much of the decade. This added to the financial pressures on the state just as oil prices and inflation worldwide were rising. In April 1979, the Tolbert administration sought to improve its finances and kick-start its domestic agricultural sector at the same time by imposing a tax on imported rice. The government told its people that the popular so-called 'pussava rice' (an imported US rice like Uncle Ben's), introduced years earlier by the Firestone company, was ruining the fine agricultural potential of the country. It promptly slapped a $5 tax per bag on the imported 'pa' boil' rice, raising the price of a bag to $27 in an economy where the average Monrovian was earning around $80 a month.

Furthermore, since most Liberians didn't grow rice and had no incentive to start (unlike in the case of other crops, rice growers did not receive government subsidies for their production), there was no

PRESIDENT WILLIAM TOLBERT, JUNE 1978 GENEVA

realistic prospect of domestic rice replacing imported rice in any reasonable time frame. While well-heeled Americo-Liberians could cope with the higher cost, for an average subsistence family the sharp rise in the price of their staple food simply meant having less to eat. Quite aside from the impact of the tax on the living standard of ordinary Liberians, the measure was seen as a cynical one since Tolbert's family operated the largest rice-importing business in the country and stood to benefit handsomely in the short term from the rise in prices.

Opposition to the measure was immediate and vociferous. Gabriel Baccus Matthews and his PAL supporters called for a demonstration against the measure, but Tolbert banned the proposed march, saying that the protestors could petition but not demonstrate. The timing of the confrontation could not have been worse for the government, as Liberia was about to host the annual meeting of the Organization of African Unity (OAU) and President Tolbert hoped for a major boost to his prestige from the event.

On 14 April 1979, supporters of PAL were joined by some 2,000 students at the University of Liberia in a show of opposition to the rice tax. Although initially organized as a peaceful protest, following a motion passed at PAL's Gurley Street headquarters, the action became a demonstration. Its ranks were quickly swelled to over 10,000 by ordinary Liberians, transforming the character of the event into a noisy and threatening mass march in the city centre. At first the Liberian army was able to control the crowds, firing tear gas to keep the marchers at bay, but as sections of the mob approached the Executive Mansion, the president's official home, the restraint of the Monrovia police broke down and they opened fire on the protestors, who then broke into full-scale rioting and looting.

The government panicked, even calling in reinforcements from the armed forces of its ally and neighbour Guinea and having their air force conduct low-flying manoeuvres over the capital.[3] By the end of the day, an estimated 200 protestors had been killed and 700 injured, with many ordinary soldiers joining the protestors in the looting spree, which continued throughout the capital for days.[4]

Many of the instigators, including Matthews, were imprisoned, but in a further demonstration of his weak position Tolbert quietly climbed down and reversed the rice tax, dropping the price back to just $20 a bag, while closing the University of Liberia and maintaining the presence of 700 Guinean soldiers in the capital, storing up resentment among the ranks of his own armed forces.

Leaving for studies in the United States

During the early 1970s, although the young Charles Taylor was still finding his way in the world of work in Monrovia, like his peers he had learned about Harvard University and MIT and the chance to go to study in the Boston area for the longed-for opportunity of a an American education was alluring. He continued to work, study and save, and with a little financial help from Liberian connections was soon on his way to the USA. First stop for Charles, however, was not an Ivy League school but Chamberlayne Junior College, a brownstone building on Boston's Commonwealth Avenue, which at the time was mostly a school for aspiring fashion designers and was popular with girls from local Boston society. In some ways this suited Charles just fine.

Upon arrival in New York the young Liberian student went on to spend some time with friends in Philadelphia, then travelled to Massachusetts to start school. However, although he had gained a place in Chamberlayne, at the time of his arrival he still didn't have the money to pay his college fees. Unlike many of his compatriots at the time, who were encouraged by their government to improve their education, Taylor didn't receive a grant to study in the USA and his savings from Liberia didn't go very far in Boston. So Charles worked to pay his way through college – and at Chamberlayne the college itself agreed to give him work to help pay his fees – washing dishes and cleaning floors.

Taylor also made contact with other Liberians in the area, and a cousin, Edwin Holder, put him in touch with a room-mate, which got him more settled. He picked up other jobs from there on, in a department store, as a security guard and on the night shift of an assembly line at a plastic bag factory in South Boston, which at that time had a reputation as one of the tougher parts of the city and indeed the country.

Being an outsider didn't stop Charles Taylor from getting out into the community at a time when American society itself was in a state of upheaval: 'I was in Boston during desegregation,' he recalled, 'and quite frankly, I don't know how I made it. I think I was one of only two or three black men to go out in South Boston at the time. I guess most of the people knew I was from Liberia. It was strange to me – I drove out there from my job at eleven at night and never got attacked.'[5]

Somehow, it helped being known as an African rather than a black American, and Taylor played the part to take advantage of people's attitudes. Already some American blacks, especially in the South, were adopting African dress and vocabulary in an attempt both to emphasize their cultural 'roots' and to avoid discrimination, so being a natural African made it all the easier, and Charles Taylor milked it to the full. He later said: 'The people of South Boston formed a kind of cult around me. As soon as whites realized I was African, they changed their attitude about me. It was truly very strange.'[6]

Charles quickly warmed to the American way of life. He developed a taste for some of the finer things and, when he could, he loved to buy the best. Sometimes, instead of paying his rent, he would spend his earnings on buying a nice suit to wear to weekend parties. Later he managed to get enough money to buy a car, so he got himself a silver Chevrolet Cougar, which made him more popular still with fellow students riding home from campus.

But studies were second to outside activities, and by now for the good-looking, outgoing and personable young West African man, women and parties combined with expatriate political activism to absorb the bulk of Charles Taylor's free time in America. In Boston, in Rhode Island, in New York and in Philadelphia, there were friends and compatriots to socialize with at parties, peers to converse with and to inform as well as to persuade at meetings – and Taylor was hungry to build his network of followers interested in the Liberian situation. 'When I got to Massachusetts, I realized that Liberians needed to keep in touch with the political climate in Liberia', said Taylor.

Bentley days and family life

After Chamberlayne, Charles decided to go on and try to get a full college degree. He applied to Harvard Business School but didn't get in. So he went on to attend Bentley College (now Bentley University) in Waltham, Massachusetts. There, his personal life was also very active. Shortly after moving to Bentley, Charles met Burnice Emmanuel, a Trinidadian American, with whom he moved into an apartment on the top floor at 58 Cheney Street in the Dorchester neighbourhood.

Burnice recalls how they first met: 'I was walking out of one of his neighbour's buildings and he just asked me for my phone number.' Their relationship was to flourish. In February 1977 the couple had a child, Chucky Taylor, who weighed 12 lb 4 oz at birth, his mother recalls, and scarcely resembled either of his parents. The complexion and features of Chucky seemed more to reflect those of Burnice's white grandfather than the copper-coloured skin and dark eyes of his parents.

Burnice recalled that when Charles arrived at the hospital, 'He didn't believe the boy was his kid. He didn't look like he was a black baby.' As Chucky grew up, his father may never have given him quite the tender care and attention that might have been expected from a normal doting parent. Once, when the child was still less than a year old, Chucky's mother related that Taylor saw his son drinking from a baby bottle and suddenly grabbed it from Chucky, declaring: 'You're too grown up for bottles' and then threw it straight out of the window.[7]

Charles and Burnice never married. They lived together in what Charles referred to as 'French cohabitation' in Dorchester for three or four years. In the early 1990s, Taylor invited the family to Liberia; so mother and son visited Taylor in his new home in the Liberian bush after nearly a decade of separation.

Charles had other girlfriends too, both black and white. While living in Dorchester with Burnice, who later said she was 'considered his common law wife', the upwardly mobile Liberian socialite met a 16-year-old girl called Enid Boikai, known by her second name Tupee, whom he immediately took to, although he didn't date her until later. That was in Mattapan in 1975.

When Charles did start courting Tupee as a girlfriend he spoiled her, took her on trips to New York City and quickly the couple were making plans. He moved out of Burnice's place and into an upscale apartment with his new Liberian belle. She suited the profile of a partner for the ambitious young Liberian, and she had family links with prominent members of the dissident community back in her native Nimba County. One such connection was Thomas Quiwonkpa, a young Liberian who was an army sergeant back home – and another who held progressive views about the future of his country. In 1980, after his return to Monrovia, Taylor married Tupee, cementing his personal life and giving him a foothold in an important constituency in the countryside too.

Delores Adighibe, a fellow Liberian student who lived downstairs in the same Dorchester apartment block on Cheney Street, was another woman whom Taylor impressed. Initially a classmate at Chamberlayne, Delores was persuaded to sign up for Bentley once he had decided to go there. She recalled having plans to attend a different school, but Charles told her: 'No, Bentley's the place to go – it'll be the school of the future.' So Adighibe went too. 'It had a high academic outlook', Charles said, not suffering from the least inferiority complex about the more prestigious nearby Ivy League schools which he hadn't managed to get into. He said: 'you know at

Bentley we like taking on the Harvard boys. We used to go and sit and argue with the Harvard students around Davis Square.'[8]

Delores and Charles talked about Liberia a lot together and were members of the Liberian Community Association of Massachusetts, a social organization in the early 1970s which later became a political group. Adighibe remembers how he was also proud of America, proud of his place in it and ambitious to make Liberia more like the United States. He believed that if Liberia had been founded by settlers of American origin, it could also develop to become more like America, with the right kind of leadership.

While at Bentley, Taylor switched from accounting to economics – he got bored with accounting and was really always interested in politics, but chose to do development economics, a field where he felt he could 'return to Liberia and be of some help to our people'. During his studies he was particularly impressed by the work of the economist W.W. Rostow, and thought he might be able to apply some of Rostow's theories back home. 'The "Big Push" was a very interesting theory', Taylor testified at his trial in The Hague. 'I felt utilizing it in the Liberian setting would help a lot.' But, whatever his academic training, Taylor's political ambitions were uppermost. 'I saw myself in the future being part of a government that would help to enable our people.'[9]

Outside school, Taylor also started to become much more political, attending rallies and demonstrations up and down the East Coast. The marches he went on typically had as their destination the Liberian embassy, although one time the protesters ended up taking an empty mock coffin bearing the name of President Tolbert up to the front of the White House.[10] One of Taylor's other ploys was to sit on the steps of the US Capitol and wait for congressmen who might listen to his accounts of the difficult times of his fellow Liberians and the need for democratic government in his country.

A fellow New England Liberian activist during Taylor's time, Maureen Hutchinson, knew him well during those years, and particularly remembers how he was always on his way to meetings, running for office in associations – and not always winning, initially at any rate. But, she recalls that 'he was a man of charm and words'.

Charles Taylor saw himself as a leader and a visionary from the outset. Already in those days he talked ambitiously to peers about 'one day going back home to free my people'. Like other contemporaries, Maureen Hutchinson also remembered Taylor more as activist than academic. 'He never missed meetings', she said: ' they were something he looked forward to. He made sure his voice was heard in a senatorial manner.'[11] After graduating from Bentley with his Bachelor's degree Taylor went on in 1978 to enrol in an MBA programme in Manchester, New Hampshire – a course he never finished.

But Charles also found his way around the world of real business quickly enough too. After his undergraduate years of doing manual jobs and factory work, he began moving up in the world – suddenly he always seemed to have money and 'he started buying more expensive clothes – not like that one suit and same pair of shoes we remembered him in for years', former neighbour Delores Adighibe recalled. He got a job at the Liberty Mutual Insurance Company in downtown Boston, which paid well apparently.

He also became involved in some more lucrative dealings on the side. He was in the car business for a while, Dolores said, 'sending cars home to Liberia'. Working together with his Liberian cousin Edwin Holder, and with his experience in the insurance industry, Taylor soon learned how to put together authentic-looking documentation and arrange to get the goods overseas and into the hands of their new owners. There was also a related insurance scheme generating 'intentional losses' and arranging 'car accidents', as his former Dorchester neighbour put it. A business based on exploiting loopholes in the system, it nevertheless provided a stream of ready cash. That was in the days when, as Dolores put it, 'the insurance firms didn't check quite as carefully as they do now'.[12]

ULAA and expatriate activism

By the end of the 1970s, the two very different worlds of arm's-length opposition to a rapidly evolving but still repressive society at home and a life of expatriate activism overseas came together for

Charles Taylor. Taylor was ambitious by nature – mostly for his own advancement, but also to play a big part in bringing change in the land of his birth. With his degree from Bentley College and his network in the United States, he was steadily accumulating credentials and had by now built up a following through years of proactive socializing, lobbying and campaigning. He had friends, followers and connections not only in the Liberian diaspora in the USA, but also in the wider community of dissidents seeking change in their homeland. What he had lacked until now was the means to take his ambitions further.

Taylor also admired the American way of life and had developed a flair for business through his various work experiences as a student. But politics came naturally to the young college graduate, and as a Liberian he sought to build influence in political circles in the United States, at a time when the policies of Washington DC towards his own country and Africa as a whole were undergoing radical change.

The official umbrella organization for participation in Liberian affairs by expatriates in the USA was the Union of Liberian Associations in the Americas (ULAA), which was founded in July 1974 with its headquarters in Philadelphia. Among the officially expressed aims of the ULAA are to promote 'national reconciliation, integration and unification; preserve and protect Liberian culture, history and traditions; uphold and defend fundamental rights, including the human rights and civil liberties of Liberians'.

While intended as a national forum and umbrella organization for the disparate but numerous community of Liberians in the United States – estimated at some 35,000 by the late 1970s – as the decade wore on it increasingly became the vehicle through which educated but politically disenfranchised – mostly indigenous – Liberians could voice their disapproval at the conduct of their nation's affairs, and agitate for change. The opportunities for advancement within their own country for those from outside the settler ascendancy – the Christian fundamentalist, Freemasonic, True Whig elite of Liberian society – even for those indigenous Liberians with a foreign education, were still severely limited, despite President Tolbert's declared policy of enhancing access to opportunities for those of non Americo-Liberian origin.

After joining the ULAA in his student days Taylor eventually became head of the Boston branch of the association. Then, in 1978, well established in his New England power base, he ran for national office in the organization. However, despite his enthusiasm, intelligence and ambition, by now Charlie Taylor was also attracting opponents as well as followers within the ULAA. Even more importantly, he was not an indigenous Liberian, having an Americo-Liberian father and more of the complexion as well as the attitude of the Americo-Liberian rulers in Monrovia – despite his mounting opposition to the way they ruled.

Bai Gbala, who together with Moses Duopu defeated Taylor in the 1978 campaign for the post of National Executive President of the ULAA, had mixed feelings about Charles Taylor the activist candidate. Describing him as 'highly patriotic in his ambition to transform the country', Gbala cooperated with Taylor in many aspects of the ULAA's programme. But he often warned Taylor that the mainstream of the organization would not accept him because of his origins. Like it or not, he told Taylor, whom he considered a friend, the ULAA at the time was dominated by Liberians of indigenous origin.[13] They were the people who had been waiting the longest and were in the biggest need of change. And the grievances that the organization sought to express were essentially those of indigenous Liberians. Gbala himself came from Grand Gedeh County, in the south-east of Liberia. He later served as ULAA president in 1979–80.

Charles Taylor believed that the genesis of Liberia's severe crisis of the late twentieth century lay in the mistakes made in the early development of the country, when the settlers kept their distance and failed to integrate with native Liberians. Rather, by choosing to subdue them, dominate the interior and exploit its people and resources, they stored up big problems.

> An opportunity was lost by the settlers that came from the United States to bond with the traditional people ... There was not this social integration ... it was a real big tussle. Aborigine Liberians

did not have an opportunity to go to school ... that opportunity was lost ... sadly it exists to a great extent in Liberia today.

It was clear that Taylor also believed that this unfortunate aspect of Liberia's historical evolution made him special when, in the late 1990s, he took power as the leader of his country as its first president of truly mixed Americo-Liberian and native origin. 'This is why I succeeded', Taylor declared, 'because I am about the first president of Liberia that fell almost dead centre. Half Americo-Liberian and half aborigine, so I mean I could fit in any camp.'[14]

Charles Taylor may have thought that he broadly straddled the two feuding camps of Liberian society, but many of his peers did not. Although he was born of a native Liberian mother, being brought up in an Americo-Liberian household from before his first birthday, attending the top high school in the country where Americo-Liberians studied and going on to spend his formative years in college in the United States was not, for them, the blueprint of someone who was in close touch with the aspirations of native society.

Furthermore, unlike his peers from either the True Whig Party in Monrovia or the native opposition with roots in the countryside, Taylor had no natural constituency of his own in Liberia. With only tenuous links to the Gola tribe through his mother, he could call on neither the core Americo-Liberian community nor one of the powerful tribes such as the Kpelle, Gio, Mano, Bassa or Loma, who had significant populations in the north and centre of Liberia.

While at this time there were also many Americo-Liberians suffering hardship inside the country who had grievances to voice, it was always going to be an uphill struggle for Taylor as an Americo-Liberian to be elected to the ULAA's highest office. That didn't stop him trying, however. Although he was never elected as executive president, Taylor did become national chairman of the organization for a brief period in 1979. Whereas some of the establishment were hesitant, Taylor and a handful of others were resolute and willing to both take and implement decisions, often on their own authority.

Beyond Taylor's social and ethnic profile, there were other early misgivings among fellow ULAA members about his intentions, despite his proactive efforts and declared desire to see change in Liberia. Bai Gbala further recalls that 'He was patriotic, a friend ... but democratic principles were not in his mind' in describing the fast-evolving political philosophy of the revolutionary-in-waiting. But if Taylor was frustrated in his attempts to gain recognition abroad, developments at home in Liberia were soon to give him a chance to take a big step closer to the real prize – a stake in the emerging new order in Liberia.

Showdown with the president

In May 1979, President Tolbert went to the United States to address the United Nations in New York in his capacity as president of the Organization for African Unity. The ULAA had banned contact with the Liberian head of state in protest against the brutal suppression of the rice riots the previous month and the introduction of a new anti-sedition law banning criticism of the government.

But for Taylor the opportunity for direct confrontation was appealing. He and his fellow ULAA leaders organized a protest march on the Liberian Mission where Tolbert was due to go after making his address, to protest against the policies of the Liberian government. Moses Duopu the ULAA president, Taylor as chairman of the board of directors, Blamo Nelson the secretary general, Bai Gbala, Tom Woewiyu and others all participated. Their supporters were aggressive and rowdy.

When the president's limousine arrived at the Mission, Tolbert tried to defuse the increasingly threatening mob by inviting the protest's leaders inside. The members of the ULAA delegation paid their visiting president differing degrees of courtesy as they expressed their opposition to his policies, but Taylor was by far the most outspoken and the least respectful. First Tolbert tried to hold a debate with the protestors in front of the media, but Taylor, brazen and articulate, outclassed his ageing adversary. Then, to the shock of the bystanders and with Tolbert already in a corner, the young ULAA agitator announced that he was taking over the Liberian Mission. Tolbert protested, warning Taylor that he would be prosecuted. 'Now listen, this has to stop', he said. But Charles Taylor simply said: 'We just want to make sure that our views are known.'[15] Then the police moved in, breaking up the demonstration, and Taylor was arrested. President Tolbert later decided not to press charges and Taylor was released.

The raucous New York protest was by no means a one-off display of Taylor's anti-Tolbert disobedience. At the time of the rice riots in April, he had reportedly advocated buying arms and storming the Liberian embassy, according to a fellow ULAA board member.[16] But Taylor's performance that day in New York marked the first step on a path to power which would increasingly be characterized by assertiveness as well as brute force and which would blend the power of his natural popularity with a more ruthless approach to the achievement of his goals.

'In the United States, I was very forceful', he said. 'It was a non-violent movement. We defended the rights of individuals in Liberia who had been arrested trying to promote democracy. It was just a matter of wanting to see things better.'[17]

Indeed, it was a global age of agitation, and protests in New York and Washington DC against repressive regimes were increasingly commonplace, as was the tactic of attempting to occupy diplomatic missions of detested regimes. Following the revolution in Iran in 1979, the mood was one of political change in much of the developing world, and Liberians, Ghanaians and protestors from other African countries, all fed up with dictatorships at home, marched for change from their American stage.

On 1 October that year, Tolbert met his critics again at the Liberian embassy in Washington DC. A group led by Gbala, including Taylor and other ULAA delegates, was received by the president, who early in the meeting asked each of them: 'How long have you been in the USA?' as if to suggest that the dissidents were out of touch with the big changes he had been making at home. When it came to his turn, Taylor replied: 'With respect Mr President, this is none of your damn business.' Gbala extended an apology to Tolbert afterwards for his fellow delegate's display of bad manners.[18]

Invitation to return

Despite these warning signals, in February 1980 the elderly President Tolbert, perhaps still believing himself secure in his position, and thinking that his youthful upstart critics in the USA had been away so long they would be surprised to see how different Liberia had become, invited Taylor, Gbala, Nelson and other ULAA delegates to come home and lend their skills and education to the country, as well as having a chance to see the situation for themselves. Tolbert invited them to advise him how to bring about the reforms within the country which he said he was sincerely trying to achieve, and committed to paying their expenses in Monrovia as well.

Despite initial concerns regarding their security, particularly in view of the laws in force banning criticism of the government, an amnesty was granted for the visitors and the ULAA delegation travelled to Monrovia at the Tolbert government's invitation.

The Liberia in which Charles Taylor found himself in early 1980 was rife with rumours and political dissent, with an all-pervasive mood of impending change. While some of the ULAA delegation went home after their consultations with the Tolbert administration, Taylor and Nelson stayed on, perhaps sensing potential in the tense and rapidly evolving political situation. Nurturing his ambitions and determined to be at the centre of any radical shifts that might occur, by then Taylor could not have been blind to the potential opportunities which might be created in the event of an abrupt change of government in Liberia.

Tolbert, despite his avid desire to see through a reforming agenda, had been overtaken by the speed of events. The bold steps he had taken to make Liberia more 'African' in the world and less segregated as a society at home had failed to satisfy the competing constituencies on whom his survival depended. Distancing himself from American influence crippled his regime at a time when he gambled on appeasing dissidents at the risk of losing his traditional domestic power base. Ineffective and unpopular, he became withdrawn in the presidency, with his friends in the government steadily abandoning him. Former allies discussed his impeachment openly in the

Executive Mansion when he was out of town. Despondent but still out of touch with reality, the president soldiered on.

By now, there was talk of plotting against him from all sides, and observers both foreign and domestic were sensitized to the strong possibility of the regime's overthrow.

Coup of April 1980

The coup of 12 April 1980, which ended 133 years of rule by the Americo-Liberian ascendancy, was instigated by a group of non-commissioned officers under the command of Sergeant Thomas Quiwonkpa. Unlike some of the other plotters who sought to displace Tolbert at the time, Quiwonkpa and his fellow plotters could be confident of the backing of the rank and file of the army as well as of many of the progressives seeking change in the country. With the impending anniversary of the rice riots on 14 April widely expected to cause more unrest in the country, the Quiwonkpa group pressed ahead quickly with their plans.

At the head of the leading group of nineteen army insurgents who assaulted the Executive Mansion late in the night of 11 April was another sergeant, Samuel Kanyon Doe. With some inside help from collaborators in the Executive Mansion Guard, the group first climbed the fence into the mansion grounds, neutralizing the security and shooting out the telephone wires used to communicate with the army barracks. They then fought their way into the building itself and upstairs to the presidential offices. Most of the soldiers on duty walked away from their posts or simply didn't react, as they were for the most part friends of the attacking party, or at least sympathetic to the mission.

Once inside the mansion, Doe's group reached the eighth floor where President Tolbert and his wife Victoria and their family were sleeping. The First Couple heard shooting, and President Tolbert became more concerned, receiving no response as he attempted to call around the various mansion security posts from inside his suite. But the presidential quarters were fully secured and no one could get in. Trying to gain access, the intruders knocked on Tolbert's door to get someone to open it. 'Mother, mother, open the door', said a man's voice on the other side, as the First Lady questioned them, demanding to know who was there. 'We want to talk to you Mother, we won't harm you', the voice outside said.

For some minutes the voices outside ceased as the attackers left to get a key to the suite from the mansion security office. Returning to unlock the door, six men burst into the suite, shot the president in his chamber in front of his wife, then pushed her aside. The invaders were scantily dressed, with painted-on war masks, typical of the native Kru warriors from Liberia's past conflicts. Roaming on through the presidential quarters, they rounded up the president's family, killing two of his children, then herding the others out of the premises to jail.[19]

There are active conspiracy theories of CIA involvement in the Tolbert overthrow. It has been alleged by a former Liberian government official, for example, that the USA provided the coup-makers with maps of the Executive Mansion,[20] while an early version of Victoria Tolbert's biography referred to the 'white hand' of a masked assailant stabbing her husband in the Executive Mansion murder. The latter reference was, however, removed from the published version of her book.[21]

What is also known is that one of the other coups under preparation in April 1980 was one led by Major William Jarbo, who had trained as a ranger in the United States. With good links inside the US intelligence establishment, his military takeover might have been favoured by the US intelligence community had it been successfully launched before Quiwonkpa's.[22]

Taylor, in his trial testimony before the Special Court for Sierra Leone in The Hague, took up the account of that night of bloodshed. Recalling the quarters he himself would occupy years later, he described how he thought the assassination must have happened:

> Now, I know that place because I lived up there myself ... The eighth floor is the family living floor of the president. It is very, very secured. All of the glasses up there are bullet proof glasses. The doors are sealed, so when the president enters, there is the

living room, his bedroom, his wife's bedroom, the entire area ... once the president ... once he enters ... it is secured.

Taylor continued his account, as related to him at the time by Thomas Quiwonkpa. The first shot that was directed at the president that night came from a soldier named Nelson B. Toe, but Corporal Harrison Pennue, who fired the second shot, was the president's actual assassin. Pennue then proceeded to slit open the Liberian leader, in a display of ritualistic disembowelment that was to be a barbaric foretaste of the methods of the Liberian regime about to take power.

Although Quiwonkpa had been instrumental in planning the coup, and Pennue was Tolbert's killer, it was Master Sergeant Doe, the highest ranking of the group leading the Executive Mansion assault, who first went on the radio to announce the overthrow of the president. A friend of Quiwonkpa since their schooldays, Samuel Doe received his comrade's backing for the leadership and he swiftly emerged from the chaos as Liberia's new ruler, going on to announce the formation of a 'People's Redemption Council' (PRC), of which he became chairman, and which was henceforth taking over the reins of power in Monrovia.

Taylor, by then already seeking an involvement with the new regime, was proactive from the outset, directly approaching the inexperienced Doe to recommend that the country's borders be sealed. He then personally directed trucks to be sent with troops to prevent a counter-coup from a neighbouring country.

As news of the coup spread, the streets of the capital erupted into a carnival-like atmosphere of drunken celebrations, with revellers dressed in tribal masks and native costumes rampaging through the streets of Monrovia in a frenzy of looting and hysterical partying. One of the first actions of the incoming Doe regime was to call members of the former cabinet and their deputies to the Barclay Training Centre (BTC), the main army barracks in Monrovia, for questioning.

Nine former ministers were sentenced to death following sham trials at which they were not allowed a defence. But in the mood of upheaval and vengeance that seized the country's new rulers, justice was not a necessary precondition for execution of the symbols of the old order. And so, ten days after the coup, with Monrovia's entire foreign media invited to attend, thirteen of William Tolbert's ministers were marched down from the barracks to the nearby Barclay Beach, nine large wooden poles were erected in the sand, and the first ministers were lashed to them to be executed.

Delirious natives ran forward to get close to the scene of the executions, while hundreds of dancing and singing local women gathered nearby repeating their favourite chant: 'Who born soldier? Country woman! – Who born minister? Congo woman!' Drunken soldiers milled around in party mood waiting for the executions to begin.[23]

Included in the list of victims was the president's brother, Frank Tolbert, who suffered a heart attack as he was lashed to the pole. Slumping forward over his bindings, he was then cut down and shot while unconscious on the ground. There were other ministers, some of whom Taylor remembered from his early days in Monrovia. He testified that these were people he knew, recalling that he had dated one of Frank Tolbert's daughters and been at his house many times. Taylor recalled: 'I had never seen anybody killed. I have seen dead bodies before as in normal death. It was a very chilling experience for me. I stood on the balcony of the commanding general's office and looked over to where it – the execution – occurred.'[24]

Each of the ministers was then shot at by Doe's soldiers in a botched firing squad execution. The army detail that was charged with the task had already joined in the drunken orgy of celebration which was taking place on the beach, and when their moment came some members of the firing squad proved incapable of hitting their targets. In at least one case, the assigned firing squad enlistee was replaced by another, who walked up to his victim with an Uzi machine gun and fired directly into his face.

Charles Taylor, at his trial in The Hague, described the debate that ensued between progressives and hardliners in the wake of the coup. He recalled one day when Quiwonkpa came back from a PRC meeting to say there were plans to execute 'up to 200' people. Taylor

EXECUTIONS AT BARCLAY BEACH, 1980

said: 'I fought for my end to tell them that it was not [necessary] ... that Tolbert's death was sufficient.' But clearly the prevailing view in the PRC was not one of clemency. Taylor went on: 'the vast majority ... of the aborigines were happy and wouldn't care less ... they probably wanted more to go. People saw this as an opportunity at last to vent the anger ... from over the years.'[25]

If Charles Taylor was so opposed to the brutal display of retribution by the new regime, why did he not leave and return right then to the United States? That was a question he was asked at his trial, almost thirty years later. His explanation was, first, that 'pulling out would have been a very glorious act to do.... but it would not have made any difference'. Second, he stated that '[we] would have lost the opportunity to bring about the meaningful change ... Imagine ... all the progressives are on board. I am in the system. I am respected. I speak freely to all of them.' It would also have been a glorious opportunity missed, after having networked and manoeuvred his way back to within an inch of the corridors of power at a time when the whole country and its economy was up for grabs – and when there were few others around with the same skills and experience as he had to take advantage of the situation.

So Taylor stayed on, initially working under the wing of Quiwonkpa, trying, as he put it, to 'get the soldiers back to the barracks'. In the days and weeks immediately after the coup, there was a veritable flood of country-based army recruits, uneducated, untravelled and ignorant, who now wanted to get to Monrovia for a piece of the action, to loot and to steal from the properties of the recently deposed ruling classes.

Native power: the People's Redemption Council

Soon, sitting in his army fatigues and reflector sunglasses looking out over the ocean from the Executive Mansion balcony, the wiry army sergeant and country boy head of state Samuel Doe began to experience the headaches of high office. Leader of a junta that had just overthrown a dynasty, Doe may have felt he was bulletproof – but while he was able quickly enough to gain the loyalty of many of his peers, his real challenge came in grappling with the realities of assembling and managing a new administration for Liberia. For a semi-literate 28-year-old from Tuzon in eastern Liberia's rural Grand Gedeh County, the task was daunting indeed.

While many Americo-Liberians had fled the country in the wake of the takeover, others initially threw in their lot with Doe, seeing the chance for personal advancement in this new government, an opportunity which had been denied to so many in previous times. While the new president sought to construct his cabinet using as many of his ethnic insiders as possible, often, like their leader, they were illiterate, until recently village dwellers or soldiers, with little experience of city life, let alone running the affairs of state in a mineral-rich, geopolitically important West African nation.

Doe's People's Redemption Council (PRC) cabinet was initially composed of fifteen ministers, all but one of whom was a native Liberian. It included former student activists from the ULAA and the Progressive Alliance of Liberia who returned and took up cabinet posts. Gabriel Baccus Matthews became foreign minister; Henry Boima Fahnbulleh Jr, a friend of Charles Taylor, became minister of education; while Togbah-Nah Tipoteh became minister of planning and economic affairs. Amos Sawyer became president of the University of Liberia, rather than entering government. The PAL and MOJA wing of the cabinet had much more of a hard-line 'Marxist–Leninist' complexion to it, according to Taylor, while the ULAA returnees like himself he considered more moderate.

Overall the PRC initially had a very hard-line and radical tone to it, as its earliest actions quickly demonstrated. It made no pretence of making concessions to civilian democratic administration and it put a firm military stamp on government. Each cabinet minister was given a military rank, starting from lieutenant colonel and going up from there. Whatever their prior background, all of Doe's ministers became military men overnight. Decisions were made by decree at the highest level of the PRC, which comprised Chairman Doe, Commanding General Quiwonkpa, the speaker and the vice chairman of the PRC. Other ordinary members of the cabinet took the orders that were handed down and implemented them rather than engaging in discussion and debate of affairs of state.

Despite its apparently radical political complexion, the PRC adopted a pro-United States stance from the beginning. Indeed, sensitive to the frustrations of Washington DC with his predecessor, Samuel Doe made all the right noises about security and loyalty to US geopolitical aims, a move which helped to secure his position domestically, as the US embraced the takeover, for the most part prepared to ignore the bloodshed of the regime's earliest days.

Liberia would never be the same again after April 1980. But just as the Americo-Liberians were violently dislodged from power by the events of that month, those from other indigenous groups who had hoped that change would benefit them were soon to be disappointed. Truly the long-hoped-for indigenous Liberian revolution quickly dissolved after Samuel Doe's takeover in 1980, and if briefly it was a reality, the triumph of the dispossessed was to be quickly replaced in the early 1980s by a despotic Krahn tribal ascendency.

Initially, Doe relied on the educated 'progressives' who had endorsed regime change and whom he installed in his cabinet. Together with these, he invited into government the returnees like Taylor and the other ULAA activists with American education and working experience, handing over the reins to those whom he thought were equipped to take charge of the administration of the country. However, rather than taking a firm grip on rebuilding the economy and reshaping Liberian society, the early months following Doe's takeover were characterized by rivalry and infighting between the American-based returnees and those progressives who had stayed during Tolbert's rule. Ultimately, in frustration, Doe decided to take back power from these ineffectual progressives and 'green card' revolutionaries, replacing them with less experienced but more trusted deputies from his own inner circle.

The new order of the Doe years was to be even more built on patronage than those of the Tolbert and Tubman administrations in the 1960s and 1970s, and it soon became many times more violent, unrepresentative and inhumane in its conduct. The Doe junta and its ruling members became drunk both on power and on personal greed. In the early 1980s Doe's Liberia went on to become one of the most repressive regimes in Africa, as well as one of the biggest recipients of US aid on the continent.

PART TWO

FROM DICTATORSHIP TO ANARCHY

FOUR

SERGEANT-IN-CHARGE: SAMUEL DOE'S PRESIDENCY

> The country had the opportunity to give the black race leadership but instead ... they were like swine who had pearls and either did not know their value or could not make use of them.
>
> Phillip Davies in Nnamde Azikiwe, *My Odyssey*

In the immediate wake of the coup Taylor already had a powerful ally in government through his connection to the head of the army. Former Sergeant Quiwonkpa was now General Quiwonkpa, commander of the armed forces and one of the four senior members of the People's Redemption Council, of which Samuel Doe was chairman. Doe thought that the ULAA students who had recently been brought by President Tolbert to Liberia should have a voice in the new government, partly since they had originally been critics of the ex-president's rule. Furthermore, the skills and connections of Americo-Liberians or other city-reared, foreign-educated Liberians were in demand in the new administration.

Initially, however, Charles Taylor was not offered an appointment in the PRC administration, having been stationed at the barracks with Quiwonkpa helping out on the administrative needs of the military. But there were more interesting assignments available, ones involving responsibility for some of the considerable amounts of cash which the new regime was beginning to receive from its chief backer, the United States. Business, unlike the army, was an area in which Taylor had proven skills, and his desire to get ahead naturally drew him to seek out opportunities in an area where he could benefit personally and perform visibly.

According to Taylor's own account, some three months after the coup Quiwonkpa enquired of him whether he had found a job in the new government yet. When Taylor said he hadn't, the commanding general said initially that nearly all the jobs – that is, cabinet posts in the government – had already been parcelled out by Doe, except for the post of head of the General Services Agency. So he took Taylor to see Doe, who said: 'Oh my God, you still don't have a job?', adding, 'I've just been told there's a position open, its not a ministerial position, its a director-generalship ... would you like that position?', to which Taylor replied: 'I will work wherever you send me.' Doe replied, 'well okay, we'll make it a ministry ... or at least we'll raise it to a ministerial level.'[1]

And so Charles Taylor became director general of the General Services Agency (GSA) of the Republic of Liberia, with cabinet rank as a politician and the military rank of major. He initially attended ordinary PRC cabinet meetings and later, because of his special status as a 'leader from America', he was also invited to attend full PRC meetings.

Thus, from being invited on a short-term assignment to come to 'look and learn' about the policies of the Tolbert government less than six months earlier, Charles Taylor was now in his first position of power, and at the heart of government, one of only two non-native Liberians in the Doe cabinet.

A new career in procurement

Once appointed as head of the GSA, an agency modelled after the United States General Services Administration, Charles Taylor had control over the purse strings of an important operation. As head of procurement for a government which was already being promised millions in support by its superpower ally the United States, he

**PRESIDENT SAMUEL DOE
SEATED IN THE EXECUTIVE MANSION, 22 APRIL 1980**

ended up in charge of a pivotal agency and occupied a position of significant influence among his peers.

Taylor asked for an assistant, requesting that his ULAA colleague Blamo Nelson be brought in as deputy director, and at the same time he hired a friend from his US college days, Delores Adighibe, as financial director. Nelson was the former secretary general of the ULAA, and just what Taylor needed as an administrator. He was, as Taylor said in The Hague, 'very useful, a man who really loves paper'.

In office as head of Liberia's GSA, Taylor was able to give full expression to his by now well-honed business sense and acumen for deal-making. In a government which rapidly became devoured by patronage and greed, the ability to deliver material perks and distribute favours put the newly appointed director in a powerful position. He also used the GSA post to earn favour with the new president and his inner circle, for example purchasing a consignment of new Toyota four-wheel-drives for delivery to every office holder in Doe's administration and at the same time refurbishing ex-President Tolbert's stretch limousine for Doe's own personal use.[2]

Under Taylor, the GSA initiated centralization of much of the government's purchasing operations, allowing the bulk procurement of ministry supplies, which would save the government money. However, since requisition-related kickbacks were a major source of income for individual ministers approving their departments' purchases, at a stroke Taylor's new arrangement deprived them of an easy source of creaming off the top from departmental supply budgets.

The position soon also earned him the jealousy and resentment of his fellow ministers, particularly since, as an Americo-Liberian with education and management experience, he tried to keep aloof from Doe's mostly uneducated inner circle of indigenous Liberian ministers. The latter's jealousy soon took a more concrete form when, in January 1981, Taylor was linked by his rivals to the release of a government document and detained, while the Taylor residence in Sinkor was ransacked by a group of Doe's heavies. Thomas Quiwonkpa was in hospital when the incident occurred, but when he learned of his political protégé's arrest he immediately had him released and disciplined the soldiers involved.[3]

By now, Taylor had also marked himself out among his fellow ministers, for a time at least, as one of the few still maintaining some semblance of financial management standards and accountability for the resources his department had at its disposal. The majority of Doe's ministerial appointees, once in office, quickly came to treat their position in government as a golden opportunity to live a life of unbridled luxury at the country's expense.

When Taylor decided to enforce some discipline in the use of public resources, he made enemies. Official vehicles were routinely used by ministers and ministry staff around the city out of working hours, in contravention of government rules. But in one incident, following a complaint from President Doe that there were insufficient vehicles for a planned presidential trip upcountry, Taylor ordered troops to requisition for the presidential fleet all available government cars that were in use around the capital. Suddenly, in the course of an afternoon, disgruntled ministers found themselves temporarily without transport as a result of the GSA's action. In a separate incident one of the ministers whom Taylor crossed was the deputy minister of commerce, Clarence Momolu, whose personal request for an office refurbishment had been rejected by the GSA on grounds of budget restrictions. Provoking Momolu's ire soon proved to be a costly action for Charles Taylor, by now rapidly exiting his honeymoon period in office with the Doe junta.

Once Doe was established in office, his purge of the former True Whig elite continued. A later high-level assassination, which occurred months after the coup, and which would cost Doe dearly while benefiting Taylor, saw the killing of Adolphus Benedict Tolbert, 'A.B.', President Tolbert's son. The husband of the Ivorian President Houphouët-Boigny's adopted daughter, Désirée 'Daisy' Delafosse, A.B. had gone into hiding in Monrovia after the coup, and then later sought refuge in the Ivorian embassy in Monrovia, which gave him asylum.

The Ivorian ambassador took the further precaution of transferring A.B. Tolbert to the French embassy, which he believed to be an even safer haven. Three days after the coup, Désirée appeared at the barracks, captured by the soldiers, who knew she was a member of the Tolbert family. Taylor was the one who recognized her, and he immediately told Quiwonkpa to leave her alone. Taylor recalls saying: 'General, we can't touch this woman. Turn her over immediately to the Ivorian ambassador and quickly.'[4] Taylor, together with his fiancée Tupee, escorted Daisy to the Ivorian embassy. Houphouët-Boigny sent a plane to bring her back to Côte d'Ivoire. Meanwhile, her husband, A.B. Tolbert, remained in the French embassy. Houphouët-Boigny was soon in touch with Doe to get his personal assurance that no harm would come to his son-in-law and Doe gave his word. Tolbert remained in asylum in one of the embassy buildings for a year, until Doe finally gave the order to break into the embassy to get him. Against the protests of the French ambassador, the army stormed its way into the embassy and took Tolbert, placing him in detention in the army central barracks prison. Several months later he was executed.

The action infuriated Houphouët-Boigny, who never forgave Doe; he vowed revenge against the Liberian head of state. Charles

Taylor, saviour of his daughter from the Doe junta in 1980, was to be the man who gave him the opportunity years later to exact that revenge.

Sitting up and taking notice in Washington DC

For the first time the United States was beginning to make major investments in the country whose former masters had always looked to it as its model in terms of society, economy and culture. All the more paradoxical was that during many long decades the United States had effectively ignored political developments in Monrovia, but now, with the Cold War in full swing in Africa, Liberia came into its own, at least militarily. For the first time in its history, the Republic of Liberia was becoming more like a true colony, not just an anomalous outpost on the other side of the Atlantic Ocean with distant historical connections to early-nineteenth-century freed American slaves.

Although the USA formally made it a condition of its support that Liberia should make steady progress towards a return to civilian rule and democratic government, in practice the Reagan White House turned a blind eye to the PRC's rapid evolution towards totalitarian government. The US administration was more concerned with reinforcing its West African military base and strategic communications installations, including the Omega transmission station which was used in navigation for naval as well as civilian aircraft over the Atlantic Ocean. Omega was crucial in the Reagan administration's official as well as covert support for anti-communist regimes in Africa and was one of only six such installations operated by the USA in the world. In Angola, the civil war had become a superpower proxy confrontation and Washington increased its military support to the anti-Moscow UNITA[5] rebels fighting there. US planes refuelled at Monrovia's Robertsfield airport en route to Kinshasa, from where they flew onwards to UNITA supply bases in southern Zaire.

However, once it became clear what kind of government Samuel Doe was truly intent on imposing on Liberia, many of the country's international businesses began to close up and relocate. Controlling positions in government and strategic industries were increasingly allocated to appointees from Doe's own Krahn ethnic background, at the expense first of Americo-Liberians then of rival native Liberians from other parts of the country. The modern side of the economy of Liberia had in effect been run by Americo-Liberian families, Middle Easterners and other foreigners, most of whom now fled. Leaving key industries in the hands of an inexperienced, incompetent, ethnocentric and increasingly corrupt junta, foreign investors and customers of Liberia soon became nervous and government revenues from export and processing businesses slumped.

But, despite economic collapse, the pace of looting of Liberia's resources by its new masters accelerated relentlessly. At the same time the United States, eager to maintain its Cold War African ally, began to contribute heavily to the military budget of the PRC and largely ignored reports of human rights abuses and the rapid shift of the country away from any semblance of democracy in its early years. When he took office Doe, although undeniably strong on street smarts, was at a disadvantage due to his lack of education. On taking the reins of power, however, he wasted little time before adopting the authoritarian ways of his predecessors in the Executive Mansion. Above all, he read Washington well, made the right noises and acted accordingly.

Reversing the policy initiatives of his predecessor William Tolbert, with his ill-fated 'balanced' approach to foreign policy, shortly after taking office Doe closed the Libyan People's Bureau and re-established ties with Israel. Israel sent military advisers to Monrovia, who trained Doe's elite presidential guard, composed exclusively of his Krahn tribe co-ethnics, and the guard soon became a loyal and formidable fighting unit upon whom their president could rely.

Naturally, with the opportunity of wielding such vast political and military power after a century and a half of being confined to a subsistence life in the bush by their oppressors, Doe and his native Liberian inner circle could ensure that the material spoils of office flowed freely and lavishly in their direction too. The responsibilities of righting the injustices of the country's previous Americo-Liberian governments were quickly forgotten in the headlong rush to self-aggrandizement and the accumulation of wealth. In total control of the country and its economy and with a willing superpower to bankroll its leader's every whim, it seemed there was no limit to the wealth that the chairman of Liberia's PRC could amass.

Meanwhile the progressives, such as Sawyer, Tipoteh and others, failed to make their mark and gain any substantive influence over Doe's policymaking. In the same way that they had failed to capitalize on the climate of dissent against Tolbert and the TWP in the 1970s, they were now marginalized by the new cadre of native military rulers, and lost the initiative in government.

Just as the previous True Whig administrations and partners had become rich on exploiting the country's wealth and sharing out a fat chunk of Liberia's business profits among themselves, Samuel Doe's regime saw no reason not to benefit personally from government too, and the mere detail that the economy was falling into ruins was not about to stop anyone from getting rich. Doe was simply able to substitute the new source of income now being derived from the US taxpayer for the prior wealth contributed through real economic development.

In Samuel Doe's first five years in office, the USA contributed in total almost half a billion dollars directly to his government, yet it has been estimated that, over the course of the decade he ruled, members of his regime embezzled some $300 million of government funds for their own personal use.[6] Unfortunately, or at least embarrassingly, Liberia's new ruler, to whom the USA had decided to give its full backing, appeared to many outsiders to be little more than a youth from the countryside with brutal tribal instincts. He and his Krahn ethnic inner circle came mostly from Grand Gedeh County, a part of the country which had received almost no exposure to the culture of metropolitan Liberia. A senior American diplomat who dealt closely with Doe and US policy towards Liberia at the end of the 1980s and in the early 1990s described the Krahn as 'Liberia's most backward ethnic group'.[7]

Although he may have had strong instincts, Doe had little knowledge of politics, let alone the geopolitics that were his Washington master's overriding motivation for backing him. From the outset in 1980, in exchange for the hefty upgrade in assistance it had committed to giving to Liberia, Washington principally demanded loyalty, while accepting a vague undertaking from Doe to move towards democracy and improved human rights for all Liberians.

George Shultz, secretary of state in the Reagan administration in the 1980s, came away from his first encounter with President Doe in Monrovia in January 1987 with an unreservedly negative impression. According to James Bishop, the US ambassador in Monrovia at the time, Shultz found the Liberian president to be 'unintelligible', and as a result of the Doe encounter reportedly even began to have second thoughts about his own judgement in choosing diplomacy as a career.[8] Herman J. Cohen, then senior director for African affairs at the National Security Council, who accompanied Shultz, recalled Doe when he got frustrated with his American visitor's complaints about his regime's shortcomings. He described Doe as 'a short man ... screaming in a high pitched whine' in front of his distinguished guests.[9]

Samuel Doe was a zealous practitioner of both traditional and mainstream religion. While in office he spent much time consulting various types of traditional priest, as well as attending both mosques and churches. He wore charms and amulets to protect himself from bullets, while cultivating a mystique about his invincibility and special powers.

However, Doe was apparently willing to make efforts to improve himself. He took adult education classes organized by the Susu Kuu movement of Togba-Nah Tipoteh. And, at Washington's behest, the US embassy sent advisers to help the president improve his reading and writing. William L. Swing, US ambassador in the early 1980s, remembered how he tutored Doe in statecraft and found him to be 'an endearing boy'. The US embassy arranged for Doe to have a satellite dish so that 'he could watch Ronald Reagan's speeches', which the Liberian president apparently enjoyed immensely.[10]

There were other reasons to doubt Doe's capacities of judgement in government. He was impulsive in his actions and at the same time did not always display a strong grip on matters in his cabinet.

In one incident early in his time in office, the president reportedly ordered an aide to summon the minister of finance to his office, only to be told, 'But Mr. President, you had the Minister of Finance shot last week.'[11]

Nevertheless, Doe did get invited to Washington DC in August 1982 and met Ronald Reagan on the White House lawn. At the beginning of the reception in the Rose Garden, President Reagan, another head of state not always known for his precise recollection of detail, introduced his distinguished African visitor to the White House press corps as 'Chairman Moe', much to the chagrin of the Liberian leader.[12]

Charlie tap-dances as Nancy rocks

As for Charles Taylor, he was the exact opposite of his boss in the administration in Monrovia. He was smooth, quick-thinking and sharply dressed. Sometimes Doe would notice a suit Taylor was wearing, and to prevent his superior becoming envious Taylor would offer it to him. The Boston-educated government operator was also willing to take risks. When Delores Adhigibe got into trouble with security at the Executive Mansion one day, a group of soldiers burst into her office at the GSA and told her she was fired. Taylor was confident and ready to stand by his deputies: 'If she goes, I go', he insisted, forcing the guards to back down.[13]

In his early years, while Doe struggled over his English jotters and with his personal tutors to improve his reading and writing skills, his wife Nancy went about her First Lady's duties in her own style, in between shopping trips to London and visiting their four children who were at school in the UK.

On one occasion, Nancy invited a group of ambassadors' wives to a reception shortly after the new First Couple moved into the Executive Mansion. While the elegantly attired guests were shown upstairs to admire the view, a rock band composed of militarily clad artists wearing reflector sunglasses blasted out grinding rhythmic tunes in the corridor, making conversation impossible.

The formal introductions complete, guests were offered hard liquor to drink – Nancy Doe and most of her Mansion entourage preferred their brandy neat on such occasions. Then the First Lady made an announcement to her assembled diplomatic guests, shouting out 'And now ladies, we're gonna shake our boodies!' The ambassadors' wives were shown back into the hallway and the band kicked into a loud reggae number while Nancy and her friends boogied to the beat. The distinguished guests awkwardly did their best to join in, but apparently weren't quite able to match the mood well enough to the First Lady's liking; after a couple more numbers they were promptly shown out and the reception was over.[14]

PRESIDENT SAMUEL DOE SPEAKS TO THE MEDIA

The mood towards Monrovia hardens

As Samuel Doe consolidated his power base with an increasing concentration of his own Krahn loyalists in the PRC cabinet, he continued forcing out the remaining progressives from positions of power. At the same time, his army continued to mete out brutal treatment to adversaries from all groups in society, including civil organizations and students. However, realizing that eventually he would need to make moves towards democracy to appease his paymasters in Washington, Doe also began to manoeuvre domestically in preparation for an election, to ensure that no apparent rivals could position themselves for a possible challenge in any future vote.

By now there was indeed a mounting climate of distaste, not to say embarrassment, in Washington DC, still not officially expressed, at the wanton and decadent conduct of the Doe administration. The Reagan White House was becoming increasingly uncomfortable with media reports from Liberia detailing the human rights atrocities and other totalitarian practices of its West African puppet. At the same time there was growing hope, if not belief, among Liberian dissidents that the USA would support a coup that could topple Doe without Washington having to get directly involved.

As American funds continued to flow to Monrovia at an unrelenting pace, the remaining progressive politicians, student dissenters, professionals and ethnic Gio and Mano citizens of Liberia were fleeing the country in increasing numbers. Like Charles Taylor, many of the political survivors of the coup had stayed on in 1980 to join the first Doe cabinet, believing in a new start for the country, or at least a continued role for themselves in the new order of things. But by now many were leaving to seek refuge and alternative opportunities back in the United States if they could, or, if not, in neighbouring West African countries.

Some went further. Thomas Quiwonkpa, co-instigator of the 1980 coup, had initially worked hand in hand with his friend Samuel Doe and at the outset had used his influence as head of the PRC armed forces to have Doe confirmed as Liberia's new president. While Samuel Doe increasingly turned only to those from his native Krahn ethnicity and set about displacing others in his administration, Quiwonkpa, who was a Gio from Nimba County, in turn tried to offset the trend by arranging the recruitment and promotion of people with links to his own region and ethnicity.

By 1983, however, the political landscape in Liberia was changing. Under pressure from his paymasters in Washington DC, Doe was beginning to acquiesce in the imperative of transitioning to civilian rule. As there would have to be elections eventually and the Krahn and related groups in the country only comprised a small minority of the population, Samuel Doe was going to need much tighter control of the process in order to be sure of dictating the outcome.

At around the same time, Doe presented Quiwonkpa with an effective demotion to the post of secretary general of the PRC, by implication weakening the power of the armed forces in national decision-making and diluting any possible threat from that source. Quiwonkpa refused to go, but the political rift with the president was irreparable and it meant that his days in Doe's government were numbered. In addition to being outmanoeuvred in the factional strife in Monrovia, Quiwonkpa also sensed the vulnerability posed by his ethnic status as a Gio, a group increasingly being marginalized in the ethnically partisan Doe regime.

At the same time as Quiwonkpa was being inexorably forced out of office, Taylor was being outmanoeuvred by his enemies in the cabinet. He compounded the situation by going a step too far in his manipulation of the government contracting process, soon becoming the victim of his own financial missteps. Taylor's position of executive power at the GSA offered a strong temptation to go beyond routine kickbacks and he soon found new ways of siphoning off cash. As Delores Adighibe, his friend and former finance director at the GSA, put it, 'vendors were coming in with bribes to get him to buy their goods ... he fell into that trap ... but then it became a matter of just receiving the money ... and no goods would arrive'.[15]

Succumbing to temptation at the GSA

In May of 1983 the Liberian Ministry of Finance discovered an overpayment by the GSA in a multiple procurement order from a United States company for parts for government-owned equipment. This was seized upon by Taylor's rivals as evidence of mismanagement and corruption. The payment at issue, in favour of International Earthmoving Equipment Inc. (IEE), based in New Jersey, was for a total of US$922,382 and it was discovered that an overpayment of some $22,000 had been made by Taylor's department. Taylor, as head of the GSA, was instructed by the Treasury to rectify the overpayment, which did not happen. His enemies smelled blood.

That August, Taylor was demoted to deputy minister of commerce and industry and his rival Clarence Momolu took over at the GSA. By now there was a growing lobby within government that was out to get Taylor, and, with popular support from fellow anti-Taylor activists, Momolu lost no time in going through the books of the department and shining the spotlight on its accounting irregularities under his predecessor. Soon he was publicly denouncing Taylor's embezzlement of the funds in the case of the IEE contract, for which, months after payment was made, no parts had been delivered to Liberia. Momolu called for a full government investigation but Taylor, always adept at public relations, at the same time called a press conference to defend himself in the eyes of the people, even if the battle for his position in the government was by now all but lost.

Outflanked and with Quiwonkpa, his most powerful ally in the administration, also under attack, Taylor knew he had no choice but to get out of the country. Sooner was better than later in the dangerous and unpredictable world of Samuel Doe's dictatorship.

Getting out of Liberia required all of Taylor's acumen for scheming and outwitting his persecutors. With the star of his mentor and protector Quiwonkpa now very much in the descendent, the risk of apprehension by Doe's cronies was high and the end result of the spare parts scandal unlikely to be favourable. Taylor, however, continued to report to his Ashmun Street office in his new capacity as deputy minister of commerce.

On the afternoon of 25 October 1983, some journalists had been invited to the deputy minister's Ashmun Street office for a briefing, and upon arrival were instructed by his secretary to wait while Taylor returned from a lunchtime engagement. No one in his department was aware of his exact whereabouts or his true movements. The guests waited at Taylor's office for their appointment for an hour, then another hour, but with no word from the deputy minister, it seemed as if Taylor had been held up across the city.

Taylor's wife Tupee, who had been ill, was planning to fly out of the country and was on her way to Robertsfield Airport to catch an afternoon flight. Taylor accompanied her and, despite not being officially listed on the flight, bluffed his way past the departure security on the pretext of comforting his sick wife and helping her onto the plane. He boarded with her and never got off. Taylor's guests, still patiently waiting in Ashmun Street, would never get their meeting.

Although Taylor said later that he did not flee the country as a result of the embezzlement accusation, but out of fear for his personal safety, the political implications were clear, and in December 1983 Doe issued a warrant for Charles Taylor's arrest.

Thomas Quiwonkpa went to his Nimba County home initially after leaving government, before events forced him to flee to the United States. Shortly after he left Monrovia, on 21 November 1983 a group of fellow dissidents led by Samuel Dokie, an ethnic Mano from nearby Saniquellie, in northern Nimba County, staged a cross-border raid into Nimba from neighbouring Guinea, attacking the strategically important iron ore mining facility at Yekepa. Dokie, like Quiwonkpa, had until recently been in the Doe cabinet, serving as assistant minister of local government until his boss had tried to coerce him into a major diversion of the ministry's funds into the president's personal account. The Yekepa raid itself resulted in a handful of deaths and achieved little for its organizers. However, the fallout from the incursion for the local civilian population was devastating.

Punishing Nimba

By now, ordinary Mano and Gio citizens, in Nimba County, Monrovia and other parts of the country, were increasingly targeted by Doe's forces on purely ethnic grounds, rather than for any identifiable offence or to any obvious political advantage. The Armed Forces of Liberia (AFL) were sent into Nimba on a reprisal raid, killing civilians and looting properties as punishment for their alleged complicity in the raid, in what amounted to a purely ethnic attack of Krahn against Gio and Mano. It was the confirmation of the beginning of a much bloodier phase in the Doe regime's management of Liberia's internal affairs and one which was to intensify further during the later years of his rule.

Quiwonkpa, while not a raid instigator himself, realized that his presence near Yekepa at the time of the attack would make him suspect and so he fled the country, ending up in the United States and registering as a student in Maryland. From there he restarted life in exile and actively networked among Liberian dissidents in the United States, increasingly intent on engineering Doe's overthrow by force.

Doe's mounting determination to remove any threat from Charles Taylor was provoked further by a letter which the fugitive Taylor wrote to the president in January 1984, exposing the corrupt ways of the entire government, and accusing Doe himself of being responsible for the wanton mismanagement and looting of Liberia's public purse. In his letter to Doe, Taylor wrote:

> You know very well that I did nothing without specific verbal or written instructions ... up to this point I have behaved responsibly ... I have kept my mouth shut while newspapers have hypothesized and made guesses as to what happened at the agency over the three years under my leadership. You and I know what happened and why. I am not prepared to become the whipping boy, just because I fled to save my life.[16]

From this point on, Doe seems to have realized that Taylor was much more than a nuisance on the sidelines who could be exiled and forgotten.

Now a fugitive from his native land, Taylor lay low in the United States while Doe raised the stakes against him, calling in the assistance of Liberia's powerful ally to reinforce the evidence against Taylor and arrange for the issuance of an international arrest warrant against him. In January 1984 Taylor travelled to Côte d'Ivoire in connection with some business transactions and was apprehended on his return while changing planes at Heathrow Airport. The UK authorities had received the extradition request for his arrest from the Liberian government. But after a review of the case, they concluded that the alleged embezzlement of public funds which Monrovia was charging him with was an internal Liberian affair, and they let him return to the USA. The FBI was going further on behalf of Samuel Doe, however, and they obtained the relevant US bank records of Taylor, the International Earthmoving Equipment

Inc. and its bank account signatories. In fact, it transpired that the FBI had already been investigating Taylor's financial transactions before Doe's formal request.

After the Heathrow incident, Taylor returned to his home in Brunswick, New Jersey and continued to live normally for a while with Tupee, although the calm did not last long and soon he thought it better to go underground in case the US authorities decided to act.

With investigations under way and the possibility of a manhunt looming, Taylor also realized he was soon going to need legal help to defend himself in the USA and, above all, to prevent his extradition to Liberia, for which Samuel Doe was now clamouring. Taylor called Ramsey Clark, a well-connected public figure and a practising attorney, who was critical of the US stance on Liberia and who would potentially be sympathetic to the detainee's plight.[17] Clark, an influential Democrat and Washington DC insider for decades, also served as secretary of state during the Lyndon Johnson administration in the mid-1960s.

Taylor apprehended on his adoptive home turf

In the spring of 1983, with Interpol and the FBI on his trail, Charles Taylor was finally tracked down by US law enforcement, in – of all places – his old college stomping ground of suburban Boston. Federal marshall Frank Dawson had already been trailing Taylor for a time and had followed his maroon Volvo on a number of occasions to houses in Roxbury and Boston's South End. On 24 May 1984, Dawson decided to make his move as Taylor entered a house in Somerville belonging to Agnes Reeves, a girlfriend and supporter from ULAA days.

The Feds used the tactic of saying they had run into a Volvo in the parking lot and wondered if the owner was inside – and when Taylor came to the door he was arrested. Reeves and three other women were in the house at the time. Dawson, recalling the arrest, said: 'Everyone was very nice, no one caused us any problems ... you could tell he lived well, he had a nice wardrobe.'[18]

Taylor called Ramsey Clark right there and then, even as he was being taken away to detention in the Plymouth House of Correction. Two weeks later, extradition proceedings were initiated by Doe's solicitor general against the detainee and Taylor appeared in court shortly afterwards. Clark had to work quickly to head off the efforts to return Taylor to Liberia and the clutches of Samuel Doe's junta.

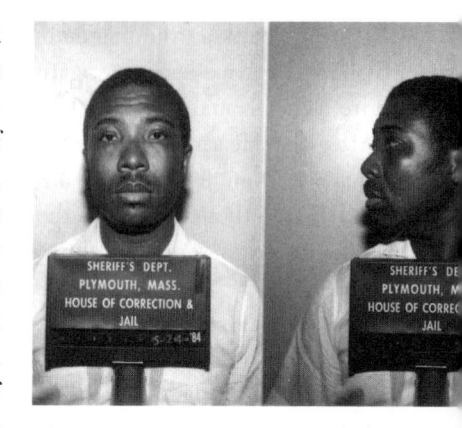

CHARLES TAYLOR, 1983 PLYMOUTH HOUSE OF CORRECTION MUGSHOT

The evidence against Taylor initially looked damning. In the first instance, it seemed that IEE, which received the money from Monrovia, had a zero balance until the Liberian GSA transaction. Further, the president of IEE, Mr B.S. Dhillon, an Indian, was a personal friend of Taylor's and a businessman established in Monrovia. It was Dhillon who was to arrange the delivery in Liberia of the parts purchased from IEE via his local company, Dhillon Brothers. Then, it was discovered that on the day following the first transfer from the Liberian government in respect of the transaction, 12 January 1983, an outgoing transfer of $100,000 went from Dhillon Brothers into Taylor's personal account. On 24 February 1983 a further $616,572, including the fatal overpayment amount, was wired from Liberia to IEE. Less than a week later, $600,000 went from the company account to Dhillon's personal account.

Taylor had opened an account at Citibank in July 1982, using Dhillon as a reference, and documents provided later to the US courts showed that over $800,000 was deposited in his account between January and September 1983.

There was another side to the story, however, as Taylor claimed that he did not personally receive benefit from the money wired from the Liberian government, and that it went to various people whose names he did not want to disclose in order to protect them.

The $100,000 that did go into Taylor's account was, he asserted, a transfer in replacement of money owed to Taylor by Dhillon in respect of earlier transactions. Furthermore, it transpired that the Liberian government had been tardy in making payments for shipments of goods in the past, giving the company a plausible reason to delay sending the goods. Either way, the bank records obtained by the FBI did show that most of the $922,000 had not gone to Charles Taylor, which was what Samuel Doe was claiming.[19]

The problem was that in the case of this shipment, the $922,000 had been paid and no goods received, and, whatever the ultimate destination of the funds, it looked as though the money had gone to Taylor, or to him via Taylor's interest in the IEE, where the bulk of the funds had been sent.

In his own subsequent affidavit, Taylor sought to prove his innocence by suggesting the fact that he had stayed on in Monrovia for some time after his demotion to the Ministry of Commerce was evidence that he had nothing to fear and he was innocent of any wrongdoing. Although Taylor did in fact flee the country a few months later, it was because he learned of the plot against his friend Thomas Quiwonkpa, he said, rather than on account of any financial impropriety. Rather than fleeing justice, he stayed on to help the country 'through its difficult times ... no sane person would have stayed in Liberia in my position if he knew that a contract like that with IIE might cost the government $900,000.'[20]

Representing Taylor, Ramsey Clarke stressed that agreeing to the extradition demands of America's African ally and unelected strongman President Samuel Doe would almost certainly lead to summary justice for Taylor in Liberia, resulting in his execution if he returned. Taylor himself argued that he was a political prisoner and that he had always acted in the interests of his country.

Speaking in his defence hearings regarding the destination of the embezzled Liberian funds, Taylor refused to explain where the rest of the money went, since he felt it could endanger the lives of people targeted by Samuel Doe. Clarke argued that it would probably have gone to others opposed to Doe supporting Taylor's contention that his motives throughout the affair were entirely patriotic, if not exactly above board. Taylor contended that, although he served in Doe's government, he was now 'an adversary of Doe, who had tried to speak out against the injustices he saw'.

However, the presiding US magistrate at the court proceedings, Robert J. DeGiacomo, was not impressed by the ostensible show of patriotism. In his report he said that 'there is no evidence that [Taylor] acted as a principled opponent of the government. He can best be described as a once-prodigal son.'[21]

Throughout the first year of Taylor's detention, a tug-of-war had been going on between the forces of international law and the extradition demands of the Doe administration, on the one hand, and the representations of Taylor's influential friends such as Ramsey Clarke, on the other. But the USA could neither detain Taylor indefinitely without trial, nor try him in the United States without proper jurisdiction for the alleged crimes committed. The impasse looked set to continue for some time longer. As Peter Flynn, sheriff of the Plymouth correctional facility during the time that Taylor was held there, said years later: 'The Feds didn't know what to do with Taylor. They couldn't ship him back to Liberia because he would have been shot the minute he was on the ground, creating a diplomatic problem. They left him at our jail for months.'[22]

Business as usual despite criticisms

Thus, as Samuel Doe mismanaged and misspent his way through his early years in office, brutally eliminating rivals with increasing impunity, the hapless Charlie Taylor, an apprehended but untried international fugitive, was languishing in a Massachusetts prison. Taylor spent a total of sixteen months in the Plymouth correctional facility not many miles away from where he had earned his college degree a decade before and where his charm and personal abilities had made such a keen impression on his New England peers.

At home on the campus of the University of Liberia in Monrovia, voices of dissent were also rising. Following a student protest on 22 August 1984, led by Amos Sawyer, Doe sent 200 soldiers to the university campus. Doe's solders flogged scores of students with rattans, and then shot at the scattering protestors, killing over fifty, while female students were assaulted and raped. The university was ransacked, causing some $2 million worth of damage and Amos Sawyer was arrested and imprisoned for two months.

The US Congress reacted with criticism, and, feeling the pressure, Samuel Doe finally agreed to call elections in 1985 to secure a mandate for his regime and ensure a stamp of legitimacy for its actions. But at the same time he set about ensuring that there was almost no climate for dissent, nor any realistic prospect of opponents mounting a campaign against him. He promulgated a presidential order – Decree 88A – banning protest and criticism of the government in any form. Amos Sawyer was rearrested, as was the Harvard-educated economist Ellen Johnson Sirleaf, also a strong critic of Doe's government.

Sirleaf, who had worked in the Tolbert administration in the Ministry of Finance before leaving to join the World Bank, had provoked the ire of Doe when, some months before, she had made a speech before the ULAA in Philadelphia on Liberian Independence Day. In the course of a broad-ranging discourse on the mismanagement of the Liberian economy she referred to Doe and his ministers as a bunch of 'fools and idiots', which particularly enraged the head of state, who by this time had become highly sensitive about his lack of education. When Sirleaf returned to Monrovia she was summoned before Doe, taken to task for her comments, placed under house arrest, then imprisoned at the Barclay Training Centre.

With the arrest of Sirleaf, the United States took direct issue with Doe. The detention of the respected international banker with allies in Washington was too much of a provocation for the US opponents of Doe's regime, and Washington suspended $25 million in aid to Monrovia in response.[23] Ellen Johnson Sirleaf was released – and Samuel Doe got his $25 million in aid; he then went about ensuring that he would win the elections in another way.

By the second half of 1985, however, a confluence of events in Monrovia and in the United States would bring about a controversial change in Taylor's circumstances and herald the launch of a new and even more volatile chapter in the young Liberian's career.

FIVE

DOE'S DECLINE, TAYLOR'S TRAVELS

'General Doe, you promised the people so many things, and you are not keeping those promises.' Ellen Johnson Sirleaf

'I didn't promise them shit.' Samuel Doe[1]

On 15 October 1985, Liberia went to the polls. Or, rather, on that day Liberia finished casting its votes in an election the outcome of which had already been decided. For days beforehand, ballot papers were being manufactured to ensure that the incumbent head of state, Samuel Doe, would win. In what was by all accounts one of the most blatantly stolen elections in recent history, even by African standards, Doe and his National Democratic Party of Liberia officially took the magical figure of 50.93 per cent of the electorate's votes, beating the Liberia Action Party (LAP) led by Jackson F. Doe (no relation, he was a Gio from Nimba County) into second place.

All independent observers on the scene as well as many Liberians believe that Jackson Doe was elected president of Liberia that day, but, as Samuel Doe's vice president Harry Moniba put it, 'the boxes were filled before the elections ... the LAP was cheating too ... but we did it more carefully.'[2]

Both houses of the US Congress also rejected the result of the election and voted to cut off aid to Liberia as a result. But Ronald

Reagan's obsessively anti-socialist, anti-Soviet administration wanted to keep its African ally at, it seemed, almost any cost. The sham Doe election was given the stamp of approval by the White House; Ronald Reagan's administration even praised the 'positive aspects' of Liberia's election campaign, saying that the result 'demonstrated that Doe seemed to have the authority to govern'.[3]

Testifying in December of that year to the Africa Subcommittee of the US Senate Foreign Relations Committee, Chester Crocker, assistant undersecretary of state for African affairs, referred to the stolen Doe election as 'movement in a positive direction' and condoned the sham as a 'beginning, however imperfect, of a democratic experience'.[4]

While successfully dealing with one important issue for Doe's masters abroad, the result of the 1985 poll thus gave a green light for the intensification of the already repressive behaviour of his ruling junta and a heightening of the persecution of its ethnic rivals and political critics at home.

Thomas Quiwonkpa's coup

From his exile at the end of 1983, former general Quiwonkpa had been spending his time in suburban Maryland in the United States, plotting against the government in Monrovia. He raised money and assembled a group of dissidents with the aim of overthrowing Doe's regime. Needing a friendly neighbouring country from which to launch his coup, he first sought help from Côte d'Ivoire, which, however, refused to become involved. He then found a more sympathetic audience in Sierra Leone where army chief General Joseph Momoh, who later became president, showed a keen interest in the plot and promoted the idea with then president Siaka Stevens.

The confidence of the plotters in what they assumed was a dislike for Doe in the United States turned out to be a delusion, however. Furthermore, US intelligence had already learned of an impending coup and was sharing information with Doe. Nevertheless the Quiwonkpa team forged ahead, sometimes in bizarre circumstances. At one point in the preparations, the chief plotter even ran into senior

US military officers in Freetown, who recognized the coup leader from his time in Monrovia, as if any further tip-offs were needed as to Quiwonkpa's intentions.

Driving to the border from Freetown on 11 November 1983, Quiwonkpa and a force of about two dozen rebels managed to enter Monrovia the following day, taking over the Barclay Training Centre (BTC) and the Liberian Broadcasting System (LBS) transmitter. Quiwonkpa came over the airwaves and pronounced a takeover of power by the 'National Patriotic Forces of Liberia', convincing many Monrovia residents that the Doe government had been overthrown.

Thousands of civilians spilled out onto the streets, and senior ministers, including the vice president, Harry Moniba, were detained by the rebel forces and taken to the BTC. Quiwonkpa toured the city in an open car, basking in the adulation of the crowds, while ordering that violence should be avoided. His failure to focus on delivering the killer blow to the hated Doe regime, however, was to cost him and his supporters dearly.

President Doe was still in the Executive Mansion protected by a cadre of his loyal mansion guards. Fatally, the rebels had failed to cut his communication lines with the army, and Doe summoned reinforcements from Camp Schefflin, about 25 miles to the southeast of Monrovia. Within hours, his tanks were rolling into the suburbs of the capital and the AFL retook the radio station. To the stunned crowds, still celebrating in the streets, Doe's voice came over the airwaves just as some were still tearing down his posters and celebrating the dictator's demise.

The coup attempt was quashed by the government's well-equipped Krahn-led army units and Israeli-trained Executive Mansion guard, who remained fiercely loyal in support of their head of state. Soon, those who had come out joyfully but prematurely into the streets of Monrovia to celebrate Doe's overthrow met with the bloodiest of reprisals at the hands of the president's forces. Quiwonkpa was captured, slain, dismembered and paraded through the streets of Monrovia to demonstrate to all the power of Doe's junta and the consequences for those who tried to oppose it.

Quiwonkpa's death rituals contained all the horrific brutality and cannibalistic embellishments of the Liberian tribal traditions at their most savage. Samuel Doe's troops reportedly hacked off and consumed parts of the traitor's body after his death, while a Nigerian reporter who witnessed the scene was horrified at what he saw, observing: 'Astonishingly, in these modern times they [Doe's soldiers] still believe that by eating bits of a great warrior's body, some of the greatness would come to them. The heart of course was the prize delicacy and it was traditionally shared on a hierarchical basis.'[5]

The failure of the 1985 coup signalled a turning point in the Doe administration's conduct of government. Now, with an election successfully behind him and continued US military backing, units of the AFL embarked on a phase of uninhibited ethnic massacres against the grassroots supporters (actual and assumed) of former general Quiwonkpa, principally the Mano and Gio tribes. Official estimates of the death toll that resulted from the 1985 ethnic reprisals in Nimba County were put in the hundreds, but local accounts point to a number closer to 3,000.

The political fallout for Liberia was equally severe, as the populations of those persecuted tribes now had no voice in government, not even the right to be heard at district level via a Monrovia-appointed commissioner, let alone through an elected local representative in the national parliament. Thus, uniquely in Liberia's history, including the times of the most blatantly exploitative True Whig Party administrative structures, whole sections of the country were now not represented at all in Liberian national affairs.

In the second half of 1985, while the preparations for the Liberian elections were under way and the Quiwonkpa coup plotters were plotting, Charles Taylor swept dramatically if briefly back into the limelight of Liberian–American affairs.

Breakout and flight: New England getaway drama

Late on 15 September 1985, Taylor and four of his fellow prison inmates broke out of the house of correction in Plymouth, Massachusetts, and sped off into the night in a getaway car towards New York

City. The entire breakout band was ultimately recaptured, except for one: Charles McArthur Taylor. Days later, Taylor's by now estranged wife Tupee and her sister-in-law Lucia Holmes Toweh were arrested and jailed for allegedly driving the getaway car that picked them up in the grounds of Plymouth's Jordan Hospital, a mile away from the prison. The two women were later identified as the drivers of the car by Thomas DeVoll, one of the recaptured escapees. DeVoll also stated that he and Taylor reached Staten Island in New York together that night, where they parted company.[6]

In New York Taylor then went to see a Liberian girlfriend, Anne Payne, who helped him stay under cover and later drove with him across country to the Mexican border, from where Charles Taylor left the United States.

There had never been a breakout from the red-brick correctional facility in Obery Street, Plymouth, and the controversy over how Taylor and his group managed to do it was to continue for years afterwards. Divergent accounts of the Taylor escape and conspiracy theories involving the US authorities' complicity in the breakout were in abundance, emanating both from within and from outside Plymouth.

Sheriff Peter Flynn, who was reticent when talking about the Taylor breakout from the facility he was in charge of that night, said he appreciated the US authorities' dilemma, with Taylor by then incarcerated for some fifteen months without trial. He said, 'They left him at our jail for months … I think they were almost relieved when he escaped.'[7]

Flynn's successor, Peter Forman, initially thought that the US law enforcement authorities had been briefed on the breakout in advance. In October 1997 he told the local press that they were 'told by a reliable source that a story of the planned escape was told to another law enforcement agency prior to the event'.[8] Although Forman later clarified that the stories circulating did not mean that the escape was actually planned in cooperation with the authorities, the suggestion of conspiracy lingered on.

Others in the jail said that the escapees cut through prison bars with hacksaws and then lowered themselves to freedom with knotted bedsheets before scaling the perimeter fence. Fuelled by local media in the area, the controversy grew and the lore fed on itself, with reported versions including Hollywood cliché escapes and a late-night manhunt involving Taylor eluding the yapping dogs of the police force in the woods around Plymouth.

Whatever the profile of the other escapees, these accounts didn't quite seem like Taylor's style. It is more likely that he planned a behind-the-scenes deal, with subterfuge rather than drama, and with a clean exit from captivity rather than a panting getaway from the jaws of sniffer dogs. More likely still is the account given by the superintendent of the Plymouth guards at the time, Brian Gillen, who said he 'used to talk to Taylor on a nightly basis' inside the prison and described him as 'outgoing, charismatic … very sharp, the executive type … you know, not like a Rambo'. He stated that Taylor had convinced a guard to escort him to a low-security wing of the prison 'because he wanted to play bridge with a fellow inmate' and then managed to get out of the guard's sight for long enough to complete a pre-planned escape with other inmates already waiting in that wing. But so far as any complicity by the authorities was concerned, Gillen thought that there was 'no reason to suspect that a breakout was planned'.[9]

White-collar prison life

Certainly life for Taylor was not too hard in Plymouth, where he was kept in very low security conditions. Delores Adighibe, his old student friend and former GSA assistant, paid him a visit one day, along with her brother Elmer Johnson, who later became a key military leader in Taylor's rebel incursion. She found conditions in Plymouth to be rather surprising, in fact she recalled thinking the whole set-up was odd. 'It didn't seem like a prison, it was just a big room with Taylor sitting openly with others.' She recalled how the guards in Plymouth would bring him African newspapers, even cigars – 'they treated him like a superstar'.[10]

Sheriff Peter Flynn was asked again in 2009 about Taylor's possible prior contact with persons who could have helped plot the escape and the results of any subsequent internal investigation into the breakout. But he remained tight-lipped, not wanting to go 'back into that whole Charlie Taylor thing', as he called it, while nevertheless mentioning that he thought his former colleagues' comments to the media closer to the time would have been right.[11]

But others were more forthcoming with their views about the breakout. Prince Johnson, a member of the NPFL in the earliest days of its insurgency campaign in 1989 and now a senator in the Liberian government, testified before the 2008 Liberian Truth and Reconciliation Commission that he thought the USA had released Taylor to help mastermind the overthrow of the Doe regime.

As for the fugitive himself, years later, speaking in the midst of his rebel campaign from the central Liberian bush in 1992, Taylor described how he got out, alleging that the CIA engineered his departure from Plymouth.

> I wouldn't even be in the country today if it weren't for the CIA. My escape ... I think they must have arranged that. One night I was told that the gate to my cell wouldn't be locked ... that I could walk anywhere. I walked out of jail, down the steps out into America. Nobody stopped me. I came home to Liberia. What was I in jail for? My dear, I don't remember.[12]

But Taylor remembered very well why Samuel Doe had sought to extradite him. Although his fellow ministers in the Doe government had also been siphoning off funds from the state, the uncovering of Taylor's irregular dealings gave his enemies the opportunity they had been waiting for to eliminate him. Now, out of prison and at large once again, he could set about planning his revenge.

Taylor's testimony before the Special Court for Sierra Leone goes even further in suggesting official US complicity in his escape. On 15 July 2009 in The Hague, the defendant said that he was *led* by guards in to the minimum security area and then escaped to a waiting car, which he 'assumed to be a government car', suggesting complicity but contradicting the sworn account of his own fellow escapee Thomas DeVoll, who spoke of Taylor's wife and another woman driving the getaway car. Taylor said he didn't even consider that the incident could be described as an escape, stating: 'I am calling it my release, because I didn't break out.'[13]

Boima Fahnbulleh, who served as foreign minister under Samuel Doe, reportedly was told by Taylor that he had paid his fellow fugitives from Plymouth $50,000 to help get him out and across the border to Mexico.[14] Agnes Reeves thought that it was Tupee who was supposed to bring the money on the night of the breakout to pass to the accomplices. In response to the allegations that a bribe was paid to arrange for Taylor's escape, the Special Court defendant again refuted this allegation: 'I did not pay any money, I did not know the guys who picked me up. I was not hiding afterwards.'

Whichever variant of the Plymouth breakout story is true, the embarrassment to the US authorities of the successful Taylor escape was not as great as the embarrassment of his continued presence. As Sheriff Flynn said in March 2000: 'They couldn't ship him back to Liberia because he would have been shot the minute he was on the ground, creating a diplomatic problem.'[15]

Tupee and Lucia were soon released, and charges were never brought against them. While the other escapees were easily recaptured, the US authorities seemingly didn't pursue Taylor with any great vigour, if at all, as he remained in the USA for several weeks before making it to Mexico and thence returning to Africa.

Taylor confirmed in his Special Court testimony that from Massachusetts he was driven to New York, where he spent one night with an old Liberian friend from his home region named Eric Scott. The prosecution alleged that he put his photo into Scott's passport and used this for his onward travel, although Taylor denied this in The Hague.

From New York Taylor continued on to Washington DC and then to Texas, where he spent a 'few weeks', his movements going undetected, or perhaps detected but undisturbed. The Special Court prosecutor in 2009 put it to Taylor that he used the Eric Scott passport to travel to Mexico then onward to Europe, but Taylor insisted that he used his own passport. 'I had my own name in my passport and moved about freely. Nobody asked me any questions', he stated.

While the authorities had retained Taylor's Liberian diplomatic passport at the time of his detention, his girlfriend in Somerville, Agnes Reeves, held on to his original one for him. The FBI interrogated Reeves in Boston right after the breakout, but by then the fugitive was out of the area. Some days later, Ann Payne came up from New York to see Reeves and collected Taylor's passport for him, thus giving him legitimate documentation for his onward travels.[16]

At the Special Court trial in The Hague the prosecution also tiptoed around the subject of his breakout, not revisiting in detail what could have been an altogether sensitive subject for those most responsible for ensuring that Taylor's apprehension and trial happened in the first place. Taylor himself strongly suggested before the trial that he knew things that could be embarrassing for the USA, when he bragged that he would reveal evidence damaging to the superpower, which he saw as trying to frame him.

Taylor's skilful exploitation of a network of contacts built up since his early years in Massachusetts, in the corridors of power in Washington DC, and through connections with revolutionary heads of state in North and West Africa, were a key element in his later ascent to military and political power in Liberia. A consummate lobbyer, networker and schemer, Charles Taylor cultivated friends in many of the right places at the right times in order to achieve his goals. Capitalizing on his commanding personality, intelligence and ambition, he could ultimately count on the loyalty of trained professional soldiers, teenage rural fighters and ordinary citizens, as well as a good share of his fellow Liberian dissidents, to back his bid for power.

Taylor's allies in the United States, both from among the Liberian community and in the US Congress and business communities, also served him well in the early years. Following the escape from Plymouth and during his subsequent years of revolutionary wanderings, it was a different type of backer who was to become the most important for Taylor's ambitions. Not surprisingly, in the context of Cold War geopolitics, the leader of a radical movement seeking to overthrow an American-backed African despot had to look far and wide for new friends – and to forge relationships which could only provoke the ire of his formerly accommodating North American hosts from those formative expatriate years.

In West Africa in the late 1980s, President Samuel Doe had already accumulated a number of enemies when the campaigning Liberian fugitive returned to the continent of his birth to look for allies. By contrast, before the decade was out, Taylor had the support of an assortment of leaders from across Africa, notably Burkina Faso's Blaise Compaoré. Côte d'Ivoire's Félix Houphouët-Boigny, although not a revolutionary, was sympathetic, and had his own reasons for wanting to see the back of Doe, not least of which was a desire to avenge his son-in-law's murder. Most importantly, Taylor would soon gain the support of the strongest ally any anti-Western rebel of the times could hope for: Libyan revolutionary Colonel Muammar Gaddafi.

Each of these heads of state, at different times, hosted, financed, supplied or supported the military preparations of Taylor and the December 1989 NPFL incursion into Liberia. In Sierra Leone, Foday Sankoh was a kindred spirit who passed through the same training camps as the NPFL in Libya, and who would become a firm revolutionary ally of Taylor once their twin rebellions in Liberia and Sierra Leone got under way.

Running spy rings around Ghana

Charles Taylor disappeared from the scene after making his exit from the USA in late 1985. Receiving help from Boima Fahnbulleh, a prominent member of MOJA and another former Doe cabinet-member-turned-defector, Taylor soon arrived in Ghana, at that time the favoured regional base for many Liberians exiled from the Doe regime. Flight Lieutenant Jerry Rawlings had taken power in Accra in a coup in 1981 and established a government called the Provisional National Defence Council (PNDC), a dictatorship with a declared radical, leftist leaning in both internal and external affairs, which eventually led to Ghana's political alienation by many regional and international partners. The PNDC reopened Ghana's relations with Libya and was critical of the Liberian regime of Samuel Doe. As such, it was a favourable environment for the leaders of the fugitive dissident community from Monrovia, most of whom were members of MOJA and were given a safe haven by the Ghanaian authorities. For the same reasons, Samuel Doe's spies, and by extension those of the United States, were keeping tabs on developments in Accra in the mid-1980s.

Taylor, however, distanced himself from MOJA in Ghana, preferring to do his own thing on the expatriate political scene, which clearly irritated some of his fellow Liberian dissidents in exile. Shortly after arrival in Ghana, Taylor was arrested on the orders of Jerry Rawlings's strongman chief of security, Kojo Tsikata. Allegedly the detention was the result of a false tip-off from a Doe associate, who, paradoxically, got Taylor arrested by claiming that they were friends, thereby implicating them both as pro-Doe informants.[17]

He may also have been the victim of an ongoing climate of distrust between the security services of the United States and Ghana, which had recently led to the arrest of spies in both countries' capitals. In 1985, before Taylor's arrival, the special forces working for Jerry Rawlings's PNDC uncovered a group of Ghanaians who had been working for the CIA; they had been compromised by a Ghanaian agent by the name of Michael Soussoudis, a cousin of Rawlings, who had in turn had been lured to the USA and found guilty of working on behalf of the Ghanaians. There then followed a 'spy swap' between Washington and Accra, which had just taken place at the time of Taylor's arrival.

Not surprisingly, then, Taylor was suspected almost right away of working for the CIA. His barely credible story of 'escape' from a US prison in Boston, his unobstructed travel during the course of several weeks across the United States, and his unhindered departure for Mexico and thence to West Africa on the face of it did not seem to add up. Along with his timely departure from the USA just two months before the attempted Quiwonkpa coup which so nearly overthrew Samuel Doe, these factors all suggested official complicity. To the Ghanaian authorities, some form of espionage role on behalf of the US government seemed the likely explanation.

Taylor himself alleged that his arrest in Accra was engineered by MOJA, irritated at his failure to join their ranks and wary of the plans he may have been making for a rival movement.[18] At the same time, since Taylor was an escaped convict from the USA, a country with which Ghana maintained diplomatic relations, any extradition request would have to be considered very seriously; none was forthcoming, however. Fortunately, with the assistance of Boima Fahnbulleh, Taylor was able to engineer his release. Fahnbulleh, now in Accra, made representations to the authorities on Taylor's behalf. Once again the agitator, campaigner and fugitive had regained his liberty.

Established in the Ghanaian capital, Taylor moved around the expatriate Liberian community, expanded his network of contacts, developed a following among the young radical Ghanaian community and enjoyed the Accra nightlife. He was also reacquainted with Agnes Reeves, with whom he had been developing a romantic relationship in the USA since his separation from Tupee. In 1986 Agnes Reeves and Charles Taylor married in a civil ceremony in Accra, after which she went to work on her husband's behalf. While in Accra, she made a significant contribution by securing an introduction to the ambassador of Burkina Faso, Mamouna Outtara, and thus opened channels to Blaise Compaoré in the Burkinabe capital Ouagadougou. The connection proved crucial when, once again, a few months later, Taylor was detained by the Ghanaian police in connection with alleged subversive activities. Compaoré, at the time the right-hand man of Burkina Faso's president, Thomas Sankara, intervened personally to secure Taylor's release.[19]

In 1987, Charles Taylor moved to Ouagadougou, where he established his base for the next two years. This departure was a convenient development for the Rawlings government, which was increasingly embarrassed by his presence. Taylor's revolutionary rhetoric and energetic presence among Ghanaian radical groups had made the Ghanaian authorities increasingly uncomfortable at a time when the Ghanaian economy was on its knees and President Rawlings was trying to restore his country's standing in the international community

With Liberia's Samuel Doe hot on Taylor's trail and the USA potentially also about to request his handover at any moment, his departure from the country came as a welcome relief to Rawlings. Other anti-Doe Liberian dissidents migrated to the Burkinabe capital too, and soon more serious preparations for organization and training of a rebel movement got under way.

The diaspora regroups

The Liberian dissident community in the region was still in considerable disarray at this time, particularly in the years following the failed Quiwonkpa coup attempt, and initially Taylor was neither particularly prominent nor influential among this scattered community of anti-Doe activists. Steadily, however, with the regrouping of the diaspora's disparate elements, Taylor's connections and forceful efforts at putting together resources and getting backers helped him to gain greater prominence in the emerging movement.

In Burkina Faso, more bloodshed and political intrigue surrounded the Liberian rebel presence. The president, Thomas Sankara, was assassinated on 15 October 1987, ostensibly by Compaoré, his deputy in the Burkinabe government.[20] While a rivalry between the two men was assumed to have led to the assassination, with Compaoré issuing a long list of grievances about how Sankara (a revolutionary socialist, also known as 'Africa's Che Guevara') was ruining the economy and destroying relations with key regional allies, NPFL operatives were also implicated in the murder. Among those colleagues of Charles Taylor who was involved was Prince Johnson, in Burkina Faso at the time helping in the effort to find a regional base for the NPFL's attempt to remove Samuel Doe from power.

On the day of the assassination, a group of Sankara's own presidential guards based in Poe, near the Ghanaian border, visited the president to try to persuade him to step aside and allow Compaoré to take power. According to Agnes Taylor's account, during the ensuing argument, the president drew his gun and shooting broke out, during which Sankara was killed.

Thomas Sankara had not been interested in providing the Liberian dissidents with a base to overthrow Samuel Doe. However, the pro-Compaoré rebels had the backing of Félix Houphouët-Boigny of Côte d'Ivoire, who, also wanting Doe removed, could have supported a plot to remove Sankara. And so it was logical that the NPFL might help Compaoré engineer the overthrow of Sankara.

Others alleged a more explicit NPFL involvement. According to Prince Johnson's public testimony before the Truth and Reconciliation Commission in Monrovia in October 2008, 'Our only option for remaining in Burkina Faso was to respond positively to the appeal from Blaise [Compaoré] to get rid of Sankara, who was against our presence.'[21]

The violent overthrow of Thomas Sankara was a major boost for the Liberian rebels. Sankara, a pan-Africanist, was seen by Washington as among the most anti-Western of the new African leaders emerging at a time when the Cold War was in full sway, with the Ronald Reagan White House competing against Moscow for allies and influence across the globe. Compaoré, however, was more amenable to Western tastes, despite being close to Libya's Colonel Muammar Gadaffi. The Libyan dictator, for his part, was now taking an active interest in revolutionary anti-Western movements in West Africa, having recently been frustrated in attempts to dislodge French influence in his neighbouring Chad.

Compaoré, who, unlike his former boss, was able to play both sides in the geopolitical game, owed a great deal of gratitude to the Liberians for their support during his takeover, and he returned the favour when introductions to Tripoli were needed by the steadily emerging Liberian rebel movement.

Building a movement

During the year and a half preceding the December 1989 NPFL invasion, Charles Taylor criss-crossed West Africa recruiting allies, gathering resources and manoeuvring, as well as for the most part successfully outmanoeuvring, his potential rivals for the leadership of the NPFL. He spent time in Ghana, Guinea, Sierra Leone, Côte d'Ivoire and, particularly, his rear base of Burkina Faso, where he adopted the pseudonym Jean-Michel Some and had a passport issued for himself in that name.[22]

Most important of all, because of his base in Ouagadougou, Taylor was able to take advantage of a regular flight schedule to Tripoli. Taylor's visits to Libya soon resulted in the NPFL being invited to participate in Colonel Gadaffi's training for African anti-colonialist rebels. Ultimately it was this ability to secure a place for the NPFL in the Libyan camps for pan-African revolutionaries which put Taylor in the driving seat with his peers and allowed him to assume the leadership of the movement. Taylor himself received military training in the Tarjura base as well as attending sessions in al-Mathabh al Thauriya al-Alamiya ('World Revolutionary Headquarters'), a school for revolutionary political instruction set up by the Libyan secret service.

However, the rivalry for the NPFL leadership was still alive and well, despite Taylor having emerged as the most prominent candidate in the early Burkina Faso days. Among the other contenders for the leadership were his old rival from the ULAA presidency race, Moses Duopu, and the Sierra Leone-based Harry Yuen. They and several others, including Prince Johnson, who led a party of recruits that went independently of Taylor for training in Libya, were jealous of Taylor's influence and connections, while distrusting him intensely.

Back in the United States, the exiled opposition was also organizing, but along different lines and in a much more hesitant manner. Amos Sawyer, Ellen Johnson Sirleaf, Tom Woewiyu and several others formed an organization called the Association for Constitutional Democracy in Liberia (ACDL). While its aim was to bring about an improvement in Liberia through lobbying the US government to force Doe into change, some of the ACDL's membership was also in favour of armed action. When Tom Woewiyu brought to their attention the plans being hatched by Charles Taylor and his embryonic rebel force and asked for financial support for the new movement, the expatriate dissident leadership was split.

Some opposed the resort to violence while others could see the merit of armed force in the furtherance of a broader freedom struggle. The ACDL ultimately committed to supporting Charles Taylor's cause and worked to extend both political and financial support to Taylor's rebels.[23]

In 1988, during his regional shuttling back and forth, Taylor was again detained and imprisoned in Accra after another clash with the Ghanaian authorities, when he tried to recruit a group opposed to President Rawlings, known as the Boys' Brigade. Prince Johnson and other rivals took advantage of his absence from the Libyan camps to fabricate a document purportedly showing that Taylor worked for the CIA. The Libyans, however, did not fall for the attempted defamation and Taylor was tipped off in time, before he swiftly outflanked the plotters by promising some of their number positions of power in his future government.

While Colonel Gaddafi's Libyan training camps were the most important link in the military preparations, access to connections in Abidjan, Danane and San Pedro were for Taylor the key to his financial readiness. His ability to tap into the powerful networks established in Côte d'Ivoire over decades by Liberia's Americo-Liberian and Lebanese business families was an important asset. Taylor's ability to earn the confidence of the exiled True Whig Party business aristocracy helped him to reach clients for Liberian commodities, the critical source of the foreign exchange he would need to finance his military campaign.

Ivorian President Houphouët-Boigny, being staunchly pro-French and anti-Doe, was a solid soulmate for Charles Taylor. With the help of his rapidly improving French, through his successful cultivation of Ivorian, French and Lebanese trading connections in Abidjan, by late 1988 Taylor's business network inside Côte d'Ivoire was taking shape. In the town of Danane in the west of the country, close to the Liberian border, the strong Liberian element in the local community provided support while in San Pedro he cultivated expatriate businessmen, many of whom used the port's major hotels as their local headquarters.

Houphouët-Boigny was not committed to hosting a dissident Liberian armed movement, though, and he was clearly aware of the risks of such a presence inside his country's borders. Samuel Doe periodically threatened Côte d'Ivoire for the potentially belligerent stance it was taking by harbouring the fledgling NPFL, and the Ivorian authorities periodically reacted and harassed the Liberians inside their borders lest they became too comfortable or took their freedom of movement for granted.

But preparations went ahead and with Burkina Faso as a reliable rear base, it only needed the Ivorian authorities to turn a blind eye to the movements of the small groups of rebels making their way across their territory towards Liberia's northern border. By late 1989, with arms and men and the support of neighbours, the NPFL was ready to strike at Samuel Doe.

SIX

CHARLES TAYLOR'S WAR

'When wartime come and I say, get-from-daway, you m'sit down there and say "fwenken".'

'I won't say "fwenken", I will say "foot help de body".'[1]

On Christmas Eve 1989, 168 scantly armed NPFL insurgents crossed into Liberia from Côte d'Ivoire to launch an invasion of their homeland which they hoped would lead to the removal of President Samuel Doe. The first significant rebel success was achieved by a group under the command of Prince Johnson and commander Paul B. Harris, who attacked the frontier post at Butuo near their crossing point in Nimba County, giving their force a supply of arms and ammunition with which to continue its advance. Charles Taylor, at the head of a separate unit, which according to plan should have been advancing in parallel, was delayed initially because of weapons supply problems, and retreated after a firefight with the AFL at the Côte d'Ivoire border. Taylor himself backtracked to Ouagadougou in the final days of December to complete the purchase of his group's arms and ammunition, before returning some days later and crossing back into Nimba County.[2] From then on the advance went more smoothly. 'I started with a shotgun and three rifles and a few dozen men behind me', Taylor related two years later.

they thought we had a multitude ... it was dark, and they just assumed. Their guilt and their corruption magnified their enemies in their sight ... they ran without a fight. Now we had arms to take the next garrison. General Varney and Prince Johnson, seasoned military men, joined our cause. Suddenly we'd become formidable![3]

From there the rebels moved further into the country, linking up with reinforcements arriving from Côte d'Ivoire to boost their numbers for a further advance. The Liberian rebels were supplemented by hundreds of Burkinabe troops provided by Blaise Compaoré's government as well as fighters from Gambia, Sierra Leone and Ghana. The latter group included idealists who felt they were joining a pan-African revolutionary cause, others who had no option but to sign up, mostly migrant workers finding themselves behind the front line, while others joined the attack as mercenaries, in the expectation of some war booty rather than through political motivations.

The population of northern Nimba County, composed mostly of the Mano and Gio tribes, were sympathetic to the incursion, given the persecution they had suffered at the hands of Samuel Doe and his army over the past several years. Many were eager for revenge against the regime that had conducted the massacres of local people in the county in 1983, 1985 and periodically since then. Prince Johnson himself was from the Yorm subgroup of the Gio tribe (sometimes his middle name is expressed as 'Yormie'), and after his arrival he led soldiers from his group into this friendly home turf, which they were able to use as a base for the next stage of operations.

When news of the rebel attack reached President Doe, although he realized that this invasion was not a minor incursion by a mere raiding party, he reacted in a familiar way – by punishing the civilian population in the surrounding regions rather than dealing with the rebels head on. Doe's AFL exacted a severe punishment on the population of Nimba County, prosecuting what amounted to a scorched-earth campaign, which soon led to widespread food shortages in much of the country. Bodies of Nimba County civilians littered the roadsides as tens of thousands fled to towns for safety, or over the border to Guinea and Côte d'Ivoire as refugees.

But when the fighting initially broke out, with Monrovia in the Christmas holiday mood, nobody paid much attention to the reports of a rebel attack hundreds of miles away in the north, and life went on more or less as normal – as far as things could be normal in the surreal world of Samuel Doe's West African dictatorship.

All this time Doe's government waged a crude propaganda war in the capital, initially denying reports that the rebels were advancing, issuing broadcasts that the country's borders were secure; then, as it became clear that there was significant fighting taking place, the president issued statements that the rebels had been pushed back and that everything in the countryside would soon return to normal.

The world – and, at the same time, the people of Monrovia – learned about the NPFL's Christmas Eve 1989 invasion not from any local newspaper or from a Liberian radio station, but through reports made by Charles Taylor via the BBC Africa Service from his front-line bases in the bush, which were then re-broadcast around the country and the region.

Samuel Doe continued to issue denials and counter-statements to reassure the population that he and the AFL were in complete control, but, whether or not people believed his reports rather than the second-hand versions of Taylor's bulletins that were also reaching them, the reality soon became evident. Despite logistical difficulties early in the campaign, by March of 1990 the NPFL was making serious advances into the centre of Liberia and was able to make life increasingly uncomfortable for the government in Monrovia.

In the countryside, once again, the Gio and Mano populations had to bear the brunt of the AFL's reprisals against the NPFL invasion force. Doe's AFL swept through their home region of Nimba County, killing, raping and looting, just as they had often done in the past – only this time, with a real enemy posing a serious threat just beyond, they went much further and civilian casualties were heavy. The AFL troops made little distinction between Gio fighters and Gio civilians, massacring both as they moved through Nimba County, spraying villages with machine-gun and mortar fire, bayoneting civilians and driving residents across the border or into the bush.

Doe's forces had already moved against civilians in the capital early in the fighting, following a thwarted coup plan by NPFL infiltrators, which was meant to coincide with the Nimba County campaign. Taylor had arranged for the Monrovia group to launch an anti-Doe uprising, but all of the plotters were arrested and made to confess on television, disclosing their Libyan training and Burkinabe connections. Doe now had an even greater pretext to pursue his attacks against potential enemy sympathizers or NPFL spies, and his security squads went into full swing against suspects.

The Nimba County massacres soon had their mirror image in Monrovia, with army thugs conducting door-to-door raids of Gio and Mano households, taking away families for questioning and abducting the men, who were often never heard of again.

Prominent opposition leaders or suspected sympathisers were beheaded at night in their homes with increasing regularity, their severed heads often discovered by neighbours in the streets the following morning. There were widespread defections of Gio, Mano and other non-Krahn enlistees from inside the AFL, which depleted its ranks as well as further polarizing the conflict into an ethnic, rather than an ideological or purely political, struggle. In response, Samuel Doe stepped up a recruitment campaign to boost the AFL's numbers, absorbing former convicts, drug dealers and other social marginals previously deemed unsuitable to serve. This intake of undisciplined recruits intensified the propensity for his army to brutalize civilians as well as take advantage of the opportunity for looting and extortion from ordinary citizens.

In Nimba County, unlike in 1983 and 1985, the AFL's purges of civilians backfired badly. As the NPFL received reinforcements and as it consolidated its supply lines in the countryside, rebel leaders were able to distribute arms to local supporters and so the force grew rapidly, while steadily increasing the territory under its control.

Taylor the adoptive Nimbaian

In Nimba County, where the incursion began, most of the local population had never heard of Charles Taylor. And those who had perhaps only remembered his name as a former Monrovia civil servant who had fled the country for the United States following embezzlement charges several years before. But his forces were effective and the rebels gained territory steadily.

Key to the Taylor military campaign was the leadership of Elmer Johnson, a US-trained soldier who held dual US and Liberian nationality and had served in the US Marines in the 1980s. Taylor had kept in contact with Johnson since he had visited him while in detention in Plymouth, and as preparations advanced he called Johnson frequently to get him interested in joining the movement, to help Taylor in his plans for making revolutionary changes in Liberia. With most of the professional Liberian soldiers operating under Prince Johnson's command in a separate sector, the leadership of a trained military officer with experience in the US Army was to be indispensable in assuring that Taylor's attack succeeded.

In late 1989, Elmer Johnson, still at home in the USA, had received a call from Charles Taylor in Côte d'Ivoire. Taylor convinced him that it would be a 'quick and easy' affair and they would soon overthrow Doe and would be in power running Liberia. Finally, in March 1990, Johnson boarded a plane to Côte d'Ivoire and joined Taylor in Liberia to help lead his rapidly advancing NPFL forces. On the battlefield Johnson's skills were invaluable, and he was also popular with the rank and file. 'He had the confidence of the men in arms', his sister, Delores Adighibe, recalled.

Supplies of basic goods from the interior became short as the main logistical arteries to the capital were cut and the AFL's military position steadily worsened. In town after town Doe's deception was shattered with the sound of approaching gunfire followed by the arriving columns of NPFL fighters advancing down the roadsides from the bush.

Doe's army also deployed tactics that were ill suited to countering the guerrilla warfare of the NPFL. While the rebels would usually advance in thin lines well separated from each other, walking long distances from skirmish to skirmish, the AFL preferred not to walk and rode huddled into open trucks to the battle front. This made them more vulnerable to ambush and caused greater casualties, making it easy for the rebels to hit them with RPG and artillery fire as they rolled through the countryside.

As the NPFL gained territory, the composition of the advancing army radically changed from its initial combination of Libyan-trained, exiled Liberian fighters, regular Burkinabe troops and assorted foreign camp followers, to one increasingly dominated by bands of local youths who now had the opportunity and the excuse to go killing and looting in the countryside.

CHARLES TAYLOR IN BUCHANAN, 29 MAY 1990

Swelling ranks, declining discipline

A force which had begun with a core of less than 200 insurgents had first been swollen with around 500 trained recruits from inside Liberia, then further reinforced with a thousand or so local camp followers, mostly armed with single-bore shotguns. Many of its rank-and-file recruits wore trademark red bandanas when going into battle, while the more professional elite units, under the command of Prince Johnson, took the name 'the Black Scorpions' and displayed emblems on their uniforms accordingly. But the character as well as the composition of the NPFL was changing and so was its behaviour, both on and off the battlefield. Indiscriminate looting and attacks against civilians became more frequent, and, as news of atrocities being perpetrated by the rebels reached the outside world, tensions within the original leadership of the NPFL began to emerge.

The AFL attacks on civilians in Nimba had left hundreds of orphans, many of whom were recruited into the ranks of the NPFL, some of them only 14 or 15 years old. As these teenagers began to sign up with the rebel army, they were mostly drafted into support roles, such as manning roadblocks, carrying ammunition and spying on enemy positions. However, in the later stages of the civil war they increasingly joined the adults on the battlefield front line as regular combatants, adding a further source of controversy and condemnation of the NPFL.

Taylor's force was not always successful on the battlefield, however. In April 1990, the notorious Krahn General Charles 'the Rock' Julu, head of Samuel Doe's Executive Mansion Guard, was dispatched to Nimba County to assume command of the flagging AFL defence, and scored a victory in Ganta, defeating and temporarily driving back the NPFL. The setback caused increased tension between Charles Taylor and Prince Johnson. Relations between the two leaders, which had been strained since the outset of the campaign, were further heightened over another incident in February 1990, when Johnson executed men under his command for theft and desertion, enraging Taylor.[4]

Finally, the two commanders split and Prince Johnson broke away from the NPFL to form the Independent National Patriotic Front of Liberia (INPFL), which went on to fight against the AFL independently, also with the sworn objective of removing Doe, but remaining a smaller, generally more disciplined army than Taylor's force. Prince Johnson, however, paid a price for his disloyalty to the assumed leader of the Liberian revolution: within weeks, his parents had been killed, reportedly assassinated at the hands of the NPFL.[5] In terms of personal temperament, however, Johnson was the more unstable of the two leaders; although a religious man given to regular prayer, he was also a heavy drinker and with a volatile temper. Taylor, by contrast, while bold and determined, was altogether a more sober and calculating leader, a teetotaller since his early adult years who described his only personal vice as a liking for the 'occasional fine cigar'.

For the next two months, the two armies would advance in parallel, but under different commanders and along separate routes. Early in the southward advance along the main Ganta-Gbarnga road, which leads to Monrovia, Johnson's men separated from NPFL in the area of Kpatawee, just south of Gbarnga.

The AFL, in disarray now, changed tactics and gave up trying to defend territory in favour of protecting the capital and other strategic locations. In Gbarnga they scuttled a huge munitions dump to allow a faster retreat, leaving the rest of the city to the rebels. For the best part of two months, the INPFL followed backroads westwards before converging on the capital, while Taylor's forces outflanked the retreating AFL on the main Monrovia road, wheeling across country to Buchanan, before circling back towards the west and attacking Monrovia via the coastal route.

As Samuel Doe's army retreated, the NPFL was able to make rapid progress, with a clear run through the countryside in several areas. The capture of Buchanan in May 1990 was a milestone in the campaign – giving the NPFL a major port and confirming that they had effectively now split the AFL forces in two. The remnants of the AFL in the east of Liberia were cut off and the NPFL could set about taking economic and administrative control of the countryside.

The rebel communicator

Unlike those he sought to replace, Charles Taylor was in many ways quite well prepared for leadership. With experience in both government and business, he was equipped to run the economy as well as the structure of the new administration he longed to put in place. Furthermore, he believed there was no reason why, with the instruction recently received in Libya and with the help of some able deputies, his rebel force would not be able to capture and control the whole of Liberia.

Also, after several years in obscurity following his jailbreak and flight from the USA, Charles Taylor in Liberia after the invasion once again deployed another skill that he had honed while an activist and agitator in the United States: public relations. Since the very beginning of the NPFL incursion, he had made a habit of calling the BBC in London on his satellite phone to inform them of his successes in – and his plans for – the new Liberia he intended to create.

Charles Taylor also used his sat-phone to keep in regular contact with Washington DC, which he regarded as tacit backer of his rebellion and which he hoped to keep as an ally as he came closer to his ultimate goal of a complete takeover of power. Indeed, the satellite equipment had been provided to Taylor by the USA, as they deemed it as much in their interests as his to keep up to date with the military progress his forces were making as they battled through the countryside. At the US State Department's Bureau of African Affairs, senior officials would have 'regular chats' with Taylor in the early months of 1990, which the NPFL leader used to brief them and, initially at least, seek their guidance on his unfolding moves.

While officially not backing the rebellion, the US administration of George H.W. Bush, spurred on by an anti-Doe US Congress and the vociferous dissident Liberian community in the USA, was favourable to the idea of Doe's departure being brought about internally, if not by elections or a coup, then by a successful rebellion and civil war as the next best option. The USA gave powerful satellite communications equipment to Taylor, then, to help him keep in touch with Washington DC and to keep abreast of the status of any of its strategic installations inside Liberia.

Now with clear successes on the battlefield the NPFL was ready to tell its story to the outside world and Taylor wanted to set his communications skills to work at full stretch.

Calling a group of foreign journalists to a press conference in Tapita, Nimba County, in May 1990, he arranged for dozens of overseas and West African pressmen and a CNN camera team to cross from the Ivorian side near Danane to come to see his operation: 'I want my name to be littered over the pages of history as being the man who started out the way it should be started out', the NPFL leader declared. 'We in the National Patriotic Front of Liberia have political ambitions too and there will be elections when the time is right. The NPFL will be the transition government.' Taylor went on: 'I'm not going to go down in history as a man who brought this country to war and then screwed up.... Nobody has been willing to risk fighting – so, we're trying ... it's easy to make a dictator in Liberia and I'm not going to let myself be one.'[6]

There was a lot to brag about and it seemed as if nothing could stop this new fighting force which sought to take over the country. Down on the coast to the east of Monrovia, NPFL fighters mopping up around the port of Buchanan were now preparing to take control of the international airport at Robertsfield, just an hour away by road and less than an hour from the capital.

AFL crumbles on the battlefield

Proof of how far the situation had gone against Doe was the cancellation of his May 1990 plans for a presidential birthday celebration in Zwedru, in his home region of Grand Gedeh County. The event was cancelled at the last minute with the birthday boy citing what he thought were intense 'sensitivities' at the time, which would mean it was better not to organize a celebration in the countryside. The fact that he could not guarantee security either for himself or for any of his intended guests on the road to Zwedru was never doubted as the real reason for abandoning the feast.

The advance of the NPFL into the south and east of Liberia was also having a devastating impact on the civilian population of the region, upon whom the long-persecuted Gio and Mano, the core group of the NPFL fighting force, now took revenge for the atrocities of the past. As the rebel advance spilled into Grand Gedeh County, many villagers from Nimba County followed them, flooding into their rivals' territory with machetes and small arms, looting and exacting revenge on the Krahn and Mandingo populations. The Grand Gedeh massacres continued into 1991 and 1992, and civilians were indiscriminately slaughtered by the NPFL forces in locations such as Duegee Town, Zwedru, Putu and Tumbo. In consequence, at Liberia's eastern border another huge exodus took place in early 1990, with Krahn civilians flooding in their tens of thousands into Côte d'Ivoire.

NPFL massacres occurred in the west as well, with hundreds of Mandingo civilians being butchered in Badeku and other locations in Lofa County, causing a refugee flight towards Sierra Leone, while in Grand Cape Mount County a group of seventy-five refugees and IGNU rescuers were massacred in June 1991 by the NPFL as they attempted to save 3,000 refugees stranded at Sulima. When the NPFL took Buchanan, atrocities were also carried out against the Mandingo population as they fled the port into Grand Bassa County.

The fatalistic nature of the Liberian ethnic tragedy was summed up by a Krahn farmer, speaking to a US journalist four years before the civil war, in the midst of Doe's regime. 'There will have to be revenge', he said. 'We know that something is in the making. When that thing explodes, then God have mercy on all of us.' Now the revenge was under way and 'that thing' was exploding with mighty force.[7]

By May of 1990, Samuel Doe was a defeated president with only the vestiges of power remaining around him. Charles Taylor's NPFL as good as controlled Liberia and the gates to Monrovia would crash open, it seemed, with one last great push. Taylor's main rival in the anti-Doe rebellion, Prince Johnson, had continued his campaign to the west, steadily gaining ground and consolidating his position but holding nothing like the amount of territory which Taylor could now claim for the NPFL. At this stage most Monrovians were still not even aware that a second rebel faction was operating independently of Charles Taylor, also closing in on the capital in tandem with Taylor's forces.

Charles Taylor, as always, was in touch with the outside world via the BBC Africa Service and the Voice of America to broadcast his successes; most of all, he was in contact with the United States, directly by phone as well as through their embassy in Monrovia and their recently arrived ambassador-designate Peter Jon de Vos. The USA wanted to avoid large-scale bloodshed while protecting its substantial assets in the country, and it believed that the key to a peaceful transition was getting Doe to agree to leave – a notion that the embassy was now tasked with warming Doe up to gradually.

But Doe ultimately rejected US entreaties to leave in security, initially believing he could hold on but later, even as the reality of defeat filtered through, preferring to stand beside what he now thought of as his Krahn nation, ready to fight to the finish.

With arms shipments to the NPFL now arriving unhindered at Robertsfield airport on a regular basis, mostly from Burkina Faso, and with the AFL in total disarray on the battlefield, now down to only a small rump of loyalist Krahn troops, there was apparently nothing holding the NPFL back except perhaps their leader. Even the majority of European and other foreign embassies were now not in favour of a ceasefire, believing that a swift takeover by the NPFL and a transition of power to new leadership would be more likely to end the bloodshed, and to avert the continued daily massacres of non-Krahn citizens inside the capital.

Although less flamboyantly brutal, less extensive and less widely publicized by the international media than the excesses of the NPFL, the brutality of the AFL and Doe's associated urban thugs was no different in kind than that of the advancing rebel armies. After the war, following extensive hearings as well as a long phase of victim and witness interviews under the auspices of Liberia's Truth and Reconciliation Commission (TRC), it was recorded that during the conflict the NPFL was responsible for a total of 63,843 violations of international human rights and humanitarian law and war crimes, a total of 39.2 per cent of all violations and three times greater than the second worst offending faction, LURD (Liberians United for Reconciliation and Democracy), and compared to the 8,794 violations of the AFL, a total equivalent to 5.4 per cent of all crimes recorded.[8] Although accurate accounts of atrocities, and indeed of total fatalities, during the war are extremely hard to come by, the work carried out by the TRC researchers represents one of the few comprehensive efforts made to quantify and attribute the suffering of Liberia's wartime victims.

Doe's internal purge intensifies

As the rebels tightened the noose around Samuel Doe's forces in Monrovia, inside the AFL the remaining non-Krahn or Mandingo soldiers who had not defected were being persecuted and often executed by their fellows. Inside the city ordinary Gio and Mano citizens were increasingly being dragged from their homes and taken off to be slaughtered, often on the pretext that they were rebels or that they had been harbouring rebels.

In one particularly bloody incident, a group of masked soldiers smashed their way into the UN compound, where many Gio and Mano civilians were taking refuge, and dragged off scores of victims for killing, in front of the watching UN guards. The following day, Doe, claiming that these atrocities had not been carried out by AFL soldiers, ordered a 'full investigation' into the incident, as if there somehow existed in the city a renegade band of his own army disguising their identities and carrying out unsanctioned eliminations of civilians.

The president even visited the UN compound to address the remaining Mano and Gio and to promise them protection in the future. The crowd shouted him down with retorts of 'Who is gonna believe you?', and the president was forced to make a hasty exit from the area in his waiting limousine

While Taylor remained committed to staying on the side of the USA, heeding their call to let diplomatic efforts with Doe run their course, there was nevertheless a strong military argument for pushing ahead, rather than risking losing the initiative on the battlefield. Taylor's rival insurgents from the INPFL were getting closer to the capital and there was now a serious risk that delay could be disastrous for the NPFL. Taylor argued with his own commanders about their next move.

In a 1992 interview with an American journalist, Taylor recounted:

> we camped a few dozen miles from Monrovia and fell to arguing about strategy. Varney [a senior INPFL general] and Prince Johnson elected to move in, to take the city. They ... began shelling randomly and stupidly. It looked as though we might have to move against them. But your American Ambassador from Ivory Coast came to see me in the middle of the night with a bunch from the CIA. Oh yes. They just appeared at our perimeter suddenly from the darkness, out of thin air.
> What your ambassador told me was that if I waited, if I didn't plunge the capital into a bloody battle, the US would back me one

hundred percent. They and the West African peacekeepers would quickly take care of Prince Johnson and I would be installed as President of Liberia. So I waited in the bush ... the rains started and it was too late to move ... they lied to me. Why did they do that?[9]

However, in the month prior to the NPFL's arrival outside Monrovia, there was another problem coming to the surface in the group. A further deterioration in the rebel army's discipline at the bottom end, and of cohesion among its leadership at the top end, threatened to stall effective decision-making. Contributing to the decline in morale was the untimely death of the NPFL military leader, Elmer Johnson. Managing battlefield success as well as working to instil discipline into the expanding ranks of the NPFL as it advanced, the well-connected Americo-Liberian Johnson was popular with the troops and known to the United States. Taylor had concerns about his loyalty, however, and may have thought that Johnson might try to race ahead to take Monrovia with a breakaway faction of the troops under his command.[10]

On 4 June, Johnson was leading a small convoy of about thirty NPFL fighters towards Robertsfield after the capture of the Firestone plantation when they were ambushed by a much larger force of AFL soldiers. The rebels had no chance as their vehicles were blocked on the road and some 500 government troops opened fire with machine guns and explosives. Doe had Johnson's body brought back to Monrovia and immediately hailed the death of the NPFL general as a great victory for the AFL against the rebels.

But not everyone was convinced about the AFL's ability to pull off such a stunning success. Suspicions were aroused at how easily the experienced Johnson had fallen into such a deadly trap. Fingers were pointed at Taylor's camp, with rumours that Johnson's popularity with the NPFL rank and file could have been a threat to the NPFL leader's supremacy, particularly as victory seemed in sight.

Whatever the truth behind Elmer Johnson's killing, his demise hastened the disorder and chaos in the NPFL ranks in what had only six months before been a relatively well controlled and effective fighting force. What had begun as sporadic incidences of atrocities against civilians by the advancing NPFL troops in the insurgency's early days now became their horrific modus operandi. Unpaid, unruly and undisciplined, they had been promised by their commanders that they would have the right to loot in enemy areas as compensation, and many had by now been in the campaign for months – it was time to get paid. As the rampaging bands of young fighters claiming affiliation to the NPFL approached the capital, their brutality against civilians intensified, and the rebels pillaged and raped their way southwards.

Taylor continued to claim that he was in control of his forces as they advanced, and that any perpetrators of atrocities among his ranks were being punished. At the time, before the international media, as well as later in his trial in The Hague, he consistently denied a systematic resort to terror tactics and inhumane treatment of civilians by his forces, saying that wherever such incidents occurred those responsible were brought to justice before NPFL military tribunals.

CHARLES TAYLOR GIVES V-SIGN, 10 JULY 1990 IN MONROVIA

But in mid-1990 these claims appeared less and less credible, with citizens fleeing Taylor's forces and reaching Monrovia, testifying about their experiences not only to fellow Liberians but, worse still for Taylor, to the international media stationed in the capital.

In addition to taking the port of Buchanan, Charles Taylor's NPFL had by now overrun the Firestone complex at Harbel, outside Monrovia, taking control of the radio station ELWA (Eternal Love

Winning Africa). As the rebels encircled Monrovia, they set up checkpoints or 'gates' at key exits from the capital as well as at several strategic countryside crossroads. These became a further focal point for massacres of stranded or fleeing Mandingos and Krahns, identified and singled out by the NPFL and tortured, mutilated or killed by the roadside as they made their futile attempts to pass. The notorious 'God Bless You' checkpoint between Monrovia and Harbel and 'Gate 15' on the road to Kakata in Margibi County were just two of the bloody points of no return for many of the civilians caught up in the fighting.

Inside Monrovia, at least for the non-Krahn and Mandingo populations, Taylor's advance offered hope for many in escaping the clutches of the AFL and Doe's death squads. But now, as word spread of indiscriminate attacks against civilians close to the capital by the advancing NPFL, no one could consider himself safe from the advancing rebel fighters.

The INPFL, also camped outside Monrovia to the west of the city, was now identifiable by the civilian population, and Prince Johnson's forces, smaller and with a higher proportion of professional soldiers, were perceived by many as a more disciplined army. For a time the US embassy considered Johnson a potential transitional leader of post-civil-war Liberia.

The military split within the advancing rebel forces, dug in outside Monrovia in two distinct sectors, was thus now evident to all observers. However, less obvious to outsiders were the increasing tensions developing within the NPFL both on the ground and among its all-important backers in the diaspora abroad.

Internal tensions and rivals' disappearances

The PR spin from the NPFL camp was that Taylor had called on his advancing army to pause to allow time for mediation between the warring parties and to let the NPFL enter and secure Monrovia with as few civilian casualties as possible. While the United States certainly asked Taylor to halt his advance, his drive for power may also have stalled for other, non-military reasons.

Crucially, key backers from among the Liberian diaspora who had supported the NPFL both administratively and financially, now began to draw back. In the wake of adverse humanitarian reports about the rebel army's conduct reaching the world's media, backers became increasingly unwilling to be associated with the NPFL's actions, while nevertheless continuing to support the aim of removing Samuel Doe from office. This loss of public support impacted Taylor's authority as well as the NPFL's ability to keep the United States and the international community from intervening to stop its grab for power.

Taylor, the ambitious driving force at the head of the NPFL's advance through the countryside for the past six months, was in no doubt as to who should lead the country after the fall of the Doe regime. However, other key NPFL figures both within and outside the country now posed a greater potential threat to Taylor's leadership of the movement and could potentially still derail his plans to emerge as Liberia's new ruler after the fighting ceased. The defection of Prince Johnson, although not a political aspirant himself, had already caused problems within the military campaign, while the late arrival of forces commanded by Cooper Teah, another Libyan-trained NPFL commander, represented a further possible threat to Taylor's supremacy. Dealing with these dissenters distracted Taylor at a crucial moment from the necessity of consolidating his military gains and resupplying and preparing his army for its final advance to victory.

Former allies in the rebel movement were now potential rivals for leadership, and in the space of a few weeks in mid-1990 potential contenders began to disappear, believed eliminated by forces loyal to Taylor, if not on his direct orders. In addition to the controversial death of Elmer Johnson, Moses Duopu, Taylor's rival from ULAA days in America, died during fighting in Nimba County. Non-NPFL politicians such as Gabriel Kpolleh, a founder of the Liberia Unification Party and a contender in the 1985 elections, also vanished, killed during the rebel campaign. In June 1990, Duopu had called for leadership elections for the NPFL, announcing that he would be a candidate for the position, thereby marking himself out as a clear rival to Taylor, by now established as the autocratic figurehead of the movement and with less tolerance for the existence of dissenters in the ranks.

Ellen Johnson Sirleaf, who visited Taylor in the Liberian bush on a number of occasions in 1990 and helped raise raised hundreds of thousands of dollars intended for the NPFL early in the campaign, became publicly more distanced from Taylor while still remaining close to the anti-Doe armed rebellion and, if at least one of her closest colleagues is to be believed, aspiring to assume its leadership from the battlefront.[11]

The most odious disappearance of a Taylor rival was the presumed killing behind NPFL lines of Jackson Doe, who, with proven democratic credentials from his 1985 election performance, could also have become a future civilian president of a post-Samuel Doe Liberia. Jackson Doe was also favoured by many in the diplomatic community as well as moderate Americo-Liberians who saw that someone of his stature would receive the backing of America if he emerged as a future leader of the country.

Jackson Doe was a popular son of Nimba County, and for Taylor he represented a challenge for the hearts and minds of his rural power base. When the news broke that Doe had crossed the NPFL lines from Fendell to Kakata in Margibi County to come over to Taylor's side, it was claimed by the NPFL as a further confirmation of its legitimacy and acceptance by the wider population. Right away, Doe was brought to Taylor's base at Harbel outside Monrovia to meet the NPFL leader, who offered him refuge in a safe house in Buchanan.

In fact, Doe was taken to Buchanan and detained pending execution, rather than protected. He never believed that Taylor or those close to him would order his killing. According to a fellow detainee, Donald Johnson, a Sierra Leonean musician who was held by the NPFL at the same time in Buchanan, Charles Taylor 'sent packages to Doe during our time in jail, but it didn't matter. He was beheaded [along with] two Nigerian journalists in August [1990] anyway.'[12]

Doe was not a rival of Taylor only because of his electoral popularity. It has been alleged that early in the fighting, he and Ellen

First battle of Monrovia
July - August 1990

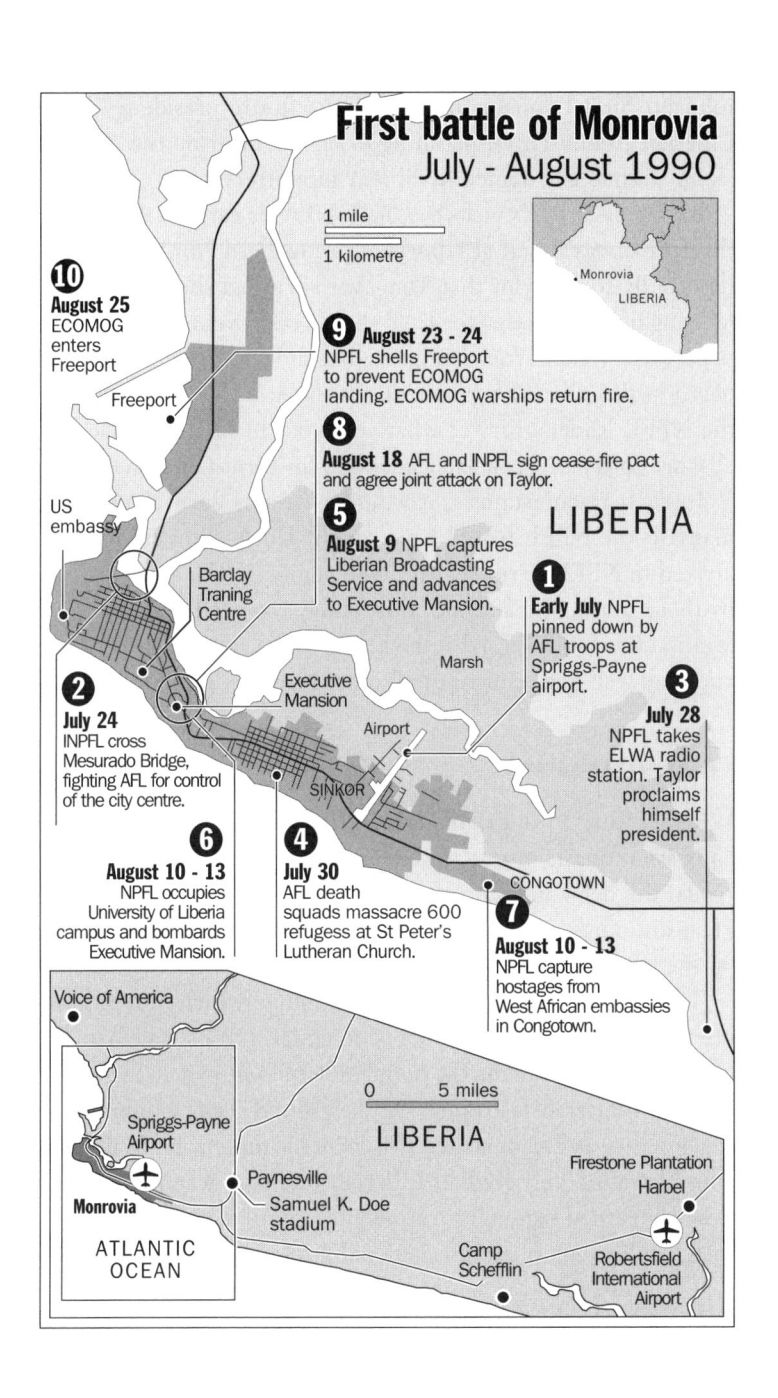

10 August 25 ECOMOG enters Freeport

9 August 23 - 24 NPFL shells Freeport to prevent ECOMOG landing. ECOMOG warships return fire.

8 August 18 AFL and INPFL sign cease-fire pact and agree joint attack on Taylor.

5 August 9 NPFL captures Liberian Broadcasting Service and advances to Executive Mansion.

1 Early July NPFL pinned down by AFL troops at Spriggs-Payne airport.

3 July 28 NPFL takes ELWA radio station. Taylor proclaims himself president.

2 July 24 INPFL cross Mesurado Bridge, fighting AFL for control of the city centre.

6 August 10 - 13 NPFL occupies University of Liberia campus and bombards Executive Mansion.

4 July 30 AFL death squads massacre 600 refugees at St Peter's Lutheran Church.

7 August 10 - 13 NPFL capture hostages from West African embassies in Congotown.

Freeport · US embassy · Barclay Traning Centre · Marsh · Executive Mansion · Airport · SINKOR · CONGOTOWN · LIBERIA

Voice of America · Spriggs-Payne Airport · Paynesville · Samuel K. Doe stadium · Monrovia · ATLANTIC OCEAN · Camp Schefflin · Firestone Plantation · Harbel · Robertsfield International Airport

Johnson Sirleaf conspired to seize the future presidency for their Liberian Action Party, planning to leave Taylor on the sidelines, a claim strenuously denied by Sirleaf supporters.

In one of Sirleaf's visits to Charles Taylor early in the war, when the NPFL was based at Gborplay in northern Nimba County, she reportedly told Taylor that Tom Woewiyu and she had agreed in a meeting in Virginia that the LAP should take over after Samuel Doe's departure. When Woewiyu arrived at the front some time later, he heard of this alleged 'agreement' for the first time and encountered the NPFL leader's fury at what appeared to be a ploy used in his absence to try to wrest the leadership for Sirleaf and Jackson Doe.

In such circumstances, it would have not been a surprise that many in the NPFL would have sought Doe's elimination when he arrived in NPFL territory. Although claimed to be entirely fictitious by those in the Sirleaf camp, this widely reported and damaging allegation was first released at the height of the 2005 election campaign and may well have contributed to her losing in the first round.[13]

Fatal distraction

Whether due to a calculated military decision, because of US embassy requests or due to the necessity of dealing with leadership rivals, the delay in entering Monrovia was to prove one of Taylor's great undoings, as the NPFL's momentum and strategic advantage on the battlefield were quickly slipping away.

Two developments now occurred, both of which were to contribute to ensuring the beginning of a long, frustrating stalemate for the NPFL – and to condemn the population of Monrovia to many months of humanitarian catastrophe. On the ground, Prince Johnson seized the initiative as Taylor stalled; while on the diplomatic front, the Doe administration and civilian Liberian interests acceded to the calls from concerned regional governments – particularly Nigeria – for the early deployment of an international military intervention force.

The international community remained passive and non-interventionist at this stage of the mounting crisis, following the lead of the United States, whose apparent lack of will with regard to military involvement, no matter what the risk of inaction, was setting the standard for all potentially concerned international actors.[14]

Members of Liberian religious and civil society, exposed on the front line and without the comfortable option of adopting a concerned observer role, took the initiative in trying to avert the looming bloodbath in Monrovia. Sitting in the Sierra Leonean capital Freetown and attempting to mediate between the warring factions for weeks, in late June the Inter-Faith Mediation Committee was still trying in vain to get the protagonists to reach a peaceful resolution of the crisis. Both the Liberian Council of Churches and the Liberia National Muslim Council called on Samuel Doe to resign for the good of the country. And LINSU, the Liberian National Students Union, in unison with the Press Union of Liberia (PUL), together with numerous other civil society groups, jointly sponsored a petition to impeach the president.

On 27 June, the Citizen's Committee for Peace and Democracy, the umbrella organization for the civil groups, organized a march on the Capitol to press home their demands. As they approached, however, government forces opened fire on the crowd, causing a number of fatalities.

The intransigence of Doe as he clung on to power proved impossible to overcome. Among the factors in his obstinacy was the increasingly belligerent lobbying of the isolated and encircled Krahn community, who faced annihilation in the event of a violent takeover of Monrovia by the NPFL. On numerous occasions, when the USA came to implore him to step into a waiting helicopter and leave the scene, he retorted that he would only agree to leave if he could take his Krahn people with him – a clearly impossible demand, but one which indicated how firmly in the grip of his supporters he was.

The second rebel faction appears

A further surprise for shell-shocked Monrovians was the appearance, in mid-July, of the INPFL, who advanced from the west to the outskirts of Monrovia and occupied Bushrod Island. The splinter faction had hitherto rarely been heard of, but their presence on the scene was now a real if complicating factor, both for Doe and for the NPFL in its ambitions to become sole heir to the government it was struggling to overthrow.

By July 1990, Monrovia was a divided city, with the AFL dug into a few remaining key sections, including central parts, the Executive Mansion, the Freeport and still holding some other key installations such as Spriggs-Payne Airport, the domestic airport some 10 miles from the capital which served surrounding West African capitals.

Much of the AFL had long since defected, leaving a rump of the President's Elite Guard and his hard-core, faithful Krahn tribesmen, who now had no choice except to stay and fight. With depleting numbers of regular soldiers, Doe took to arming Krahn and Mandingo civilians in order to bolster the dwindling ranks of his defending force.

This development proved to be a further motivation for atrocities, as the undisciplined and newly armed vigilantes took to carrying out their own form of urban reprisals and ethnic attacks. On the night of 29–30 July, one such band, led by the self-styled 'Captain' Tailey Yonbon, a personal selection of Doe's, led an attack on some 2,000 displaced Gio and Mano civilians who were taking refuge in St Peter's Lutheran Church, Sinkor. The attack, which took place within the International Red Cross compound, and as such clearly designated as neutral territory, was discouraged by some of Doe's senior officers from the regular AFL. A horrendous night of butchery took place as terrified fleeing civilians were slaughtered and bayoneted to death inside the church and within the surrounding compound, with women and infants massacred alongside the male refugees, all of whom were 'suspected' of having been infiltrated by rebels. Among the approximately 600 fatalities that night was Charles Taylor's own father, Neilson, who was caught up in the humanitarian nightmare like so many other ordinary Monrovians taking refuge at the time in the church.

For most of July Taylor was unable to break through the AFL's final defences around the capital. The Executive Mansion, where Doe was bunkered, was a virtual (some said actual) nuclear shelter, heavily fortified and almost impossible to penetrate by conventional assault. Built by the Israelis in 1964 at a cost of some $20 million, it was both the last bastion of power in Liberia and a fitting fortress from which an embattled president could make his final stand.

Taylor claims the presidency

Whether brimming over with optimism or perhaps hoping that words might hasten the reality, on 27 July Taylor made a bold and historic pronouncement on the recently captured radio station ELWA, previously an American-owned evangelical station, which listeners across much of the region tuned into.

Announcing to his fellow citizens that a new government, the National Patriotic Reconstruction Assembly Government (NPRAG), was being formed to replace the rump of the Doe administration, he at the same time proclaimed himself president of Liberia. Despite the deluded nature of his claims, the very fact that such a pronouncement could have any credibility shocked many outsiders, on whom it was belatedly dawning that Charles Taylor might soon be the leader of a new mineral-rich anti-Western rebel state with backers in Côte d'Ivoire, Burkina Faso and Libya. For many, particularly the Nigerians, who cherished their influence in English-speaking West Africa and had prospered in Liberia under Doe, this was a sudden wake-up call and a major spur to action. In stark contrast, the proclamation was met with derision and disbelief by ordinary Monrovians, still trapped between the front lines and enduring successive months of living hell. For those on the ground it was plain to see how far Taylor still was from realizing his claims.

Given the rapid advance of Charles Taylor's NPFL, leading to the fragile but bloody stalemate of late July 1990 and with some 3,000 of their civilian nationals still trapped behind the NPFL lines, the governments of Nigeria, Ghana and Sierra Leone pressed the Economic Community of West African States (ECOWAS) to take action in the face of the continuing crisis. This led to the formation of the regional body's conflict mediation committee and shortly thereafter the signing of an agreement on 7 August 1990 in Banjul,

Gambia. Established within the structure of an overall ECOWAS Peace Plan, which included the assent of the AFL, INPFL and Liberian religious and civil groups, but the vehement opposition of the NPFL, the plan's key element was the authorization of the dispatch of an ECOWAS intervention force to Liberia.

An Interim Government of National Unity (IGNU) was formed under the leadership of Amos Sawyer, the leading progressive and former president of MOJA, who, like Ellen Johnson Sirleaf, had been in exile in the United States. The IGNU included representatives of the signatories to the Banjul Agreement and received the recognition of the international community as the legitimate government of Liberia.

At the Banjul summit, Côte d'Ivoire and Burkina Faso, Charles Taylor's main allies in West Africa, strongly opposed the intervention plan that Nigeria proposed to the ECOWAS committee. The leaders of the francophone dissenters argued that military action in a member country could only be approved by a meeting of ECOWAS heads of state, not by their representatives at committee level. But Nigeria and its anglophone allies, together with Guinea, were eager to act, and they passed an agreement committing troops to the intervention force, the Economic Community of West African States Monitoring Group, or ECOMOG. The ostensible purpose was to assemble a neutral, disinterested multinational force, able to gain the confidence of all sides and to bring about a quick cessation of hostilities.

A total of five countries from ECOWAS agreed to participate by sending troops, while several French-speaking member countries either opposed intervention, as was the case with Côte d'Ivoire and Burkina Faso, or declined to participate unless funding was made available to them. In the end an overwhelmingly Nigerian-constituted intervention force was assembled, together with troops from Ghana, Sierra Leone, Gambia and Guinea.

While ECOMOG was a mostly Nigerian force in composition, its commander, General Arnold Quianoo, was Ghanaian, perhaps to give at least the appearance of some balance of nationalities in the command of the intervention army.

Côte d'Ivoire, the dominant francophone country in the region, not to mention France itself, was perpetually suspicious of Nigerian domination of West Africa, and any extension of anglophone hegemony in the region was inevitably met with unease. Furthermore, decades earlier, Côte d'Ivoire's President Houphouët-Boigny had supported the secession of eastern Nigeria, which had led to another, even greater, humanitarian catastrophe than the one now unfolding in Liberia.

The war between Biafra and Nigeria caused the deaths, mostly by starvation, of some 3 million people of Igbo ethnicity in the breakaway republic. The Biafran leader, General Odumegwu-Ojukwu, was given asylum in Côte d'Ivoire after the Nigerian government, with the staunch support of the United Kingdom and others, ultimately overran Biafra's crumbling defences and the secession collapsed.

Also, at a personal level Houphouët-Boigny had supported former President Tolbert, but most of all was Samuel Doe's sworn enemy following the execution of his son-in-law, A.B. Tolbert, following the 1980 coup.

Nigerian element drives a wedge between Taylor and the USA

The problem for Taylor was that, given the Nigerian president's long-standing support for the government of Samuel Doe, ECOMOG with Nigeria calling the shots was far less likely than the USA to be an impartial facilitator of the future order of things. Taylor would lose his key superpower ally if President Babangida in Abuja took over from the US ambassador and Taylor's contacts in Washington DC in the role of Liberia's principal peace-broker.

When Nigerian and Ghanaian civilians in rebel-held zones tried to cross to the government-held areas, they were held hostage by the NPFL, taken as bargaining chips to prevent the dispatch of a potentially hostile intervention force, or at least that was Taylor's reckoning at the time. Taylor also used his domestic and international media connections to denounce the impending arrival of ECOMOG as a 'foreign invasion', and Tom Woewiyu, NPFL defence spokesman, lobbied hard against the dispatch of the peacekeepers. Following meetings in Banjul, Woewiyu said: 'There is no way we are going to let them enter Liberia. We're going to fight them with knives, guns, cutlasses, anything we can find ... another armed force entering Liberia is just like putting explosives to fire.'[15]

After the intervention force arrived and attacked NPFL positions, Taylor made a radio broadcast, on 14 September, threatening to kill one ECOWAS national from among the hostages he held, in retaliation for every NPFL fighter killed by ECOMOG.

Taylor's ranting and his deputies' hectoring, together with the hostage-taking plan to prevent ECOMOG's deployment, all backfired, however. The governments of Nigeria, Ghana and Sierra Leone were determined not only to protect their citizens, but also to prevent the takeover of a new leader in Monrovia and the creation of a Liberia–Côte d'Ivoire–Burkina Faso axis opposed to their interests in the region.

The force was finally dispatched on 24 August, from its staging base in Sierra Leone, and headed directly for the Freeport on Bushrod Island. The NPFL began a heavy bombardment from land as well as sending a gunboat to harass the incoming ECOMOG ships, but with the assistance of the INPFL, who defended the Freeport fiercely in support of the ECOMOG landing, the white helmets of the 3,000 peacekeepers were soon visible in parts of the capital, and the regional forces secured a beachhead on the edge of Monrovia.

The INPFL supported the peace process from the outset and its leader, Prince Johnson, in contrast to Taylor, had never said that he sought the leadership of the country. Furthermore, Johnson and the AFL came to a seemingly unholy agreement on 18 August, to join forces in opposing the NPFL. The AFL itself was also particularly compliant with the ECOMOG presence, given the close relationship between the Nigerian president and its own beleaguered commander in chief, President Doe. All of these elements, combined with Johnson's control of the Freeport as a result of earlier campaigns, allowed the combined defending forces to beat back the NPFL and allow a successful ECOMOG landing in the capital.

As ECOMOG soldiers fanned out through the streets of Monrovia, a degree of calm which the city had not known for several months began to return. Food was distributed to the starving local population and foreign nationals in the government-controlled sector of Monrovia, mostly those from neighbouring West African states, began to be evacuated. Despite ECOMOG's ostensible neutrality, the AFL now had the effective support of a well-armed foreign peacekeeping force, which also was allied to the INPFL, giving Doe the benefit of a degree of breathing space that he had not known for many long weeks.

Assassination of Doe

ECOMOG's force commander, General Arnold Quainoo, was nevertheless careful about his relations with the other factions present in Monrovia, and took care to avoid meeting with Doe in order to avoid the appearance of taking sides with the incumbent regime. The ECOWAS peace plan called for the organization of an all-party conference to establish and install an interim, civilian-led government, followed by elections after one year. Therefore, favouritism to any side could be seen as acting counter to the terms of the plan.

However, the INPFL had taken and held the Freeport and surrounding territory prior to the arrival of ECOMOG and therefore was in close proximity to the new force's command when it finally installed itself there in late August. Prince Johnson thus enjoyed close communications with the intervention force, although the INPFL's official presence at the port was down to a nominal twenty troops, as demanded by ECOMOG immediately upon their arrival in early August.

Following the bilateral ceasefire between the AFL and INPFL two weeks earlier, in the first week of September a meeting was arranged between Johnson and Doe at the Barclay Training Centre, the AFL's headquarters. The men shook hands and embraced, and formalized their agreement to make a joint effort to support ECOMOG and push back the NPFL from Monrovia. Even at this late stage, Doe apparently still entertained ideas of a comeback, perhaps heartened by the thought that the two men, both indigenous Liberians, could work together to rid Liberia of what the president saw as the predominantly Americo-Liberian-backed NPFL.

A few days later, on 9 September, an unusually clear and gunfire-free Sunday afternoon in the capital, following a meeting between Sellee Thomson, Doe's principal spokesman, and General Quainoo, Doe decided to visit the Freeport to see the ECOMOG force commander. Thomson had arranged a meeting between the two men and Doe decided to take the unusual step of driving from the Mansion, which he rarely left these days, with a relatively light security detail and without informing General Nimely, chief of his Executive Mansion Guard.

Driving through the deserted streets of Monrovia in a long motorcade, sirens blaring, past rotting corpses and scattered groups of starving refugees huddling under makeshift roadside shelters, many of those with the strength to do so got up and shouted abuse at their despised and deluded head of state as he passed by waving in his open-top stretch limousine. Even on the way to the Freeport, Doe took what would previously have been considered the reckless decision to drive through areas controlled by the INPFL.

Arriving at the ECOMOG headquarters, Doe's detail of bodyguards, over seventy men in total, were required to disarm, while the president went inside to see General Quainoo. Prince Johnson and a squad of his rebel soldiers arrived at the Freeport shortly afterwards. The INPFL were heavily armed, but they had concealed their weapons inside the jeeps upon arrival, and, unlike Doe's bodyguard, managed to bring their weapons inside the compound.

Johnson initially went upstairs to the force commander's office, but then soon burst out and ran downstairs, shouting an order to his men. Johnson's troops then opened fire on the AFL. In a firefight that lasted some two hours the INPFL carried out a comprehensive slaughter of the president's entourage and bodyguard, before moving on to seek out Doe himself. The ECOMOG contingent was near-powerless to control the situation. Justifying his troops' decision to take cover, the Ghanaian force commander recounted: 'I was being expected to deploy the outnumbered ECOMOG soldiers at the Freeport at the time between the Armed Forces of Liberia and the INPFL rebels ... no general rank officer can be that stupid and inconsiderate, especially in a peacekeeping operation.'[16]

Gruesome ending on videotape

Doe was found hiding in Quainoo's office. He was promptly shot several times in the legs and bundled into the back of Johnson's jeep and taken to the INPFL's headquarters at Caldwell for interrogation. What followed counts as one of the most gruesome and well-publicized tortures and executions in contemporary history, as Johnson arranged to videotape Doe's interrogation, subsequently distributing copies of the president's final ordeal to the foreign press corps and ultimately to much of West Africa and around the world.

During the video scenes, shot at close range with the voices of both Doe and his interrogators audible, the terrified, flabby president can be seen stripped to his underpants, arms bound behind his back and forced onto the floor, then ordered to speak by his interrogators about what he had done to the Liberian economy and where the people's money had been sent. During other scenes, Prince Johnson can be seen sipping a can of Budweiser and being fanned by a young woman as he directs the interrogation, while other rebels hold down Doe, screaming at him to talk as well as shouting at each other.

Doe is filmed begging to be released to talk, and desperately assuring his captors: 'Gentlemen, gentlemen, we are all one!' as Johnson retorts: 'I don't want to shoot you, I'm a humanitarian. But don't fuck with me!' Then Johnson loses patience, saying: 'that man won't talk – bring me his ear'. He orders his men to first cut off one, then the other, of the president's ears, provoking screams of agony from the heavily bleeding victim. Johnson proceeds to raise one of the ears to the camera before putting it inside Doe's mouth.

Johnson then orders his men to get Doe out of his sight and the president is dragged off to the patio for further interrogation by other rebels. 'What did you do with the Liberian People's Money?'

demands one, with Doe, fading fast, still imploring to be set loose. 'I'm in a lot of pain, my ears are cut', he mumbles. Doe is then told to order his forces to surrender to Johnson, with more screaming and shouting from the rebels, before the video ends.

Doe died later that night from bleeding. His body was taken the next day to the Island Clinic and put on display for all to see, in case any rumour spread about a possible escape or the assassination not really having taken place. The myths were still very much alive about Doe's immortality and ability to protect himself through his juju charms and amulets.

When Doe was first captured, Johnson had wanted to hand him over to ECOMOG or the Americans to be put on a ship or a plane and taken into exile, but then there was disagreement among his commanders over what to do, based on the fear that he might be able to escape using his mystical powers, including, it was said, possibly flying away from his captors.[17] Thus, the exhibition of his body was final and indisputable proof that the 'bulletproof' Doe, who had so often proclaimed his invulnerability due to spiritual protection, had at last succumbed to his mortal wounds.

Just days before Doe's assassination, it was widely rumoured that there had been an imminent plan by ECOMOG together with the US embassy to remove Doe from the scene, and discussion of such an arrangement may have been behind his precipitate departure for the Freeport that afternoon.

For his part, Taylor also seems to have been aware of a Doe escape plan. In a radio broadcast two days before Doe's death, he referred to his repeated demands that Doe be taken away by ECOMOG but that they had failed to do so. Now, Taylor said, it would be wrong to allow him simply to leave the scene without first being arrested and tried for all the crimes that he had committed and the devastation he had brought to the country.[18]

SEVEN

THE PANTOMIME OF PEACE

> ECOWAS has established a record of restraint and professionalism sorely needed in Liberia ... we continue to meet our obligations to the Liberian people, while recognizing that the historical relationship between our countries has changed irrevocably.
>
> Leonard H. Robinson Jr, deputy assistant secretary for African affairs, before the House Foreign Affairs Committee, subcommittee on Africa, 19 November 1992

For the two years following the NPFL's retreat to Gbarnga in October 1990, a series of initiatives were undertaken by the interim government, the regional community led by ECOWAS and Liberian civil society groups as well as the international community, all aimed at bringing a lasting end to hostilities, disarmament of the warring factions and a return to more stable conditions in the country in preparation for elections and a permanent civilian government. These included the Bamako Ceasefire of November 1990, the Banjul Joint Statement of December 1990, the February 1991 Lomé Agreement, and the Yamoussoukro I–IV Accords of June–October 1991.

With Amos Sawyer's IGNU the official government of Liberia, but in reality a puppet government kept in power by ECOMOG, Taylor responded by establishing a governmental structure of his own to administer the extensive territory occupied by his forces. The NPFL established a rival capital in Gbarnga, which became the seat of Charles Taylor's National Patriotic Reconstruction Assembly Government (NPRAG). Militarily, it consolidated its grip on much of the rest of Liberia, extending its control into the south and east of the country as well as westwards towards, and later across, the Sierra Leone border.

With the onset of the war in Sierra Leone in 1991, the NPFL extended its territory of operations, as Revolutionary United Front (RUF) forces and NPFL fighters jointly attacked parts of Liberia's western neighbour. At home, it continued to face ECOMOG across a front line which in places ran little further than along the outskirts of Monrovia, thus putting Taylor's forces in charge of 95 per cent of the country, including the only international airport at Robertsfield and the two major ports of Buchanan and Harper.

Ghanaian General Arnold Quainoo stood down in the wake of the Samuel Doe assassination, and his replacement, the Nigerian General Dogonyaro, continued in Monrovia in the capacity of ECOMOG's force commander until March of 1991, when he in turn was replaced by General Rufus Kupolati. From that time onwards until its departure from the country, ECOMOG was always led by a Nigerian, despite the supposed multinational nature of the force, and the ECOMOG commander was chosen directly by the Nigerian president, not by a joint decision with Nigeria's participating partners in the internationally sanctioned force. Dogonyaro, in the name of the IGNU, succeeded in disarming the INPFL and getting the remnants of the AFL to return to their barracks. Prince Johnson's faction then lost military relevance in the country, although his followers continued to maintain a strong presence in the western suburbs of Monrovia.

Increasingly, therefore, ECOMOG was conforming to Taylor's portrayal of the intervention force when it landed in August 1990: a Nigerian army attacking another country in support of its widely hated dictator whom his NPFL fighters were trying to oust.

In the course of the dozen or more peace conferences that took place in the next three years the struggling factions old and new would constantly manoeuvre behind the scenes to improve their bargaining positions, and, while there were lengthy lulls in hostilities, serious fighting continued to erupt between the posturing at peace summits and intermittent ceasefire agreements. One of the main problems in achieving any kind of peace deal was that Taylor, now in such a powerful position in the countryside, refused to participate on an equal footing with the other interests and factions, some of whom he had just defeated or outflanked in the fighting of the previous year. He had equal disdain for others, including the 'puppet' IGNU, whom he didn't recognize as the rightful rulers of the country; Amos Sawyer's official interim government was regarded by the NPFL leader more as a front for the interests of ECOMOG.

Brute force prevails in negotiations

Therefore, when the all-Liberia Conference was convened in Monrovia in March 1991 by the interim government, together with ECOMOG, the INPFL and members of Liberian civil society, the NPFL initially refused to attend. This delayed the start, since it would obviously have been meaningless to have a conference on the future of Liberia if the ruler of almost the entire country's territory was absent. For its part, the IGNU and its president, Amos Sawyer, initially objected strongly to the inclusion of representatives of warring factions in a future interim government, but since the NPFL rejected such a condition outright and the country was in any case 100 per cent under occupation by armed forces of one colour or another, Sawyer was forced to concede that military leaders had a voice, and from then on a new principle was accepted that armed faction leaders could also be the country's interim politicians, a development with ominous implications. Following further negotiations, assurances and concessions to the NPFL, the rebels agreed to participate, but Taylor refused to attend the Monrovia sessions personally, citing lack of adequate security.

Unable to achieve real progress without his authorization, the NPFL delegation shuttled almost daily between Gbarnga and the capital, a three-hour journey by road. At the same time as the Monrovia Peace Conference convened, the NPFL in Gbarnga announced and published its own 'Peace Plan', the essence of which was that there were truly two sides to the negotiations, the NPFL and the ECOMOG-backed, Monrovia-based supporters of the IGNU. The dormant remnants of the AFL and the now demobilized INPFL had been absorbed into the Monrovia structure, and as such were no longer valid negotiating entities, according to the Taylor declaration.

The conference itself, held at the showpiece Hotel Africa Centre, was a highly contentious affair, with constant disruptions, fighting among delegates and the ultimate defection of the NPFL delegation leader, McIntosh Gayewea, to the Monrovia government side. He was replaced by the hardliner Tom Woewiyu, the NPRAG's minister of defence. While the entire NPFL delegation soon walked out of the conference, they had clearly established their control over the character of the future peace process. The NPFL could not be forced into any deal which it did not find acceptable. In Woewiyu's words: 'The Monrovia politicians should realize that this is no business as usual.'[1]

From that time onwards a calmer mood descended on dealings between ECOMOG and the NPFL, with the new Nigerian force commander General Kupolati proving more diplomatic and more willing to accommodate the rebel position. He travelled to Gbarnga several times for talks with Taylor, and during the ensuing period ECOMOG forces were invited to make 'confidence visits' into NPFL-controlled territory.

During the later part of 1991, the negotiations moved onwards to Côte d'Ivoire and a succession of four summits in the elaborate surroundings of Félix Houphouët-Boigny's capital Yamoussoukro. Taylor, unable to make military progress against the superior power of Nigeria's heavy artillery and jet bombers, now made the removal of heavy weapons from the war theatre one of his main negotiation demands in this phase. The other negotiating aim on which the NPFL was close to achieving progress was the recognition that there were effectively two sides to the discussion, Taylor's own NPFL and the Monrovia coalition politicians together with ECOMOG.

It was around this time that former US president Jimmy Carter brought his influence to bear seriously on the Liberian situation, entering into discussions with both sides, facilitating negotiations and in 1991 establishing the Carter Center in Liberia, which ultimately remained active in the country for almost a decade. Taylor and Carter struck up a rapport during Carter's several visits to the country and, as fellow Christians and Baptists, sometimes the two men took the time to pray together. Charles Taylor could count on Jimmy Carter's moderating influence in the matter of heavy weapons, as he also could on that of his Yamoussoukro host and old ally, the now ageing and frail President Houphouët-Boigny.

In contrast to the more familiar situation of UN peacekeeping missions in conflict regions, bound by rules of engagement and unable to be proactive in confronting the enemy, ECOMOG's command felt neither constrained militarily nor obliged to show regard for the safety of civilians. Because the NPFL had opposed their presence violently from the outset, ECOMOG's character had already been defined at an early stage more as one of a combatant pro-government faction than of an impartial mediation force. They took the battle to the rebels, and whatever and whoever lay in rebel-held territory was potentially vulnerable to their assaults. From their base at Lungi Airport outside Freetown, ECOMOG jets carried out missions into the Liberian countryside, firing rockets into villages and forest areas from where the NPFL was believed to be operating.

Due to the hosting and harbouring of ECOMOG inside Sierra Leone, which allowed these raids to be carried out, Taylor became openly threatening towards his counterpart and adversary in Freetown, President Joseph Momoh. In an October 1990 broadcast referring to the bombing raids, he declared: 'My patience is running out, what I will do is anybody's guess ... President Momoh will soon find out what we will do to stop Sierra Leone from being used to conduct air raids on Liberia.'[2]

The situation in Sierra Leone itself was tense, with a rebel insurrection of its own imminent. The instability being fomented by its Revolutionary United Front, allies of the NPFL, was compounded by tens of thousands of Liberian refugees flooding across its eastern border to escape the NPFL. The refugees fleeing ahead of the advancing NPFL forces and entering Sierra Leone were mostly from the western counties of Liberia, where there is a large Muslim population. In time-honoured fashion their able-bodied youths and adults soon regrouped and resurfaced as a new fighting (and looting) force, known as the Liberians United Defence Force (LUDF). Another exiled Muslim group led by a former Doe administration information minister, Alhaji G.V. Kromah, known as the Movement for the Redemption of Liberian Muslims (MLM) also emerged across the border in Sierra Leone at around this time.

Both groups fought alongside the Sierra Leone Army against anti-Freetown rebels, before turning their attention once more towards their homeland. The LUDF and MLM merged to form the United Liberation Movement for Democracy in Liberia (ULIMO) and were later joined by other groups of anti-NPFL forces, including Krahn soldiers from the remnants of the AFL.

ECOMOG, the civil war's imported faction

In September 1991, ULIMO crossed the border back into Liberia, waging an effective campaign that was to soon give them control of most of Grand Cape Mount and Bomi counties, opening up a second front against the NPFL and seriously reducing the extent of Liberian territory under Charles Taylor's control. As with the NPFL and INPFL before it, ULIMO was then in a position to exploit the diamond and other commodity wealth on both sides of the border where it controlled territory, which helped sustain its advance financially.

ECOMOG established a so-called 'buffer zone' along Liberia's western border with Sierra Leone, in principle to keep ULIMO and the NPFL separate. Although the zone was supposedly demilitarized to prevent cross-border attacks, when ULIMO began its campaign in Liberia, ECOMOG granted the new rebel faction safe passage, facilitating its infiltration into the country allowing it to mount surprise attacks on Taylor positions inside Liberia.

At the negotiations, Jimmy Carter lent support to Taylor on the issue of ECOMOG's transgressions as well as the devastation being wrought by their use of heavy weapons in civilian areas. Blaise Compaoré, himself now under international pressure to desist from fuelling the regional conflict, urged Taylor to sign a deal in Yamoussoukro, despite his Liberian ally's strong reluctance to allow an ECOMOG presence in the territory under his control.

The 1991 Yamoussoukro IV accords served an ostensibly useful purpose for both the NPFL and the Monrovia–IGNU sides. From Charles Taylor's point of view the recognition of the fact that there were two parties to the discussion and two effective governments with their own 'sovereign' territory in existence in Liberia was a propaganda coup, which he trumpeted for weeks to come across the airwaves. For his part, Amos Sawyer emphasized the portion of the agreement which included disarmament of forces and the deployment of ECOMOG throughout the countryside. He held a champagne reception to celebrate this success on the night after the summit concluded.

The bubbles of optimism were soon to burst in the ever-evolving atmosphere of the intermittent conflict. With the advance of ULIMO on Taylor's western flank, viewed by ECOMOG and Monrovia as a godsend, in their overall aim of weakening Taylor, the concept of disarmament and an ECOMOG presence in Greater Liberia became harder and harder to sustain.

ULIMO generated a political sensation as well as delivering a propaganda blow to Charles Taylor when in August 1992 its forces appeared on the outskirts of Monrovia at Brewerville. Citizens flocked towards the front line just to catch a glimpse of this new force that had done the seemingly impossible – defeating the NPFL and driving Charles Taylor out of two of Liberia's western counties. ECOMOG naturally also welcomed the ULIMO presence close to the capital and their forces enjoyed a good rapport with the rebels in the zones where their armies came into close proximity with each other.[3]

After a period of bloody infighting during the ULIMO campaign in Liberia, Alhaji Kromah emerged for a time as the movement's overall leader, although he was strongly associated with the faction's founding MLM component and its pro-Mandingo constituency. Due to this infighting and because of the different ethnic and religious complexions of its component parts, ULIMO soon splintered into a Krahn-centric faction, ULIMO-J, under Roosevelt Johnson and a Mandingo–Muslim faction, ULIMO-K, under Alhaji Kromah.

The latter faction had a philosophy which went well beyond the typical desire for revenge and material compensation of the other fighting groups in the Liberian civil war. As Muslims excluded from the mainstream of Liberian life for generations, Mandingos had for long been regarded by much of the Liberian population as not officially Liberian citizens but rather as itinerants with their roots in Guinea and other countries to the north. Thus, for their ideologues, the ULIMO mission took on much more of a 'jihadist' dimension, to strike back against the infidels whether of Monrovia, the NPFL or other parts of the country.

Operation Octopus

By mid-1992, distrust was on the increase between the two main opposing armies, the NPFL and ECOMOG, based respectively in Gbarnga and Monrovia. ECOMOG was supporting as well as arming the anti-Taylor factions more and more overtly, with palpable effect. Inside the capital, too, Prince Johnson found himself losing leverage in his uncomfortable détente with ECOMOG, while the IGNU, supposedly a bastion of civilian government order in a sea of armed factions, also began sponsoring its own armed group known as the Black Berets, who received training in Guinea with ECOMOG assistance. The sincerity of all parties to the peace process, never strong, was increasingly being strained.

Taylor believed that it was only a matter of time before ECOMOG launched an all-out attack on his forces, and so he prepared a pre-emptive strike. He reopened talks with Prince Johnson, who, despite his split with the NPFL two years earlier, had remained in communication with his rivals. With Taylor's forces under threat and

Johnson sidelined, their interests once again became more closely aligned, and the two leaders agreed to collaborate in staging an attack on ECOMOG to retake control of the capital. On 15 October 1992 NPFL fighters infiltrated the outskirts of Monrovia by passing troops through INPFL territory to the west of the city, while other units advanced from the east by wading across alligator-infested swamps to outflank the ECOMOG defences.

Surrounding Monrovia, the rebels attacked with full force at 3 a.m., in an assault known to the NPFL as 'Operation Octopus' because of the tentacle-like infiltration strategy of its protagonists. Having failed so narrowly to take control in 1990, but with the tide of war in the rest of the country turning against them, Taylor's forces had to succeed now or the prospects of military victory would soon be beyond their grasp. In the renewed fighting, Monrovia, which had enjoyed relative calm for over two years, was devastated, and, as ECOMOG and its allies counter-attacked with heavy force against the NPFL in the northern suburbs, casualties were heavy.

General Olurin, the new force commander of ECOMOG, and his new Nigerian chief of staff, Brigadier Samuel Victor Malu, were resolutely determined to rally the anti-Taylor forces in an all-out defence of Monrovia and its 1 million-plus population. After a sustained firefight across the city, which dragged on for weeks, the NPFL finally began to run low on ammunition and was pushed back, leaving Taylor once more thwarted in his goal of sealing a final victory.

Using heavy artillery, cluster bombs and napalm in the Monrovia suburbs to flush out the relatively small number of NPFL fighters, General Malu lost no sleep over the consequences of civilian casualties in his counter-attacks. Operation Octopus cost thousands of lives, with some 6,000 alone estimated to have been victims of ECOMOG bombing of civilian positions.

In the midst of Operation Octopus, Taylor reneged on his recently renewed alliance with Prince Johnson and attacked the INPFL, having ensured the defection of many from within its ranks, most notably General Samuel Varney, a key commander since the beginning of the campaign. Splintering into two, then finally dismembered, the INPFL ceased to exist, and Johnson, with nowhere left to hide in Liberia and ECOMOG on his back in Monrovia, surrendered to the Nigerians and was placed in custody, eventually being put on a ship and detained in Lagos for the next several years. Despite his detention by ECOMOG, Johnson was, however, never held to account for the murder of President Samuel Doe.

The ECOMOG counter-attack meanwhile gained momentum, and this time Malu was not content to let his forces rest at pushing the NPFL to the outskirts of the capital. Using their devastating ground and aerial firepower, his counter-attacking forces pushed Taylor out of Robertsfield Airport, out of his forward headquarters in the Firestone complex in Harbel and out of the port of Buchanan. Gbarnga was bombed, and ECOMOG pushed deep into NPFL territory. Taylor was even forced temporarily to abandon the NPFL capital, moving his government to remote northern Nimba County.

As ECOMOG and its allies among the anti-NPFL factions steadily cut off Taylor's access to arms supplies, for the first time since the outset of the campaign he was forced to accept that the best chance for an outright military victory had slipped from his grasp. No longer able to call the military shots in the country, he prepared for a new phase of conflict in which he also had prior experience and was arguably even more skilled at than military confrontation: bargaining, negotiation and manoeuvring towards peace and democracy while at the same time not reneging on his long-standing aim of achieving total power.

Not only did the NPFL now have no choice but to negotiate, it probably wanted negotiations as soon as possible to avoid further annihilation on the battlefield at the hands of the re-energized, reinforced and rampant ECOMOG. It was also losing territory fast to the other factions, ULIMO and the LPC, who were effectively now fighting as ECOMOG proxies in the west and south-east of the country respectively. By the end of 1993, the NPFL had given up about two-thirds of the territory that it had won in 1990, and the more it lost the less bargaining power it would be likely to have at the negotiating table.

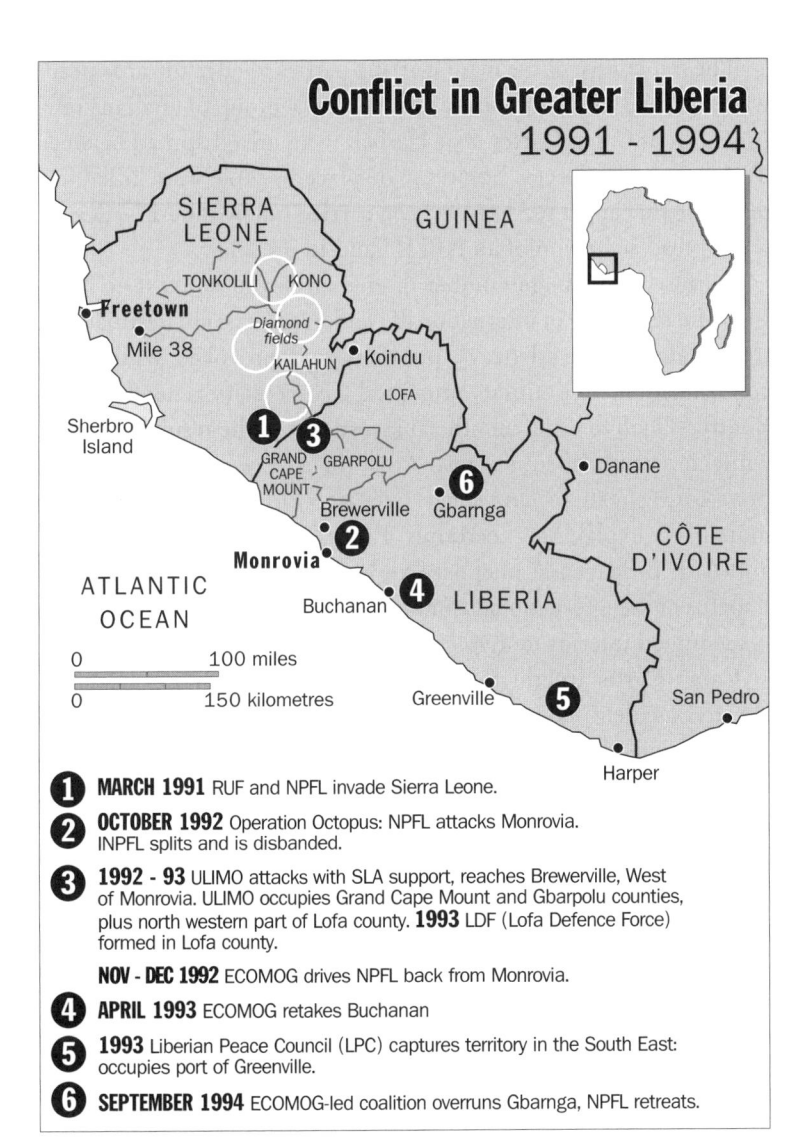

Conflict in Greater Liberia
1991 - 1994

1 **MARCH 1991** RUF and NPFL invade Sierra Leone.

2 **OCTOBER 1992** Operation Octopus: NPFL attacks Monrovia. INPFL splits and is disbanded.

3 **1992 - 93** ULIMO attacks with SLA support, reaches Brewerville, West of Monrovia. ULIMO occupies Grand Cape Mount and Gbarpolu counties, plus north western part of Lofa county. **1993** LDF (Lofa Defence Force) formed in Lofa county.

NOV - DEC 1992 ECOMOG drives NPFL back from Monrovia.

4 **APRIL 1993** ECOMOG retakes Buchanan

5 **1993** Liberian Peace Council (LPC) captures territory in the South East: occupies port of Greenville.

6 **SEPTEMBER 1994** ECOMOG-led coalition overruns Gbarnga, NPFL retreats.

The imperative of the main warring parties to edge towards peace was catalysed by a major atrocity involving a group of civilians on 6 June 1993 at Camp Carter near Harbel, in an area disputed between Taylor and AFL forces. Some 547 displaced people were killed in a massacre that appeared to have been carried out by the AFL, despite widespread suspicion of an NPFL hand in the affair.

Because of the huge number of civilian deaths so close to Monrovia during a time of internationally endorsed ceasefire negotiations, the incident received heavy publicity and provoked widespread condemnation. The atrocity prompted UN secretary general Boutros Boutros-Ghali to order an official investigation, the results of which, while never published, suggested that the AFL was to blame. Other private investigations have suggested that NPFL involvement was the more likely explanation; certainly Taylor used the incident both for anti-AFL propaganda purposes and to benefit from the increased impetus of the international community towards arranging a ceasefire, his assumed ulterior motive.[4]

Camp Carter caught the headlines but it was by no means an isolated incident. Human rights abuses continued to be committed by all factions throughout the period of negotiations and intermittent ceasefires. Despite a public apology in 1992 from Charles Taylor for atrocities, the actions of forces under his control,[5] his fighters continued to terrorize civilians. Abductions and massacres continued in the course of NPFL attacks around Buchanan, in Lofa County, in Grand Gedeh and in an attack on Pleebo, Maryland County, in 1994, all involving at least dozens and sometimes hundreds of civilian murders. In 1995 when Taylor's forces laid siege to Bong mines during a six-month period, thousands of people were killed or kidnapped in the area, including a slaughter on 7 March 1995 of some 300 civilians near the Heindi market in Bong County.

Cotonou Accords offer amnesty to perpetrators

On 25 July 1993, an agreement ending the existence of the Interim Government of National Unity was signed in Cotonou, Benin, providing for the establishment of a Liberian National Transitional

Government (LNTG) and an amnesty for the warring parties in Liberia. The NPFL and ULIMO, together with the hosts and observer signatories, agreed and declared 'a ceasefire and the cessation of hostilities ... within and without the perimeter of Liberia' and at the same time expressly recognized 'the neutrality and authority of ECOMOG and the UN Observer Mission', thereby granting the latter bodies and their personnel complete freedom of movement throughout the country.

The Cotonou Agreement stipulated that, concomitant with disarmament, a five-member Council of State would be constituted to replace the IGNU, its members to be elected by the factions, and should take power until such time as elections could be held. A 35-member transitional parliament would be set up, which would contain 13 representatives of the NPFL and the interim government and 9 from ULIMO. However, it took the next eight months for the parliament to be convened, as disagreement over the allocation of key posts and manoeuvring between the factions continued.

A UN Observer Mission in Liberia (UNOMIL) was created in 1993 to monitor the agreement in conjunction with ECOMOG, whose force was expanded and reinforced by troops from outside the region. The UN created the post of Special Representative to the Secretary General (SRSG), mostly to assist ECOMOG and the other parties in peace negotiations. The Organization of African Unity (OAU)[6] contributed some 1,700 Tanzanian and Ugandan troops, who were deployed alongside the West African peacekeepers. By March 1994 demobilization of fighters had begun but the process was to be short-lived, and only a reported 3,500 fighters turned in their weapons before hostilities resumed.

By now weary of war, sceptical of peace and above all cynical about every one of the factions' motivations in the ongoing dance of negotiations, the people of Liberia said goodbye to the IGNU – popularly derided as the 'Imported Government of No Use' and prepared to receive its successor entity, the LNTG. The recognition that an all-civilian government could not succeed in bringing peace to a country ruled by the gun was now official. Liberia's new leaders were all factional strongmen with a power base built on pillage; it

CHARLES TAYLOR IN GANTA, DECEMBER 1994

the south-east, where they captured large chunks of territory in Grand Gedeh and Maryland counties and also threatened Harper, by now the only port still remaining in the NPFL's hands. In the north-west, Alhaji Kromah's ULIMO-K had displaced the NPFL in parts of Lofa County, spawning the creation of the Lofa Defence Force, also outside the accords, headed by François Massaquoi and allied to the NPFL.

The ongoing negotiating climate encouraged the creation of splinter factions such as the LPC, since an allocation of resources from ECOMOG could be secured, and, if successful, control over territory and a probable seat in future government arrangements would follow. This in turn would guarantee a share of the spoils of the next peace deal for each faction's leadership, which would not have otherwise been on offer to, for example, mere regional offshoots of the AFL or former Doe deputies, which was essentially George Boley's profile.

ECOMOG's approach was spawning new factions on all sides. In addition to creating more enemies on the battlefield, the consequence for the NPFL was that it would soon have more rivals to contend with in a future peacetime government. Senior NPFL leaders doubted Taylor's strategy of continuing to fight on all fronts rather than negotiating a peace deal, now believing that it was time to stop fighting.

The situation came to a head in mid-1994, when Taylor's longtime ally and Gbarnga defence minister Tom Woewiyu, together with Sam Dokie and Laveli Supuwood, moved to Monrovia with the NPFL-CRC or 'Central Revolutionary Council' and declared that Taylor was no longer one of the council's members. The CRC had already been in existence in Gbarnga, with Charles Taylor as its chairman. But the members of the breakaway group now declared him expelled from the council, stating that they were going to take up their allotted NPFL seats in the interim government in Monrovia.

Woewiyu became minister of labour in the LNTG and, once over on the other side, criticized Taylor publicly in a press conference in Monrovia, blaming him for prolonging the war. Woewiyu also made a statement to the LNTG which reopened the issue of Taylor's alleged involvement in the controversial 1990 killing of Jackson Doe behind NPFL lines. Referring to his own return from a Sierra Leone peace conference to Taylor's HQ in Harbel a week after Jackson Doe's arrival, Woewiyu said:

> Taylor informed me that Jackson Doe was with him and that I should inform Amos Sawyer, Ellen Johnson Sirleaf and all the politicians that he was safe, only for me to arrive in Harbel one week later and he could not tell me where Jackson Doe was.[7]

In Taylor's Special Court trial in February 2010, in response to a direct question from the lead prosecution counsel, Brenda Hollis, he denied both having had a hand in Jackson Doe's death and responsibility in the 1990 killings of Gabriel Kpolleh and Moses Duopu: 'That is not correct. Jackson Doe was a very well respected man', Taylor responded. He contradicted the 1994 testimony of Woewiyu stating: 'Tom Woewiyu made a lot of wild allegations that later he apologized for ... I am aware of the nonsense he wrote.'[8] Tom Woewiyu, for his part, has denied apologizing to Taylor and retracting the statement he made in July 1994.[9]

Taking advantage of the defections from the NPFL central command, in August 1994 ECOMOG coordinated a joint attack on Gbarnga by the other factions and, while Taylor was still in Ghana for peace discussions, they succeeded in expelling his forces from the city. Although Gbarnga was later recaptured, the power of the once mighty rebel army had been dealt a serious blow and it was time for Taylor to adopt new tactics in his continuing pursuit of power.

Developments to the east on the other side of the Gulf of Guinea were also favourable to a more lasting ceasefire. In Nigeria in June 1993, in a botched attempt to return the country to civilian rule after General Babangida's long reign, the northern political ascendancy was defeated, in one of Nigeria's freest, fairest and most decisive elections ever. Chief Moshood Abiola, a Yoruba businessman and philanthropist from the south of the country, was overwhelmingly elected in a country which has typically been divided between a Muslim-voting north and a Christian south. Babangida annulled the result of the election, plunging the country into crisis, with a new military dictator, Sani Abacha, eventually taking over in Abuja.

The situation that the 1993 Nigerian political crisis provoked was compounded by the issue of the costly and unpopular involvement in Liberia, and when Abacha took the reins of power the impetus to extract Nigeria from its controversial ECOMOG involvement was heightened, whist restoring some of the country's badly tarnished international image, earned in the engagement's early years. Abacha proved more accommodating towards Taylor in the ongoing negotiations process in contrast to his predecessor, the hard-line anti-NPFL Babangida, whom Taylor considered his sworn enemy. The changeover of power in Abuja was thus a further facilitating factor in persuading the NPFL to sign a serious peace agreement, while eventually also leading to improved relations between the NPFL and the Nigerian ECOMOG contingent on the ground.

After another year of attempts at disarmament and intermittent fighting, on 19 August 1995 leaders of the warring parties, which now included seven factions in all, together with representatives of the Liberian civilian interest groups, met in Abuja. They signed a new agreement, based on the original Cotonou accords, and established a revised version of the 1993 transitional government, headed by a six-member Council of State, including the three main factional leaders, Taylor, Alhaji Kromah of ULIMO-K and George Boley of the LPC. The Council of State was chaired by Professor Wilton Sankawulo, and included two civilian representatives, while leaders of the smaller factions received ministerial posts and responsibility for various government agencies. Disarmament of the factions was provided for, leading to elections then scheduled for August 1996.

Taylor returns to Monrovia

On 31 August 1995, Charles Taylor entered Monrovia for the first time since 1983. Dressed all in white, to reinforce in the minds of his victim-followers the quasi-biblical aura surrounding his second coming, his reception was rapturous. Cheering fellow Liberians lined the route to the capital, and by the time the Taylor caravan reached the outlying communities of Monrovia the throng had thickened and their anticipation was mounting. At Paynesville junction, amid hazy late rainy season heat, women tore off their *lappas*[10] and cast them into the road in front of the NPFL leader's limousine, enhancing the imagery of virtual beatification that many Liberians accorded to the Dakhpannah, Charles Ghankay Taylor, even as their city, their children and their lives still bore the terrible marks of the butchery that his several thwarted attempts to rule by force had wrought upon them.

Taylor settled into Monrovia in the grand style to which he hoped to become accustomed – presidential, that is. Although only one of six members in the transitional administration, in practical terms Taylor, as speaker of the parliament and leader of the largest wartime faction, held the upper hand in the ruling council.

He was by a long way the most well-heeled of the factional representatives, both figuratively and literally. Ostentatious in dress as well as behaviour, while sharing space with the other transitional representatives in the Executive Mansion, Charles Taylor believed in the trappings of power almost as much as he hungered for power itself. He retained his taste for snappy dressing, first developed on those New York City social trips and the New England party circuit, now adapted to embrace an African element acquired during his time in government in the bush. Taylor often dressed in white or grey two-piece suits, buttoned at the neck. His favourite accoutrements included snakeskin shoes with gold buckles, gold-rimmed sunglasses and a diamond-encrusted gold watch, as well as his carved oxblood swagger stick.

Also a sportsman and fitness fanatic, Taylor both as aspirant and president played tennis and basketball on personal courts at his Congotown home. A formidable table-tennis player, when in government he once challenged the Liberian national champion to come to his home for a game. Even after years in Liberia, he remained a fan of the Boston Celtics, and like most young Liberians then and now he was an ardent soccer fan too. He sometimes sported a black baseball cap declaring 'President Taylor' in gold braid. Despite his long years in rural Liberia, the Dakhpannah also enjoyed music, saying at the time that his all-time favourite was the iconic African-American gospel singer Mahalia Jackson. He also developed a taste for classical music, including Handel and Bach. In film, perhaps less surprisingly, his preferred character on the silver screen was Dirty Harry.[11]

As well as a swimming pool, Taylor's expansive suburban compound also housed its own chapel, particularly useful for a president who was also a devout Evangelical Christian as well as a Baptist deacon, needful of hosting coreligionists and influential fellow believers such as Jimmy Carter and Jesse Jackson.

Transitional government no. 2: new game, same rules

For the various actors in this long-drawn-out political-military drama, the stage was shifting. Just as Taylor had seized the early initiative when the conflict had taken on a primarily military character, now that the struggle was returning to the world of political rather than battlefield manoeuvres he was once again quick to get ahead of the game. Furthermore, his new rivals and co-presidents in

THREE PRINCIPAL LIBERIAN WARLORDS: CHARLES TAYLOR
(NPFL), ALHAJI KROMAH (ULIMO-K) AND GEORGE BOLEY (LPC) IN
MONROVIA TAKING OATH TO RESPECT THE PEACE PROCESS SIGNED
19 AUGUST 1995

the transitional government, Alhaji Kromah of ULIMO-K, with its largely Mandingo power base, and Roosevelt Johnson of ULIMO-J, while both also originally products of the pre-war Monrovia elite, were less able to wield power than the assertive and internationally savvy Taylor. George Boley's Krahn-dominated LPC was still only a supporting player, acting in alliance with others rather than as a force on its own.

This scenario gave Taylor leverage in the next phase, which he was able to exploit to his advantage. Furthermore, despite his recent reverses, Taylor still had the largest number of troops and the most money, giving him automatic senior status among his rivals in the eyes of the majority of Monrovia's political cadres.

Under the new LNTG configuration, while each of the factions had its allocated ministerial portfolios, the true balance of power was still determined in the countryside and in the barracks, and according to how much brawn the faction leaders could bring to bear in promoting their political interests. Alliances were struck and broken between the players to further their goals in the evolving transitional government power play.

Roosevelt Johnson's ULIMO-J faction, a relatively weak player in the Monrovia hierarchy, had been benefiting from military and financial assistance from the NPFL in the areas it controlled in Bomi County to the west of Monrovia. Scheduled to disarm and withdraw from an area containing diamond fields, on 28 December 1996 Johnson's forces instead launched a surprise attack on ECOMOG in the Tubmanburg area where they were being deployed. This major breach of the countrywide ceasefire jeopardized the credibility of the ULIMO-J leadership and led ECOMOG to evacuate the Tubmanburg area over the coming two days, in a reversal of its objective of nationwide deployment to monitor the peace process.

The ULIMO-J Tubmanburg attack may have been staged in response to encouragement by, or possibly in a deal with, Taylor. Since Taylor and Johnson had been collaborating behind the scenes in recent months. Taylor may have induced Johnson to strike at ECOMOG, to create confusion and to reinforce the NPFL's contention that a foreign occupation force was more of a liability than an asset now that Liberia had a government (of sorts) of its own once again.

Third battle for Monrovia

Taylor soon turned Johnson's actions to his advantage and began to play the role of statesman, adjudicator of disputes and policeman all at the same time. While Johnson, minister of rural development in the transitional government, was now distrusted by ECOMOG, he also had to contend with infighting in his own party, which flared up in early 1996 shortly after the Tubmanburg attacks.

General Armah Youlo had attempted to take over the faction from Johnson following an internal disagreement over the allocation of the post of chairman of the National Bank of Liberia, a post allocated to ULIMO-J, an earlier dispute which Taylor had already played a part in defusing.[12] Taylor convened the Council of State to demand recognition of Youlo's faction and Johnson's suspension as minister of rural development.

Flare-ups of violence broke out in Kakata, 45 miles north of Monrovia, while supporters of General Youlo clashed with Johnson supporters in Sinkor, the area of Monrovia where both men lived. During the clashes Dweh Gbawu, a Youlo supporter, was killed and Johnson was held responsible for the killing.

The entire situation had given Charles Taylor's NPFL the opportunity it had been waiting for, to present itself as the true 'government forces'. All earlier cooperation with Johnson was now cast aside, and Taylor, as the dominant member of the LNTG, convened an emergency meeting of the Council of State and demanded Johnson's arrest, giving him until 5 April to turn himself over to ECOMOG. Johnson refused and explained his position, bitterly accusing Taylor of hijacking the government and perverting the process of justice at the same time: 'we have not submitted ourselves', he said, 'because councilmen Kromah and Taylor have now become policemen, jurors and judges ... we will not submit ourselves like chickens to be slaughtered at the hands of the NPFL'.[13]

Taylor then ordered truckloads of his troops, totalling some 5,000 fighters, into the city in anticipation of a showdown. When Johnson failed to turn himself in by the following day, Taylor proceeded to lead the operation to apprehend his fellow faction leader, whom he now branded as a peace-deal violator turned murderer.

However, on 6 April, Johnson's men, supported by former AFL troops and LPC fighters, resisted the attempts to capture their leader and Monrovia was quickly plunged once more into full-scale warfare. Among the groups who appeared on the streets of Monrovia at this time in support of Johnson were his 'Butt Naked' brigade, soon a popular feature in the dispatches of the international press corps who reported to the world on the group's (lack of) battledress and chalk-painted faces.

The NPFL's fighters, many of whom had failed to cash in on the early campaigns and had thus not benefited from the climate of relative peace since 1992, now converged on the capital in an assault which, on their side, quickly became known as 'Operation Pay Yourself'. Accurately so, because Taylor's unpaid fighters only got paid when there was looting to be done, and lately good looting had been harder to arrange without warfare. In the ensuing weeks of fighting, some 80,000 Monrovians were forced to flee their homes.

The ULIMO-J forces, beaten back, retreated to the Barclay Training Centre (BTC), along with the forces of the LPC and some 10,000 Krahn civilians, who, as in the previous assaults on the capital, were sure to be the first victims of reprisals following an NPFL triumph. An all-out bombardment of the BTC followed, with horrific scenes inside the centre as the attackers fired artillery, mortar and RPG rounds into its perimeter. An evacuation of foreign nationals was once again organized from Monrovia as the fighting spread, with the total destruction of the premises of almost every embassy and organization that had tentatively re-established its presence since the recent return of peace.

International community trapped in Monrovia inferno

In early 1996, in contrast with the lesser international involvement prior to previous attacks on Monrovia, there was by now a considerable international aid community presence as well as a partial return of the pre-war diplomatic community to Monrovia. Encouraged by the peace agreement and eager to play their role in the post-conflict reconstruction process, numerous NGOs, UN agencies and their staff were caught off guard by the sudden resumption of fighting in the capital.

Dozens of four-wheel-drive vehicles, together with supplies and equipment, recently purchased and shipped to the country in renewed programmes of post-conflict assistance, were stolen or destroyed, with jeeps being driven by fighters around the city, careering through Monrovia in a frenzied motorized rampage before being crashed or left burning around the capital's streets.

Fighters captured VHF handsets of international personnel and monitored the UN's every movement as its staff communicated desperately with each other in search of a passage to safety. Unfortunately the UN security contingency plan had not taken account of the eventuality of the eruption of a city-wide explosion of factional fighting and looting, and soon the scores of international staff

KRAHN BEING SHOT BY NPFL MILITIA, MAY 1996 FIGHTING

dispersed around Monrovia converged on the Mamba Point district, the location of the only true safe haven, the US embassy.

One African international organization worker, Guilherme Mambo, a Mozambican working for the International Organization for Migration (IOM), related his experience of the desperate days in Monrovia around Easter weekend 1996:

> I was cut off, on my own, in the upstairs of the premises we had been using as office space. I salvaged the car battery out of our vehicle to charge the satellite phone, which remained my only means of communication, and taking advantage of an apparent lull, I quickly moved over to the house where dozens of other international workers were mustering before making a dash to the US embassy. Together all the foreigners made a break for it, running with a few belongings the 800 metres or so towards the embassy, the only possible hope for security and an eventual evacuation.

In a bizarre scene, as the foreigners rushed towards the embassy, hundreds of Liberian civilians passed them in the opposite direction, desperately pursuing what was *their* perceived best option, flight into the countryside and away from the fighting.

Initially the foreigners were allowed only into the embassy's outer Greystone compound, where some 20,000 Liberians were congregating in the hope of safety. Vulnerable to attack at any time inside the unsecured compound, they waited for clearance to enter the main embassy grounds. Initially only Americans and Canadians were permitted. Waiting in line behind them were the Europeans, with the other West Africans – as was the usual protocol – the third category to be offered asylum. Some Liberian families with children born in the United States were screened for asylum. The children who held American passports were allowed through to safety; their Liberian parents and siblings had to stay behind.

Not in a favoured position as an African, worse still as a Mozambican, not even from an ECOWAS nation, Mambo was unlikely to be allowed entry. Banned by the US marines guarding the compound from making communications while inside the US perimeter, he was still able to make one last call to some colleagues at his Geneva headquarters. Their call over the weekend to connections in Washington DC worked like magic, and when the word to allow entry of the next group of the waiting foreign workers finally came, one Mozambican was among the selected few on the list. From there, an evacuation was authorized, and US Navy helicopters, under threat of being shot down by factional fighters surrounding the area, shuttled the international workers out of Liberia to Freetown's Lungi Airport, from where they made their way homewards.[14]

At one stage, NPFL fighters broke into the US embassy compound and a few attempted to enter the ambassador's residence, where they were fired on by American marines, who killed three insurgents. Now ECOMOG, which had initially backed Taylor and Kromah in their operation to capture Johnson, realized that if the BTC fell, it was likely that Taylor would effectively be in a position of total control, and it began to reinforce the besieged Johnson garrison. The USA thought the same: after all the international efforts at building peace, the prospect of a Taylor takeover by force was horrific. Deviously engineered under the guise of a national policing and security operation, Charles Taylor and the NPFL were once again close to becoming the masters of Monrovia.

Using their privately contracted logistics and civil police proxy corps, the Pacific Architects and Engineers (PAE), the US embassy used helicopters to shuttle in supplies to Johnson's men at the BTC to help them defend themselves. Some of the helicopters were shot at by the attacking forces outside. The Krahn soldiers inside, as in previous confrontations, had become desperate, with no hope of survival in the event of an NPFL takeover.

Taylor's forces, however, failed to press home their attack. Too many of the boys on 'Operation Pay Yourself' were busy in the suburbs looting instead of fighting to ensure victory. Taylor himself was distracted, deciding to take some wealthy agricultural land in the vicinity of Kakata as well as grabbing control of gold-producing areas in the south-east. Meanwhile Johnson succeeded in mobilizing his allied remnant AFL forces based at Camp Schefflin outside Monrovia to move in on the capital to relieve him. Once again, the NPFL had lost its opportunity to deliver a knockout punch.

Taylor called a unilateral ceasefire on 6 May, although fighting continued around the capital. Ghana's President Rawlings arranged a peace summit, which Taylor and Kromah didn't attend, while ECOMOG offered Johnson asylum in Nigeria, which he turned down, returning to Monrovia after the Ghana talks. Finally, a reinforced ECOMOG imposed its own ceasefire on 26 May, retaking the key bridges to Monrovia, relieving the BTC and restoring a semblance of order in the capital.

Another triumph for the strongmen

Monrovia's Easter uprising had nevertheless served a purpose for its perpetrators. Taylor and Kromah, the instigators, had enhanced their power in the capital, by engaging in a bloody feud. The civilian actors and the minor factions had to face the new reality. George Boley saw the writing on the wall; he melted away for the time being and left Liberia.

Taylor and Kromah in the meantime called for the Council of State to be renamed the 'Collective Presidency' to reflect the fact that its members were the true executive power in the land, and for the term 'LNTG' to be suppressed and replaced with 'Government of the Republic of Liberia'. Such a move would have elevated the status quo, and negated the essence of the 'transition' which the current arrangement was supposed to represent, an intermediate step on the path between conflict and democracy. It suited those with military muscle, but not the country's surviving civilian actors.

Despite its inauspicious beginning, 1996 was the last full year of interim government arrangements in Liberia. In August, ECOWAS brokered a deal between the still feuding factions and in September Ruth Perry, an experienced senator, former Chase Manhattan banker and Sande society elder, took over as chairwoman of the Council of State. Less than a year later, Liberia would have a taste of true democracy for the first time in its history.

PART THREE

POWER IN GREATER LIBERIA

EIGHT

GREATER LIBERIA: PROSPERING AND ASSIMILATING

> Fail not to use every opportunity to gain a position of prosperity for yourselves, and to open to civilization and Christianity the great continent of which you occupy the border.
>
> Edward Wilmot Blyden[1]

From mid-1990, by which time the NPFL had secured control over 90 per cent of Liberian territory, until 1994, when the movement for the first time fragmented seriously after a period of territorial losses, Charles Taylor was at the head of a military-economic operation which remained well managed at its core, despite the indiscipline displayed by its front-line recruits and NPFL fighters' indiscriminate use of violence against civilians. The NPFL machine had access to hard currency through its exports of timber, minerals and agricultural commodities, in turn keeping well supplied with arms from the proceeds, in order to continue its periodic assaults on the outskirts of Monrovia and to defend itself from attack by ECOMOG or its rival warring Liberian factions.

Administratively based at Gbarnga in Bong County, the National Patriotic Reconstruction Assembly Government (NPRAG) organized 'elections' and constituted its own parliament, with all the trappings of an official democratic state and with Charles Taylor as its president. While the Interim Government of National Unity in Monrovia was the officially recognized government of Liberia, it remained confined to an embattled enclave little greater in area than the perimeter of the capital itself. After a short time, Greater Liberia was booming, while its rival city state on the Atlantic Ocean was a burned-out shell shackled with debt and dependent on outside military and financial sustenance.

One enormous economic bonus of the NPFL's unofficial but very real and very lucrative commercial operations was the fact that, not being the official government of Liberia, the NPRAG did not have to assume any of the approximately $3.5 billion of debt that the previous regime had run up with its international creditors and for which the IGNU, with Amos Sawyer as its president, was now responsible as the 'legitimate' government of the country. Thus, the IGNU was cash-strapped, suspended from the International Monetary Fund (IMF) and the United Nations and with no domestic economic activity to speak of on which it could collect revenues. Its annual budget was estimated at less than $20 million.

By contrast, the NPFL had secured most of the hinterland, the deep-water port of Buchanan, as well as effective control of the other main ports of Greenville and Harper and the key land export routes to the north and east through friendly Côte d'Ivoire. It also had the international airport at Robertsfield under its control, into which flights of arms from Libya and Burkina Faso landed unhindered, in order to keep the rebel military operations supplied.

Security returned to much of the countryside, and the lucky rebel returnees who came home with life, limb and loot intact could settle down to a reasonably normal existence. Schools reopened in many areas, and for a time many former child combatants could pick up the threads of a normal youth. But with the NPRAG still very much dependent on its military for defence, there were constant movements around the countryside of NPFL fighters being deployed to put down what were at first minor insurrections, and later major incursions by newly formed rebel factions. These NPFL movements in turn brought on periodic bombing sorties from ECOMOG's Sierra Leone-based air force jets, who flashed across the bush firing

TAYLOR IN THE GBARNGA PRESIDENCY

rockets at their intended targets, rarely with regard to the presence or otherwise of civilians in the vicinity.

Now, although frustrated in its key objective of capturing Monrovia and with total power in the countryside, the NPFL was in a position to exploit resources commercially in the lion's share of the Republic of Liberia. The territory that the NPFL controlled became known as Greater Liberia, and indeed it did comprise the greater part of the whole country's lands and economy.

Getting down to foreign deals

The initial economic imperative was to obtain foreign exchange to buy arms. In one regard, the NPFL was at the disadvantage of not being a sovereign entity with the right to sell concessions on behalf of a country, and collect taxes on the proceeds of shipments made by overseas corporations. But, on the other hand, Liberia had the great advantage of having an existing financial structure where the US dollar was the accepted currency for transactions, which helped blur the distinction, for those who cared, between dealing with the official as opposed to the unofficial government of the country. Furthermore, the commercial ineptitude and lack of entrepreneurial capacity of the Doe regime had left a vacuum of latent business opportunities and unexploited resources, with valuable mineral and agricultural projects run down or abandoned since the early 1980s and waiting to be reactivated.

It was in such abandoned or dormant minerals projects that the NPFL got its start as a functioning financial economy, capable of transacting serious international deals with the outside world. The first major business deal of the NPFL was in the cannibalization of the abandoned Bong iron ore mine, which had once been a German-owned enterprise. Taylor arranged for the dismantling and resale abroad of the equipment from the disused mine, earning valuable foreign exchange in the process, with which he then effectively founded his future foreign exchange operations, via a financial entity known as the 'Bong Bank'.

The former jewel in the crown of Liberia's mineral economy, the Nimba Mining Company (NIMCO), based at Yekepa, close to the Guinean border, had been a resource of hundreds of thousands of tons of some of the highest grade iron ore available globally. Iron ore was historically the mainstay of the Liberian economy, accounting for 40 per cent of the country's GDP in 1975.[2] The Yekepa mine, now partially depleted, had been a major revenue earner for the governments of Presidents Tubman and Tolbert, when the Liberian–American–Swedish Minerals Company (LAMCO) operated the business. In 1979 a group of potential international investors began negotiating with Doe's government to reactivate the Yekepa mine. However, it had been disused and was eventually abandoned during the 1980s, but when Taylor took control of the area he picked up the discussions. He began to deal with a group of international investors, including American, Japanese, British and South African interests, who could provide the financing for mining operations.

The bigger prize, however, was access to the Guinean side of the border, where some 60 per cent of the total Mount Nimba iron ore resource, as yet unexploited, was located. The consortium that dealt with Taylor for the Yekepa operations certainly would have already had its eye on the larger Guinean reserve, to which they could aspire to gain access after the war, although logistics were a problem in wartime. The alternative route, by rail through the Guinean port of Conakry, involved a journey of 640 miles, a costly and time-consuming detour.

One advantage of the international interest in large commodity projects such as the NIMCO operation was that it added to the de facto international recognition of Charles Taylor's administration via the commercial involvements of reputable international corporations. Indeed the former management of LAMCO readily provided consulting services to the new local iron ore operator, the Liberian Mining Corporation, seemingly without reticence over the identity of their new business partner.[3] More generally, the willingness of international corporations to deal with Charles Taylor was motivated not by ideological support for his movement, but on a calculation that he would soon be the leader of the legitimate government of the country, and as such it was necessary to establish links now rather than being shut out at a later date.

The multinational business presence in Taylor's Greater Liberia also undermined the Monrovia government's attempts to curtail the financial and arms procurement activities of the NPFL, since the governments of some of the same countries who were sponsoring the IGNU also hosted companies which were now involved in a lucrative mining business with its rivals, and so would be unlikely to take action to bring a halt to the flow of commerce through Taylorland. The IGNU nevertheless tried to curb Taylor's business activities, and brought lawsuits in foreign courts against businesses which dealt with NPFL associates in Liberia. In 1991, Amos Sawyer's government also tried to act against Taylor's economy via its currency, issuing a new banknote called the 'Liberty' dollar, in competition with, and intended to replace, the existing Liberian notes known as 'J.J.s' after J.J. Roberts, the republic's first president.

CHARLES TAYLOR'S GBARNGA HOUSE

While the IGNU ordered existing J.J. notes to be destroyed in an attempt to disrupt the Greater Liberian economy, the scheme backfired, as the NPRAG declared the Liberty notes invalid in its territory and they quickly began to lose value. Soon the original J.J. circulated in Monrovia alongside the Liberty dollar bill at approximately double the new note's value, adding to confusion in the IGNU enclave and further demonstrating its powerlessness against the Taylor-controlled Liberian economy.

Solidarity with Francophonie

The one exception to the purely longer-term commercial motivations of businesses that were willing to get involved in contracts with Greater Liberia concerned France. The French remained committed to their key ally in the region, Côte d'Ivoire, which in turn was concerned about the sudden large Nigerian presence in Liberia and its economic as well as military implications. That presence, established under the guise of the ECOMOG multilateral peacekeeping operation, involved looting of Liberian assets and takeover of businesses in areas under ECOMOG control. Nigerian involvement in Liberia was rapidly morphing into a commercial presence to rival the prominent role that Côte d'Ivoire had hitherto enjoyed.

The French state-owned corporation Sollac participated in the NIMCO project which in March of 1991 bought 70,000 tons of iron ore, paying $80,000 per month to Taylor for its shipments. Accused by the Paris media of using its state firm as a back-door method of funding the NPFL, France nevertheless continued to be proactive in both financial and diplomatic support of Taylor during his early years as the alternative government in Liberia. France also provided diplomatic help to the NPFL for its business activities, such as when in 1992 the United Nations tried to mount opposition to the Liberian mining operation on environmental grounds.

Abidjan was the business centre for much of Charles Taylor's commerce, as well as his main foreign banking base, while San Pedro, a strategic port on the Ivorian side of the border, did a roaring trade in Liberian commodities.

Timber, and in particular the African hardwood so prized in the European furniture industry, found ready buyers operating through Côte d'Ivoire, and vast amounts of wood were hauled through Danane across the Ivorian border to the north or directly to San Pedro for shipment to Europe. Charles Taylor's brother Bob played the key role in handling forestry operations and managing timber exports from the Liberian side, while much of the wood thus exported was handled in Côte d'Ivoire by French and Lebanese businesses. Exiled Americo-Liberian businessmen and former ministers from the Doe government were among those to set up business in San Pedro, and British, Chinese and Russian interests also had commodity dealings with Taylorland through Côte d'Ivoire.

In Paris, President François Mitterrand's son Jean-Christophe, who was minister with responsibility for Africa at the time, directed many of the country's commercial operations in francophone Africa, including Liberian deals that passed through Côte d'Ivoire. In this way official France indirectly gave its blessing to French commodity dealers and produce importers operating in Liberia.

Taylor also used major Ivorian financial institutions such as Société Générale de Banques in Côte d'Ivoire (SGBCI) and the Ivorian branch of the transnational Ecobank in Abidjan for his financial dealings. He also controlled an account at Citibank in the Ivorian commercial capital.[4]

In NPFL-controlled Buchanan, Taylor reportedly subcontracted out the handling of port operations to a Western-owned operator, the Associated Development Corporation.[5] Again the foreign management role provided an added measure of legitimacy as well as offering new business referrals, which included Lebanese and American concerns with an interest in using the port.[6] Business continued until ECOMOG finally captured and ransacked Buchanan in 1993, putting an end to iron ore shipments.

Following the NPFL's capture of the Firestone plantation at Harbel, which had effectively stopped running during the war, it is thought that Taylor negotiated a deal with the ownership in order to recommence production of rubber, the export of which was again an excellent source of foreign exchange for the Greater

Liberian economy. Through NPFL control of the workforce a form of 'protection' was imposed on the company, whereby it collaborated with Taylor. With what degree of willingness it did this is hard to determine, but the company defended itself afterwards by saying that it had to cooperate with the rebels to protect its assets. Whatever the motivation, Firestone provided both rubber revenues for the NPFL and a forward military base within striking distance of Monrovia from which the NPFL could attack the capital. The IGNU was particularly indignant over the role of Firestone in what it saw as its facilitation of the October 1992 'Operation Octopus' attack on Monrovia.

The commercial influence of Greater Liberia soon extended beyond the official territory of the country itself, and what had been a historically established cross-border trade in diamonds with Sierra Leone, mostly conducted by small-scale nomadic traders, now took on a new and more strategic dimension. With diamonds flowing from Sierra Leone, as well as from Guinea and even as far away as Angola, where Jonas Savimbi's UNITA rebels also sought a commercial outlet for the gems they extracted, Liberia became the official export source for many more times the quantity of diamonds than it actually produced. Helped by its US dollar-based economy, not to mention a regular flight schedule operated by SABENA, the Belgian national carrier, by 1994 Liberia was the third largest supplier of diamonds to Antwerp, and in the following year supplies from the country grew by 227 per cent in carat terms.[7]

During the period of NPFL control of the commodity economy of Liberia from 1990 to 1993, the estimated value of timber, diamonds, rubber, iron ore and other commodity business ran into hundreds of millions of dollars. Accordingly, it has been estimated that the taxes that Charles Taylor's government was able to levy on this trade could easily have exceeded $75 million annually.[8]

Furthermore, the trade in looted items, such as automobiles, zinc roofs, doors, house fittings and even street lamp posts added millions more to the total value of items exported from Greater Liberia. Most of the looted household fittings went to Nigeria initially, then later were sold to Guinea and Côte d'Ivoire. Looted house fittings and roofing materials transformed the Guinean countryside and also helped to expand Danane with building projects.

While some refused to recognize Taylor's control of the majority of Liberian territory and its economy, and officially dealt only with the financially impotent Monrovia regime, those who had serious business to do in Liberia in the early 1990s had to come to Gbarnga, Charles Taylor's rival capital in Bong County. It was not only business people but also diplomats and of course the coveted media visitors that would come, in order to access the influence and contact the power that was driving events in the country as well as those of Liberia's neighbours.

Friends and family also came to visit, and the Gbarnga house was often full of Taylor's children from his various partners, American and Liberian, official and unofficial. He invited Burnice Emmanuel here with their son Chuckie in 1991 so that the family could be reunited. Although Emmanuel, remarried by then, stayed elsewhere, Chuckie stayed with his father, an experience which made a great impression on the young African American, and which was to lead him back to Liberia as he entered adulthood a few years later.

Charles Taylor had started rebel life at the head of a loyal and dedicated army, proud of his media image before the world and meticulous with the messages spun by his PR operation. What is more, he was popular, at least with some in Monrovia and with many in the parts of the countryside that he had 'liberated' from the terrors of the Doe regime.

However, after two years in the bush he became known internationally as the leader of a group of out-of-control fighters, motivated by looting and destruction more than liberation, and brutal with its enemies as well as bizarre in style of warfare and attire. His army, people were being told, went into battle high on drugs, coerced children to join its ranks and conducted atrocities against civilians around the countryside. Meanwhile its leader, it was alleged by the international media, financed his operations by plundering the countryside to pay for his war effort while working with arms dealers and pariah states to keep his breakaway Liberian state supplied.

The importance of countering the anti-NPFL media onslaught at this point could never have been greater, and effective public relations once again became a priority for the president of the NPRAG. To this end, Charles Taylor became more proactive in his interaction with the media and in his use – and misuse – of intelligence.

With his satellite phone and fax machine operating twenty-four hours a day from NPFL headquarters in Gbarnga, Taylor received intelligence from allies and collaborators globally which gave him military, commercial and diplomatic superiority. He had informers in Monrovia and other world capitals, including Washington DC;[9] and often members of the rival pro-IGNU government media in the Monrovia enclave would contact the NPFL for more complete and reliable information about developments on their own side of the front line than their government sources could offer.

The Taylor communications machine operating in the heart of Bong County also frequently leaked information to the Monrovia press while its leader continued his regular dialogue with the BBC Africa Service and other Western media outlets. The official NPFL newspaper *The Patriot* was a professionally produced publication and contained business news as well as a regular diet of political propaganda.

For its part, the Monrovia-based media remained active, and continued to be critical of the NPFL. Charles Taylor's information minister, Joe Mulbah, kept channels open with his rivals in the capital and visited Monrovia periodically. There were even times when it was thought that the media could become a force for uniting the country, rather than a tool in the hands of adversaries sworn to wresting control of the country from one another.[10]

In international relations, Taylor milked his high-level international connections for propaganda benefit too. Showcasing his legal counsel, Ramsay Clark, a former US attorney general, to add kudos and legitimacy, he also leveraged the 1991 visit of Jimmy Carter to Liberia to maximum effect. Prior to his meeting with the former US president, the NPFL had special T-shirts printed for distribution. Other shirts of NPFL simply said: 'Ghankay is OK', and his Liberian beneficiaries, happy at the free distribution of fresh clothing, happily wore them as the media looked on.

Ghankay-Leaks, a media operation ahead of its time

In addition to the bitter military struggle against the ECOMOG invasion force, as Taylor characterized it, he waged a constant propaganda war against the Nigerian peacekeepers. Aware that publication in the world's media of the brutality of their methods and the corruption of the force's leadership would help to undermine its presence, his ability to publicize embarrassing details about its less laudable activities served the NPFL's cause well.

Also able to leak information obtained from stolen US State Department cables about Washington's concerns over Nigerian tactics in the pursuit of their anti-NPFL campaign, Charles Taylor added credence to his contention that ECOMOG was an invasion force, while exposing the true thinking of US diplomats on the ground at the same time.

In the early 1990s the USA had a vague and ambiguous approach towards Liberia, one which reflected both inter-agency conflict in Washington DC and discomfort at the consequences of its own past actions and omissions. While resulting policy was non-committal, official comments could be evasive. In such a context, the leaks of diplomatic cables which Taylor propagated may have unwittingly served a wider purpose beyond those of the NPFL's own strategic interests in the war in Liberia. For example, when ECOMOG proved itself to be nothing more than another ill-disciplined, pro-government looting and racketeering faction, Taylor's leaks exposed official US preoccupations over the corruption and unsuitability of the Nigerian peacekeeping force for its intended mission. In part, these actions probably served to alert the USA to the need to take a more controlling role in the crisis. When it did, by for example dispatching the Pacific Architects and Engineers[11] force to assume supervision of ECOMOG logistics in 1994, the latter force's illicit commercial activities were notably curbed.

The NPFL's financial management was as personalized around the figure of its leader as was its political control, such that, besides a select few of his closest deputies, family members and collaborators, in its heyday in 1991 to early 1993 the economy of Greater Liberia was to a large degree the personal economy of Charles Taylor.

The management of the Greater Liberian economy was always fluid, relatively efficient and highly lucrative for the NPFL, with no taxes to pay and few constraints on the free flow of goods, as long as friendly governments and border authorities were paid off and as long as the NPFL's fighters and their civilian allies could maintain control of their territory of operations and export channels.

To the east, the border with Côte d'Ivoire, while never one that the NPFL had to transgress or defend in the military sense, remained porous from the commercial point of view. With all the contraband of conflict flowing across it unhindered, and its government and financial institutions fully disposed to accepting the business of NPFL companies and associates, the latter operated in their eastern neighbour's territory much as if they were legitimate concerns based within Côte d'Ivoire itself.

Barter deals were common, as was the coercion of firms with logistics capabilities into providing transport, equipment and fuel to NPFL fighting units. In general, while firms were encouraged to stay in operation or even, for those who had fled in 1990, to return to Liberia to do business in Taylorland, once they were involved it was made clear to them that their businesses were an integral part of his military operation and should make their resources available to the NPFL accordingly.

In areas such as south-eastern Liberia, particularly where ethnic or recent commercial links to the Doe administration could have proved an obstacle, former Doe units were absorbed into the Special Forces Commandos of the NPFL, who oversaw logging and port operations at Greenville and surrounding areas. The proximity of Sinoe and Maryland counties to Côte d'Ivoire, and to San Pedro in particular, made regional operations relatively easy to supervise, and the financial side of deals could be handled without major hindrance through Ivorian banks.

Working conditions were also improved for many, particularly those involved in key industries such as agriculture. At the Firestone plantation in Harbel workers received a guaranteed minimum rate paid in US dollars. In other industries such as logging, considered key to the foreign exchange earnings of the economy, Taylor established a minimum wage of $2 per day, more than workers had previously earned.[12]

A testament to the value of the business of Greater Liberia was the fact that, following ECOMOG's capture of Buchanan and other economic assets from the NPFL starting in 1993, senior officers in the Nigerian-led force soon restarted almost identical businesses, often with the same partners, receiving lucrative commissions from commodity exporters for the right to access Liberian ports. Buchanan itself was partly out of operation after its capture by ECOMOG, due to the removal to Nigeria of much of the heavy equipment and port infrastructure, which the regional intervention force dismantled and shipped wholesale out of the country during its looting of the city.

The wealth of war

Although the NPRAG established an administrative structure in the territory under its control, in an informal state such as the Greater Liberia of 1990–94 the degree of personal control over the occupying armies by a single commander-in-chief was pronounced, and the degree of delegation of authority was restricted and often accompanied by the threat of capital punishment for failure or the transgression of loyalty. While the NPRAG did establish a bureaucracy with a police force and a civil court system in Gbarnga, at grassroots level the resort to violence or the threat of it was an important instrument of control of civilian populations by Charles Taylor's rebels.

The citizens of Bong and Nimba counties, the NPFL's natural support base, particularly those who joined as NPFL fighters and went on to loot and rob in other parts of the country, were the first ordinary material beneficiaries of the war. Indeed, for the two years following late 1990, not only did many of these areas of the country enjoy relative peace, their militarily more 'proactive' citizens enjoyed a boost to their material standard of life through new possessions recently acquired from sections of Monrovia or other conquered towns and villages. Homes were refurbished and equipped, repairs were made, equipment and appliances were installed and new small businesses were launched.

In places, particularly zones close to the front lines between factions, looting became almost systematic, down to the last detail. A town would be cleared of its population by one side, looted, abandoned, and then, after the population moved back, it could be invaded by the other faction, once again to dispossess residents of any items they had managed to take with them on the first sweep. Rarely in this pattern of looting and counter-looting did rival factions actually do battle with each other. For the most part they saved their energies for the acquisition of property from their victims.

Even at the height of the civil conflict there were probably fewer than 100,000 active fighters at most, out of an original Liberian population of around 3 million (which soon fell to closer to 2 million after the huge refugee exodus). So it could be said that even at the bottom end of the scale, only about 3 per cent of the population was actually involved as combatants in 'warfare'. Every family in all communities across Liberia was in some way tragically affected by the war through the death, disappearance, injury or exile of a family member or close friend; the beneficiaries were few and for the most part their gains, as it turned out, were fleeting.

The tactics of control used by the NPFL, while often giving the appearance of being wartime lawlessness, arguably had similarities with the methods of Liberian administrations in the past, as well as those of colonial administrations in the wider African continent over half a century before.

The Liberian Frontier Force, in the early twentieth century, had neither the motivation nor the resources to police the entire countryside properly, and it certainly could not hope to win the allegiance of local populations through popular civil administration. Nevertheless, due to the African colonial order established at the end of the nineteenth century, successive settler administrations in Monrovia were committed to defending, if not administering, the entire territory that fell within the agreed boundaries of the Republic of Liberia.

At the 1884 Berlin Conference, European nations, after dividing up the entire patchwork quilt map of Africa among themselves, were thereafter forced to exert control over their new possessions' vast perimeters. More often than not, these formed the boundaries of economically uninteresting and ethnically illogical subdivisions of ancient Africa, but nevertheless became inviolable territorial touchlines, the defence of which was essential to anchor the commercially lucrative coastal outposts which were the original reason for the Europeans' presence on the continent.

In both the nineteenth-century colonial case and the governments of the early Liberian republic, where the resources required for the administration of a territory were unavailable and the challenge of maintaining control in the absence of infrastructure was great, the resort to violence as a means of control may have been the only option available from the point of view of the ruling authority.

A key difference from the colonists' methods was the NPFL's attribution of the right to loot, delegated to its fighters usually in lieu of pay. In contrast to the colonial armies of earlier times, nearly all of Charles Taylor's fighters were unpaid, except when there were battles and it became time to 'Pay Yourself'. This reinforced the dimension of plunder in the logic of the Liberian civil war, and in turn contributed to the relative attraction of fighting to children and adolescents. Often orphaned, with no farms and businesses to sacrifice and little prospect of material survival through peace, they were the most willing recruits to rebel armies and also the cheapest to retain. Around Charles Taylor's Gbarnga headquarters or when fighting in the bush, there were always groups of children hanging around their leader, running errands and sometimes fighting alongside the adults, devoted to their 'Papay' who in the midst of the wartime destruction had given them a living and a father figure to look up to.

Connecting with country spirits

As the leader of the NPFL and contender for the presidency of his country, Charles Taylor was confident of ultimate success. But, after 1990, installed as president of the NPRAG in the heart of the Liberian countryside, it became more important for him to establish himself in the traditional society of native Liberia and assimilate its customs, trappings and rituals.

The unique way of life of the traditional inhabitants of the Liberian interior, the importance of the Liberian indigenous system of beliefs, together with secret societies, their rituals and an emphasis on the invisible as well as physical experience, was a world far removed from Charles Taylor's previous adult environment. Although he is the son of an indigenous mother from the Gola tribe, his early education, formative years in the United States and brief spell in government in Monrovia had given him little if any contact with the ways and beliefs of the native majority of Liberia.

Centuries before, in traditional rainforest West Africa, no aspiring ruler could expect to achieve power without ascending through the traditional tribal hierarchy and gaining the loyalty and respect of local chiefs in the process. Normally this would have involved lengthy initiations in bush schools and time spent climbing the hierarchy of a Poro society in a rural location, as well as preferably a display of adulthood through success in battle. While not lacking in credentials in the latter department, Charles Taylor had neither the time nor the temperament for the traditional route to achieving the formal recognition by native society which he now felt he needed to command respect and to rule the country.

Now based in the Liberian heartland, Taylor could more easily see that the deputies and foot soldiers whose loyalty he depended on in battle today could one day be the citizens and voters of the country he planned to rule. To access the traditional networks of power in the interior, it would be both expedient and indispensable for him to know and understand the 'Other Liberia'.

Taylor saw that he would need to gain the support of a wider group of Liberians than did most of his Americo-Liberian predecessors, especially in a Liberian society that had become more ethnically polarized since the early 1980s. Transcending tribal boundaries of support and synthesizing geographical loyalties had never before been achieved by Liberian rulers, and indeed, rather than healing the divisions in Liberian society, the Doe years had greatly aggravated tribal enmities and regional antagonisms across the country.

Soon after pulling back from the Monrovia front line in September 1990 and retreating to establish his new capital in Gbarnga, the NPFL leader set about engineering his transformation. The process first involved names, then appearances, and later beliefs: Charles McArthur Taylor was now Charles Ghankay Taylor; the Ghankay – 'strong one' – forename better fitting the purposes of his native social assimilation than the American-sounding McArthur.

Public appearances saw more white robes and traditional attire and less the business suit for official engagements. During his campaigns in the bush he began to carry a carved, oxblood-coloured chieftain's stick, said to be hewn from the wood of a mystical tree under which nothing ever grew. The stick remained with him all the way through his campaigns and ultimately into the Executive Office in Monrovia.

Taylor had less access to the formal process of adoption into the Poro or other secret societies of Liberia and less time to establish himself within traditional communities than his predecessors, being unable to 'climb the ladder', as it were, to the top echelons of traditional religion from his temporary rebel base in Gbarnga. To expedite matters, he leapfrogged the system by creating an association of officials of traditional societies, then proclaimed himself supreme chief of the new group – achieving instant canonization with none of the red tape of lengthy and complex inductions and initiations. His new self-conferred title, the 'Dakhpannah', confirmed that he was now the overall chief of all the tribes of Liberia's interior.

Other societal memberships held by Taylor from earlier days included the Grand United Order of Odd Fellows (GUOOF), a fraternal order founded in 1843 in the United States with a charter from its counterpart Grand Lodge in Manchester, England. Like other African-American fraternal societies at that time, the GUOOF was set up originally by former slaves in the American South to provide mutual assistance and to further its members' academic, social, and economic prospects.

As Taylor grafted on his new identity in the traditional native world, he also paid attention to maintaining and indeed renewing his Christian credentials, equally important for acceptance among his Americo-Liberian constituency at home and abroad, especially in the United States. Liberian Christians are Baptists, Methodists, Presbyterians, Episcopalians or Evangelicals. Taylor had been baptized at age 12 as a Baptist and attended the Baptist Ricks Institute as a schoolboy. But in adulthood he realized particularly that the maintenance of a strong profile in the Christian community could be crucial to cultivating friendly links with key religious-political supporters in the United States, including former president Jimmy Carter, Reverend Jesse Jackson and Pat Robertson among others.

His apparently flexible and evolving approach to religious affiliation continued in later years, and during his period in exile Charles Taylor adopted yet another faith, converting to Judaism in 2005. He did this, he said, 'because of my background' and 'because my ancestry links me to Judaism', while declining to elaborate on what those links might be.[13]

Excesses in the interior

In the context of Charles Taylor's assimilation of native culture and his ascent to the Dakhpannah of the Poro, suggestions emerged that, while he was based in Gbarnga, rituals were being carried out at his headquarters which went well beyond usual traditional secret society practice and included cannibalism. One such reported accusation named Taylor as an actor in 'ritualistic consumption of human body parts', later stating that 'these bloody rituals were allegedly carried out in Charles Taylor's house'. The accusations appeared in an article published in *The Times* on 2 November 1999, citing the Stephen Ellis book, *Mask of Anarchy* as its authority.

When the article appeared, Charles Taylor was in the midst of his presidency and particularly sensitive to any attempts to further damage his already battered reputation in the international media. He saw the cannibalism allegations, together with a second claim that appeared in the book, referring to involvement in the death of Jackson Doe, as libellous and deliberately aimed at damaging his reputation. He decided to sue *The Times*, Ellis and the UK publisher Hurst & Co., for libel.

Taylor was represented in the trial by London-based Ghanaian lawyer Azanne Kofi Akainyah. As the two sides began to face up to each other, another commentator and former visitor to Taylor in Gbarnga, perhaps in a foretaste of the UN Special Court proceedings to come, told the press: 'If Charles Taylor were not an African leader, *The Times* would, in no way, run such a libellous story. It knows it can't prove it, yet it ran it willy-nilly because it knows African leaders can be ridiculed at will, and for free. That must stop.'[14]

Taylor's representation and the defendants started to amass evidence and prepare witnesses for their respective legal arguments. Raising the stakes, Chief Justice Gloria Scott in Monrovia vowed to file further lawsuits against any witness who testified against President Taylor in connection with the trial.[15]

However, the defence held a trump card that Taylor's people would have extreme difficulty handling: the strong possibility that witnesses could be drawn into expanding their testimony at length, and to make statements about wider aspects of the conflict, including human rights violations ordered or condoned by the NPFL's leader. At a time when Taylor was battling for acceptance by the international community and struggling to have sanctions against his government lifted, the disclosure of even partially credible accusations of abuses in front of the world's press could risk the defection of the few remaining allies he had in the international community.

In the end it was the daunting financial obstacle to pursuing the case which finally forced the Taylor side to throw in the towel. First, the court required Taylor's side to post a £185,000 deposit to offset court costs because he was a foreigner and a person with no assets in the European Union. Second, it seemed highly likely that an appeal against any decision could be expected to follow, raising the prospect of significant additional costs. In assessing their prospects, in January 2001, Mr Akainyah wrote to his client and, while stating his confidence in the merits of their case, advised that

> the current political climate in England has become even more hostile to you than when the allegations were published.... You are being required to litigate the whole history of the Liberian Civil War ... this will be prohibitively expensive ... the defendants claim that their fees alone will be £1 million.

Taylor decided to call off the lawsuit. His statement explaining the decision stated:

> Counsel has advised me that the effect of these decisions is that the English High Court has refused to allow me what can be regarded as a proper opportunity to vindicate my reputation, because it has insisted on a form of proceedings which would be too broad, costly and time consuming.

President Taylor's financial constraints did indeed seem considerable; he also left the solicitors' firm of Akainyah & Co. with an outstanding account for £78,000 in legal fees, a bill which remained unpaid over a decade later.

Master of stagecraft

Even though it has been established that cannibalistic acts have existed historically in Liberia as part of traditional self-protection rituals in warfare, and that the practice of cannibalism increased dramatically during the recent Liberian civil conflict, what was being referred to by the defendants in the 2000 London libel case went far beyond the ordinary, suggesting the possibility of an elected sitting president, or those close to him, personally engaging in cannibalism.

There was further embarrassment to come during the Special Court proceedings in The Hague in March 2008 when one of the prosecution's witnesses, under cross-examination, divulged that he had been in the same secret society as Charles Taylor, and stated that he and Taylor had eaten human hearts together on more than one occasion. Dramatic courtroom scenes accompanied the testimony of Joseph 'Zigzag' Marzah, who claimed to be a senior NPFL commander, in direct contact with Taylor and close to him at his Gbarnga headquarters. Following heated exchanges with lead defence counsel Courtney Griffiths, Marzah detailed specific instances of eating human hearts, before crossing himself, apparently in remorse for having breached Poro society law and revealing its secrets. Taylor's defence counsel denied the claims and argued that Marzah was never close to him.

Notwithstanding the cannibalism accusations that occurred years later, once Taylor had become president of Liberia, the aspiring head of state learned a lot about the world of the supernatural during his Greater Liberia years and combined it to positive effect with his aptitude for showmanship once back in Monrovia during the transitional administration. In late 1996, following a particularly traumatic year in which the capital had once more been ravaged by destruction, death and insecurity just eight months before, as Christmas approached in the capital a strange but powerful rumour grabbed the attentions of a tense and naturally superstitious population.

At church pulpits and in the shops and streets of Monrovia, a rumour spread that darkness would engulf the city on 8 December, with unpredictable consequences. The prophesied occurrence was widely associated in the minds of many with the possible outbreak of yet another terrible wave of violence. The ECOMOG commander, Victor Malu, put his forces on alert and deployed them through the city the preceding day, as a tense population awaited the spectral occurrence.

On the day that darkness was rumoured to descend, Charles Taylor erected a large Christmas tree in a prominent location in the capital and invited the press to see him turning on the lights. In the midst of their anxiety and at the moment of maximum tension, suddenly their would-be leader appeared in the press, dressed in white and smiling broadly as his face shone with the lights of Christmas in the background. By a simple, well-orchestrated act of public relations, Taylor enhanced his 'supernatural' image in the eyes of a populace prone to spirituality and a belief in the importance of 'juju' or black magic in their lives.[16]

NINE

SIERRA LEONE:
LIBERIA'S SISTER REVOLUTION

> Liberia will not support any armed group in Sierra Leone. Liberia will make sure that its borders are protected and that no one will be permitted to operate in and out of Liberia to carry on acts of aggression against Sierra Leone.
>
> Charles Taylor, president of Liberia, December 1997

What became the most controversial of all of Charles Taylor's foreign misadventures stemmed from the NPFL's cooperation with and support for anti-government revolutionary fighters in Sierra Leone. From connections made during his leadership of a group of rebel trainees in a North African camp, to military collaboration with Sierra Leone's rebels, to invasion and thence to direct interference in a neighbouring country's civil war was a progression of events which had consequences for Taylor that far outlasted his rise to and fall from power in Liberia.

At around the time that Charles Taylor was walking out of prison in the United States in 1985 to make his way back to West Africa and Liberian plotting, the political landscape was also beginning to change across the Mano river, in his homeland's western neighbour. Sierra Leone was a country with a colonial history under Britain, which had led it to independence in 1961. Like Liberia's, its society and domestic politics were dominated by a coastal elite, and pressures for change had built up over the decades, ultimately leading to anti-government youth movements in the interior, which in turned provoked supression of dissent and the exile of the regime's opponents when President Joseph Momoh took over the reins of power in 1985.

The autocratic Siaka Probyn Stevens had ruled Sierra Leone since 1967. Momoh, from the same political dynasty as Stevens, was his hand-picked successor. Taking over the reins of power, he was then confirmed in a one-party election in November 1985 in which he officially took 99.9 per cent of the vote. For the country's frustrated political dissenters this hastened an inexorable drift towards insurrection, and for some, including activists like Corporal Foday Sankoh, it led to the welcoming arms of the Gaddafi revolutionary training organizations in Libya. Sankoh went on to become the leader of a rebel movement, the Revolutionary United Front (RUF), whose armed struggle destroyed his country, ravaged its youth and outraged the world with its atrocities, in much the same way as his allies and collaborators to the east, the NPFL, did in Liberia.

Forming Corporal Sankoh

Sankoh joined the Sierra Leonean army in 1956 and was promoted to corporal in 1962, the only promotion he would receive in his military career. His international experience began when he was sent to the Congo in 1963 as part of Sierra Leone's contingent of a United Nations peacekeeping force. While there he had an opportunity to see the international community in action in a country struggling through the pangs of its post-independence trauma. Corporal Sankoh soon became disillusioned by his experience of the UN operation, having observed them acting in what he saw as their thinly disguised role as the proxy of colonial interests in Africa. The outrage and embitterment he felt, in common with most Africans at the time, at the murder of Congo's Patrice Lumumba contributed to his views on African self-government and post-colonial international involvement in the continent's affairs.

Lumumba, newly independent Congo's first elected prime minister, was murdered while in the custody of the Belgian military in eastern Congo in January 1961, a short time after giving a stirring Independence Day speech which snubbed the Belgian king and highlighted the Congolese people's suffering under colonialism.

From the founding of the British colony in 1808, the great natural wealth of Sierra Leone was always both its blessing and the source of its people's greatest misery. Rich in bauxite, gold, diamond and rutile reserves, as well as offering fertile plantations for palm oil, timber, coffee and cocoa cultivation, Sierra Leone was a naturally wealthy land. 'Serra Leoa', or 'Lion Mountain' as it was originally named, was first encountered by Europeans in 1462 when the Portuguese explorer Pedro da Cintra harboured his ships there as he navigated the West African coastline. He named the place he stopped at after the roar of the oceans that could be heard crashing along the beach beneath a range of hills running along the country's coastline.

Sierra Leone was not unlike Liberia in the diversity of its ethnic composition too, with the largest group, the Mende, from the east and south of the country, counterbalanced by the second main ethnicity, the Temne, dominant in the north. The Krio, descendants of freed slaves returned from the oceans around West Africa's coast in the nineteenth century, formed the metropolitan elite. Together with the Lebanese African population, the merchant classes of the country, they composed the administrative and commercial centre of gravity in Freetown.

During colonial times, most of the country, known as the Protectorate of Sierra Leone, was ruled by a British governor, while the colony of Freetown was administered by Sierra Leone's Krio. Similar in many respects to the Liberian ruling class, although without the injection of a great number of freed slaves from a far-off Western country, Sierra Leone's Krio did not yet have their own independent republic. Nevertheless they participated in the running of their settlement in much the same way as their Liberian counterparts in Monrovia, operating a trading outpost for the outside world and maintaining a political economy with respect to the interior based on the extract-and-exploit model.

Sierra Leone's descent into an enduring cycle of rampant, chronic, all-pervasive corruption leading to civil strife began soon after the departure of its first post-colonial ruler, Milton Margai, in the mid-1960s. At the time of independence, Margai, a native Sierra Leonean of the Mende ethnicity and a qualified physician with a degree from Newcastle-upon-Tyne, was practically the only indigenous Sierra Leonean in the country with a university degree. Already an older man when he took office, Margai commanded respect, succeeded in striking a balance between the country's different ethnic interests and ran the country with relative restraint, keeping corruption at a moderate level.

After his death in 1964, Milton Margai was succeeded by his brother Albert, under whom things began to slide more noticeably into a pattern of tribal favouritism and the inevitable accompanying corruption. 'Big Albert', as he was known, was ousted following the March 1967 elections and replaced fleetingly by Siaka Probyn Stevens, leader of the Sierra Leone All People's Congress (APC), the main representatives of the Northern Temne ethnic constituency. Almost immediately after his swearing-in, Stevens was in turn the victim of an army coup which installed a military regime called the National Reformation Council, a pro-southern coalition of interests under the chairmanship of Colonel Andrew Juxton-Smith, a Krio.

The following year, Siaka Stevens, who came from the smaller northern ethnic group the Limba, and whose APC had been the numerical winners of the 1967 poll, forced Juxton-Smith out with the help of pro-northern junior army officers. The army rank and file coup-makers created a National Interim Council, which handed over power to an APC-dominated civilian government, and in April 1968 Siaka Stevens was once more sworn in as prime minister in Freetown.[1]

Stevens's early years in power were relatively stable, although characterized by a struggle to consolidate power whilst keeping increasingly volatile elements within the Sierra Leone Army (SLA) under control. One of the strategies Stevens used was to bring in members of the Guinean military to protect himself against a possible coup by opposing interests in his own military. Following the arrival of such a detachment from Sierra Leone's western neighbour in March 1971, Stevens's Freetown home was attacked by renegade SLA soldiers who saw the presence of foreign troops as a provocation. Although the dissidents were beaten back by loyalist forces, Stevens went into hiding whilst calling on Guinea for further reinforcements.

In the Guinean president, Ahmed Sekou Touré, Stevens had a powerful ally who soon helped him back to power. With the help of Guinean paratroopers and reinforced by menacing flyovers of Freetown by Guinean MIG jets, he then stamped hard on dissent, beginning an era of iron rule over Sierra Leone which lasted for the next decade and a half. Under Siaka Stevens, stability was restored at the cost of the establishment of a virtual police state, together with a system of extensive patronage and corruption throughout the country.

From then on, the country never looked back. Its ingrained system of patronage in public life and partisanship for the benefit of the ruling elite, the Lebanese business community (who began to arrive in their numbers in the 1920s and 1930s), and foreign business interests allied to the Freetown government became firmly established as Sierra Leone's way.

This was the Sierra Leone to which Foday Sankoh returned after his service in the Congo; and as he reintegrated into Sierra Leonean life, increasingly he didn't like the society that he saw. He determined to enter politics, but at that time entering politics at all was a risk unless you supported the ruling party. In 1971 he was implicated in the coup against President Siaka Stevens and was imprisoned for six years in Freetown's Pademba Road prison. While in prison Sankoh had time to reflect, to read and to ponder his country's fate as well as his options for the future. He read Mao Tse-tung avidly and developed his ideas on revolution and society. By the time of his release, he was a firm believer that neither a civilian kleptocracy nor a military dictatorship – Sierra Leone's only two systems of government since independence – held out much hope for the future. Under the status quo the lot of ordinary Sierra Leoneans was always going to be that of the downtrodden and the disenfranchised.

What had never been tried in Sierra Leone, what was lacking there as in many other failing post-independence African states, he decided, was the idea of a third way: a popular revolution, an uprising of the ordinary people.

Connecting in Libya – launching from Liberia

Sankoh began to recruit, drawing followers from around the country, establishing his base in the southern provincial capital of Bo, Sierra Leone's second city. Soon he was ready to make the next move, and, like his revolutionary soulmate from Liberia, it was not long before he connected with the biggest and wealthiest backer of revolutionary movements in West Africa at the time: Libya's Muammar Gaddafi. From 1988 Sankoh and a core group of his revolutionaries-to-be visited Libya, where they trained and prepared for their return. It was during this time that members of the Revolutionary United Front almost certainly came into contact with the NPFL for the first time.

Although Charles Taylor testified that he did not meet Sankoh personally in Libya, others in the UN Special Court proceedings have stated that Taylor and Sankoh first met during this time in the Libyan training camps. The prosecution at the Special Court for Sierra Leone, in its efforts to demonstrate a 'joint criminal enterprise' between Taylor's NPFL and Foday Sankoh's RUF dating back to the late 1980s, sought to demonstrate Taylor's contacts with Sierra Leone's rebels from the earliest times. Contrary to Taylor's contention that he 'never knew about the formation of the RUF and never met Foday Sankoh in Libya',[2] defence witness Issa Sesay testified: 'According to Mr. Sankoh, he said he met Mr. Taylor in Libya and later in Liberia because Mr. Sankoh and his men were also training in Libya.'[3]

Taylor maintains that the two men first made contact when ULIMO attacked the NPFL in Liberia in 1991 with Sierra Leone government support, and that he sought RUF cooperation in countering their offensive. Sankoh, in any case, had yet to emerge as leader of the RUF at the time Taylor attended the Libyan training camps, and, given his lack of education and low military rank, the Sierra Leonean quite possibly never attracted the attention of an NPFL leader preoccupied with building an army to invade Liberia. During his Libyan visits Taylor did, however, admit to meeting the more prominent Sierra Leone rebel leader at the time, Allie Kabbah, whom he described as a leader of the 'Sierra Leone Pan-Africanist Movement'.

There is little to suggest that the NPFL and the RUF had any joint operations in prospect in 1988; although they already had parallel objectives, their military collaboration did not begin until three years later. In the timing of the launch of their respective insurrections, it was the NPFL that moved first; Charles Taylor, Prince Johnson and their 168 trained rebels left Libya in three or four groups, first moving back to Burkina Faso, between April and June of 1989.

Thus Sankoh and his 200-plus cadre of Sierra Leoneans were still in preparation by the time the Liberians moved out. But the Sierra Leoneans were not far behind in launching their own rebellion, and RUF vanguard units soon returned to eastern Sierra Leone. While Sankoh worked from his base in Bo, others infiltrated Kono District, where they took the first steps towards fomenting an uprising among the local population. They agitated particularly among the diamond workers, who would be key to the success of their planned insurrection. Over a year later, the main RUF invasion group was assembled inside the borders of Liberia, by then under Charles Taylor's control, from where they had a secure launch pad for their attack.

At around the same time as he was in a position to forge connections with Sierra Leone's rebels in Libya, however, Charles Taylor tried to solicit the cooperation of the Sierra Leonean head of state for the deployment of his force to invade Liberia. The NPFL's first plan was to attack Liberia from Sierra Leone, with the main force seaborne, targeting Robertsport in Grand Cape Mount County, some 10 miles from the border and only 50 miles north of Monrovia. To secure backing for this strategy from Momoh, in 1988 Taylor attempted to travel to Freetown via the Guinean capital Conakry, journeying overland.

Taylor's intention was to speak to the president and secure approval for the plot. He met with a less than warm reception from the authorities, however, and his request for a meeting at the presidency was turned down. A later attempt to see Momoh in Freetown was equally unsuccessful, resulting in Taylor's deportation to Côte d'Ivoire.

Taylor's resentment at the rebuff in Sierra Leone only intensified when shortly afterwards Momoh granted Doe access for the deployment of his forces along the Sierra Leone–Liberia frontier. Taylor had to shelve his plan to invade Liberia from Sierra Leone. His feeling towards Momoh did not diminish with time, and his desire for revenge against the Sierra Leonean regime would soon resurface in more concrete form.

In 1990, when the government in Freetown gave its support to ECOMOG as it made its landing in Monrovia, the leader of the NPFL was further incensed. In particular, the stationing of Nigerian bomber jets at Freetown's Lungi Airport, which were used to attack and harass the NPFL as it retreated from Monrovia, led to Taylor making particularly belligerent remarks. It was then that he openly vowed to 'send the war' across the border to Sierra Leone. And send it he did in the following year, with NPFL fighters crossing the border in support of Foday Sankoh's rebel army.

The Sierra Leonean civil war began on 23 March 1991, with around a hundred Sierra Leonean and Liberian rebels crossing the border from Liberia to attack Bomaru in Kailahun District, while a second incursion was made further south near Pujehun. Initially, the RUF was unknown to most people in Sierra Leone and it was thought that the incursions might be spillover border disputes from the Liberian fighting or even localized violence related to disputes over cross-border commerce. After the first incursions, the RUF fighters, together with well-armed NPFL troops, developed their raids, attacking rural farmers, villagers and local mining communities, driving out their inhabitants, while at the same time drawing new recruits, often by violent coercion, from among the male youth of the territories they conquered.

The initial response from President Momoh, himself a former head of the army, was to ask for outside help, both regionally and from the UK. He knew the capabilities of the Sierra Leone Army (SLA), which at that time was a poorly organized force of around 4,000 men. Furthermore, standards of morale and loyalty in the SLA were questionable, and he rightly doubted its ability to repel a well-organized rebel offensive. Britain, however, despite its military ties with Sierra Leone, which had included the Royal Navy using Freetown as a staging port for the invasion of the Falklands in 1982, turned him down.

While also calling on his ECOWAS allies to help fight back the insurrection, Joseph Momoh then sent troops to the border area to repulse the RUF attack. The result was a miserable failure: ordinary soldiers, many with little in common with the regime and nothing to gain from keeping them in power, defected to the rebel side, swelling the RUF's ranks.

Valentine Strasser's coup: another boy soldier takes over

The following year, in the capital Freetown, a junior army officers' coup led by Captain Valentine Strasser ousted Momoh and installed a regime known as the National Provisional Ruling Council (NPRC). The war-wounded 26-year-old junior officer walked into Momoh's office on 29 April 1992, to register complaints about soldiers' conditions as well as the levels of corruption and nepotism at senior levels in the army. As Momoh objected, Strasser's soldiers overwhelmed Momoh's guards while other rebel units captured the government radio station on the other side of the capital. Strasser took charge of the government, becoming the youngest head of state in the world at the time.

Captain Valentine Strasser tried to take on Foday Sankoh's advance with outside help while rallying the ordinary population behind him. To help restore the people's jaded faith in their rulers, his new NPRC government, like nearly all Sierra Leone's governments both before and after it, pledged to work to eliminate corruption. However, more importantly for his own survival, the forces of his NPRC also failed to curb the incursions of the RUF, which soon moved further into the country, capturing mining areas and taking effective control of the majority of the territory.

Responding to Strasser's appeal, Nigeria, which had been a supporter of the Stevens and Momoh governments, moved to help Strasser against the RUF under the auspices of ECOMOG. Sending two battalions to bolster the ranks of the SLA, Nigeria also stationed Alpha fighter jets at Freetown's Lungi Airport to support the government army. In November 1992, they together succeeded in pushing the rebels out of the diamond fields and back across the border into Liberia. However, as in Liberia, the Nigerian presence was a double-edged sword for Sierra Leone, and elements of their force were economically active in the diamond fields of eastern Sierra Leone, extracting their own share of the gems while officially on a mission to protect the region from the RUF.

As with the NPFL two years earlier in Liberia, the Nigerian intervention force was seen by the RUF as a foreign invasion force, a powerful militarized faction with a licence to pillage the countryside of its wealth. After its initial reverses, the RUF soon regrouped and successfully counter-attacked, adapting its tactics to guerrilla warfare against the Nigerians, many of whom were enlisted men from their country's arid savannah, less familiar with the type of terrain and less able to adapt to the humidity of Sierra Leone's tropical forest.

In January 1994, Strasser initiated a recruitment drive to reinforce the SLA in a renewed effort to counter the insurgency. He effectively began to conscript child soldiers, bringing large numbers of orphans and young teenagers into the army, tripling the SLA's ranks to around 14,000 troops. But the expanded government army was still barely trained, badly equipped and poorly motivated, and problems stemming from this soon resurfaced for the government side in the war.

Sent to the front line, but underpaid and with no real interest in the status quo, many of the SLA soldiers began to fight for the government by day, while operating on the side of the rebels by night. The government troops who acted in this way became known as the 'Sobels'. The phenomenon of changing sides between factions, also common in Liberia, was familiar enough, but the simultaneous service for both sides which the Sobels undertook was a new departure, underlining the total disenfranchisement of the youth fighters and ordinary army recruits from the interests of their leaders.

The RUF again built on its successes, and pushed its attacks closer in towards the capital. Its force was gaining in number and by early 1995 numbered around 1,500 fighters. On 15 April 1995, it launched an offensive towards the west, capturing the strategic crossroads of Mile 38, pushing into the rutile, gold, diamond and productive agricultural regions. In effect, what the RUF had done was to gain control of nearly all of Sierra Leone's economic resources. As the NPFL had done a few years earlier in Liberia, the RUF now owned the productive capacity of the country, so there was no need for peace. Financially, Strasser's government in Freetown soon came to resemble Amos Sawyer's government in Monrovia – it had all of the debts and none of the resources. It was garrisoned in the capital but had no control of the countryside. Its military was in a shambles and its finances were shot. Its state of crisis was complete.

Diamonds are a warlord's best friend

Sierra Leone's Kono District, rich in diamonds and next to the Liberian border, became the focal point of much of the fighting. While the RUF had no legitimate outlet for shipping and trading diamonds overseas through Sierra Leonean channels, for a time, while Charles Taylor controlled most of Liberia's ports and borders, there was little to hinder the extraction and export of diamonds from eastern Sierra Leone, no matter who was in power in Freetown. In consequence, Sierra Leonean diamonds were able to flow out of Taylor-controlled territory, officially exported by Liberia but in reality originating from Sierra Leone's mines.

In early 1995, with the rebels only 12 miles outside Freetown, Strasser asked for help from Executive Outcomes, a private South African military company run by Eeben Barlow and formed mostly of recruits from the former South African Defence Force during its apartheid days. Barlow knew a thing or two about destabilizing African governments, having done it for a living in Southern Africa in the 1980s in his previous job.[4] With an internal mandate to provide military security services only to recognized governments, Executive Outcomes was for a time the answer to Strasser's problems; in March 1995 it first provided training for the Sierra Leone army then went on the offensive against the RUF. In the following months it succeeded in wresting back control of most of the country's diamond fields from the rebels, in effect creating a corridor for the safe transit of precious stones through rebel-held territory.

By the end of 1995, Valentine Strasser, politically and financially bankrupt, decided to play the last card he held: the appeal for democracy. Against the tradition of all his predecessors and in marked contrast to the way in which he personally had come to power, Strasser decided to call a national conference and launch a bid for UN-supervised elections. Elections were scheduled for 25 February 1996 with UN support, but the plans were met with derision by the RUF. Strasser was desperate, and his sudden conversion to statesman and peacemaker didn't fool Sankoh; nor did it restrain the RUF. Holding all the economic cards in the country, Sankoh refused to have anything to do with Strasser's conference or his elections.

Sankoh had nothing to gain by participating in elections or democratic government and much to lose, as he was able to control a good slice of the countryside as well as access to its most valuable resources. In addition to rejecting the call to the ballot box, Sankoh also demanded the expulsion of the representative of the UN from the country, as well as the departure of the ECOMOG and foreign mercenary forces.

The government's credibility was at an all-time low. By January 1996, Valentine Strasser was gone, slipping out of the country more with a whimper than with a bang, forced out by his deputy, Brigadier General Julius Maada-Bio. Maada-Bio, who was close to Nigeria's President Abacha, had a sister, Agnes Jalloh, who was a negotiator for the RUF. He was suspected of engineering the takeover in an attempt to prevent the return to civilian rule which his predecessor had pushed for. Pro-election demonstrations, including a heavily attended market women's protest through the streets of Freetown, evidenced the impatience of the people with endless civil war and the country's military rulers, whether government or rebel. The women's leaders threatened to expose a group of politicians who had been bribed by the military to argue in favour of postponing the ballot.[5]

Maada-Bio ultimately did respect the election timetable that the international community had put in place, and voting went ahead as scheduled the following month. Sankoh, however, still refused to participate. But the first round of the elections went ahead and the people of Sierra Leone came out to vote in droves.

With thirteen parties presenting themselves in the first round, no single candidate achieved the required number of votes to secure the presidency. Sankoh, furious, had by then become desperate to prevent the second round, which would confirm the legitimacy before the international community of a new president of Sierra Leone.

How could he stop the people from voting? His RUF guerrillas mounted fresh attacks, targeting civilians with brutal methods and with the primary aim of preventing people from going to the polling booths. This time, with the macabre war cry 'No arms, no elections', the trademark RUF practice of amputation of its victims went into full swing. As they moved through an area, the rebels were brutally effective in provoking panic through the tactic of sending their mutilated victims ahead to the next village to spread terror in advance of their attacks.

Defiant Sierra Leone goes to the polls

The Freetown government also panicked and Maada-Bio called on Côte d'Ivoire's President Henri Conan Bédié, the successor to Félix Houphouët-Boigny, to come to his aid. The logistics of bringing Sankoh from the bush to attend peace talks was a stumbling block, as no one wanted to take responsibility for Sankoh's transfer to Côte d'Ivoire. Ultimately, Sankoh agreed to a ceasefire and was lifted from his position in the bush by helicopter to Yamoussoukro, where he met Maada-Bio for the first time and a peace deal was struck. But a short time later he called off the ceasefire and reversed his position, saying he had agreed to nothing. It was not in Sankoh's interests to talk democracy.

But in the meantime, the second round of elections proceeded. The people voted again, amputees with their hands cut off ('long sleeve' as the rebels called it) or 'short sleeve' (cut off all the way past the elbow), streaming into the polling stations with the others, led to the booths to vote by family and friends who helped them to register their votes, in a moving show of defiance of the rebels and a display of their determination not to be excluded from the process by violence.

As a result, Ahmed Tejan Kabbah, an ethnic Mandingo of Muslim upbringing, a lawyer and former UN bureaucrat, was elected president on 17 March 1996, with his Sierra Leone People's Party (SLPP) taking over 60 per cent of the vote. Upon taking office, he immediately called for a resumption of the peace talks in Côte d'Ivoire, but Sankoh refused to recognize the result of the elections; above all, he refused to recognize Tejan Kabbah, the long-time salaried servant of the international community and now, to him, the perceived agent of the West's interests, as president of the Sierra Leone for which he had sought a radical future.

In Freetown, the Kabbah administration kept on the various foreign military advisers and special forces, including the Nigerian ECOMOG contingent, as well as Executive Outcomes, who together with the SLA went on to counter-attack the RUF. The South African private military group also played a part in training the Kamajors, a traditional ethnic Mende fighting group who sided with the government and came to represent a significant force in the next stages of the war. Kabbah increasingly used the Kamajors as his de facto presidential guard, and promoted their leader, Hinga Norman, to the position of deputy minister of defence in his new cabinet.

The prominence of the Kamajors in the government became counterproductive for Kabbah after a certain point, causing friction with the SLA, which began to fracture into pro-Kabbah and pro-RUF factions. The announcement of plans to reduce the size

FODAY SANKOH DURING 5 MAY 2000 PRESS CONFERENCE IN FREETOWN

of the army further raised tensions, seen as favouring the unofficial Kamajors over the SLA, while public criticism over the slow pace of reform in the countryside was also mounting. Matters came to a violent head in October 1996 when clashes between the SLA and a group of rival Kamajor troops led to over a hundred deaths.

Another issue that developed into a scandal for Kabbah was the extremely high cost of maintaining the foreign forces in the country – with Executive Outcomes alone reportedly costing some $1.8 million a month to keep in operation. The South African mercenary force was effective though, and, together with the SLA, the Kamajors and ECOMOG, their battlefield successes did finally help to bring Foday Sankoh to the negotiating table.

The Abidjan peace talks, stalled by the elections and Sankoh's constant change of posture, had nevertheless continued as fighting in the countryside periodically erupted. But as the tide turned against the RUF, Sankoh was forced to look for a way out, and peace became a more acceptable option.

On 30 November 1996, the RUF and the SLPP government of Ahmed Tejan Kabbah signed a peace deal in Abidjan. Under the accords, the RUF agreed to disarm in exchange for amnesty and assistance in reintegration. To achieve this, the deal provided for a process that brought members of the RUF into talks on demobilization commissions, established jointly with the government side.

Importantly, Kabbah now agreed to the departure of all 'foreign forces' from the country, a point upon which the RUF had always insisted. The decision to dispense with the services of Executive Outcomes was one which Sierra Leone's president would soon come to regret.

With the RUF now an accepted group in the political discussions, the government falteringly continued with its programme for a return to civilian rule. There was an atmosphere of hope that the endless cycle of violence was finally coming to an end. Little was achieved, however, with Sankoh still bellowing against his opponents from a distance and the RUF leadership in Freetown observing a pattern of constant obstructionism in the implementation of the agreement. The ceasefire was barely respected by the RUF and sporadic fighting continued in the countryside as the discussions on implementation continued.

Sankoh goes AWOL

On 2 March 1997, Foday Sankoh disappeared from the Hotel Ivoire in Abidjan. He remained incommunicado for some three weeks, destination unknown, until it emerged that he had flown to Nigeria. Although supposedly on an official mission, upon arrival in Lagos he was arrested by the Nigerian authorities on suspicion of gun-running. During his detention, efforts were made to accelerate the pace of progress towards disarmament and demobilization, but ultimately his deputies proved to be just as intransigent without him as with him.

During Sankoh's absence in Nigeria in early 1997, a group of his RUF deputies who were impatient with the slow pace of peace negotiations conspired to do a deal with Freetown to end the fighting. The group, which included Philip Palmer, the former RUF head of security at the Abidjan talks, was encouraged by the UK and other embassies to betray Sankoh, and came to a meeting in Guinea to negotiate a deal, they thought, with the Sierra Leonean government. The plan was thwarted, as Sam Bockarie, Sankoh's loyal deputy, had been aware of their plan and had the defectors surrounded and captured on arrival. Bockarie, nicknamed 'mosquito', who trained with the RUF in Liberia in 1990, continued to be one of its leading members and remained in charge of the organization in his boss's absence.

Sankoh's presence in Nigeria was not simply the consequence of random flight, it transpired. There were considerations of regional diplomatic rivalry as well as domestic political pressures to consider. For both reasons, it seems likely that Nigeria's President Abacha did not wish to be upstaged by the francophones as peacemaker in the region.

Just as in Liberia, Nigeria's forces had been making a lot of sacrifices in the name of peace in Sierra Leone, at considerable financial cost and, particularly in Liberia, with little gain in terms of diplomatic recognition or enhanced international prestige.

Abacha imprisoned Sankoh in Abuja and at the same time tried to coerce him into accepting peace. The ploy failed, with Sankoh continuing to make anti-Freetown pronouncements from foreign detention, enforced by Bockarie on the ground at home and remaining as intransigent as ever to the idea of disarmament of his forces.

On 25 May 1997, African Liberation Day, a force of Sierra Leonean rebels from the newly formed Armed Forces Revolutionary Council (AFRC) in Freetown blew down the gates of the Pademba Road Prison with mortars, freed their imprisoned rebel comrade Major Johnny Paul Koroma, whom they declared their leader, and stormed through the capital, mounting a successful *coup d'état* against the Kabbah regime. Kabbah himself fled the country to neighbouring Guinea. Koroma took over as head of state and invited his fellow rebels, the RUF, now dispersed in pockets around the countryside, into government with him. Sankoh, still calling the shots from detention in Abuja, instructed his commanders to join forces with the new group. For just under a year the AFRC–RUF alliance ruled Sierra Leone. Foday Sankoh was appointed vice president of Sierra Leone *in absentia*.

The coup was a major affront to the peacemaking efforts of the international community and underlined the fragility of the democratic process in the absence of true disarmament. In particular, the newly elected British government of Tony Blair stepped up its involvement in Sierra Leone on behalf of the ousted Kabbah. Furthermore, in June of that year the Organization of African Unity met and overwhelmingly approved a Nigerian military response under the auspices of ECOWAS. Nigeria sent warships and bombarded Freetown from the ocean, blasting rebel-held and civilian areas alike. Their troops moved in, and by March 1998 the rebel government was defeated.

Upon the expulsion of the rebels, Ahmed Tejan Kabbah returned to the country and was restored to office. He immediately took reprisals against members and supporters of the junta, carrying out dozens of executions of soldiers who had sided with the rebels. Kabbah's grip on government remained tenuous, however, and he relied heavily on the remaining forces of ECOMOG to keep him in power and on the backing of the British government.

Cry Freetown: New Year's massacre of 1999

Yet RUF and AFRC rebels were still operating freely in many parts of the countryside and, despite the Nigerian presence, were able to threaten the capital at any time. It was not long before another coup was mounted, and this time Freetown took one of its bloodiest blows of the long civil war to date. On 6 January 1999, in a well-planned attack which involved large-scale smuggling of small arms from the countryside into the capital in advance, AFRC rebels first infiltrated the city and then mounted a massive onslaught on Freetown's civilian population. ECOMOG failed to detect the rebels entering in force among ordinary civilians, and then were taken by surprise as the AFRC rebels sprang into action, rampaging through the streets and taking over much of the city, while carrying out hundreds of amputations on their civilian victims.

At one stage the rebels tricked their way into a barricaded Nigerian peacekeepers' base where thousands of civilians were taking refuge, by posing as fleeing civilians themselves; when the compound gates were opened, they stormed inside in force wielding machetes, and running amok through the huddled throng of terrified refugees. From there they had free rein to unleash a punishing wave of killings and mutilations on their trapped and defenceless victims. Afterwards, open lorry loads of traumatized, limbless people rolled through the streets of Freetown as attempts were made to deliver hundreds of the wounded to medical aid in the city's overstretched hospitals.

The city was plunged into chaos and widespread bloodshed continued, with insurgents occupying half of the capital and the Nigerians reeling in disarray, struggling along with the remaining operational elements of the SLA to restore order. It took six traumatic weeks for the government side finally to regain control. The toll on the civilian population, not to mention the impact on Kabbah's credibility, was devastating. Much of Freetown was totally destroyed in the fighting. Sierra Leone's rebels had proven once and for all that the elected government could never guarantee the security of its population without their consent.[6]

By mid-1999, all sides of the never-ending Sierra Leone conflict were in the mood for peace, with the warring parties exhausted, its civilian population both physically shattered and demoralized, and the international community thoroughly tired of the enormous cost of the never-ending cycle of negotiations followed by broken ceasefire upon broken ceasefire.

In Nigeria, whose ECOMOG contingent had paid a heavy price for their engagement in Sierra Leone, the mood was strongly in favour of withdrawal. Following President Sani Abacha's death in mid-1998, the issue of foreign interventions became central to the election campaign for a new leader, with candidates voicing their support for withdrawal from Sierra Leone as a sure-fire vote winner at the polling booths.

Across the border in Monrovia, President Charles Taylor also sought to act as peace facilitator, calling on all parties to the dispute to seek dialogue. Now under international pressure and publicly committed to an ending of his country's involvement in Sierra Leone's civil conflict, Taylor was a potentially valuable mediator in the forthcoming peace process because of his close links with the RUF leadership.

In London, Tony Blair's government had invested diplomatic effort, as well as money to the tune of some £30 million in the previous year alone. It had also incurred considerable embarrassment, notably over the Sandline affair. Sandline, a UK private security firm, had arranged a deal with President Kabbah which included the shipment of some 35 tons of arms to the government side to help fight the rebels. However, under UN resolution 1132 of 8 October 1997, an arms embargo was in force in Sierra Leone. The UK's ambassador in Freetown, Peter Penfold, had coordinated the meetings between Kabbah and Sandline, and stated that he informed the UK government that arms were included in the transaction. Penfold's position was that he believed that the embargo applied only to the RUF and AFRC rebels, and not to arms shipments made to the democratically elected government of Sierra Leone.

Nevertheless, in March 1998, a scandal erupted in the UK over the deal, as Foreign Secretary Robin Cook denied both knowledge and involvement, and blame was ultimately laid on the Foreign Affairs Select Committee of the House of Commons, for failing to inform the government. The chief civil servant responsible, Sir John Kerr, was dismissed from his post. Penfold, regarded as a hero by Sierra Leoneans for his role in the defeat of the RUF, was denied a further career posting and was effectively forced out of the diplomatic service.[7]

Regional blunders by the Reverend Jackson

The United States supported the British in their desire to see an early negotiated end to the conflict. ECOWAS and the OAU were also determined to see an end to the endless instability in Sierra Leone and lent their support to the Anglo-American effort. President Clinton deployed his special envoy and secretary of state for the promotion of democracy in Africa, Jesse Jackson, to help bring Kabbah and Sankoh together to the peace table. Jesse Jackson, already controversial in the region for his uncomfortably close ties to Charles Taylor in Monrovia, as well as for his prior contacts with the RUF in 1998, now appeared to compound his radical stance and take an almost inexplicably pro-rebel line. He had recently demonstrated his unfamiliarity with the politics of the continent by comparing Foday Sankoh with Nelson Mandela, in remarks which he later disavowed as 'misunderstood'.[8]

Perhaps euphemistically explained by 'powerful lobbying' on behalf of the RUF or perhaps out of inexperience and naivety, Jackson was instrumental in supporting Sankoh's release from prison, a condition which the RUF demanded in order to participate in peace talks. A free man again, Sankoh went to Togo, where he was hosted by Togolese president Gnassingbé Eyadéma, the new self-styled francophone regional peacemaker, since the death of Côte d'Ivoire's Houphouët-Boigny in December 1993.

Kabbah, initially reluctant to make concessions to the rebels at a time when Freetown was relatively secure and with more experience of the RUF than his international backers, was figuratively 'kidnapped' by Jackson and his aides while attending an African-American Summit in Accra and flown by helicopter some 100 miles to Togo, where Sankoh was waiting. From there Jackson, with other West African leaders in attendance, helped coax Kabbah into signing an almost laughably generous peace agreement with the RUF leader in Lomé on 7 July 1999.

The RUF leader couldn't have got a better deal if he had bargained for years. The key terms of the accord included an amnesty for the RUF and its leadership and provided for Sankoh to take up a key position in the proposed new government, as well as awarding him the vice presidency of the country. Benefiting from the tailwind of the international community's eagerness for peace at any price, Sankoh was appointed chairman of the board of the Commission for the Management of Strategic Resources. The Commission was intended to be responsible for 'securing and monitoring the legitimate exploitation of Sierra Leone's gold and diamonds, and other resources that are determined to be of strategic importance for national security and welfare'.

Provision was also made for the invitation of a UN peacekeeping force, the United Nations Mission in Sierra Leone (UNAMSIL), to be dispatched to the country, and for a process of disarmament, demobilization and reintegration (DDR) to be implemented for the country's ex-combatant population; and the UN and the government of Sierra Leone jointly agreed to set up a Truth and Reconciliation Commission. Later, the government asked the UN for assistance in establishing a Special Court, whose mandate would be to bring to justice those who 'bear the greatest responsibility for the commission of crimes against humanity, war crimes and serious violations of international humanitarian law, as well as crimes ... within the territory of Sierra Leone since 30 November 1996'.

In October 1999, the United Nations sent the first contingent of 6,000 peacekeeping troops to Sierra Leone; its numbers increased soon afterwards to over 10,000 and UNAMSIL went on to become the UN's largest peacekeeping mission in the world. Its early months in the country were not easy ones for the multinational force, and DDR did not get off the ground, as provided for in the peace accords.

Foday Sankoh, on the one hand in office as vice president of Sierra Leone, and on the other hand with a cabinet position supervising the country's natural resources shipments, was in position to act as gatekeeper for access to the diamond trade of the country. Furthermore, his RUF rebels continued to have a presence in the diamond-producing regions, and for many months after the Lomé agreement the government and the UN forces remained unable to wrest complete control of those areas from them.

Taylor works to free UN hostages

As ECOMOG's Nigerian troops at last withdrew from Sierra Leone in April of 2000, clashes with the rebels in the countryside resumed. The RUF took seven international aid workers and missionaries hostage, and then, in a major incident in May 2000, some 500 UNAMSIL soldiers were abducted by the RUF in Kailahun in eastern Sierra Leone. In June, UN secretary general Kofi Annan and Nigerian president Olusegun Obasanjo requested Charles Taylor to assist in securing the release of the mostly Zambian UN hostages, due to his prior connections with the RUF leadership.

Taylor responded positively. 'I have said to them that I will do everything within my own strength to help release the hostages in whatever way I can',[9] he told the international media. Sure enough, within weeks, the hostages were slowly released, mostly into Liberia and the custody of Liberia's security forces, before being shuttled back to Freetown to rejoin their units.

At around the same time as the UN hostage-taking, a shooting incident occurred outside Sankoh's house in Freetown, which led to his arrest by the Sierra Leone police. On 8 May 2000 a huge crowd of anti-RUF protesters, demonstrating against continued violence and their betrayal by Sankoh, who had reneged on his promise to accept peace, chased the RUF leader from his home and clashed with armed RUF supporters outside the vice president's house. The confrontation led to the pro-Sankoh group opening fire on the demonstrators, and twenty people were killed. Sankoh was captured and imprisoned, together with several of his senior cabinet colleagues, who were stripped of their government positions.

In support of the effort towards peace, in July 2000 the UK dispatched 800 troops to the country in response to the continuing crisis; and a senior British police officer, Keith Biddle, was placed in charge of the Sierra Leone national police force in an attempt to improve its accountability and enhance its efficiency. Together they were able to assist the government troops in regaining control of the greater Freetown area, as well as securing key routes to the provinces. After this, they initiated a period of training and joint manoeuvres with the SLA and UNAMSIL. However, there was trouble ahead for the UK contingent: on 26 August a splinter group of former rebel fighters calling themselves 'The West Side Boys' took eleven UK soldiers hostage and held them for two weeks, until UK forces stormed the rebels' base, freeing the men.

Sierra Leone was largely pacified by the end of 2001, due to a large extent to the continued UK military presence and the flooding of the countryside with UNAMSIL peacekeepers – Sierra Leone became the UN's largest peacekeeping mission globally by 2002, with some 15,000 international personnel at the peak of its operations. The UK forces stayed on during the transition to peace and finally left Sierra Leone at the end of 2001.

In light of the breaches of the ceasefire and with the RUF's credibility and popularity greatly diminished, renewed peace accords were negotiated and signed in Abuja in November 2000. In January 2001, Charles Taylor declared the end of his support for the RUF and that March had his forces seal the border with Sierra Leone. In August 2001, Issa Hassan Sesay took over the leadership of the RUF and the following month met President Kabbah in Koidu, shaking hands with his former adversary and declaring the fighting over.

In January 2002, President Ahmed Tejan Kabbah was able to declare officially to his country's people in their patois that 'De war don don'. The civil war was finally at an end, and the DDR process finally got under way. By early 2002, some 72,000 combatants had been disarmed and demobilized. In May 2002, Kabbah won a landslide re-election, in which the RUFP (Revolutionary United Front Party), the political successor to the outlawed rebel force, failed to gain a single seat in the government. Sierra Leone was ready to move on, even if regional fighting had now returned to Liberia and was also breaking out in a new civil war in Côte d'Ivoire.

Also at the beginning of 2002 UN secretary general Kofi Annan announced his intention to establish a war crimes tribunal to punish those most responsible for the Sierra Leone civil war. That set in motion a process which the following year led to the indictment of thirteen alleged masterminds of the conflict, including one non-Sierra Leonean, Charles Taylor, then president of Liberia.

The record of Charles Taylor in relation to Sierra Leone while he was president of Liberia remains the subject of intense controversy, with the focal point his arrest in 2006 and subsequent trial before the Special Court for Sierra Leone, discussed in Chapter 14.

A further controversial aspect of the Sierra Leone diamond trade during the Taylor presidency was the alleged link between diamond dealing and global terrorism – an aspect which first fell under the spotlight following the 1998 al-Qaeda bombings of the US embassies in Nairobi and Dar es Salaam. With the growing role of Middle Eastern and other foreign interests in West Africa's diamond trade, the possibility of an al-Qaeda terrorism link with

Sierra Leone's diamonds became the subject of heightened interest for US intelligence.

Subsequent media reports and UN investigations made reference to the presence of al-Qaeda operatives sent to Liberia to buy Sierra Leonean diamonds from the RUF since 1999 and who were allegedly escorted by Taylor's government to make their deals. The story first came to prominence in 2003 in an article by a US reporter, quoting the US Special Court for Sierra Leone prosecutor David Crane, who told him that 'Charles Taylor is harbouring terrorists from the Middle East, including Al-Qaeda and Hezbollah and has been for years ... he is not just a regional trouble maker; he is a player in the world of terror and what he does affects lives in the United States and Europe'. The report also said that al-Qaeda dealers had been dispatched to Liberia to 'buy all the diamonds that the RUF could produce'.[10]

On 25 July 2004 a group of al-Qaeda agents were arrested in eastern Pakistan, including Ahmed Khalfan Ghailani, who was wanted in connection with the 1998 African embassy bombings. Ghailani, together with Fazhl Abdullah Mohammed, had travelled to Liberia in March 1999 to coordinate the diamond purchasing operations of al-Qaeda, according to the report, which was prepared by UN investigators for the prosecution side in the trial of Taylor. The document went on to allege that the two operatives who were received by Taylor in his Congotown residence were staying at the Hotel Boulevard in Monrovia.[11]

When al-Qaeda struck at New York's World Trade Center in September 2001, US intelligence was galvanized into action. A raid into Liberia was planned and authorized by the Department of Defense using agents from its special forces already stationed in Guinea, with the objective of capturing the al-Qaeda operatives under Charles Taylor's protection, according to officials who cooperated anonymously with the 2004 UN investigation.[12] The raid was later called off, but al-Qaeda supposedly continued to deal through Liberia with the knowledge and assistance of Charles Taylor, who reportedly received $1 million for harbouring Ghailani and Mohammed following the World Trade Center attacks. The two men, by then on the FBI's most wanted list of terrorists, were kept at the Gbatala military training base in Bong County.[13]

Corroboration for the story came during the Liberian Truth and Reconciliation Commission hearings on Economic Crimes, in February 2009, when it was also alleged that the two operatives had been introduced to the RUF's Sam Bockarie through Taylor. According to the TRC Testimony of the Global Witness representative, Patrick Alley, the two al-Qaeda operatives were escorted to Sierra Leone when they arrived in 1999, introduced to the RUF's Sam Bockarie, giving him $100,000 in cash for a parcel of diamonds. Alley also said that his organization's research revealed that al-Qaeda had been buying diamonds globally in a strategy of 'commodifying' its assets, diversifying away from financial accounts, which are more subject to the surveillance of international authorities.[14]

UK search for scapegoat in Sandline affair

In his testimony before the Special Court in 2009, Taylor denied press reports linking him to Sierra Leone diamond dealings during the 1998–2002 period. He referred in particular to the 2003 *Washington Post* article which linked him to al-Qaeda and explained that, following the allegations, his government cooperated with the US authorities investigating the matter. He said that 'by the time of the 2003 article, the matter had already been investigated and dismissed.' Furthermore, he suggested that the article had not produced any factual evidence to support its claims.[15]

In the same testimony, the defendant went on the attack against those whom he saw trying to use him as a scapegoat, denying that arms reaching Sierra Leone during his presidency were coming through Liberia. Referring to the links between UK Ambassador Penfold, Sandline and its shipments of arms to Sierra Leone from the UK in violation of the UN arms embargo, Taylor said: 'The explanation of how arms are flowing into Sierra Leone is that they are coming from Liberia. They will bring in these arms and build this lie that the arms are coming from Liberia.[16]

TEN

ELECTION VICTORY AND THE TAYLOR PRESIDENCY

> The prince told them about the need for government. His government did not require taxes but order and discipline. The prince organized the land and it became a kingdom in its own right. Prosperity and peace dwelt in the land and the prince's fame spread throughout the world.
>
> Wilton Sankawulo, *The Marriage of Wisdom*

'He spoil Liberia – so let him fix it': so rationalized three-quarters of Liberia's voters on 19 July 1997, overwhelmingly electing Dakhpannah Charles McArthur Ghankay Taylor as president of their devastated country. In an election which was free and deemed by most fair, Taylor took 75.3 per cent of the votes of the 622,000 Liberians who participated. His National Patriotic Party (NPP) won 49 out of the 64 seats in the House of Representatives and also swept the Senate, gaining 21 of the 26 seats in the upper chamber. To his personal as well as the NPP's organizational credit, in the final count Taylor's party won 50 per cent or more of the votes in every single one of Liberia's counties – and over 80 per cent in some – while other candidates could only struggle to garner a few per cent in the one or two counties with which their interests or ethnic power base were associated.

The decision that Liberians took at the polls and that perhaps took even Taylor by surprise certainly stunned much of the Western media, who had spent many column inches and much broadcast air time over the previous seven years deriding him. Despite a near-ubiquitous foreign media portrayal of Taylor as a brutal warlord responsible for gruesome human rights abuses and atrocities against civilian populations, the foreign observer community on the ground found little to fault in the conduct of the July 1997 polling. Some 500 international observers from the Organization of African Unity, the Carter Center, the EU and other bodies such as the US-based Friends of Liberia, and including over 200 observers from the United Nations, found limited irregularities, and former US president Jimmy Carter, present in Liberia for the polling, described it as a 'uniformly excellent election process'.

Nevertheless it remains true that irregularities in elections, whether in Africa, the United States or elsewhere in the world, can often take place well before polling day and thus leave the monitoring process ineffective or at least vulnerable to a relative shortage of long-term (early arrival) observers. In the 1997 Liberian election, there was little time for extensive pre-campaign coercion or gerrymandering, but the candidate who had the broadest existing network in the countryside, namely Taylor, was at a definite advantage. That said, in the case of the 19 July 1997 election result, a final count for the winner of over 75 per cent left little room for dispute as to whom the Liberian people had chosen that day to run their country.

Furthermore, considering that Taylor had only been sharing office in a temporary interim government, and thus that he was technically not even the incumbent in the race, the 1997 outcome stands in stark contrast to Liberia's previous election in which Samuel Doe could only declare himself as winner of 50.9 per cent of the votes cast in 1985, and this even with all the counting behind closed doors carried out by hand-picked officials of the ruling government and no foreign observers allowed.

Taylor's nearest rival in the election, the recently returned expatriate Ellen Johnson Sirleaf and her Unity Party, came a distant second with some 10 per cent of the votes, while four other candidates polled relatively modest, single-digit percentages. Some initial accusations of vote-rigging and other irregularities were lodged by rival candidates, but these were for the most part perfunctory and each ultimately withdrew their objections and accepted the result, with some declaring support for Taylor afterwards and vowing to work together with his government.

Considering the compressed timetable for organizing the poll and the huge numbers of Liberians who were still displaced around the country or in exile outside its borders, the participation rate was good. The population of Liberia was estimated at little more than 2.5 million in 1997, and of that number there were still almost a million refugees living outside the country's borders. Nevertheless, in the weeks and months before the voting, many Liberians returned from neighbouring countries, both by road and by ship. Returnees were particularly facilitated in making the journey from Ghana, where the United Nations High Commission for Refugees (UNHCR) and its partners, such as the International Organization for Migration (IOM), conducted several repatriation operations from its refugee camps in the weeks prior to the election. Earlier requests to allow voting to be held inside refugee camps in Guinea and Côte d'Ivoire were rejected by the host governments on security grounds, but, all told and considering the devastation of Liberia's infrastructure and communications, Liberians abroad and at home made serious efforts to exercise their democratic rights on election day.

If the result on 19 July 1997 made no sense to sections of the foreign media who had unswervingly demonized the very name of Charles Taylor, and if rational outsiders could see little logic in a country choosing as president one who was so clearly a prominent orchestrator of its recent destruction, then perhaps more basic, alternative explanations have to be sought from among the ranks of the voters themselves. While detractors in Washington and elsewhere brushed off the Taylor triumph as largely achieved through 'intimidation' – although hardly any overt intimidation or serious violence was reported – the true state of mind of ordinary Liberians might better explain the voters' true motivations in electing Taylor so unequivocally in July 1997.

Family values versus fear of violence

Perhaps people simply voted for the leader who seemed strongest and most likely to return Liberia to order and stability. Certainly the 1991–94 experience had brought some stability to much of Liberia, and people in the countryside appreciated what Taylor had done for agriculture, for example, where he had shown generosity in raising wages and improving conditions. Furthermore, among ordinary Liberians, their preferred candidate had gained a reputation as a family man, and a soft touch with children, earning his nickname 'Papay'. This was a refreshing positive in an increasingly dysfunctional post-civil war society where many men lost interest in providing for the home and took off with young women, leaving their wives and families. The electorate believed that, despite his faults, Taylor was a man who would not abandon his 'Liberian family' when times got tough.

By contrast, the electorate was also not impressed by the new breed of politicians that now aspired to represent them. The melting pot of wartime had exposed people to new faces and new personalities, whether from their experiences in refugee camps or in the cauldron of Monrovia. A former regional peace facilitator who observed the scene commented:

> Given the calibre of those Taylor was competing with, voters were left with no alternative to Taylor himself. They had time to reflect on the goings on within the nouveau political class in Monrovia and could not have been impressed. The discerning electorate would not be deceived by the rhetoric of the middle-class leftists and socialist opportunists who stuffed transitional governments, whose backbone was externally composed and therefore could not provide a sense of permanent security. They desperately wanted their broken-down society reordered but were left with Taylor to depend on … Like [President Jerry] Rawlings in Ghana, at the right time Liberians could have seen off Taylor and his machinery on a level democratic playing field. Liberians, like their counterparts elsewhere in Africa, do read their situation far better than they are credited with.[1]

Thus the seeming injustice of the situation where one who bore so much responsibility for the carnage and suffering should then benefit by being handed the reins of power was not uppermost in the thoughts of a majority of the people on election day. Another factor at the front of voters' minds was the near certainty that a Taylor failure at the polls would result in a resumption of hostilities by the NPFL, and so there was more to the decision than just choosing the strongest leader – it was also a calculated risk which entailed a high element of insurance against further insecurity.

Taylor, when interviewed just prior to polling, said that in his view 'the question of a run-off doesn't arise' – referring to the stipulation that a second round of voting would take place if any candidate failed to gain an outright 50 per cent of votes cast at the first ballot. If a second round were required, many thought that anti-NPP parties could unite to defeat Taylor by supporting a single alternative candidate.

The imperfect pre-election disarmament process had left potentially disgruntled election contenders with an alternative to accepting the result peacefully. Indeed, it was widely feared that only the 'ugly' weapons – arms which had been damaged – would be handed in by the factions, and that they would keep their good guns in hiding. Charles Taylor could not have been oblivious to the fact that his NPFL had managed to store significant caches of arms out of reach of the ECOMOG forces monitoring the pre-election disarmament process, some of which the peacekeepers unearthed within weeks of polling. These discoveries of NPFL were testament not only to the flawed pre-election process but also to the unspoken threat to post-election peace which the born-again democrat Charles Taylor might pose should he not achieve his objectives at the ballot box.

Intimidation by another name perhaps, but in tarnishing the Taylor success at the polls in 1997 with this assessment, his detractors could not ignore the fact that, in addition to the NPFL, many other factions and forces had also been responsible for the trauma of the Liberian civilian population since 1990. In particular, the looting and destruction unleashed upon them by the ECOMOG force throughout the early years of their deployment must also have been a major consideration for ordinary Liberians trying to give their country a fresh start under a strong and experienced national leader. After all that had happened in the previous seven years, at the hands of outsiders as well as home-grown warlords, Liberians had decided to give Charles Taylor one more chance.

Granted the population was in a situation of extreme pain and desperation, many seeing Taylor as both Satan and saviour. They only knew that had his takeover of Monrovia in July–August 1990 succeeded, it would at least have brought an end to the starvation and the inhumanity of life in a city under siege by rebel armies on the outside, and ravaged by the rampaging remnants of its own government's army on the inside.

The president-elect, reflecting on the turn of events shortly after the elections, was not slow to remind outsiders that he had also been close to the presidency in 1990, again with much popular support, albeit of a different kind. Speaking in December 1997, Taylor said:

> It proved one thing. The Liberian people, in the final analysis, stuck to their convictions. The Liberian people decided six and a half years ago what they wanted to do and where they wanted to go. They decided that I presented the best framework for building this country, the best framework to take them into the next millennium.
>
> For some reason, however, certain individuals at home and abroad tried to indulge in king-making here with the sole objective of sidelining the decision made by Liberians six and a half years ago. It worked for some time. People were appointed presidents here, foreign countries came in with their fighting forces, they dictated policy, they subdued the Liberian people – but only for a time.
>
> In the final analysis, when the people had the opportunity to come out and speak in the last elections, they said [to the foreigners], 'you've wasted our time for six and a half years; we've always wanted this man to lead us; you did not give us the chance to express it, you came and dictated your policies, now we are speaking: that's the man we want.[2]

With memories of the Easter 1996 bloodbath still fresh in the minds of Monrovians, and for the Krahn, Mandingo and other groups in the countryside still particularly vulnerable to a return to violence, it was less a case of the man they wanted than the man they knew through bitter experience. The logic of support for Taylor can better be explained by his NPP's presence deployed effectively across the country, his perceived power as a leader as much feared as loved and the sheer exhaustion of the electorate with the prospect of continued inter-factional chaos.

Life-or-death calculation by the electorate

Taylor's view was that an indecisive result in 1997 and a return to internal struggles could have prolonged the presence of ECOMOG, whose departure a clear and uncontested election result would facilitate. However, despite his long-standing antipathy towards the regional force, by the time of the elections ECOMOG had become an altogether much better behaved occupying army than it had been in 1990-93, and without its presence the elections could almost certainly not have taken place.

But in choosing Charles Taylor as president the people at least had a better chance of bringing an end to the constant state of personal insecurity as well as the regular looting of their homes by rival armed groups. One researcher summed up their thinking, characterizing it as a logical calculation rather than an endorsement of the NPFL's past atrocities, describing Liberia's choice as: 'a reasoned ploy by the electorate to maximise the possibility of improved living conditions'.[3]

Clearly in Liberia in 1997, unlike elections in more normal circumstances, voters were not choosing from alternative philosophies of government, nor selecting one set of policies over another in choosing the future direction of their country; rather, they were deciding how best to give it and themselves a reasonable chance of physical survival for the foreseeable future.

The door to an internationally supervised poll in Liberia was opened in January 1997 when Charles Taylor agreed to participate in the disarmament process, to which other factions had already signed up. Under the process, the role of the Nigerian ECOMOG commander, Major General Victor Malu, was instrumental. Energetic, motivated and showing a determination to overcome any obstacles to the disarmament objective mandated under the August 1995 Abuja Peace process, Malu persuaded, cajoled and finally coerced each of the faction leaders in turn to comply.

By early February 1997, General Malu's strong-arming of the more reluctant armed groups appeared to be bearing fruit and an estimated 10,000 weapons and 1.4 million rounds of ammunition were handed in to the ECOMOG peacekeepers, paving the way for peaceful election preparations.

In a confirmation of the mood of the country at the time, many combatants encountered by ECOMOG declared that they were turning in their guns against their leaders' wishes, because they were tired of the war and wanted to go home to what was left of their villages and families. The sentiment of the fighters was mirrored by the feelings of the civilian population, who were happy to risk anything for peace.

Next, the ECOWAS 'Committee of Nine', consisting of representatives from Nigeria, Niger, Mali, Côte d'Ivoire, Sierra Leone, Guinea, Ghana, Burkina Faso and Gambia, dispatched Nigerian minister of foreign affairs Tom Ikimi to Monrovia for discussions with Liberian head of state Ruth Perry, the ECOWAS-appointed chairwoman of Liberia's Council of State since September 1996, to agree on further preliminary measures to be taken to lay the ground for elections.

They reached an accord providing that any current members of the power-sharing Executive State Council must resign and nominate non-candidate substitutes if they intended to run in the forthcoming elections. Accordingly Charles Taylor promptly resigned from the State Council, appointing Victoria Reffel to take his place as representative of the National Patriotic Party, the newly formed political wing of the NPFL. His deputies appointed and formalities for his candidacy completed, Taylor immediately left for Taiwan on an election fundraising trip.

As the pre-campaign manoeuvring began, in opposition to Taylor's NPFL there was aligned a potentially powerful Krahn coalition composed of George Boley's LPC, now reconstituted as the National Democratic Party of Liberia (NDPL), Roosevelt Johnson's ULIMO-J and former vice president Harry Moniba's New Democratic Party. The popular former foreign minister Boimah Fahnbulleh also declared himself a candidate. From the non-Krahn side of the opposition was Alhaji Kromah's All Liberian Coalition Party. The pro-foreign business interests and formerly pro-Taylor True Whig Party remained popular in Monrovia and outlying suburban areas, together with the Liberia Action Party (the party of the 1985 election winner Jackson Doe) and the Unity Party. These groups formed the main anti-NPP contenders in the north and west of the country.

In terms of campaign tactics, resources deployed and incentives offered to voters, there were clear differences between candidates and across areas. Charles Taylor soon proved himself savvier, better organized and more powerful than his opponents. With little distribution of newspapers and no television to speak of outside Monrovia, radio stations were the primary means through which most Liberians gained their information. The two largest stations available were Radio Liberia International and Taylor's own music and news station, KISS-FM. The NPFL broadcasting enterprise had its origins in 1990, when its rebels overran the Firestone plantation outside Monrovia and were able to convert its looted communications equipment to begin radio broadcasting operations.[4]

Mastering the airwaves

As KISS-FM was the only option in many areas, and in others the only station that continued to broadcast throughout the day and night, Taylor's NPP effectively controlled Liberia's airwaves, despite the existence of other local stations and valiant efforts from the international community to redress the imbalance. The Swiss-based organization Radio Hirondelle sponsored the establishment of Star Radio, which was headed by a former chief of the BBC Africa Service, George Bennett. Intended to be active during the election campaign, after delays in its launch, it ultimately only became operational in July 1997, just days before voting began. Its presence therefore had little effect on the unlevel pre-election broadcasting playing field.

Furthermore, Taylor's financial resources also proved decisive, allowing him to disburse largesse across the country prior to polling. Indeed rivals criticized him for overspending the maximum $3.5 million per candidate permitted in the campaign. Lively rallies, at which bags of rice were distributed liberally to voters by NPP activists, helped earn favour in the rural areas; while bigger-ticket stunts such as chartering a helicopter to take the national football team to Togo to play in a match just at election time – at a reported cost of $23,000 – certainly caught the attention of many voters as well as raising the eyebrows of rivals and observers.[5]

Charles Taylor also disbursed funding through a private 'charity' which he had founded for war victims and the resettlement of displaced people, raising outside funds to support its pre-election handout. Contributions came in from Taylor's overseas business backers associated with the Liberian Maritime Board, which operated in both Europe and the USA, with funds being credited directly to the charity.[6]

The Firestone rubber plantation had also been 'protected' by the NPFL at a cost during the years of fighting, and by 1997 this protection force was transformed into an NPFL-affiliated security company, providing handsome revenues to the party machine. In the Executive State Council Taylor also held some of the more financially interesting ministries, allocated to the NPFL at the time of the 1994 Akosombo accords and confirmed at Abuja. These included defence, information and maritime affairs, each of which, while unable to pay its civil servants on time, was nevertheless a source of bribes or commissions which could be extracted from foreigners or those able to pay for facilitation of their needs.[7]

By the time of the official start of the election campaign on 16 June there were more realignments among the parties, which for some seemed to offer a chance of success for an anti-Taylor candidate. The Krahn Coalition broke up by May 1997, which provided an opening for expatriate Ellen Johnson Sirleaf to return to the scene with a chance of victory. Viewed as being largely untarnished by wartime involvements, she was favoured by the United States and the international community, with whom she had served as chief administrator of the United Nations Development Programme and senior loans officer at the World Bank. Sirleaf was able to attract a variety of natural supporters when she returned to Monrovia to launch her campaign.

Originally a founder member of the LAP, Sirleaf nevertheless switched allegiances and stood as the candidate of the Unity Party (UP), gaining the support of the True Whig Party, the Liberia Unification Party, the Liberian People's Party of Togba-Nah Tipoteh and other groupings. She also had the natural support of her home base of Lofa and Montserrado counties, as well as of the professional and business classes in Monrovia. The latter realized the importance of external relations and the return of Liberia to international creditworthiness. Clearly, in order to attract the necessary resources to restart its devastated economy, Liberia would need capable financial management; Sirleaf had also worked as an executive with Citibank, another experience seen by outward-looking Liberians as in her favour.

Ellen Johnson Sirleaf stood on a platform of recovery, social development and economic advancement, an ambitious programme at the time for Liberia and in stark in contrast to that of all of her rivals, most of whom stood on what were in reality regional, ethnic or military-based allegiances.

Sirleaf's platform was based on a Five-Point Plan, including a revival and strengthening of the regional association with neighbours Guinea and Sierra Leone. However, in the context of starving, war-weary Liberia, such proposals demonstrated Sirleaf's greater comfort with promoting sophisticated solutions and moving in the corridors of international development organizations than grappling with the challenge of how to resuscitate the moribund torso that was Liberia's economy and society in 1997.

In contrast to the restricted, parochial appeal of most candidates, Charles Taylor was the only contender to assemble a broad power base with an effective reach into nearly all of Liberia. Taylor derided the Sirleaf candidacy, dismissing her before the electorate as inexperienced and unfamiliar with the reality on the ground after such a long absence overseas. He also branded her as the proxy candidate of the

United States and Nigeria, both by now established in the minds of many Liberians as untrustworthy and potentially destructive forces with their own agendas.

Another asset for Taylor came through developments in his personal life. Taylor got married again, this time to Jewel Howard, an economist, in January 1997, in a lavish Monrovia ceremony, which helped cement Taylor's status as presidential favourite while also giving him a popular and influential ally for the campaign.

As the campaign got under way, Taylor's supporters harassed and attacked Sirleaf's UP convoys as they tried to travel across the countryside to reach voters, making the attempts of her already poorly resourced campaign at getting a national hearing all the harder. Taylor was acutely aware of the advantage he held in organization – not only in his traditional heartland of Bong and Nimba counties, but elsewhere in the country where other candidates could not mobilize their people quickly enough to wage a truly national campaign, which Taylor's NPP was quite clearly able to do.

The election was held in July in the middle of Liberia's rainy season. There was difficulty in securing the preliminary arrangements for polling, and the Independent Electoral Commission (IECOM), which was itself under-resourced, had already postponed voting from May to July to allow more time for preparations. Registration of the 1.2 million eligible voters began in late June and lasted for a period of ten days. The IECOM asked for more time for the 1,700 polling stations to be made operational throughout the country, but the NPP lobbied ECOWAS to maintain the schedule. More time for the IECOM also meant more time for the NPP's rivals to organize and get their message out, and Taylor pressed for no further delays.

Meanwhile, as a result of his earlier trip to Taiwan, in exchange for Liberia's future vote in favour of Taiwan's recognition at the UN, among other support, he secured a donation of $1 million from the government in Taipei to help the IECOM in its set-up efforts. This pre-election diplomatic gambit showed once again that Taylor could marshal resources from an array of unlikely international allies, helping him outflank the opposition candidates in their battle for more preparation time. In addition to financial support, he also received an honorary doctorate from his Taiwanese hosts, adding another title to his collection.

Early Taylor administration

Whether with hopeful anticipation or with justifiable trepidation, the people of Liberia waited for their new leader's first steps in government after taking office. The UN and ECOMOG, now committed to stepping aside from Liberian politics to allow the country's elected president to take over, hoped it had not just overseen the legitimization of dictatorship through the ballot box and the granting of a mandate for a renewed round of destruction. But for the most part the international community was pleased that Liberia had undergone peaceful elections with a decisive outcome, and that it had been spared the need for yet another costly and ugly intervention to keep the disgruntled, power-greedy factions from returning to use of the barrel of the gun to express their dissent.

With his overwhelming margin of victory, Taylor could afford to be magnanimous to his defeated opponents, as well as to feel secure in offering a certain number of cabinet posts to leaders of rival political parties. Indeed, Liberia's new president seemed to go out of his way to bring the leading members of all the main contesting factions into his new government, under the banner of what he called 'National Reconciliation'.

Monie Captan became minister of foreign affairs, while former ULIMO-J head Roosevelt Johnson was brought into the government as rural development minister; representatives of George Boley's predominantly Krahn Liberia Peace Council, as well as François Massaquoi of the Lofa Defence Council, were also given appointments. Taylor's disaffected former defence spokesman, Tom Woewiyu, minister of labour in the transitional administration, was also kept on in his post. The very fact that Woewiyu was asked back to join Taylor's government suggested that after all he perhaps accorded a measure of respect to his former deputy's 1994 decision to break ranks.

While awaiting the verdict of the Special Court in the Hague in 2011, the former president recalled the earlier falling out with Woewiyu over the defence minister's accusations that Taylor was needlessly prolonging the war, saying:

> I disagree with him but that is his right ... Liberia is bigger than Woewiyu and me. He had something to contribute to the building of Liberia and I brought him back, which shows that I respect differences of opinion. For me, it's never been personal. After my election, I brought former ULIMO-J and ULIMO-K, LPC and opposition figures, military and civilians, into the government. Like I said, it's about Liberia. It's not personal; I respect the opinions and criticisms of others.[8]

In the first weeks folllowing his election, Taylor consistently preached reconciliation and – if cabinet appointments alone were the measure – he practised inclusivity. At the same time, what passed for inclusivity could have been aimed at disabling any potential political opposition by inviting his main rivals into the government. When charged with this accusation, Taylor rebutted with the explanation:

> What we have to do, coming out of a war, is not to go witch-hunting. What we are trying to do is not to win them over to our party. We are trying to win them over in terms of their understanding that in order to build this country, a small country like Liberia, very rich in natural resources, we don't need to be at each other's throats. ... And I think the opposition leaders also have an interest in this. They must understand that, the point here, in Liberia under our government, is that the opposition is not the enemy.[9]

Taylor toured the countryside with foreign ambassadors, and alongside respected national figures like former interim government president Amos Sawyer and his successor Professor David Kpormakor, claiming that he was doing things differently, promising true reconciliation. In the president's words, 'This has to be the spirit in Africa. In Liberia, we will have to set the examples.'

Faltering steps on the path to respectability

These were ambitious words, and at the same time ominous ones. Not all of Taylor's electoral rivals accepted the invitation to join him in government. Probably the biggest disappointment was the persistent refusal of his defeated rival Ellen Johnson Sirleaf to accept the top financial job in the NPFL administration. Monrovia badly needed to repair relations with Washington and the IMF, to have the wartime sanctions on Liberia lifted and to restore the country's creditworthiness, and no one was better placed than Sirleaf to achieve this goal, were she to take up the post of Liberian minister of finance.

However, Sirleaf refused all overtures aimed at winning her support, just as many of her backers in Washington DC licked their wounds at the abject failure of their 'preferred' candidate to make a significant showing at the polls. Sirleaf, despite having originally supported the NPFL, funded Taylor in 1990 and, it is alleged, showed interest in the leadership of the rebel movement early in the war, now spurned invitations to join the new government.

One of Ellen Johnson Sirleaf's childhood friends and 1997 election backers was Rachel Diggs, whom Taylor brought in as his ambassador to Washington DC on a spur-of-the-moment appointment made during her August 1997 visit to Monrovia for the inauguration. At the time she was working for the World Bank, having left Liberia in the 1980s. Diggs originally saw Taylor as an instigator of the country's troubles, but after meeting him was impressed by his presidential aura as well as his religious devotion – particularly the fact that while fighting in the bush he had found time to 'train a Mormon tabernacle choir', according to Diggs.

Apart from restoring relations with Washington DC and working to end sanctions, one of the new ambassador's tasks was to woo her childhood friend Sirleaf and persuade her to join the cabinet in Monrovia. But Diggs's several approaches over the coming year were 'turned down at every stage'. 'It was a dog's job', recalls Diggs, referring to her position representing Liberia in the one country that could make or break the new administration, a country which for now showed few signs of doing anything more than tolerating its existence.[10]

At home, upon entering office, Liberia's new president ordered a number of 'cleansing' measures that may have appeared symbolic on the temporal level, but in superstitious, spiritual, shell-shocked Liberia, were for many people enormously significant in a deeper sense. One such act was the removal of the 'Statue of the Unknown Soldier' from the small triangle of ground just outside the walls of the Executive Mansion and between the University of Liberia campus and the Capitol building. Erected by President Doe in the 1980s it was variously rumoured to have President Tolbert's remains buried beneath it, or to have had a child buried alive under it as a sacrifice, or, more politically – the version that Taylor himself preferred – to have been deeply symbolic to Doe, serving as a monument to his power, and an encapsulation of his 'Krahn nation'. For whichever reason, the ruins of the statue, already largely destroyed in 1996, were removed in Taylor's first year in office and replaced with a flower border.

The Executive Mansion itself underwent ritual purification by a large group of Christian clergymen, drafted in by Taylor to undertake a week of praying and fasting on every floor, as part of the process of cleansing the building. In a further manifestation of the chief executive's superstition, a total of seventy ministers and priests from a variety of denominations were invited; they were then divided into groups of seven to carry out their work of spiritually consecrating the mansion.

More verifiably, there was a spate of politically motivated murders in Taylor's first year in office, characterized either as a purging of rivals or as revenge killings, as the incoming power elite violently jostled its way into government.[11] Whatever the basis in truth of the countless other rumours that circulated throughout the capital at the time of the consecration, the process sent one message quite clearly to the Liberian people: the element of juju, so integral a feature of the fighting the country had endured over the previous eight years, was still alive and well; and the new president was as obsessive in his behaviour and as superstitious in his beliefs as his immediate predecessor, whose loathsome legacy was still so painfully carved in the consciousness of the citizens who survived him.

Another one-time rival of Taylor's and former deputy speaker of the transitional parliament, Sam Dokie, did not succeed in his candidacy for a senate seat in Nimba County, but nevertheless pledged support for Taylor after the election. However, on 28 November when travelling to a family wedding in Saniquellie, Dokie was detained by police officers on the orders of Taylor's security chief Benjamin Yeaten and subsequently driven back towards Monrovia with his wife and other family members. Their charred tortured bodies were discovered in the countryside two days later. While Taylor denied any knowledge and ordered an investigation, the atrocity represented the poorest of starts for his post-election attempts at repairing a tarnished human rights reputation.[12]

After a year in office, in August 1998 Charles Taylor took the democratic initiative once again, and convened a three-week 'National Conference on Liberia's Future', in Monrovia. He invited political opponents, regional heads of state, representatives of civil society both at home and in exile, and prominent Liberians from abroad. His US supporters were also present, including Jesse Jackson and the president's one time US legal counsel, Ramsey Clark. Taking a page out of his electioneering handbook of the previous year, T-shirts were printed up and distributed around the capital's marketplaces, emblazoned with the dove of peace and the words 'Sweet Liberia' to reinforce the message of reconciliation.

Counting the cost, forgetting the guilty

Nigeria's General Sani Abacha attended Charles Taylor's inauguration, consolidating his country's renewed friendly relations with Monrovia after many years of confrontation with Taylor under his predecessor Ibrahim Babangida. After the polling, Abacha called on all Liberians to 'accept the verdict of the people'. Nigeria was particularly pleased to be able to extract itself in an orderly fashion from its lead role in the ECOMOG military intervention, with successful election supervision to its credit after the controversy it had provoked and the tarnished reputation it had earned in the early years of the civil war. The performance that had earned the rapacious earlier peacekeepers of the ECOMOG force their Liberian nickname 'Every Car Or Moving Object Gone' was a national embarrassment which President Sani Abacha, by then serving chair of ECOWAS, was eager to dispel.

In financial terms, the intervention had been costly too. Nigeria spent an estimated $1 billion on its contribution to the ECOMOG forces over seven years of fighting, although estimates of what it had truly spent on the operations varied wildly. The USA gave ECOMOG some $31 million for its operations, but with large-scale diversion of funds and creative accounting it is difficult to know how much of the national or foreign contribution to the effort had finished up in private accounts and how much went to peacekeeping in Liberia. As early as 1995 the Nigerian government claimed that it had already spent $4 billion on the operation, which led one researcher to calculate that this would have meant it had been spending $80,000 per year for each one of the 10,000 or so soldiers it had deployed to Liberia.[13]

As for the United Nations, in September 1997 its representative in Monrovia dealt a cruel blow to Liberians hoping for some form of justice or accountability for the worst of its country's tormentors of the past seven years: its outgoing ambassador, the Namibian Tuliameni Kalomoh, revealed that the UN would now not pursue previously announced plans to investigate specific war crimes and atrocities against civilians. It was the beginning of the official outside acceptance of Liberia's post-war culture of impunity that dogged future attempts at achieving reconciliation and the enforcement of justice for years to come.

Indeed, avoiding accountability also seemed to be the mantra of the incoming Taylor administration: it quickly became clear that his government did not intend – perhaps not surprisingly – to hold anyone responsible for the officially estimated 150,000 deaths and – even less surprisingly – the wholesale looting of the country's resources of iron ore, gold, diamonds, rubber and timber over the preceding seven years. On Charles Taylor's inauguration day, rather than remembering their nation's glorious history and origins, Liberians were effectively being called upon to cultivate their collective amnesia and let the new government move ahead with its business.

Business was one thing that Liberia's new head of state certainly knew something about; just as he had worked his commercial connections in the region, in Europe, the Middle East and in the United States during wartime, he was now able to generate more profitable opportunities for Liberia and for himself once in office.

PRESIDENT TAYLOR TASTES A GLASS OF MÉDOC WITH WIFE JEWEL, IN PAUILLAC, NEAR BORDEAUX, 30 SEPTEMBER 1998

The lucrative Liberian Maritime Agency, which had been run by a United States company, International Registries Inc. (IRI), with over 3,000 ships internationally using its flag of convenience registration, previously accounted for around $24 million annually – as much as half of all of the Liberian government's official revenues. After Taylor was elected, the agency was transformed into the Liberian International Ship and Corporate Registry (LISCR), and run by US associates of the Liberian president, chief among whom was his Washington political fixer and legal counsel, Lester Hyman, who later became the Registry's chairman. Crucially the change meant that the revenues of the LISCR now began to go to non-government as well as government bank accounts, allowing Taylor the option of diverting the LISCR's revenues to purposes of his own choosing.

Uphill struggle to repair US relations

In Washington DC, however, the official position was not to forget, let alone to forgive. Charles Taylor, although indisputably now a democratically elected leader of a country with whom the USA had a long if no longer special relationship, was still a man with a record in America. Furthermore, during the climax of the Cold War when Ronald Reagan was ordering the bombing of Tripoli in retaliation for Libya's complicity in terrorist attacks against civilian airlines, Charles Taylor had been accepting Muammar Gaddafi's hospitality and his fledgling NPFL had received training in Libya.

Also counting against Taylor in the eyes of US officialdom was the fact that anglophone influence in West Africa had been outflanked if not usurped by a francophone-backed insurgent. Paris welcomed Taylor, who visited France together with First Lady Jewel in the first year after he took office. Both Côte d'Ivoire, still France's most important outpost in Africa, and Burkina Faso, Taylor's reliable rear base for much of the war, were French-speaking countries. Taylor had fomented revolt in Sierra Leone, irritated the authorities in Ghana and waged war against Nigerian forces to gain power in Monrovia, thus losing favour with three more English-speaking allies of the USA.

Nevertheless, Taylor was still able to rely on the support of influential friends in the USA, including the sympathy of ex-president Jimmy Carter. After giving his blessing to the Liberian elections in 1997, Carter lobbied for the incoming Taylor administration to be given a chance to rebuild Liberia. But US policy had changed and Jimmy Carter's influence was no longer the critical factor in securing US support.

As a diplomatic strategist, Taylor played his cards poorly in the Clinton and Bush era. He misread the cues on more than one occasion. While he continued to expect support from America when it was more the CIA than the White House that had an interest in his success, he also made enemies closer to home just as the USA was encouraging African leaders to deal with their region's problems themselves. Just as William Tolbert had paid the price for cultivating

African allies at the expense of allegiance to Washington, so Taylor failed to cultivate regional allies whilst still believing in a United States that no longer believed in him.

Elsewhere, as a result of Taylor's opportunistic embrace of Taiwan at the time of the election campaign, Beijing promptly refused to recognize his new government, guaranteeing a powerful adversary in any potential future dealings at the UN. At the other end of the spectrum, France was the first non-African country to congratulate Charles Taylor on his victory, underlining the continuing divergence in sentiments regarding the election result between Paris and Washington.

Liberian casualties had never been a motivating factor in US policy towards Liberia; nor had the lack of democracy historically been an obstacle to supporting its leaders. So when Taylor finally did triumph legitimately at the ballot box it was a bittersweet paradox that his arrival in the Executive Mansion was not taken as the signal for a time of reconciliation with Washington and a beginning of national reconstruction with US financial support. Rather, it was greeted with a sense of official disapproval of his presidency and a mood of tacit opposition to his regime.

For the president of Liberia, it was the second act in the tragedy of betrayal that characterized relations between Taylor and the United States. Left in limbo seven years before at the gates of Monrovia and now denied the material support that could give Liberia a fresh start, Charles Taylor's worst nightmare was unfolding. There was to be no Marshall Plan for devastated Liberia; nor even the lengthy breathing space that Ghana's Jerry Rawlings, another West African coup-maker turned democrat, had been allowed by the international community after his violent takeover in Accra in 1981.

Cash-strapped and cut off from aid

Now in office as a legitimately elected government, the Taylor administration had to contend with the same frustrating realities of interacting with the international community that its predecessor transitional governments had experienced. With national debts approaching $3 billion and an official national budget of only $41 million in its first year, the numbers simply did not add up. In the conventional sense of economic accounting, Liberia could not pay its way in the world, and its only chance was to seek financial help from the outside until it could get back on its feet. With the United States showing resistance, especially with the continuing shadow of Taylor's involvement in the Sierra Leone conflict, in the short term there were few prospects of kick-starting the economy back into financial health.

Borrowing from the IMF was out of the question in the meantime, with unpaid interest and arrears of the previous governments' debts still hanging over the country, and negotiations for aid with international institutions like the World Bank, especially without the backing of insiders like Ellen Johnson Sirleaf, would be lengthy and frustrating.

President Taylor was hemmed into a financial corner. The business methods that had proved so effective for him as a commodities and arms dealer when out of government seemed an increasingly attractive, if indeed perhaps the only, option. Some of the NPFL's former business partners that he could rely on represented a far more attractive short-term source of cash for his and his country's needs.

Unfortunately, some of these partners were still involved, directly or indirectly, in the war in Sierra Leone; and included in the commodities that they dealt with were diamonds for export to the international market. Meanwhile, on the import side, arms were among the goods that the Taylor government had access to through former connections.

One factor that did not change while Charles Taylor was in office was his aptitude for running government business and personal business simultaneously, despite the new constraints of having a government administration and a country at peace to impose checks and balances on his activities. Often, just as in his days in Gbarnga, government business would help finance personal deals – that is, in those cases where it was possible to tell which was which.

It was alleged by foreign observers who dealt with his government that Taylor operated a 'dual fiscal system' with an official set of books for the Liberian government and another set for his personal dealings. The latter reportedly included cuts he was able to take on government monopolies in timber, gold and diamond mining, as well as commissions taken on the exclusive control of commodity import businesses such as rice. One diplomat tracking the presidential stake in Liberia's economy estimated it as 'possibly equal' in size to the actual national budget.[14]

Perhaps in some ways the Dakhpannah Dr Charles Ghankay Taylor was happy after all that he didn't have an international economist on his team to supervise his government's finances, lest she rein in his massive off-the-books private business activities. Ellen Johnson Sirleaf, although she received a drubbing in the July 1997 elections and had spurned an offer to join Taylor in government, nevertheless kept a close eye on the goings-on in Monrovia and didn't much like what she saw. One of the few to criticize Liberia's president openly, she summed up his administration, then one year old, succinctly as characterized by 'corruption, misappropriation, ostentation, oversized security and self-aggrandizement', accusing the president of wanting to 'rape the state then give it out, to create a patronage state'.[15]

Defence and domestic order: the ATU and the SSS

In addition to filling cabinet posts, in his early months in office President Taylor built up two other agencies which helped to satisfy his appetite for heavy security in the country. The first was a special paramilitary detail called the ATU, the 'Anti Terrorist Unit', which was created and commanded by Charles McArthur Taylor Jr – young Chuckie Taylor had now been given a major job in his father's first administration. The ATU was a completely new, highly personalized force, not reporting to the Ministry of Defence nor to any other government department, but only to its commander and the president himself. Chuckie Taylor, in his status as an American citizen and the president's son, used and abused his position as its commander with near impunity.

Nevertheless, the ATU was one of the few fighting units which had recognizable uniforms and whose enlisted men received regular pay. The agency was not answerable to a government ministry, nor provided for in any part of the Liberian national budget. Made up of the more experienced fighters from the NPFL, the ATU comprised Burkinabes and Sierra Leoneans as well as Liberians, those rebel war camp followers who had become 'unemployed' following the winding down of hostilities in Liberia's western neighbour.

The other force, the Special Security Services (SSS), was the president's personal security force and charged with guarding access to the Executive Mansion, the airport and other key installations, and protecting senior diplomats and VIPs. Led by Benjamin Yeaten, the SSS also carried out surveillance duties and harassed journalists deemed to be overstepping the mark in their prying, or suspected of writing anti-government articles. Its composition and the behaviour of its rank and file were not dissimilar to that of the ATU, although rather than wearing standard security officer uniforms, they were more often recognizable by their reflector sunglasses and Kevlar trench coats.

In the wake of the scandalous assassination of Sam Dokie and his family in November 1997, no one doubted the lethality of Yeaten's SSS henchmen. In town, the officers in the SSS were known for showing hostility to the public when carrying out their responsibilities, throwing their weight around while escorting and protecting the president, as well as cajoling citizens for bribes and generally bullying the populace. In an incident widely reported by expatriates during Charles Taylor's fiftieth birthday celebrations in 1998, SSS men guarding the Executive Mansion at one stage shoved their way through the invitees from the diplomatic corps to get to the food tables and manhandled guests who were attending the event.[16]

To ordinary Monrovians, the Special Security Service was at its most visible during President Taylor's routine daily mid-morning drive from his Congotown residence to the Executive Mansion. His motorcade typically consisted of some twenty vehicles, with the presidential Mercedes-Benzes flanked by a squad of trucks and Land-Rovers, filled with SSS men sporting RPGs, assault rifles and other heavy weapons.

While the SSS and ATU received off-budget funding, paid for by the president's personal funds, the AFL, the country's official army, was downgraded in its importance during peacetime.

Chuckie Taylor created the ATU's training base at Gbatala, just outside Gbarnga, in Bong County, near Charles Taylor's former wartime headquarters, which was also reported to be where the RUF commanders were based and received training. At one point in mid-2000, according to a Sierra Leone Police Special Branch Intelligence Report dated 5 June 2000, there were a total of 4,000 fighters undergoing training at the Gbatala camp.[17]

Charles Taylor Jr, Liberia's wayward apprentice

Chuckie grew up in Florida with his mother Burnice, who remarried after Taylor left for Liberia in the 1980s. Charles Junior was a fairly normal African-American teenager, somewhat on the quiet side, attending school, enjoying hip hop and rap music and showing no particular knowledge of, or interest in, Africa. That was until his father called and invited the family to Gbarnga in 1991 during the Greater Liberia days. After that trip, while Burnice Emmanuel had no interest in staying in Liberia, Chuckie, the impressionable teenager, was excited and apparently transformed by the atmosphere of warfare going on all around him and the evident superpower status of his father.

Returning to the USA, Chuckie showed rapid signs of personality change after his Liberia experience, and he started to get into trouble. While still only 16, he began drinking, smoking pot and having run-ins with the police, getting arrested for obstruction of justice and then for mugging a fellow teenager at gunpoint. He developed anger and a meanness which worried his girlfriend and his mother, who soon got fed up with her wayward son.

After Chuckie turned 17, Burnice called Charles senior in Liberia and said: 'I've had him until he's 17 ... now it's your turn.' Chuckie went back to Liberia just as his father was coming to power in Monrovia. When he left the United States for Liberia in the mid-1990s, Chuckie was still awaiting trial for assault charges and so he became a fugitive from US justice, just like his father.

Chuckie tried his hand at the timber business in the pre-election economy but showed little aptitude. Then, after his father's election, still in his early twenties, he got the chance to 'go into security'. With an insurrection starting up in the north west of Liberia after 1999, there would be plenty of security work for Chuckie Taylor to do. That was how the mean, vicious youth with the gangster swagger, Kevlar jacket and corn-row hairstyle, also the president's son, got the job as head of the Anti Terrorist Unit.[18]

In Liberia the ATU soon gained a reputation for lawlessness and brutality, and in later years was increasingly implicated in looting and theft, as well as far worse offences on a number of occasions. The unit's men spent a lot of their time, both in the capital and in the countryside, seeking out rebels and interrogating them. Its methods included torture, often supervised and sometimes carried out by Chuckie Taylor himself. One favourite method employed by the ATU bullies in Monrovia was to tie their prey to a mattress as they were being beaten, to lessen evidence of external bruising – so that all their injuries would be internal and less easy to identify when the victim arrived at the hospital. Chuckie also employed the so called 'tabay' torture on his victims, tying their elbows together tightly behind their backs with wire until bones broke and blood oozed out from the arms.

As commander of the ATU, Chuckie ordered or committed numerous acts of torture and murder not only against civilians but on occasion against his own staff. One such unfortunate, Lieutenant Isaac Gono, was employed by Chuckie Taylor as a driver. He had gone for over a year without pay, reportedly because Chuckie kept the salary money allocated to him by his father for staff payments. Gono wrote a letter begging the ATU chief for some compensation from his superiors, which angered Taylor Jr.

On 18 September 2002 Gono was driving in town and hit a dog, splashing the animal's blood over the front of Taylor's car. When

Chuckie saw the mess he ordered his men to beat Gono severely as a disciplinary measure. Gono received a heavy punishment, after which he was taken to the John F. Kennedy Hospital, where shortly afterwards he died. As a result of the incident, two soldiers were sent for court martial. The Ministry of Defence initially denied that Taylor Jr had been involved. But he had been, and President Taylor was furious with the senseless death of an ATU member at the hands of his own son. He sent $16,000 to the family of the deceased and soon afterwards removed Chuckie from his position at the head of the ATU.

On 9 January 2009, Chuckie Taylor was sentenced by a Florida court to ninety-seven years in prison for torture and conspiracy to commit torture, under a 1994 federal law allowing US citizens to be tried and convicted for acts of torture committed overseas.

Squandering the democratic opportunity

For a country struggling to emerge from two decades of conflict and insecurity, heavily dependent on political support and funding from abroad, the Taylor administration had got off to a poor start. The new president's continued resort to unofficial security arrangements with a strong degree of personal rather than legislative control was sending the wrong signals externally and doing little to improve either the confidence or the welfare of the population internally.

Taylor's attempts at bringing former rivals into government with him were ultimately unsuccessful, and his choices of deputy soon brought more discredit than approval from the international community. Old business methods from the wartime dealing days persisted, and Liberia's finances became closely intermingled with those of Charles Taylor. In Sierra Leone, where violence and chaos persisted, there was suspicion of continued Liberian official involvement, despite declarations and assurances from Monrovia.

Charles Taylor only had a brief window of time to win back the favour of Washington DC and a White House that viewed his election to the presidency with scepticism from the outset. When he began to flounder, the USA, in concert with Taylor's enemies-in-waiting, would turn actively against him, and from that moment on the international community became Taylor's adversary, not his partner, in the recovery and reconstruction of Liberia.

The former president's view of his record and experiences in office were markedly different. While awaiting verdict in his Special Court for Sierra Leone trial, Taylor disagreed that there had been any turning point in relations with the USA, saying he felt that there had been no particular moment when things had gone 'from good to bad'. He said:

> My government never received any cooperation from the US government after my election as president. ... Liberia needs to stop waiting for the United States and others to act as Santa Claus bringing Christmas gifts. Either we are free and sovereign or we should ask to be the 51st state of the US...
>
> My government was never given a chance. We would have made a difference and Liberians, or may I say a majority of Liberians still recognize my contribution and that's a fact.

In support of his contention that his government stood unaided by the US, Taylor pointed to the example of the 1997 election itself and what he perceived as US meddling. 'There was nothing to lose in terms of favour', he stated. 'The US funded Ellen Johnson Sirleaf against me and she won less than 10 per cent of the votes.'

When asked whether an opportunity to mend US–Liberian relations had been lost with his democratic triumph and whether a better chosen cabinet might have made a difference, Taylor was unmoved. 'No, there was no squandered opportunity. My cabinet was a Liberian well-qualified cabinet and acted in Liberia's best interests. It is and never should be the business of Washington to choose the ministers of any nation!'[19]

PART FOUR

FALLOUT FROM A REVOLUTION

ELEVEN

A GOVERNMENT EMBATTLED

When we consider the record of ... the races on the other side of the Atlantic, who have frequently been prey to revolutionary disorder, there can be no doubt that the regularity with which our public affairs have been conducted has favourably impressed the outside world.

> Arthur Barclay, president of Liberia,
> inaugural address, January 1904

Intransigence over Sierra Leone

While the domestic reconciliation and government inclusivity agenda proceeded at home, abroad the Taylor administration still had a lot of work to do to repair its image and address the criticisms of its opponents over human rights abuses and its involvement in the continuing Sierra Leone conflict.

In the meantime, now dealing with a democratically elected president, the international community tried to rein in Taylor's apparent continued international military participation in his western neighbour's war, first by persuasion and then by coercion. The persuasion effort attempted by the US government was to prove an ill-judged exercise in diplomatic subcontracting. Still wary of direct involvement but eager to play a part in bringing about peace, the Clinton administration passed responsibility for dealing with Charles Taylor and Foday Sankoh to Jesse Jackson and Donald Payne, chairman of the Congressional Black Caucus, to spearhead US diplomacy in the Mano River Union. President Clinton and Secretary of State Madeleine Albright consulted with Jackson and entrusted him with a high-level mission to the region.

In February 1998, Jackson arrived in Monrovia in the capacity of US Special Envoy to the region and was warmly received by Charles Taylor and his government. Facilitating the visit was a long-standing Liberian–American connection named Romeo Horton, whom Jackson had helped get out of prison in Liberia during the rule of Samuel Doe. Now flown over from the USA and co-opted by Taylor to brief him on Jesse Jackson and be present at the Robertsfield Airport tarmac reception, the Horton link ensured that President Taylor was well prepared, and the visit got off to a smooth start. Romeo Horton was later appointed as head of Liberia's Presidential Banking Commission, as a reward for his good offices.

With Horton's help, Jackson and Taylor developed a good rapport, and right after the Clinton visit to Africa Taylor was able to leverage the relationship considerably to the advantage of his ongoing public relations efforts in the United States. Jackson organized a 'reconciliation' conference in Chicago for Taylor in April 1998, billed as an event for all Liberians living in America to come together with their new government to meet, unite and bury their differences. But as the arrangements became public, it became clear that the event would be a very one-sided affair with Taylor government speakers dominating the podium. Opposition leaders were initially not invited, but after protests by prominent US-based anti-Taylor Liberians, and a phone call to the organizers from the State Department, a token presence of opponents was included.

Nevertheless, the event had the feel of a pro-Taylor rally, and when Jesse Jackson addressed the audience his contributions came across as laden with praise for the Taylor administration. 'It's morning time in Liberia. It's morning time', Jackson cooed. Later, the voice of Taylor himself boomed across the huge conference centre as his image was beamed across a wide screen by teleconference link and his wife Jewel Howard-Taylor graced the gathering of the Taylor faithful.

Opposition speakers were cut short, despite rapturous applause for the suggestion from a representative of the New York-based Coalition of Progressive Liberians in the Americas (COPLA) that a war crimes trial for Liberia be organized. Harry Greaves, who together with Ellen Johnson Sirleaf co-founded the Liberia Action Party, said of the event that the 'general perception was ... that Jackson was a paid lobbyist for Charles Taylor'.[1]

After the return to bloodshed in Sierra Leone in 1999, the USA was less concerned about lending support to Liberia's reconstruction and more interested in removing the apparent Charles Taylor impetus behind its neighbour's never-ending civil war. The continued connection between Taylor's involvement with the RUF, the illegal export of diamonds from Sierra Leone's mines, and the shipment of weapons to the RUF rebel fighters was increasingly at the top of Washington's agenda in the region, and US diplomacy soon turned to curtailing the assumed Liberian government role in the situation.

In his 17 July visit to the Executive Mansion in Monrovia, US Undersecretary of State Thomas Pickering gave a blunt ultimatum to the Liberian government, threatening Taylor with 'severe consequences' if his actions in Sierra Leone were not brought to a halt. But President Taylor rejected the call, declaring in a national radio address the same week: 'We refuse to accept, and reject efforts on the part of any nation to muffle this country, engage in arm-twisting without facts in an attempt to subdue this nation.' Shortly afterwards, the Clinton administration responded by imposing a travel ban on Taylor, his family and his closest aides.

A week later, in conformity with the recently imposed UN Security Council resolution which had imposed a ban on any unofficial diamond exports from Sierra Leone, a UN panel convened in New York to hear testimony pointing to a Liberian arms-for-diamonds link. Sierra Leone's minister for mineral resources told the panel that Liberia was exporting annually to Antwerp alone some forty times the maximum of 150,000 carats which its own diamond mines were capable of producing. Diamonds of Guinean and Ivorian origin were also cited as being exported to Antwerp in impossibly large quantities, completing the picture of what was an apparent operation of massive illegal diamond traffic from Sierra Leone through its neighbours to the world market.

Defending his country's position, Liberia's foreign minister Monie Captan dismissed what he described as the recycled press reports and other shaky grounds for the alleged illegal diamonds link through Liberia, saying there was no 'concrete evidence' of his government's involvement, challenging the UN to give Liberian officials 'the opportunity to scrutinize whatever [evidence] is in their possession'.[2] But the US and UK ambassadors to the UN, Richard Holbrook and Jeremy Greenstock respectively, were adamant about what they had learned, and they were increasingly becoming impatient adversaries of Charles Taylor's government at the world body.

Meanwhile, the United States National Security Council (NSC) authorized surveillance of armed factional leaders in the region, which together with corroboration from satellite images of troops and materiel movements, and Sierra Leone-based UK intelligence reports, continued to build up a picture of Liberian government involvement in the evolving cross-border warfare.

A UN report on the Mano River Union's regional war, issued in March 2001, accused Liberia of supporting and fomenting chaos and crimes against civilians by shipping arms to the RUF in exchange for diamonds. The UN report contained findings that were unambiguously damning for President Taylor. Highlights included the findings that

> A Liberian is said to be President Taylor's representative in Kono [the eastern Sierra Leone diamond district] with a mandate to supervise operations; ... there are innumerable accounts in RUF written reports ... of high-level RUF meetings with President Taylor; ... the panel has found conclusive evidence of supply lines to the RUF through Burkina Faso, Niger and Liberia.

In summary, the panel

found unequivocal and overwhelming evidence that Liberia has been actively supporting the RUF at all levels, in providing training, weapons and materiel, logistical support, a staging ground for attacks and a safe haven for retreat and recuperation.[3]

The panel of experts recommended that sanctions be imposed on Liberia. However, commentators criticized the methodology of the report as well as its findings. There was too heavy a reliance on eyewitness and uncorroborated reports of persons who were themselves likely to be UN insiders or disposed to an anti-Liberia stance within Sierra Leone. One such contributor was Sierra Leone's foreign minister, James Jonah, himself a veteran of the UN system and a consistent opponent of the Liberian viewpoint throughout the conflict.

PRESIDENT TAYLOR CONVERSES WITH NIGERIAN PRESIDENT OLUSEGUN OBASANJO DURING A SYMBOLIC BONFIRE TO DESTROY SOME 1,500 WEAPONS IN MONROVIA, 26 JULY 1999

There was dissent in the UN Security Council from Russia, France and China, as well as Mali, the African member of Council at the time. France officially regarded the pro-sanctions line to be 'negative', suggesting that incentive rather than punishment would be more effective. Mali expressed reservations that the pro-sanctions Security Council members had failed to provide 'hard facts' sufficient to warrant the imposition of sanctions.[4]

However, with strong backing from the UK and intensive lobbying to ensure its passage, the US-sponsored resolution was ultimately passed on 7 March 2001. It renewed the ban on arms supplies to the country, in force since 1992; it imposed an embargo on exports of diamonds from Liberia; and the travel ban against the Taylor entourage was expanded to include a total of 130 people, including ministers, family, ex-wives and close business associates. The elected president of Liberia was then only permitted to attend international conferences of the UN, OAU or ECOWAS, but not to travel abroad for any other purpose.

The LURD is born

In September 2000, the RUF, still with apparent Liberian support, crossed the Guinean border, and mounted large-scale attacks both against towns south of Conakry and in the 'Parrot's Beak' region, the part of the country in the extreme east which runs past the north of Sierra Leone and hooks around Lofa and Nimba counties in Liberia. The Parrot's Beak region has been disputed historically, with Freetown claiming that Guinea unilaterally annexed what was rightly Sierra Leonean territory. Heavy destruction and loss of life resulted from the RUF incursion, and it was not long before President Lansana Conte, the Guinean president, prepared to retaliate against the RUF's Liberian hosts, stepping up his support for a new rebel movement with bases inside Guinean territory, Liberians United for Reconciliation and Democracy (LURD).

LURD was founded in 1999, composed mostly of Liberians of Mandingo and Krahn ethnicity. Its first significant incursion into Liberia was in April 2000, when its fighters crossed into Lofa County, attacking civilians in areas near the Guinean border.

The United States, for its part, began a programme of support and training for the Guinean military, which in turn backed up LURD in its cross-border raids into northern Liberia. Having dithered for a decade through following a policy of avoiding military involvement in Liberia, unofficially but unmistakably the United States at last had an armed proxy in the region for its battle against the rule of Charles Taylor.

LURD's leadership, under Sekou Conneh, had always sworn that its only objective was to remove Taylor from power and that they would hand back control of captured towns, plantations, mines, ports and other assets of the country as soon as he left office. It is true that Conneh was no Charles Taylor in terms of personality or ambition, but then who could say how he might act once holding the reins of power? Taylor himself had once sworn that his only aim was to remove Samuel Doe and that he would afterwards submit to democracy. Over a decade later, once he had fought to the bitter end to ensure that he did gain ultimate power, the Liberia that he pledged to save had been destroyed. If the leader of this latest group of usurpers succeeded, and their leader suddenly had a change of heart and decided to crown himself as chief, how many more months and years of war might Liberia then have to endure?

Over the course of the following three years, LURD fought a campaign against the Taylor government first in Lofa County and then in the west and centre of Liberia, ultimately capturing a large swathe of territory and moving on to encircle the capital. Its campaign further impaired the government's efforts to revive the economy, and, with an international arms embargo imposed on Liberia but not on Guinea or Sierra Leone, both of which armed and supported LURD, it was an uphill struggle to keep the rebels at bay.

In early 2002 small groups of rebels infiltrated the south of Liberia, bypassing government strongholds and attacking the towns of Klay and Tubmanburg in hit-and-run-style actions. They often held the towns only for short periods before retreating or being driven back, but their actions had a strong impact on the government in Monrovia. In February 2002, Taylor declared a state of emergency in response to the incursions. In May, his childhood home town of Arthington, only 20 miles outside the capital, was attacked, spreading fears of an imminent strike against Monrovia.

All this LURD was able to achieve with relatively small attack units, whilst keeping its power base outside major government-held towns. In Ganta, north-western Nimba County, the Guinean border is only five minutes away across the St John river. From the Guinean side, rebels could launch attacks with artillery support from the Guinean army. LURD captured the town in the early stages of the war but later in 2002 government forces were able to rearm and retake the city.

By the time of an early-2003 ceasefire, when foreign journalists were invited by the government to see Ganta, there was no civilian population left. The schools, the hospital, the mosque had all been destroyed by shelling. An observer described the scene in the town, which had once been a centre for the entire north-west region of Liberia:

> it was a town inhabited almost entirely by armed children. Some roared through the dirt streets in pickup trucks and others trailed along behind the Chief of Staff [the government army commander of the town] as he walked through the rubble; ... when he stopped they stopped, levelling their guns outwards at the gloomy jungle. ... they stood around in their snow parkas and leather jackets and flip flops ... they were probably all on drugs and none of them had much of an idea why they were fighting or perhaps that there was even an alternative to it.[5]

The resurgent regional civil war that began in Liberia in 1999, engulfing Sierra Leone and also parts of Guinea, soon dragged yet another victim into its clutches. Confronting an increasingly well-backed threat from LURD in the north and west, the Taylor government's stance towards its eastern neighbour was then polarized by a political and constitutional crisis which broke out in September 2002 in Côte d'Ivoire.

With the region now awash with Sierra Leonean and Liberian mercenaries, after over a decade of armed conflict in both countries, many who had no apparent interest in demobilization and civilian life were drawn to wherever there were opportunities to fight and, of course, to loot. The Ivorian president, Laurent Gbagbo, was fighting a civil war in his own country against northern rebels, and sent a delegation to President Taylor in Monrovia seeking helicopter support for his forces.

But the old regional alliances between formal regional francophone alliances had broken down since the days of Félix Houphouët-Boigny and his successor Henri Conan Bédié. Burkina Faso's Blaise Compaoré was now sympathetic towards the northern rebels in Côte d'Ivoire's civil strife, and maintaining US acceptance through good relations with Compaoré was now the priority for Taylor, so he turned down Gbagbo's request and sided with his opponents.

Gbagbo took his revenge on Taylor in the following year, 2003, and in the process helped to seal the Liberian president's fate, by backing and arming another Liberian anti-Taylor faction allied to LURD in the south-east of the country. The group, led by Thomas Nimley, known as the Movement for Democracy in Liberia (MODEL), succeeded in capturing the key logging port of Harper, and later Buchanan, as well as much of the territory that lay in between. By mid-2003, the combined forces of LURD and MODEL controlled over 70 per cent of Liberian territory, and it was Charles Taylor who now found himself hemmed into an enclave in Monrovia, defending the capital against well-armed and well-backed invaders.

As the fighting against LURD in the countryside continued and Taylor's military and economic position deteriorated, rebel calls for him to give up power grew louder, a demand backed by continued hostile actions as well as rhetoric from the international community. In March of 2002, two months after the official end of the war in Sierra Leone, the UN appointed an independent panel of five investigators to examine whether the Taylor government had been complying with their demands for Liberia to disengage from its involvements with the RUF and the illegal trade in diamonds since the initial imposition of sanctions.

The sanctions had hit the government's ability to beat back the rebels and also had a debilitating impact on the civilian population. Scarce resources were being used in defence instead of in attending to the run-down state of schools, hospitals, agricultural production, sanitation and nutrition needs of the population. The government further claimed that the diamond sanctions were hurting legitimate Liberian miners, who were unable to find an outlet to sell domestically produced gems. Furthermore, as President Taylor complained vehemently, his government had a constitutional obligation to defend Liberian territory against armed attack from the outside, and it needed to obtain weapons and ammunition in order to do this, something which the embargo made impossible to do legally.

In April 2002, the UN panel reported back with its conclusions. It found that the government in Monrovia was no longer fuelling a war in Sierra Leone, while noting that mercenary elements from the former conflict had drifted over the border and were now participating in the fighting in Liberia. UNAMSIL, the UN Mission in Sierra Leone, provided its inputs to the UN panel, finding 'no reason to believe that the RUF has received military or related support from the Liberian government during the period under review', while an ECOWAS verification mission noted that Liberia had expelled RUF members from its territory and had cut off contacts with the organization.[6] The OAU asked the UN to end the sanctions on Liberia because of the 'negative impact' they were having on the Liberian population.[7]

Despite this progress, the damning part of the independent panel's report remained: it found that while diamond sales had dropped off to a trickle in the review period, new weapons were still being purchased by the Liberian government in violation of the arms ban. This was enough for the enemies of Charles Taylor on the Security Council, and they brought their full persuasive forces to bear on their fellow Council members.

Sanctions crush the Liberian economy

On 6 May, the Security Council adopted resolution 1408, which extended sanctions on the government, including a modified travel ban, prohibition of diamond sales and a continuation of the arms embargo. There was a further call for a widening of sanctions to include the proceeds of the US-based Liberian Maritime agency, which registers over 1,000 ships annually under a flag-of-convenience system, as well as the proceeds of timber exports, which LURD said were being used to fuel the fighting in the civil war.

In the view of the Singaporean Security Council president Kishore Mahbubani, despite the declaration of the official ending of the war, peace in Sierra Leone was not yet guaranteed and the government of Charles Taylor had 'not yet fully complied' with its requirements, and so the sanctions needed to be renewed.

Sanctions were imposed, then, in the absence of unanimity among the wider international community with regard either to the need for their imposition or to who would bear the heaviest burden from their renewal. Powerful interests had prevailed. In November 2002 the sanctions against Liberia were renewed, and in January 2003 President George W. Bush issued an executive order extending a prior declaration of the US government of a national emergency with respect to Sierra Leone and expanded it to include the actions of the government of Liberia in its support of the RUF because, in Bush's view, 'the actions of the RUF continue to pose an unusual and extraordinary threat to the foreign policy of the United States'.[8] There was to be no letting up on Taylor or the scattered remnants of the RUF.

President Taylor was frustrated at his inability to win what he saw as a propaganda war against the USA and the UK, which in turn was preventing him from making progress at home. As one who had used the BBC, CNN and other global media sources so effectively in his early campaigns, having the tables turned on him was a doubly bitter pill to swallow. The same countries with the powerful media were backing his enemies on the ground, a devastating combination.

In Taylor's view, 'by the time you are lambasted on the CNN and BBC, you are already a demon. And then all their little organs, their covert arms, begin to take over. Its frightening!' As to the source of the covert arms being deployed against them, President Taylor as ever remained reticent to name names, always just referring to 'powerful countries'. He said of them succinctly: 'when your master is your enemy, you are doomed.'[9]

But for the UN as a body, Taylor had less respect. UN Secretary General Kofi Annan had not fully backed an extension of sanctions, warning of their impact on ordinary Liberians. But, as in other major conflicts of the day, notably the highly controversial launch of the second Iraq War in March 2003, the UN was only partly the forum for final decision-making; it was also the tool of others as well as the justification for the decision itself, which in reality was being taken outside the world body's auspices. Bitter at this evolution, Taylor criticized the sanctions decision as what he called 'a ploy by these powerful nations to interfere in the democratic process of Liberia ...' He observed, 'I see for the first time that the UN is being used indirectly to perpetrate evil against a member state because of personal reasons of other member states. Again, we don't have an opportunity to confront these allegations. It's very difficult.'[10]

Special Court closes in on its prey

In Freetown, the establishment of the UN-sponsored Special Court for Sierra Leone in 2002 marked the beginning of the end for Charles Taylor's career, as its judges and witnesses steadily amassed evidence against their neighbour. In March 2003 the judge of the court approved the indictment of Charles Taylor on seventeen counts of war crimes.

Taylor's government demanded that the warrant for his arrest be rescinded on the grounds that the president's apprehension could upset the stability of the Liberian state – a plea which was flatly rejected by the UN Special Court. The president himself was intransigent. In a live television and radio broadcast he agreed to stand down as president and depart Liberia only on condition that the international indictment against him be revoked. Defiant, on 20 June he addressed the nation:

> The indictment against me is not about Charles Taylor. It is about Sierra Leone trying to disgrace Liberia. People are asking me why I'm afraid to go to Sierra Leone and appear before the court. Why are American officials afraid to appear before the World Court in The Hague? I am willing ... to give up my constitutional right to a second term but the international community must do the same. They must make a sacrifice and withdraw the indictment.

As the fighting raged on in early 2003, rebels from LURD were increasingly able to attack and enter parts of Monrovia with ease, helped by the new supplies of rockets and other heavy weapons they now possessed. In contrast, the remaining mostly young fighters from the government side were depleted in numbers and increasingly low on ammunition.

Taylor's last Battle: Monrovia
June-August 2003

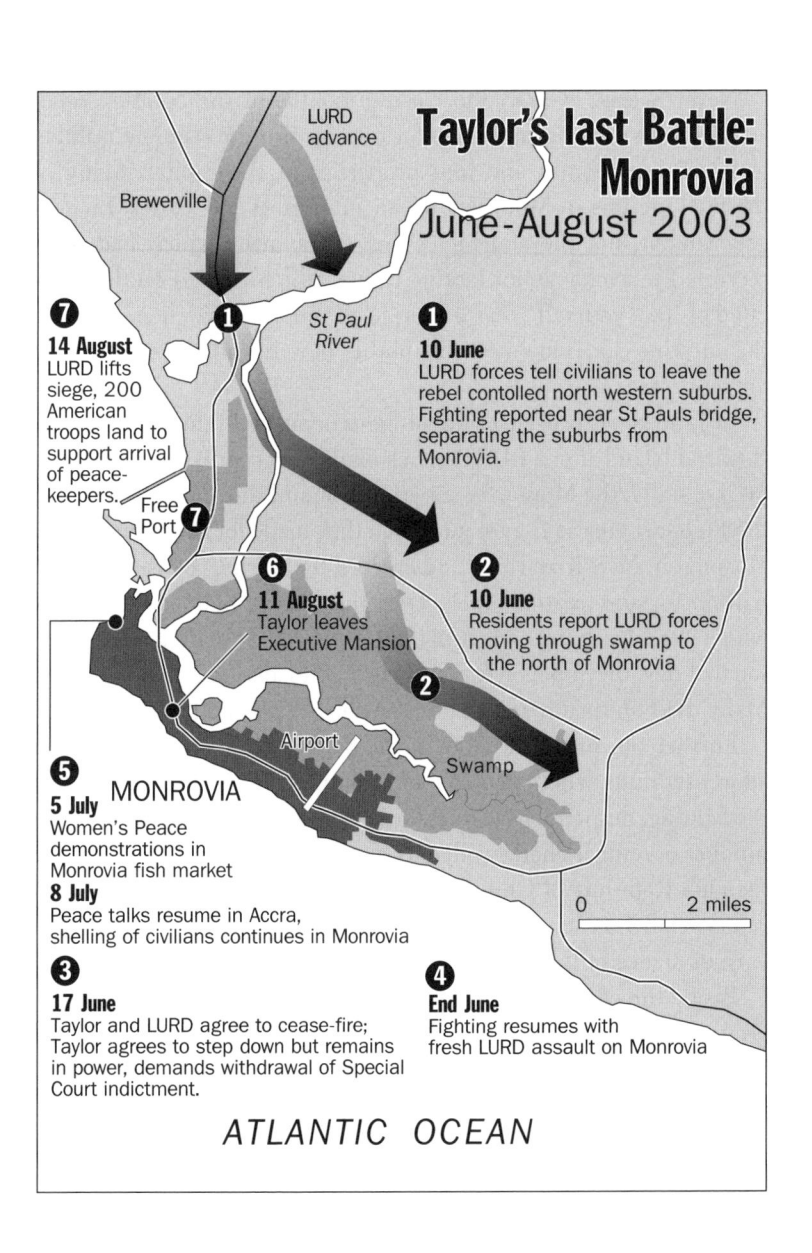

LURD advance

Brewerville

St Paul River

❼ 14 August
LURD lifts siege, 200 American troops land to support arrival of peacekeepers.

Free Port

❶ 10 June
LURD forces tell civilians to leave the rebel contolled north western suburbs. Fighting reported near St Pauls bridge, separating the suburbs from Monrovia.

❻ 11 August
Taylor leaves Executive Mansion

❷ 10 June
Residents report LURD forces moving through swamp to the north of Monrovia

Airport

Swamp

MONROVIA

❺ 5 July
Women's Peace demonstrations in Monrovia fish market

8 July
Peace talks resume in Accra, shelling of civilians continues in Monrovia

0 — 2 miles

❸ 17 June
Taylor and LURD agree to cease-fire; Taylor agrees to step down but remains in power, demands withdrawal of Special Court indictment.

❹ End June
Fighting resumes with fresh LURD assault on Monrovia

ATLANTIC OCEAN

Nevertheless, even in the closing months of the conflict, rebel attacks were used as an excuse for teenage pro-government militias to break into homes and loot properties in the capital. Many of the final victims in Monrovia fell to supporters of Charles Taylor's government, not the attacking rebels. The army which had been recruited in exchange for looting rights, which existed on the principle of 'pay yourself', was giving itself one last pay cheque before the curtains came down on yet another bloody and traumatic battle for Monrovia.

In June 2003, pro-government fighters pushed rebels back down Bushrod Island after a LURD attack on the city centre, looting shops, market stalls, the Monoprix supermarket, and the 'Club' brewery in the Freeport area as they went. Then they made for the Redemption Hospital in New Kru Town and entered the wards, accusing staff of harbouring and treating rebels. Over the protests of doctors, some of whom were operating on victims who had been wounded in the fighting that day, they opened fire, forcing staff to abandon their patients. Many died on the operating tables or on the hospital floors.[11]

Further out in Paynesville, at the Samuel Kanyon Doe national sports stadium, where people had been living under the seats to flee the fighting, desperately waiting for Red Cross food distributions, the number of refugees had swollen to 33,000. The stadium, built by the People's Republic of China in 1986, had been extensively damaged but nevertheless served as a haven for the displaced throughout the various stages of the Liberian conflict.

Inside the capital, the atmosphere continued to deteriorate, deprivation giving way to desperation. Due to a combination of neglect, financial constraints, international sanctions and mismanagement, in the six years of Charles Taylor's presidency the power and water supply to residents had never been reconnected. Everyone with a chance to get out had left long ago, leaving the wretched human urchins, the unfortunate victims of their time and location in Liberia, to scrape an existence amid the rubble and the refuse.

At last, in early June Taylor flew to Ghana for peace talks with representatives of the two main rebel groups, held under the auspices of ECOWAS. For the embattled president of Liberia, it all could have ended then, since at the opening of the negotiations in Accra, on 4 June 2003, the Special Court for Sierra Leone's chief prosecutor, David Crane, decided to authorize the delivery of the international warrant for Taylor's arrest as the president and his entourage came to the Ghanaian capital to attend the peace conference. But, by a quirk of fate, miscommunication or bureaucratic incompetence, Charles Taylor slipped through the net and received one last lease of political life, as the Ghanaian authorities claimed that the warrant had not been received in time for them to act. What could have been the detention and removal of Taylor by force was thwarted by an apparent procedural snafu, and the Liberian leader escaped on a flight back home to Monrovia to fight again. Before leaving, however, Taylor promised to step down as president to make way for peace.

Afterwards, Ghanaian president John Kufuor denied charges that his authorities had bungled the arrest, saying that the international community had 'betrayed' him through its behaviour. 'One would expect that due consultation, reparation and all that would be made before a decision of such magnitude was announced', said the Ghanaian president. 'You don't invite a president of another country to your country only to arrest him.'[12]

After Taylor's departure from Ghana, the peace talks continued, initially proving inconclusive as fighting around Monrovia and in the countryside continued. But then two weeks later, on 17 June, delegates reconvened in Accra and a breakthrough was achieved. The Liberian government representative Daniel Chea shook hands and hugged MODEL chief negotiator Tia Slanger and LURD representative Kabinah Janneh as fellow delegates cheered and burst into singing the Liberian national anthem. Again, Taylor had agreed to a ceasefire with acceptance of the condition that he would step down as president and start the process towards implementation of a lasting peace.[13]

Backpedalling from peace

But in the previous week, on 12 June, in Monrovia, President Taylor had arranged a press conference, where he again demanded that his indictment before the Special Court be rescinded as a condition for the establishment of peace in the region. Already he was evoking some of the wider issues and contradictions surrounding the Special Court and its jurisdiction, issues which were to return to cast a pall over the proceedings years later. Referring to the indictment, he said: 'It has to be removed', describing the legal instrument as 'racist, politically motivated and aimed at disgracing an African leader'.

Taylor blamed Washington and London for engineering the situation, saying that they should be the ones to provide the remedy. 'It is not about Taylor', he went on, 'it is about the question: can Africa be free? It sets an unhealthy precedent. Tomorrow it could be Museveni, Kagame, Mugabe, Gbagbo.'[14] Taylor now dug his heels in and said that he would only give up office after democratic elections, scheduled for October that year, and that his replacement should take over as provided for in the constitution, in January of 2004.

The tenuous peace was immediately shattered and fierce fighting resumed in late June, with each side claiming violations by the other of the 17 June ceasefire. Rebels once more laid siege to Monrovia, causing increasingly heavy civilian casualties. President Taylor refused to return to the negotiating table in Ghana, saying 'I have not left this city and I will not leave this city. I will remain to encourage my combatants to fight all the way. My survival is the Liberian People's survival, your survival is my survival.'[15]

On 5 July Taylor announced that he would accept asylum in Nigeria, offered by President Olusegun Obasanjo, without specifying when exactly he would leave, only declaring that he would make an 'orderly exit'. As the regime in Monrovia desperately battled on for a few more weeks, international pressure was finally brought to bear and Taylor began to discuss more seriously the terms of his departure. The US diverted the aircraft carrier USS *Kearsarge*, en route home from the war in Iraq, with 1,800 marines and attack helicopters on board, to head for the coast of Liberia. George Bush called on Taylor to accept the Nigerian president's offer and step down.

The USA sent a small military detachment into Monrovia to assess the security situation. They were on occasion obstructed by pro-Taylor fighters, but were met by much greater crowds of refugees and desperate residents of the capital who chanted 'No more war' and 'We want Bush'.[16] At the same time, outside the US embassy in Monrovia, civilians seeking a safe haven were being ripped to shreds by mortar and rocket fire landing around the Mamba Point embassy area. The humanitarian situation continued to deteriorate as rebels prevented shipments of food and medical supplies from reaching the vulnerable through Monrovia's Freeport. Thousands of refugees in Buchanan were also trapped in the fighting, as there too the government battled on with rebels during July, to try to recapture the port.

The international community was desperate for the USA to take a firm course of action, but for a time longer it seemed as if everyone was waiting for someone else to act. In Maputo, the Mozambican capital, African Union delegates added their voice to those of the USA and unanimously called for Taylor to leave, a stinging indictment itself from a body which has, for example, repeatedly defended Robert Mugabe of Zimbabwe against calls from the West for him to leave office. At last, in early August, repeating its earlier calls, the Bush administration now directly insisted that Taylor resign office and leave the country, as a precondition for the dispatch of an international peacekeeping force, to include US troops. Charles Taylor finally had nowhere left to hide.

Charles Taylor's last day in office

On 11 August 2003, Monrovians sensed a strange atmosphere in their burned-out shell of a city. An unusual quiet descended in the afternoon as preparations got under way for a ceremony that was the first of its kind in Liberia for a generation and, for most who witnessed it, unique in their lifetimes. Power was about to pass from one Liberian president to another without the death or assassination of the incumbent.

With President Thabo Mbeki of South Africa, Mozambique's head of state Joachim Chissano and John Kuffour of Ghana in attendance, Charles Taylor prepared to say his last goodbye to the

Liberian people. 'You could have heard a pin drop in Monrovia that day', said Loretta Nagbe, whose husband was killed in 1998 by Taylor forces just outside their home near Gbarnga;

> Taylor's boys had no ammunition left, he could keep sending them to the front but then they had nothing left to fire at the rebels. It was over … that day the city came to a standstill, many people just stood there, listening in shock and disbelief, incapable of imagining that Charles Taylor was about to go.[17]

The weekend before, Taylor had spoken to his National Patriotic Party colleagues for the last time, calling the forcible nature of his departure a 'rape of democracy'.[18] Until close to the end, Taylor had intended to stand again for another term in office, with presidential elections scheduled for 14 October 2003. Now, the international community was not going to give him that chance and he prepared to speak to the nation for the last time as their head of state.

As the president addressed his people in his rich deep tones, he was defiant as always, but this time with a more sombre note to his oratory, one not as familiar to most of his countrypeople. With bitterness in his voice, he complained that his people had been brought to their knees by the international community because 'something as small as a toothpick cannot be exported from our country'. Still respectful of the United States, but resentful about its treatment of Liberia, Taylor referred to himself as a 'sacrificial lamb … a whipping boy'; then, referring more directly to the USA, he said 'They can call off their dogs now. I realized that I could no longer see the blood of our people wasted.'

'I do not stop out of fear of the fight. I stop now out of love for you', Taylor said. The United States, in his view, was the 'architect of the anti-Taylor policy', but it could make a huge difference to Liberia if it spent just a tiny fraction of what it will spend in Iraq, he opined.

> There are massive resources here … gold, diamonds all that is needed to support you, our people. I have fought for you. I have resisted attempts in the past to sign agreements that would take everything. I hope they do not sign these agreements now. I

challenge George Bush, with due respect Mr President, please, you are a man of God, do something for our people.

Passing the green sash of Liberian presidential office to his vice president, Moses Blah, Charles Taylor then officially resigned his office, as many supporters around him wept. He concluded emotionally, 'I can no longer see you suffering, the suffering is enough. God willing, I will be back.'[19]

At 5 p.m. that afternoon he was driven to Robertsfield Airport and, escorted by Nigerian officials, boarded the plane which would take him out of Liberia and to exile in Calabar. LURD stopped fighting, the guns fell silent and over the coming weeks and months the roads and ports of Liberia, or what remained of them, gradually reopened for use.

Moses Blah served as acting president of Liberia in an interim government in Monrovia, which two months later ceded power to a government of transition under Gyude Bryant. This government, however, proved incapable of revitalizing the devastated and unstable country, and so the immediate post-Taylor period was marked by humanitarian crisis accompanied by rampant government corruption.

Early in the twentieth century, the Nigerian author and statesman Nnamde Azikiwe listened with youthful amazement to a story being told to him by a fellow student, a young West African named Phillip Davies. One day in 1920 when they were sitting in their classroom in the Hope Waddell Training Institute in Calabar, a colonial port city in his country's south-eastern corner, Davies turned to describing his homeland, a land where there was no foreign ruler or white European master to dictate the nation's affairs. It was 'an African country whose executive and administrative officials were black men. It was unbelievable', Azikiwe recalled. 'The president, and the governors of the counties were black men, so were all the judges, law officers and heads of department of the civil service.'[20]

That country, Azikiwe learned, was called Liberia, and the young Nigerian's fascination at the thought of Africans in control of their own destiny and managing their own affairs remained a source of enduring fascination for him throughout his early career. 'Zik'

Azikiwe went on to become a journalist, academic and distinguished public servant, publishing a book on Liberia and even at one stage applying to serve in Liberia's diplomatic service in the early 1930s. The inspiration Azikiwe took from that youthful knowledge of Liberia undoubtedly shaped his ambitions and helped build a resolve to one day become the leader of his own land, in a government where Africans ruled their own people.

Azikiwe indeed went on to achieve great things; he became the most prominent political figure of a generation in his own vast country, leading it to independence and becoming the first president of an independent Nigeria from 1963 to 1966.

Eighty-three years on from that moment in a Calabar classroom, the latest black president of the country that caused the young Nigerian such marvel and admiration sat under house arrest in a villa streets away from Azikiwe's former school, outlawed and disgraced for his part in the invasion he had abetted and the trauma he had visited upon another West African state. That man had also led Africans, and he too had for a time been in control of his country's destiny; but he had also sorely abused his power both in and out of office and now his day of reckoning had almost come.

Exile years in Nigeria

Although Taylor was out of the Liberian scene, from the outset of his time in residence in Calabar the controversy continued. There was confusion almost from the beginning regarding his exact status in Nigeria, with on the one hand an indictment pending against him from an international court, and on the other a host government offering him lavish accommodation, facilities and freedom of communication, despite the ex-president's official 'house arrest' and imposed travel ban. The Nigerian government denied that he was a prisoner, accepting that the ousted Liberian president was in their country as part of an internationally agreed settlement aimed at restoring peace to Liberia.

Charles Taylor had time on his hands as he sat in his villa in Calabar, but not much time left to evade the mounting forces of international justice that were closing in around him, orchestrated by those determined to see him stand trial for his past actions. The US and the anti-Taylor hawks in the international community were far from prepared to let matters rest with Taylor's comfortable asylum in Nigeria. On 3 November 2003 the Special Court for Sierra Leone entered into a cooperative agreement with Interpol and on 4 December a so-called 'red notice' was issued, formally requesting national law enforcement bodies to collaborate towards ensuring Taylor's arrest.

But Charles Taylor was a determined figure even though deposed; still with a loyal band of political supporters and business contacts at home, he remained constantly in touch with Liberia from his Calabar base, phoning his associates daily, negotiating deals and communicating with his remaining operational deputies. To a degree, business activity and the maintenance of his command structure could be conducted from a distance. Soon, however, steps were taken internationally to shut down the Taylor financial machine, which bitter experience had demonstrated could so quickly be transformed into a war machine under the former president's direction.

In March of 2004, Taylor's Monrovia residence was searched, leading the exiled leader to file an application to prevent law enforcement authorities from entering his property. The appeal was denied. In May of that year, Taylor's legal team attempted to have the whole Special Court for Sierra Leone indictment against him quashed. His application was turned down, a UN spokesman commenting, 'it is a matter of time ... Taylor will face justice. There cannot be impunity for Charles Taylor.'[21]

Two months later, on 23 July, the UN Security Council ordered a freeze on Charles Taylor's assets, as well as imposing restrictions on his family, wife, ex-wives and those of his key allies in government, in practical terms putting an end to remaining hopes of his organizing any kind of armed comeback.

Charles's wife, Jewel Howard-Taylor, had initially moved with him into exile, but she returned to Liberia in 2004, after which the couple could no longer meet; the travel ban prevented her from reconnecting with her husband. In July 2005, Jewel petitioned for a divorce, which was granted in January of the following year, because, according to the court, 'prevailing circumstances have deprived her of the conjugal benefit, consortium and companionship of their marriage to the extent that marital life between them had become impossible'.[22]

Jewel, who remained politically loyal to her ex-husband, went on to become senator for Bong County in the 2005 elections. However, in office she has not enjoyed the same freedoms and privileges as most of her peers: the reality of the Taylor legacy was soon brought home to her when, a few months after her successful bid for the senate, Howard-Taylor was banned from travelling to Ghana to participate in training for members of the newly constituted assembly.

For his part, Charles Taylor was not long without consortium and companionship; soon he was joined by another bride, Victoria Addison-Taylor, whom he had married in an Islamic ceremony in Monrovia in 2002. Victoria gave birth to their first child a year later. Justifying his polygamy, the ex-president stated that, as a traditional leader, he was 'entitled to four wives'.[23]

The third and most recent of Victoria and Charles's offspring was born in February of 2010, some three years into Taylor's detention in The Hague. When the news of the detainee's apparently unstoppable feats of fatherhood reached Liberia, the local rumour mill spun into action, many having assumed that his conditions of detention could not be permissive of normal conjugal contact. The new child was quickly dubbed the Taylor 'Miracle Baby'.

Foot-dragging by the old guard

In Monrovia, the posture of Gyude Bryant's transitional government in 2004 was not in harmony with the quickening pace of the international legal efforts against Taylor. Following the UN travel and financial bans and Interpol's arrest notifications, Bryant declared that Taylor's 'presence in Nigeria is part of the peace process ... he should not be removed', thereby throwing something of a spanner into the works of international efforts to end the wanted man's status in legal limbo.

The Nigerian authorities also seemed reticent to become involved in Taylor's rendition to justice. President Olusegun Obasanjo did not display the same sense of urgency as the UN and the United States, also based on the premiss that his country was playing a role in the peace process by keeping Taylor quietly on the sidelines – and with the justification that any sudden handover could potentially risk sparking renewed unrest in the region. The obstructionist approach by Nigeria, which arguably delayed Taylor's ultimate arrest by over two years, is believed by many insiders to have gone all the way to the higher echelons of government and the military in Abuja; speculation was rife that, if brought before an international court, Taylor's wartime financial and commodity dealings with Nigerian ECOMOG commanders could easily be revealed, causing huge embarrassment.

Liberian human rights groups tried to pressure the Nigerian government to hand Taylor over to face the Sierra Leone war crimes charges. But the Monrovia transitional government obstructed their efforts. Again members of parliament preferred to sit on the fence, nervous about raising tensions domestically, declaring that 'allowing Taylor to face the court in Freetown will hamper the Liberian Peace process'. Thus, caught between cooperation and caution, they contributed to a standoff which would last for over two years.

By mid-2005, however, the Monrovia government, in its last months of existence before national elections, began to come around to adopting a tougher stance on Taylor. Accusing him of abusing the terms of his asylum by making frequent calls home, allegedly posing a potential threat to the maintenance of peace, they called for a review of the terms of his asylum. Gyude Bryant convened leaders of his fellow Mano River Union states, President Tejan Kabbah of Sierra Leone and Guinean Prime Minister Cellou Diallo, to issue a joint statement for the review of the asylum.

Gyude Brant's stalling tactics to keep the old order running under new management had run out of gas, and his apparent complicity in Liberia's financial scandals, past and present, were soon investigated. After Ellen Johnson Sirleaf's administration came into power, he was questioned by police and later arrested together with four alleged accomplices on charges of embezzlement in two cases each involving of over $1 million. At first claiming presidential immunity and then trying to abscond, in 2009 Bryant was ultimately acquitted on one of the charges relating to theft from the state oil refinery and in September 2010 the second charge against him was dropped.

Finally, on 5 March of 2006, newly inaugurated president Ellen Johnson Sirleaf formally requested the Nigerian government to render Taylor from asylum. Nevertheless, since there was no indictment for Taylor in a Liberian court, she was reluctant to bring him back to Monrovia on shaky legal grounds and asked that Nigeria return him directly to Freetown. Logically and legally, she argued, he needed to be taken to Sierra Leone where his indictment had originated. But the Nigerian government had not offered to provide a plane.

Nigeria said that Sirleaf was 'free to come and take Taylor into her custody' – easier said than done for Liberia on its own and without international authority to fly into Nigeria and remove one of its citizens whom his hosts had declared was 'not a prisoner'. The indictment had been weakly drafted, without full UN Chapter VII powers, which otherwise would have allowed a United Nations plane simply to go to Nigeria and pick him up directly.

Given the major part that President George Bush ultimately played in forcing Taylor from office in August 2003, it remains curious that, even after Taylor's indictment by the Special Court for Sierra Leone earlier that year, it took fully two and a half more years for the accused man to be taken into captivity.

Charles Taylor's close collaboration with the USA in the early years of his military campaign gave him an edge which, rightly or wrongly, he relied on to see him through a lot of international flack, and, despite the ultimate let-down at the gates of the Executive Mansion in 1990, his ties with the US intelligence community remained. Despite the opprobrium heaped on Taylor by the White House in his final days in office, it is clear that, even after his exile to Nigeria, there were ties of a different kind that continued to bind Liberia's pariah president to the US intelligence community, even though half the world regarded him as a dictator and mass abuser of human rights.

While accusations of high-level corruption between Nigerian and Liberian public figures helped explain President Obasanjo's reluctance to deliver their exiled guest into justice, they do not fully explain why the international community took so long to bring the necessary pressure to bear to ensure Taylor's handover. There have been suggestions that, even though in conflict with the stance of the White House, it was the fact that Taylor had been on the US intelligence community payroll that inhibited more robust action. Specialists who spoke anonymously to UN investigators for the report which was prepared in 2004 for the Special Court's prosecution highlighted the ambiguity of the US position, attributing the reticence to act to Taylor's 'longstanding ties with the [US] intelligence community'.[24]

In his 2004 book *Blood from Stones*, the US writer Douglas Farah asked the question bluntly: 'Why hasn't the United States pressed for his handover to the Special Court? The US is funding most of it and the high powered prosecutors are led by people from the Defense Department. To get [Nigeria] to get Taylor turned over we're not going to do anything.'[25]

Dash for the border

Beginning with the statement on 25 March 2006 of Nigerian President Obasanjo to Ellen Johnson Sirleaf that her government was free to take Taylor, the hitherto ungainly process at last began to lurch into a higher gear. Obasanjo's confirmation that Taylor could be removed was the turning point in a long-drawn-out saga and a signal that the end was near. Taylor now knew he could no longer shelter under Nigeria's official state umbrella, despite the Nigerian president's earlier assurances that he was in no danger of being removed. Once again, with his enemies closing in, desperate measures were called for. Two days later, the situation began to spin out of control in a succession of dramatic events, surrounded by confusion and intrigue, in true Taylor style. The days that immediately followed the Obasanjo announcement were to be Charles Taylor's last outside of captivity.

On the morning of 27 March the international community heard the dramatic announcement that Taylor had disappeared, that he was no longer in his villa in Calabar. The news was all the more embarrassing for Olusegun Obasanjo, who was just preparing to leave for the United States on an official visit and was due to be received by George W. Bush at the White House the next day. The US authorities were furious and demanded swift and effective action from Nigeria. Tension was high and speculation was rife as to whether Taylor had truly got away, and whether he had been helped by friends in the Nigerian security service or other insiders. Where was he and where was he heading?

In Monrovia there was nervousness. President Sirleaf thought Taylor might be heading towards Liberia; despite the substantial presence of around 15,000 UN peacekeepers, he was still an influential force with the ability to pull off surprises. The American ambassador Donald Booth and the UN special representative Alan Doss were both out of the country.

One of Taylor's spokesmen, Sylvester Paasewe, said that he was still in Calabar; so did his 20-year-old granddaughter Desiree, who lived in the same house as Taylor. Another close confidant, R.A. Paul, the president's spiritual adviser and an American evangelical minister, said he had left without being able to say for where. Paul was in Ethiopia trying to arrange a fresh place of asylum for the former president; but the fugitive himself was by then in a car heading northwards. According to Mr Paul, Nigerian state security agents had 'told Taylor to leave with them', and they had supposedly escorted him to the north-eastern border of the country, arriving at 4.30 in the morning, whereupon they 'told him to go and they left him'.

However, Abuja had clearly warned that Taylor should make no attempt to leave Calabar and had urged those with influence over him that he should not try to escape. It seems that the ex-president of Liberia still had faith in his former hosts, even at that late stage when they had already decided to give him up. Just before departing Calabar, Taylor called the peace mediator Dr Akyaaba Addai-Sebo, who had earlier advised him not to leave and, referring to his trust in Obasanjo, said: 'my brother will never betray me'.[26]

But Taylor had been betrayed. As he travelled the final stretch towards Chad, at 5 a.m. on 29 March he was apprehended and detained by Nigerian border officials.[27] The master of daring escapes and evasion from international justice had finally run out of luck. The Nigerian authorities quickly got their Liberian captive onto a plane to Abuja and, without hesitation this time, returned him to Liberia.

As with Taylor's mysterious bolt from Plymouth, Massachusetts, twenty years earlier, conspiracy theories about the Calabar getaway were abundant. According to some, a fake escape and successful recapture had been staged by the Abuja authorities to distract media attention and enhance the Nigerian president's standing on the occasion of Obasanjo's visit to the United States that same week. Obasanjo was manoeuvring domestically to gain acceptance for his bid to run for a third presidential term – requiring his tinkering with the constitution – already a topic of controversy in the international media. Backed by sources in the Nigerian security forces, this version alleges that Taylor was flown from Calabar to Abuja just before the Nigerian president's US visit, then taken by the authorities to Maiduguri in the north, near the border with Cameroon, where he was allowed to attempt a border crossing – then the authorities sprung their trap and recaptured him, taking the credit and boosting confidence before the US administration and media.[28]

According to others, Taylor was in league with Nigerian security agents acting on their own authority, whose confidence and loyalty he had nurtured over the space of the past two years, a theory which is supported by the reported discovery of over $1 million in cash in the four-by-four vehicle with diplomatic plates which brought him to the border. More sinister still is the belief that Nigerians in high places who could suffer serious embarrassment from potential revelations in Taylor's trial wanted to encourage his flight, while arranging for him to be shot while attempting escape at the border.[29]

From Taylor's side, the story was that there was no escape attempt, and that he had simply left on a planned visit by road to Chad, to see his friend Idriss Déby, the Chadian president. Already in south-eastern Nigeria near the Cameroonian border, why would he travel the 1,700 kilometres to the north of the country just to flee into Cameroon? Maiduguri was en route to Chad, his intended destination.[30] He drove the whole way with two Nigerian state escorts; he was provided with some $50,000 in cash and travelled with the full knowledge of the president.[31]

Whichever version is true, the generation of instant wrath on the part of the US government at the prospect of Taylor once again being at large and dangerous in West Africa was unquestionable, and it brought swift and decisive action from Abuja to ensure the fugitive's recapture.

Upon his apprehension, there was no more ambivalence on the part of the Nigerian authorities. Taylor was arrested and flown immediately to Monrovia. Once more arriving back in the land of his birth, the Dakhpannah Dr Charles Ghankay Taylor was met by UN forces as he stepped onto the tarmac at Robertsfield airport, handcuffed and placed in a helicopter for Freetown to face justice before the Special Court in Sierra Leone. From there, he was later delivered into the custody of the International Criminal Court in The Hague, where his trial proceedings began in June 2007.

TWELVE

RELATIONS WITH THE UNITED STATES

> As they are themselves nearly powerless they must rely on the just sympathy and justice of other powers ... I should inform that the [United States] regards Liberia as possessing peculiar claims to the consideration of this government.
>
> Letter from the US government to Lord Aberdeen, British foreign secretary, December 1845[1]

US policy towards West African conflict in the late 1980s

During the decade of the 1980s, countering the threat of socialism and discouraging radical pan-Africanism was a greater priority for US policy than fostering democracy in countries with a fragile rule of law such as Liberia. But for Liberians, their relationship with the United States took on an importance which went far beyond its real status in American eyes, whether economically, politically or culturally.

One of the enduring paradoxes in the Liberian tragedy of the past thirty years has been the stark juxtaposition between the standard American view of Liberia and Liberians' views of the United States. While the US government found Monrovia a useful ally during the

Cold War and consequently financed its president, Samuel Doe, in lavish fashion to maintain his unswerving loyalty, Washington did little to improve the lot of ordinary Liberians or to champion their human rights, which were brutally trampled on by their government over a sustained period of time.

While it is unlikely that many ordinary Americans could find Liberia on a map of the world, either then or now, the esteem in which all things American were held by ordinary Liberians was often tantamount to adulation. Their imitation of the fashions, lifestyle, music and language – young Americo-Liberians in the 1970s loved to show their worldliness by speaking to each other in what they called *cullor*, an adaptation of the young black speech of the urban US South – was truly the highest form of flattery of the great nation that Liberians, particularly Americo- but also native Liberians, looked up to.

Despite a unique historical link and the strategic ties that were for a time so important, with the exception of a generation of Peace Corps volunteers, a handful of well-meaning religious leaders and the occasional burst of reactive interest by lawmakers in Washington DC, the plight of Liberians whether in peacetime persecution or in wartime suffering remained of little consequence to US policymakers.

When Samuel Doe stole the 1985 elections and the US effectively did nothing about it, while continuing to fund his regime of brutal ethnic persecution, many Liberians truly believed that the USA surely must have had some kind of ulterior plan, that this could only be allowed to go on temporarily and the ultimate intention to make the intervention that was so desperately needed must be close at hand. But they were sadly mistaken, and nobody at the top of the US government paid more than passing attention to Liberia's worsening plight as it plunged inexorably towards humanitarian catastrophe.

That limited degree of concern which was paid by the few in the US Congress who sought reform and a shift towards democracy in Liberia in the 1980s soon melted into total indifference with the ending of the Cold War in 1989 and the US invasion of Iraq in August 1990. Liberians' long-standing loyalty was taken for granted by the US political establishment and for the most part not reciprocated.

There clearly had been a desire on the part of the US State Department in the 1980s to remove the problem of Samuel Doe, and after the December 1989 NPFL invasion many thought that Charles Taylor might be the answer. Officials in Washington were frustrated at their inability, on the one hand, to remove Doe by more forceful means, since he was still needed by the White House as a strategic Cold War ally; but, on the other hand, they were unable to back him more publicly as he was clearly a highly criticized figure in the US Congress and the constant subject of antagonistic lobbying by influential US-based Liberians. Policy therefore drifted and US commitment to Liberia took no concrete form.

With the incursion of the NPFL in December 1989, the wheels of US diplomacy once again started whirring. The State Department finally had 'a problem it could get its teeth into', as Herman Cohen put it. Taylor kept in contact with the USA about his progress and, initially at least, his forces seemed to be treating US citizens and US property correctly. The official public stance of the NPFL at that stage was that they only wanted to remove Doe, and that the people of Liberia could choose their own leader after that.

The key concern for the USA was to not put the $400 million-plus worth of US strategic and communications assets at risk by pushing Doe too hard too soon, while at the same time ensuring that his successor – initially presumed to be Charles Taylor – would be stable and reliable enough to maintain them after taking over. Also, there were about 5,000 US citizens in Liberia at the start of 1990, and, while initially only recommending and facilitating departures, the US embassy had not deemed it necessary or appropriate to order an evacuation. Nevertheless, in the event of a sudden deterioration, they would have to rely on Doe's government to ensure the civilians' security, once again militating against outright opposition to him staying in power.

At one stage in late April 1990 it seemed that the president might indeed agree to go, when Doe informed the US embassy that he would leave only on condition that his inner circle and fellow Krahn in Monrovia could be guaranteed safe passage. He demanded that the US negotiate with the rebels to keep open the road to Sierra Leone and provide security for him and some 500 people in his entourage to escape to Liberia's western neighbour.[2]

The US complied and the State Department prepared an exit strategy for Doe, selecting a suitable country of asylum. President Gnassingbé Eyadéma of Togo was persuaded to make an offer of asylum and the USA had a Hercules C-130 positioned in Freetown ready to fly to Monrovia to take Doe out of the country. The mood at the American side was upbeat, but Doe kept changing his mind in response to conditions on the ground. He drank heavily, took drugs and both his judgement and perceptions of reality constantly wavered. As Assistant Secretary of State Cohen put it: '[at first] ... we felt exhilarated ... but sadly Doe lacked the capacity to understand what was required'.[3]

US suspension of arms signals end of Doe

One decisive move that the USA did make as the rebels began to advance was the suspension of arms shipments to Doe's government. In response to the blatant and mounting evidence of atrocities against civilians, the US cut off military shipments to the Monrovia regime. The NPFL took it as a clear signal of support, despite it not being intended as such. Tom Woewiyu, defence spokesman for the rebels, said that once the USA cut arms supplies to Doe, they knew they could win. Doe kept on asking for supplies just the same: as his army swelled with its rush intake of 3,000 new recruits in May 1990, he asked the US embassy for rifles to supply the new fighters. The USA refused, as did most of Doe's former allies; the embattled Liberian dictator finally managed to get one last shipment into the country, from Romania.[4]

There were also second thoughts about backing the rebel side. Early in the Nimba County campaign, the NPFL approached the US embassy in Abidjan to establish a dialogue. Their entreaties were rejected, apparently because the Libyan connection, now apparent to the USA, branded the rebels as undesirable interlocutors. By April

1990, when word started to leak to the outside world about atrocities being committed by the NPFL against civilians, as well as some of Taylor's less-than-reassuring actions in enforcing discipline within his own leadership, there were further reasons to doubt Taylor as the best choice for the succession in Liberia.

At a summit meeting in Washington DC in May 1990, an all-party delegation was invited from Liberia at which the USA proposed that a ceasefire be called, and elections in which the insurgents would also be invited to participate be organized in October of that year. Tom Woewiyu attended on behalf of the NPFL, adding his assurances that in the meantime the rebels would safeguard US property and personnel and step aside to allow elections after Doe had left. The government of Liberia's representatives, however, rejected the idea of early elections and the strategy reverted to one of luring Doe to resign with various inducements.

In late May, hopes were once again raised as Doe seemed to be accepting the US-brokered exit plan and the president of Liberia eagerly negotiated the details of his future with US officials. Bizarre in his behaviour and out of touch with reality as ever, at one stage Doe was inquiring of the USA about the possibility of a place at Harvard or Cambridge University after he left; at another moment his main concern seemed to be that he and his family should be flown abroad but only on condition that they be provided with twenty-five cases of soft drinks to go with them.[5]

By early June 1990, the US State Department plan to remove Doe was ready to be executed: Doe had agreed to asylum; he would be taken out by plane and replaced by Vice President Harry Moniba, who in turn would appoint Charles Taylor as vice president; then, after a decent interval, he too would leave the scene. That was how it was supposed to play out and Taylor had signed up to it. All that was needed was for a high-level official to be dispatched to Monrovia to give Doe that 'final push' to leave office.

Herman Cohen was the one selected for the mission. Then, just as State Department staffers were getting excited about the dispatch of their special envoy, their plan was suddenly quashed from above. At a 4 June meeting in Washington DC, deputy national security adviser Robert Gates stamped on the whole plan, attacking the very notion that the USA had any reason to be involved in Liberia's problems. Gates further refused to recognize any special responsibility to the country on the grounds of historical ties. The USA owed Liberia nothing, and there would be no US-sponsored escape plan for Samuel Doe. The following day it emerged via the National Security Council that President Bush had instructed the NSC that the USA 'would not take charge of the Liberia problem'. Official lack of interest had been confirmed at the highest level of government.

There was disappointment and dismay at the State Department over the sudden application of the brakes to their well-developed plan. There was also an apparent disconnect between information and decision-making at the highest levels. The key man in the operation, Herman Cohen, found it hard to swallow. He wrote: 'I was personally outraged, particularly by the absence of any real dialogue between those with the knowledge and those with the ultimate power of decision.'[6]

The door was slamming shut in Doe's face for other reasons too. Soon after the negotiations collapsed, an evacuation of the surrounded Krahn entourage by road to Sierra Leone was no longer an available option: Prince Johnson's forces had pushed down from the north and west of the country and had cut the Babangida Highway off. Monrovia was surrounded.

Preparations for the Gulf War: the death knell for peace in Liberia

Nevertheless, as the civil war raged on and the security of Monrovia and its large vulnerable civilian population was clearly threatened, the US embassy was still sufficiently interested in seeking a solution of some kind that it welcomed the Nigerian-led ECOWAS plan, which in effect took up the negotiations with Doe where the USA had left off a month before.

For its part, the United States had evacuated some 2,500 of its nationals and Western citizens in the first week of August 1990, although the West African hostages behind NPFL lines were still stranded. Diplomatically, Washington was now a passive observer in Liberian diplomacy, unofficially glad to give the ECOMOG intervention its backing and rid itself of responsibility, but officially still treading a cautious path. There were good reasons for this, despite the safe departure of the remaining US citizens. It was the summer of 1990 and the USA was expending its diplomatic capital in securing UN Security Council votes for an invasion of Kuwait, following the Iraqi invasion of its smaller neighbour.

Côte d'Ivoire, the principal opponent of the ECOMOG intervention plan among West African states, was one of the African members of the Security Council at the time, and the USA wanted to be sure of its support. For the White House there were bigger fish to fry than Liberia and so the USA reverted to a neutral status in the Liberia discussions, whilst publicly supporting any moves towards a peaceful solution. Furthermore, there was the added bonus of being able to encourage 'African-led solutions to African problems', a concept which was already gaining popularity in Western circles at the time and which would become almost the mantra of the non-interventionists in future African catastrophes, following the US debacle in Somalia in 1992 and the UN's ignominious retreat in the face of genocide in Rwanda in 1994.

In the case of Monrovia, the USA was in force on the ground, or just off the coast, and in a position to send in its marines to end the bloodshed and starvation that racked the city. But intervention by US marines was never authorized. From the rebels' point of view, even a token intervention would probably have been sufficient to bring an end to the fighting. Indeed, when the USA evacuated its remaining nationals in early August, it used an assembly point in central Monrovia into which it flew helicopters from its ships waiting offshore. Potentially vulnerable, the USA contacted all the faction leaders to ask that there be no shooting. The State Department called Charles Taylor to ask the NPFL to stand fire, while the US embassy called Prince Johnson and the AFL to ask for their cooperation in a trouble-free evacuation. All of them complied. When the message came through that the USA was coming into central Monrovia to retrieve its citizens, everybody stopped fighting, albeit briefly.

Charles Taylor later confirmed how easy it would have been for the USA to end the war with just a token intervention. After the events of 1990 he told the State Department: 'If you send in a company of marines, we'll all surrender.' Herman Cohen later testified that, 'I know that Charles Taylor often didn't tell the truth. [but] I think there he *was* telling the truth.'[7]

ECOMOG, the newest looting faction in Liberia's war

But abdicating responsibility and effectively handing over the role of peace broker to a Nigerian-led intervention force turned out to be yet another ill-judged policy move by Washington, as conduct of many of the force's troops was soon to prove, and not only because the main rebel faction, the NPFL, refused to recognize it as an independent party in the conflict.

The ECOMOG force was far from being a professional, disciplined, fighting force. Although drawn from several countries across the region, one thing that all the component nation troops of the force had in common with each other, and indeed with the fighters from the rebel factions whom they opposed, was that they were all ordinary, badly paid West Africans, often from rural backgrounds. The opportunities for personal material advancement were not lost on the young enlistees, and, as the force settled in and the fighting got under way, so too in a short time the fridges, air conditioners, vehicles, furniture and appliances from the Liberian capital were being loaded onto the ships bound for mostly Nigerian ports.

Monrovians, while on the one hand initially welcoming the international protection force, which saved them from murder and starvation in the summer of 1990, were on the other hand soon dismayed at the rapacious behaviour of their erstwhile saviours.

A good summary of the US record in the evolution of conflict resolution in Liberia in the first year of the civil war is provided by Liberia author and researcher Stephen Ellis:

> The US government, to compound its error of persistently providing support to the brutal Samuel Doe, massively miscalculated the effect of encouraging a Nigerian-led force into Liberia in August

1990. Once the US had lost the initiative in Liberia, it never regained it. The country remained a very low priority for politicians and officials in Washington and was generally dealt with at a relatively low level of the administration.[8]

Ex-president Jimmy Carter deplored the racist aspect of the US omissions in Liberia as much as the lost opportunities to act militarily to prevent civil war. Speaking in the late 1990s after the war and following the successful US and NATO interventions in former Yugoslavia, he said:

> we concentrate our efforts on Bosnia and we don't pay any attention to Liberia, Rwanda and Burundi because they're African countries ... they're black people and they're poor people and we concentrate our efforts on white people in Europe ... this is a tragedy.[9]

While the morality of ignoring Liberia's descent to humanitarian disaster may have been deplorable, the economics of ignoring the situation had no ground in logic whatsoever. Later, in 2003, the USA did hold a hearing on the future of US foreign policy towards Liberia. On the floor of the House, the question was asked:

> Are the people of Liberia suffering any less than those of Iraq? We can find $87 billion to rebuild a nation that actually throughout history has not even made a fraction of the same contribution to America as those individuals from Liberia. The question is especially relevant when the estimated price tag for an intervention in Liberia is only $275 million ... it becomes a question of the value of lives on the African continent ... particularly when you look at Liberia and the closeness that it has had with the United States of America.[10]

Viewed in the context of the hundreds of millions of dollars spent supporting and propagating the Samuel Doe problem, and of the many tens of millions more that the post-conflict humanitarian work of healing Liberia were to cost, not to mention the much larger bill that will be incurred for a proper reconstruction of Liberia, should it one day be undertaken, these few hundred million dollars that the USA failed to spend in 1990 represent a relatively modest sum. US humanitarian assistance to Liberia between 1990 and

1995 alone reportedly totalled around $500 million, according to a former deputy chief of mission at the US embassy in Monrovia, which could easily have been more than the cost of the intervention in 1990 that the White House was so desperate to avoid.[11]

The Taylor Project, a turning point in trust

Charles Taylor's personal admiration for the United States was never in question; from his college days to the gates of Monrovia's Executive Mansion in July 1990 until his appearance in a courtroom in The Hague, he often publicly expressed his support for and even love of America. Given the efforts expended by successive US administrations to undermine his progress, first in the later stages of the war, then again after he was elected president, and ultimately to ensure his removal from office, this almost unswerving loyalty might seem a little misplaced.

Throughout the hostilities in 1990, the USA, while eager to see the end of Samuel Doe, was equally wary of Taylor because of his relationship with Libya, the rapidly deteriorating human rights record of the forces under his command and other indications of his increasingly tyrannical style of leadership. Washington ultimately did not see him as a suitable replacement for Doe and began to look for alternatives while still urging the sitting president to leave the scene peacefully.

Because of the waning support for Taylor in Washington, it was crucial for the NPFL to avoid further antagonizing the USA if at all possible. During his 1990 Tapeta press conference for the international media, Taylor was economical with the truth when he tried to allay some foreign policy concerns that the USA might have had as he stood before the cameras of the international news media: 'We have never trained in Libya, we do not receive any assistance from Libya ... Libya must not be blamed.' Later in the same press briefing he went on to pour embarrassing praise on the White House, referring to Richard Nixon as 'one of the great presidents' and smilingly recalling President Reagan, whom he called 'good old Ronny ... I just seem to like the guy, perhaps because there's a little bit of the conservative in me.'[12] Whether this public adulation for what Taylor saw as his political mentors and for the homeland of his young adulthood had any noticeable effect on US attitudes is questionable. What was increasingly beyond doubt was that, with the Cold War over and the USA the sole global superpower, violent upheaval and mass suffering resulting from the civil conflict in Liberia were of minimal importance in American foreign policymaking. There was little incentive to intervene, except on humanitarian grounds and even then the USA preferred to play its part only as a supporter of others, not as a principal actor. But the USA had financed and condoned the rule of a brutal, torturing, murderous dictator in Liberia for a decade and turned a blind eye to his gross human rights violations throughout the 1980s – so Liberians and international observers alike were justified in questioning the logic of US policy and its seeming inconsistency.

In the protracted struggle aimed at gaining control of the country, for Taylor there was always a need to keep on the right side of the superpower. But the Taylor–US relationship goes much further than that, with what some insiders in the region refer to as the 'Taylor Project' having benefited in its early stages from the assistance of the USA, whether overt or, perhaps, inadvertent – for instance in the early stages of his rise to prominence. Whether by ensuring that he avoided extradition back to Samuel Doe's Liberia in 1984, or in condoning a 'soft exit' from Plymouth on 15 September 1985, to facilitating his rapid progress on the battlefield in 1990, the USA seems to have given Taylor a lot to be thankful for in his early years.

This part of the early Taylor story fits well with a collaboration hypothesis. The USA, at first blinded to all the embarrassing side effects of their unconditional support for the dictator Samuel Doe in pursuit of Cold War geopolitical aims, eventually realized it needed to remove him after he stole an election and human rights in Liberia continued to deteriorate. They could not do it overtly so needed someone to do it for them, someone known to them that could act reliably without endangering US interests. Taylor fitted the bill in more ways than one.

Certainly inside West Africa, speculation was rife that the Taylor Project was a CIA project. This extended well beyond the suspicions of President Jerry Rawlings's Ghanaian security forces or the NPFL's battlefield adversaries. It was a part of the core thinking of the Taylor inner circle itself. While advancing through Nimba County in the spring of 1990, and onwards to Monrovia in the middle of that year, Taylor kept Washington DC informed of his movements. It was really only in July 1990 that the USA seemed to be having serious second thoughts about him, and began shifting support to Prince Johnson's INPFL, when Johnson emerged as a serious and initially more acceptable contender to replace Samuel Doe as Liberia's new leader.

Although George Bush's administration had stamped on plans to remove Doe in favour of Taylor in May 1990, after the ECOMOG intervention in August of that year the USA returned to a more proactive role, once again flirting with bilateral communication as well as peace facilitation. After the capture and assassination of Doe, and as ECOMOG battled to push the NPFL back from Monrovia, on 20 September 1990 a US State Department regional 'fact-finding' mission landed in the Ivory Coast, met with the government and from Abidjan made contact with the NPFL. Together with Kenneth Brown, the US ambassador in Abidjan, they flew to Man in the north of the country near the Liberian border, from where the US delegation got into four-by-four vehicles and drove across the border, travelling some 10 miles into Liberia to meet with Charles Taylor.

Now under pressure from a changed military arithmetic, Taylor told the Americans he would accept a ceasefire if it was brokered by the USA and if ECOMOG was included – indeed he said that he would order his fighters to surrender to US troops, with whose involvement Taylor would find peace acceptable. The rebel with the Liberian-American heart was still a believer, and there was a chance of a real breakthrough. The diplomats went to work putting together the details of a plan – but again, as the wheels got into motion to bring the parties together on the ground, and as word got higher up the decision-making chain in Washington DC, the brakes were applied.

Bob Gates at the NSC was reportedly furious that this jungle outreach unit of the State Department had entered into talks potentially committing US forces. Calling the whole adventure 'beyond their mandate', Gates disowned the ceasefire plan and pulled the USA out from any involvement. From there, once again, momentum died and the plan collapsed. Taylor refused to attend a meeting scheduled for 27 September with the warring factions and ECOMOG, since the USA was now not going to be present. He went back to the bush and continued to fight.[13]

Efforts to implement disarmament of the rebels in the countryside under the various peace agreements signed over the years therefore rarely made much progress. Nevertheless, Taylor's distrust of the Nigerians was a stumbling block which gave the US an opportunity in 1992 to play a role once more. Co-opting the participation of Senegal, an ECOWAS member country which Taylor said he trusted and to which he would order his forces to disarm, the USA persuaded the Senegalese government to join the ECOMOG effort in its attempts to implement disarmament of the NPFL.

Better still, this time there was an involvement which the White House endorsed. President Bush had strong relations with Senegalese President Abdou Diouf, which got the wheels turning more quickly. The USA was willing to finance an intervention by a Senegalese contingent, which would take over the role of disarming the NPFL in potential flashpoint areas.

With this force duly dispatched in early 1992, there was at first progress with the new face of ECOMOG on the ground. Then in May 1992, a major incident shattered Taylor's credibility with the USA and forced the Nigerian ECOMOG command back on the warpath with renewed vigour. An NPFL arms cache, illegal under the terms of the Yamoussoukro III agreement, was discovered by a contingent of Senegalese soldiers. While the peacekeepers attempted to seize the arms, the NPFL surrounded and captured the Senegalese and later executed six of their contingent. The incident destroyed the faltering momentum towards peace. Taylor had broken his word to the USA and both Washington's and Abuja's patience with the diplomatic approach was now exhausted.

ECOWAS went to the UN Security Council and obtained an arms embargo against Liberia in November 1992. The USA halted its mediation attempts, and Nigeria attacked NPFL positions aggressively with warplanes and artillery, while stepping up its support for the other factions in the country which were now also gaining ground from the NPFL.

A protracted war with ECOMOG was something that Taylor was never going to win. By attacking the intervention force when it first arrived instead of just consolidating his hold on the Liberian territory that the NPFL controlled in August 1990, he sparked a confrontation which stiffened opposition to his bid for power, and led to the emergence of new armed enemies who gradually captured back more than half of Greater Liberia. A more reasoning and less impulsive commander-in-chief could have seen that de facto rule of the entire country outside Monrovia would inevitably have led to political acceptance if he had only shown enough patience to negotiate from what was at the time a position of formidable strength.

Not unlike the unreciprocated admiration that characterized the lopsided relationship between the people of Liberia and ordinary Americans, Taylor was soon apparently giving the USA more than he got in return, and it cost him dearly in his ambition to succeed. Instead of pressing home his advantage when he could have taken the Executive Mansion for himself in 1990, he paused at the behest of Washington DC. Months later, instead of being president of Liberia, he was back in the bush, his forces retreating and the NPFL just one of a number of forces now jostling to promote their own respective roles in the next phase of the evolving Liberian drama.

The August 1990 war against Iraq ensured that US attention would irrevocably be turned away from West African allies towards striving for success in its new military adventure in the Middle East. Not unlike its relations with Saddam Hussein, who enjoyed US support during his long war in the 1980s against Iran,[14] even up to within a year or two of the his invasion of Kuwait, official America turned from being an ally of Taylor to an enduring adversary in a relatively short period of time.

In addition to its pattern of conduct on the battlefield, which made Taylor's NPFL an unpalatable ally, from widespread atrocities against civilians to the frequent use of child soldiers, there were specific incidents which served to hasten the fall of Taylor's stock in Washington DC.

In 1990 fighting around the Executive Mansion, the NPFL reportedly shot a number of Israeli commandos working alongside Samuel Doe's presidential guard, experts who had originally been sent to train the Liberian president's elite force and who were still present in Monrovia at the time of the NPFL attack. Tel Aviv was incandescent with rage and turned its fury on the United States, which it had thought was confident of the security of Israeli personnel and was able to control the situation on the ground.[15]

Between 20 and 23 October 1992, during the mayhem that ensued in the wake of Operation Octopus, five American nuns were killed, some of whom were reportedly first raped, by NPFL forces in Monrovia. The nuns, from the Adorers of the Blood of Christ, based in Illinois, had been looking after children orphaned by the fighting in 1990. During the hostilities, hundreds of children from orphanages in parts of the city occupied by the NPFL were abducted, including those in which the American nuns were working.[16]

Further aggravating anti-Taylor sentiments in Washington was the discovery and arrest in 1993 of a spy in the US State Department working on behalf of the NPFL through intermediaries. Geneva Jones, a 47-year-old US military and federal employee of over two decades' standing, had passed confidential overseas embassy and CIA documents to two African journalists working in Washington DC, one a Kenyan and the other a Cameroonian. Jones's responsibilities included sorting and distributing classified cables from US embassies in Africa.

Taylor's Washington spy

Jones took the cables from her office rolled up in a newspaper and passed them to the Cameroonian, Dominic Ntube, who in turn faxed the documents to Charles Taylor's front-line base inside Liberia.

While much of the stolen intelligence was more likely to have been about Iraq and Somalia than about Liberia, the fact that Taylor the arch-fixer had once again subverted the US system added to official dislike for him and fuelled a mounting determination to see him out of office.

The trail to Taylor's Washington DC spy began in late 1992 when the NPFL was on the run from counter-attacking ECOMOG forces, and his command centre at the Firestone compound outside Monrovia was overrun. Among the documents left behind were fourteen state department cables and a fax cover sheet addressed to one of Taylor's aides, which included Ntube's Washington DC telephone number.

It transpired that the inside connection had been working quite smoothly for many months, with the NPFL in Gbarnga receiving copies of State Department cables destined for its African embassies on a weekly basis. Some of these were quite openly faxed to local West African media representatives by Taylor aides, which was ultimately how the US became aware of an espionage operation. A reporter for *West Africa* magazine in Liberia in 1992 said that for a time his publication 'received copies of the cables every day'. Ultimately, it was the Nigerian-owned West African magazine which tipped off the US authorities and put them on the trail of the informants.[17]

Later incidents, such as the NPFL incursion into the vicinity of American ambassador William Milam's residence during the April 1996 fighting in Monrovia, in which US marines killed three insurgents, damaged relations further, and by the time Charles Taylor was poised on the brink of the presidency in 1997, he was far from benefiting from the favour he had once enjoyed with policymakers in the USA.

Worse still was the incident in September 1998 when Taylor's security police, once again on the trail of Roosevelt Johnson, were involved in a shooting incident with pro-Johnson supporters and American marines outside the US embassy.

Johnson had been brought into the administration as minister of rural development as part of the policy of reconciliation with rivals and the inclusion of a broad range of voices in the new government. Nevertheless, around his Monrovia residence he maintained a paramilitary entourage, which effectively controlled a part of the city on Camp Johnson Road with an armed presence, road blocks and searches of those who wished to enter the area. Johnson and his mostly Krahn supporters, formerly of the ULIMO-J faction during the war, ran their own enclave within what was supposed to be a free city.

Initially tolerating the situation, Taylor finally removed Johnson from his cabinet, but tensions continued to rise as the Johnson faction engaged in evictions and harassment of the ordinary population within their self-declared zone of control. There were unsuccessful attempts to resolve the crisis through negotiation. On 18 September, it looked increasingly as though the Johnson group might attempt to mount a coup against Taylor. Government forces stormed the Camp Johnson Road area and retook it, an operation that saw fifty deaths.[18]

The following day a group of Roosevelt Johnson's armed supporters moved towards the AFL barracks at the Barclay Training Centre and engaged in a gun battle with security forces. The renegade group dispersed in the direction of Mamba Point towards the US embassy, where they tried to gain access, initially unsuccessfully. Meanwhile Liberian police attempted to arrest some of the Johnson group and further shooting erupted, involving police, US embassy guards and Johnson supporters.

Liberian government security forces opened fire on a group including Johnson and some US personnel outside the embassy compound. It appears that by this stage, with any possible coup attempt thwarted, Johnson was now seeking asylum from the USA and was being pursued by Taylor's security forces. In the incident, two US personnel, a government contractor and an embassy staff member were wounded while four of the Johnson party were killed.

The US eventually admitted Johnson and twenty-four of his followers into the compound, although Taylor initially believed that Johnson had been killed and issued a statement of regret at the incident. Shortly afterwards, as news reached the Executive

Mansion that Johnson was not only alive but about to be evacuated by the USA, Taylor issued a threat to shoot down the US helicopter carrying him out of the country.[19]

There were disputed claims from the American and Liberian sides regarding the exact cause and outcome of the incident, with the USA initially claiming that two Americans had been killed. A UN investigation followed and clarified that there had been injuries but no deaths of US personnel. Nevertheless, the incident led to calls on Capitol Hill to close the embassy and demands from the USA for an apology from the Liberian government.

The 1998 embassy shooting incident soured Taylor's relations with the Clinton administration at a time when he needed all his diplomatic capital to help resolve other issues, both domestic and regional. Yet seemingly he still held out hope that the United States, just as it had been his quiet supporter at the outset of the NPFL rebellion, now might somehow become his salvation as he at last had gained control of Liberia.

But just as the USA had at first underestimated Taylor's staying power in the prolonged struggle against Samuel Doe and later against ECOMOG and the assorted allied anti-NPFL factions, so did Taylor overestimate Washington's propensity for reconciliation when the fighting finally stopped.

Clearing the file in Massachusetts

Once in office, the Taylor administration certainly made strong efforts to mend fences with the USA, as well as to project a positive image in the American media, one which was by late 1997 severely tarnished. To that end, a media campaign and a presidential visit to the USA were high on the new president's foreign policy priority list. But, quite apart from sources of political hostility, there was one lingering, distant but nevertheless crucial legal issue still unresolved from Taylor's US past: his breakout from a US prison in 1985 while awaiting extradition to Liberia.

Charles Taylor's new ambassador in Washington DC, Rachel Diggs, tried to work, together with Lester Hyman, the Liberian president's US legal counsel, to get Taylor's name cleared. Officially, he was still a fugitive from prison following his 1985 breakout, a wanted man in the State of Massachusetts. With the importance of the US trip in cementing relationships with allies and to lobby for support from those in high places in Washington DC, it would be embarrassing if the visiting president of a sovereign country were still to be technically facing arrest by one of the US states. Although renewed detention for the prison escape of thirteen years before was a highly improbable event, the theoretical possibility of a five-year sentence still hung over President Taylor after over a year in office in his own country. Arguably, as a visiting head of state, Taylor would have enjoyed immunity from arrest under international law. But there were still potential risks. Either way, having the offence still hanging over him would not have provided a positive mood for Taylor's first visit to the United States.

As legal overtures were made on behalf of Taylor, a bureaucratic tap dance ensued, with the State of Massachusetts unwilling to take action on its own to drop the charges without the green light from the State Department, while the State Department officially claimed it had no jurisdiction over the authorities in Massachusetts and would not interfere in what was a legal matter of a US state.

Finally, following a lengthy process of nod-and-wink communication with the State Department, the Massachusetts charges were dropped in 1999, with the USA still denying it had given the go-ahead to clear Taylor's name. 'This was a decision that the Massachusetts authorities had to make on their own ... we were not involved in the process', an unnamed State Department official said at the time. However, according to Joseph P. Gaughan, the Plymouth assistant district attorney, Lester Hyman 'had the State Department talk with us', indicating that 'it would be in the best interests of diplomacy' to drop the charges.[20]

Although too late to clear his name in time for the planned 1998 presidential visit to the USA, the behind-the-scenes decision to drop the charges marked the end of a troubling chapter from Taylor's early career. However, it by no means marked the end of his troubled relations with the US administration.

Visit to United States aborted

Ambassador Rachel Diggs also had the job of making the advance arrangements for the 1998 presidential visit. An extensive programme was planned including a meeting with the Congressional Black Caucus, an encounter at the White House between Hillary Clinton and the Liberian First Lady, Jewel Howard-Taylor. There was a trade promotion event planned at the Liberian embassy and interviews were arranged with the editors of the *New York Times* and the *Washington Post*, as well as a lunchtime address at the National Press Club in Washington DC. Then at the last minute Taylor decided not to take the risk of going after all, due to the uncertainties over his legal status. Much of the programme had to be cancelled and Jewel Howard-Taylor represented her husband at the remaining official receptions and events.

At the embassy in Washington, there was hardly any money available to pay for these functions or to fund the salary of the ambassador herself, so Diggs ended up using her own funds to prepare parts of the programme. It was not that the government of Liberia or its president were necessarily broke; the challenge was more one of achieving legitimate international liquidity in Western countries. The reality was that moving money to the USA in times of international scrutiny and arms sanctions against Liberia was neither easy nor desirable when the official budget of the country was very tight and the required funds might have to come from sources potentially deemed contaminated by less above-board operations. A similar plight befell most of Liberia's threadbare overseas missions as the country's diplomatic envoys, constantly strapped for cash, struggled to present the case for their government at a time when it needed all the international support it could get. By contrast, in Monrovia, the fortunate few who were in the president's favour had lavish expense accounts and flaunted their cash at summits and functions while their colleagues and compatriots suffered in poverty.

At one of the final OAU summits in Durban in 2002, Foreign Minister Monie Captan missed much of the proceedings due to his shopping obligations, then returned to the conference hall and was observed ostentatiously unwrapping his new $600 mobile phone in front of Liberian colleagues and deputies from around the continent, some of whom lived without electricity in their homes due to lack of government funds.[21]

In the end, for Taylor's long-suffering ambassador to the USA, the task of representing Liberia in Washington was too great and the obstacles to achieving success too large. Diggs resigned her position in November 1999. Speaking to Taylor by phone at the time of her resignation, she said 'Mr President, this is very embarrassing. I don't think you have been very helpful to Liberia.'[22] Nevertheless, she offered her services to Taylor for any short-term projects he might need her to carry out and indeed continued to assist and advise the president over the coming four years, up to and during the LURD invasion of Liberia and the 2003 peace talks in Accra which marked both the end of his rule and the beginning of his future as an indicted international war criminal.

Reflecting on the former president's career and character, Diggs pointed to his achievements in rebuilding the Capitol in Monrovia, establishing the modern functions of the Central Bank and, most of all, his great talent in attracting and recruiting such a high calibre of deputies, from the USA and elsewhere, to come to work in his administration. When it came to diamonds, however, useful as they were in the Liberian government's arms-related businesses, the Taylor diplomatic effort failed. 'He worked hard', Diggs said 'to bring Liberia into the Kimberly process' (a regime established by a UN resolution in 2000 to certify the origin of diamonds as coming from non-conflict zones), but, despite Liberia finally being at peace, this was one challenge which proved to be beyond his powers.

On the president's personality, Diggs has highlighted an aspect of Taylor which others have often remarked upon: the recurring contrast between, on the one hand, the personal impression he created, when a subject was in range of the Taylor charm and aura, and, on the other, his track record, behaviour in and out of office and the nefarious acts committed during his pursuit of power. She remembers how those on the US side felt about her former boss: 'No one here wanted to make any contact with him ... but the picture they got when they sat down with him was totally different. He has a compelling personality.' He was 'extremely well-read and astute and it seemed as if he could be aware of every world event that was taking place'. In her role as ambassador she indicated that the frustrations had been great, and the memories 'sharp and painful ... because I could see where Liberia could be today with more cooperation from the United States'. The USA, she felt, influenced all other actors not to cooperate with Taylor's Liberia, and that was what ultimately ensured its downfall.

The Americans' African

With his education, his connections and the flair for winning over followers which had given him the springboard to his political career, Charles Taylor was able to cultivate and later harness the support of a wide range of Americans. Until things began to go wrong in his relations with Washington, and even after they became strained, he maintained an appeal, a natural draw, to those who believed in a US role in remaking Liberia. Unlike many linguistically distanced francophone African dictators, culturally and politically estranged southern African heads of state or unpalatable Muslim radicals from North Africa, Taylor often seemed to many to be a lot more like an American and he was willing to put his trust in the United States.

In the US Congress, some African-Americans through the years have been sympathetic, seeing the Taylor personage acting as a bridge between two continents and a figurehead for African-Americans seeking a connection with their mother continent. New Jersey representative and former Congressional Black Caucus leader Donald Payne thought Taylor was in a unique position because he 'had the knowledge of both worlds'. Payne liked Taylor 'because,' he said, 'he is intelligent; he knows what sells here, and he's from *over there*'.[23]

Whether for reasons of outlook, culture, religion, politics or business, a range of different Americans could get on with Charles Taylor. In a sense he was the closest thing there was to the American's African.

For Liberians, as painful as their experiences of living through his war had been, Charles Taylor was a leader they could respect, because as well as fearing him they also saw him as strong, decisive and powerful. He had no clearly defined single ethnic identity to brand him as being from one tribe or another, but for someone who had assimilated Americo-Liberian ways in his youth he managed through studious efforts to adopt at least the trappings of native Liberians' ways. Furthermore, he was from a relatively ordinary background, not an elite settler family, and he worked his way through his education and rose to the top by his own efforts, notwithstanding how unpalatable the consequences turned out to be. It is true that Liberians liked Charles Taylor, and even after he destroyed their country they accepted his promises that he would rebuild it, and voted for him despite everything.

THIRTEEN

LIBERIAN LEGACY

> I made my way home to a nation terrorized and grieving ...
> a nation whose entire history was being rapidly rewritten.
>
> Russell Banks, *The Darling*

Young Liberia: conflict and flight

For the militarized youth of Liberia's civil war, the young men, boys and more than a few women and girls who were drawn into fighting for one faction or another in order to survive, those who were coerced, who drifted into the war as orphans or who were taken alongside their brothers and neighbours into battle, the war years eliminated any semblance of a childhood, and for those among them who survived a return to normal adolescence was impossible.

At the end of the first four years of fighting, the total number of combatants in the Liberian civil war was estimated at around 40,000, although a 1993 UN Appeal document estimated the total as being as high as 60,000.[1] Two main rebel factions in the fighting after 1990, the NPFL and ULIMO, both made extensive use of child soldiers, often under the age of 15, in contravention of the Geneva Convention stipulation on the use of child combatants. UNICEF has estimated that some 10 per cent of fighters were under the age of 15, while other estimates suggest that 20 per cent were between 15 and 17, but with the vast majority of the balance being very young adults, aged between 18 and 25 for the most part.[2]

Contrary to the public representations of the factional leaders, children were used in front-line combat roles, as well as the behind-the-lines positions that the commanders often claimed – for example, for carrying ammunition, manning checkpoints and conducting spying missions for their seniors. The AFL does not appear to have made systematic use of child soldiers in the conflict, despite having been responsible for large numbers of atrocities against minors.

In addition to fear, hunger, confusion, coercion, peer pressure or revenge, a serious motivation for many children in the Liberian civil war was the lure of material gain – they were drawn, just as their elders were, by the promises of 'looting rights' in Monrovia and other raided towns and cities, by leaders who were unable to pay or uninterested in paying actual wages to their troops. There was a motivation related to the legacy of Liberian society from the 1980s – a highly militarized one – in which one of the few routes to advancement or a prestigious career for a young adolescent was to join the army, and so wartime offered a plethora of opportunities, not to mention often a choice of armies, for the young Liberian man looking to become a soldier.

From the rebel commanders' point of view, the extensive use of very young fighters had a practical aspect to it as well – in an atmosphere of instability and fear where most adults preferred to avoid the violence unless there was a strong prospect of material gain, it was easier to convince very young people to fight for almost nothing, other than vague promises of a share in the spoils of war. Once at the battlefront, children were given drugs to make them brave, or mentally unable to appreciate what they and those around them were doing – the distribution of 'bubbles' (amphetamines) to child fighters was an increasingly common occurrence during the conflict.

The added motivational advantage was that, unlike adults, who worry about their families back home when they are at the front line, children, with no responsibilities, just focus on the fighting without distraction, whether drugged going in to battle or not.

In the infamous Operation Octopus of October 1992, as the NPFL moved in to attack ECOMOG positions in Monrovia, they used what could be described as 'child shields' – waves of armed children sent out ahead of the adult combatants to attack the enemy positions. With their programmed fearlessness, albeit temporary and artificial, the effect on the enemy was unnerving and initially some of the defenders were reluctant to shoot at children. However, once they were fired upon there was little option but to shoot back, and the child soldiers were gunned down with their comrades in arms.[3] Later, ECOMOG forces used loudspeakers to call to the advancing children, offering them toys, sweets or the longer-term inducement of the chance of a home and a school to go to, which in some cases proved effective in getting them to lay down their arms and defect.[4]

After the war, organizations such as the Liberian Children's Assistance Programme, as well as international agencies such as UNICEF, established reintegration programmes for surviving child combatants. Interviews conducted among their caseloads provided considerable corroboration for stories of beatings of enlisted children, drugging and the use of torture against those who showed unwillingness to join the rebel army. Children were forced to commit acts of extreme violence against adult victims, sometimes as their 'initiation' into the ranks of whichever faction was recruiting them. This could include conducting torture, rape or mutilation in order to gain acceptance by the fighting force.

After 1991, when ULIMO surged from eastern Sierra Leone into Liberia, it grew rapidly at the expense of the NPFL and conquered territory quickly with promises to its young recruits of things they never had with the NPFL, if indeed ever, in peacetime. Many had been searching for their parents unsuccessfully in NPFL territory and decided to try on the other side of the front line, which necessitated switching sides and joining the opposing rebel force.

Charles Taylor became famous for his recruitment and deployment of a 'Small Boys Unit' as it was widely referred to – although official NPFL representatives would insist that it was in fact a 'Special Bodyguard Unit' – which was suggestive of a less direct role in combat operations. It is true that those who visited Taylor in the bush during the war years often remarked on the presence of a group of very young enlistees in the immediate vicinity of his base camp. Indeed, in the absence of clearer indications, the presence of the child guards was sometimes taken as the surest sign that 'the president' (of the government of Greater Liberia, the NPRAG) must be close by.[5]

The orphaned child fighters around Taylor thought of him as their father, following him around the base or when he moved inside NPFL territory, admiring and adoring him almost as a true parent and earning their commander the additional nickname of 'Papay' from his most loyal and vulnerable followers.

When Charles Taylor was elected president in 1997, after seven years of war, the population of Liberia was decimated as well as dispersed, regionally and internally. In addition to an estimated 200,000 casualties of war, there were some 700,000 in total who had fled the country, fully a quarter of Liberia's pre-war population of 2.8 million, making it the sixth largest refugee population in the world at the time. Another 50 per cent of the population, 1.4 million people, were internally displaced, according to the UNHCR.

Of the refugees who left Liberia, the majority were accommodated in camps in neighbouring countries, with Côte d'Ivoire and Guinea taking the lion's share of the caseload, receiving 235,000 and 160,000 persons respectively. In addition, it is estimated that 14,000 left for Sierra Leone and some 17,000 made their way cross-country or by sea to Ghana.[6]

A much smaller number of exiles, those who had resources, notably the Americo-Liberians, went further afield, particularly to the United States. Beyond these self-financed refugees, many with an American friend or relative, the US government stepped up its assistance to the war-affected Liberian population. Despite its unwillingness to intervene militarily in the first Liberian civil war in the 1990s, the USA became the largest donor of humanitarian assistance to Liberia, and granted legal Temporary Protective Status (TPS) to some 20,000 Liberians living in the USA, starting from 1991. TPS lasted until September 1998, when, following national elections and a return to civilian government, the State Department deemed that conditions in Liberia no longer warranted the continuation of the programme.

The US refugee resettlement programme offered permanent US naturalization to those who qualified, with applicants usually being considered in one of two main categories, either as political asylum-seekers or, much more commonly, as those with sufficiently close family ties in the USA to be granted reunification status. The UNHCR administered the asylum cases, known as 'P1', while an independent Nairobi-based NGO, the Joint Voluntary Association (JVA) sent teams to the refugee camps to conduct periodic interviews for reunification cases ('P3') on behalf of the US government. The transport arrangements for successful US resettlement applicants were handled by the International Organization for Migration, (IOM) from its regional office in Accra.

Voyage of the *Bulk Challenge* and Buduburam Camp

Following the third battle for Monrovia, which erupted in the wake of the Roosevelt Johnson shooting incident and his subsequent bloody pursuit through the capital, the return of wholesale insecurity to Monrovia in April–May 1996 provoked a large group of Liberians to congregate at the Freeport where an ageing chartered cargo ship, the *Bulk Challenge*-Lagos, had docked and was selling tickets to passengers, offering to evacuate the desperate.

The situation surrounding the *Bulk Challenge* excursion was both pathetic and problematic from the outset. Given the ship's dilapidated, dangerous and unseaworthy state, the extortionate amounts that those who sought to travel had to pay to board – between $50 and $75 for most – not counting the bribes payable at the Freeport itself, made the journey barely affordable for many. Nevertheless, its ardently anticipated docking represented a flicker of hope, a chance to escape for those caught once again in the cauldron of a brutal urban civil war. Not all were fortunate in their attempts to leave. Some 900 would-be travellers who had paid the bribes to pass the port and had already loaded their luggage onto the ship were ultimately denied boarding.[7] With its hull leaking and its final destination uncertain, and 4,000 passengers on board in crowded, unsanitary conditions, the *Bulk Challenge* set sail on 5 May 1996, and headed towards Ghana. It was largely the young and the fit – those with fewer responsibilities, not to mention prospects in Liberia, or those who had some resources saved up from the recent more stable times – who decided to make the sea journey.

The ship steamed eastwards, but by the time it was approaching the waters of Côte d'Ivoire it was leaking so badly that it had to dock at San Pedro, the westernmost Ivorian port. As the country was unwilling to allow such a large number of fugitives ashore, only non-Liberians were allowed to disembark; nevertheless, a few bolder and fitter Liberians decided to make a jump for it in any case, and swam or rushed ashore with those whom the Ivorian authorities had decided to accept.

Bulk Challenge set sail again, heading first for Takoradi, the deep-water port in the south-west of Ghana. But the government of Jerry Rawlings was unprepared for the influx, both logistically and financially, as well as being worried about the social impact of this potentially unruly band of largely young Liberians. The Liberian war with all its horrors by now conjured up unpleasant images in the minds of many in more peaceful neighbouring countries. This group were an unknown quantity arriving from a lawless and violent land, where, in the minds of some Ghanaians, teenagers didn't attend school but instead roamed the countryside wearing wigs, carrying Kalashnikovs and dismembering people.

Repulsed by Ghana and ignored by the international community, *Bulk Challenge* set sail again, this time for Nigeria, where it hoped to be granted the right to dock and the chance to unload its human cargo, by now on board for over a week and getting agitated as well as unhealthy, with food and water supplies running low and conditions becoming more insanitary by the day. But the ship's acceptance by Nigeria was not assured either; there was a dispute over the cost of harbouring such a large group and finding what could be potentially long-term accommodation for the refugees.

There was the animosity in many Nigerians' minds over the recent treatment of many of their fellow citizens at the hands of Charles Taylor's forces, stranded and cut off behind enemy lines during the war, captured, held against their will, tortured and mistreated in Liberia. And of course ECOMOG, Nigeria's proxy expeditionary army, until recently had been involved in direct combat with Liberia's largest armed faction – the leader of which was now the dominant voice in the ruling Council of State in Monrovia.

For their part, the Liberian passengers were unhappy about putting ashore in Nigeria as well. After the six-year presence of the ECOMOG force in and around Monrovia, many associated Nigeria with the looting and theft of their possessions, another form of insecurity just as bad as that which they suffered at the hands of their home-grown rebels. The point was moot: Nigeria denied the *Bulk Challenge* the right to bring its passengers ashore.

Pressure began to build to end the situation, an outcry in the international media was generated, and the need to bring an end to yet another chapter in the harrowing story of Liberia's distressed people was deemed a priority. Discussions took place among the international community and with the government of Ghana, always the more likely host country for the passengers among the ranks of the unwilling.

Ultimately international support was mustered and guarantees given, with donors coming forward to provide the necessary resources for the care and maintenance of the passengers of *Bulk Challenge*. On 15 May the ship and its exhausted, tense and agitated human cargo came ashore at Takoradi, finally accepted by President Jerry Rawlings, after fellow Ghanaian UN secretary general Kofi Annan agreed to provide the necessary funds for the accommodation of the refugees in Ghana.

The story of the passengers on board the creaking, leaking *Bulk Challenge–Lagos*, rejected and forced back onto the high seas by government after government as undesirable and destabilizing elements, is a telling portrayal of the international attitude generated by the Liberian tragedy after over six years of on-and-off warfare. The story stands out both as an illustration of the collapse of hope in the country and as further evidence of the international community's continued display of indifference to Liberia. The chartered cargo ship which ferried 4,000 Liberians away from their homeland was originally intended to bring its passengers to safer shores over a relatively short distance of five or six hundred miles, a two-day journey at most. But then, in a shameful international solidarity of reluctance which bordered on abandonment, its attempts at docking were rejected by one country after another in an ordeal lasting a week and a half, causing distress and hardship to those who endured it.

Youth on the run – and on the rampage

The first stop for the majority of the new arrivals was the nearby Krisan refugee settlement. By August 1996 most of the refugees had been transferred to the large UNHCR camp at Buduburam outside Accra, where they joined over 8,000 other refugees already in Ghana as a result of earlier waves of wartime migration from Liberia. Buduburam's population boomed again in later years when war returned to Liberia, and by 2005 the camp had an estimated 25,000 residents.

Camp life on the outskirts of Accra was very different from the portrayal of classic refugee dependency by the photo media merchants of squalor or the aid organization propagandists in their quest for heart-wrenching, fund-raising scenes of pity and despair. For one thing, the intention of the UNHCR camp managers was that the refugees should become as far as possible self-sufficient, engaging in farming activities as well as other projects to improve infrastructure around the camp as its population grew, as well as helping to provide basic utilities such as water supply and 'camp based organizations' intended to build more permanent housing, generate vocational training, or write project proposals aimed at starting small cash-earning enterprises such as chicken farms.

In addition to its football ground, basketball court and other sporting facilities, Buduburam also gave refugees the opportunity to engage in vocational training, such as computer and technical courses. But many just started businesses with the other refugees as clients. Since the camp was quite far from the city, and refugees had to travel to town to make phone calls, an important business opportunity presented itself through the establishment of phone booths in the camp and charging other refugees by the minute for their long-distance calls. The vast majority of overseas calls made were to friends and relatives in the United States, the source of regular remittances through Western Union, for whom Liberian refugees were the most important customers in Ghana.[8]

Outside the camp in the local Ghanaian economy, there were few opportunities, however, although some Liberians managed to start businesses of varying degrees of legitimacy, the aim of which was to become self-sufficient. Liberian refugees in Ghana were able, if only partially, to live the good life, and, despite their ostensibly difficult circumstances, many were able to imitate a version of that conspicuously American lifestyle to which nearly all young urban Liberians had aspired in better times.

For many younger Liberian women the process of adapting for survival took a different form, with work beginning after dark in and around the multiplicity of music and beer spots in Ghana's capital. Finding a partner (or partners), whether for longer or shorter term relationships, in a local bar was one of the few viable opportunities, and although such Liberians were often labelled as prostitutes by local Ghanaians, most would not consider themselves as such, but rather as victims of temporary and unexpected circumstances.

Around the streets, shops and nightclubs of the Ghanaian capital, the new refugee arrivals stood out from their more conservatively dressed and modestly behaved Ghanaian cousins, and if they didn't always have more money than the locals, they made every effort to look as if they were more prosperous, more successful and more fashionably dressed. The lifestyle which some were able to lead was far from that of desperate refugees with no alternatives. A visitor to Buduburam could often see the occasional BMW or Mercedes parked around the camp grounds, a further tell-tale sign of pockets of conspicuous refugee consumption.

Others with money found their way into residences in the Ghanaian capital and were accepted, although not always welcomed, by their more conservative and socially more stable Ghanaian hosts. In fact, out of a total wartime refugee Liberian population in the Ghanaian capital (and a few in Kumasi, some 150 miles north) of some 30,000, around one-third lived in private housing in the capital, which, although difficult for many, afforded an independence and sense of self-sufficiency that being tied to camp life could not. In Ghana most tenants are required to put up two or sometimes three years' rent in advance, and so many Liberians banded together, living several to a room initially, just to enjoy the option of having their own home.

However, the dividing line between the camp and town dwellers was blurred to a considerable degree, with many refugees shuttling between the two to maximize their opportunities for finding work as well as receiving benefits. For those on the list for US resettlement, keeping close to camp was important, both in order to be available for possible JVA interviews and for all important social networking and information-gathering.

From 1997 and particularly 1998 onwards, for those accepting voluntary return assistance to Liberia, their departure with UNHCR did not necessarily mean leaving Ghana indefinitely. In fact, many took IOM transportation to go home and see their families in Monrovia for a month or two and then returned privately, often by plane, to continue their lives in Accra.

This phenomenon of refugee commuters was unique to Ghana, however, as the larger numbers of refugees in the Guinean and Ivorian camps, where for the most part conditions were less agreeable, generally returned and then stayed at home if they could. Thus whereas the UNHCR voluntary return programmes were largely successful in the latter countries, in Ghana the programme failed, with 1998 representing the peak year for returns, with 2,515 refugees leaving Ghana, then only 350 in 1999 and finally zero in 2000, by which time the flow was once again reversing due to renewed fighting.

US resettlement was quite a different proposition. Since Ghana was the processing centre for regional departures, those close to the administrative hub tended to be the best informed about regulations,

LIBERIAN REFUGEES IN GHANA AFTER BEING ARRESTED OUTSIDE BUDUBURAM REFUGEE CAMP FOR DEMONSTRATING AGAINST UN PLANS FOR THEIR REPATRIATION TO LIBERIA, MARCH 2008

quotas and opportunities, and refugees based there were often the most successful at attending and passing interviews in order to be accepted. With the US Congress raising its quota for Liberians in the late 1990s, from 12,000 in 1999 to 20,000 in 2001, the programme was busy and well subscribed. Out of those totals, on average between 10 and 15 per cent of departures were Ghana-based refugees, with a total of 3,230 such resettlements to the US recorded in 2001.

The disrespect of the displaced

The character and position of Liberian youth were transformed in the war years, affecting all young people whether refugee, combatant or victim. The shattering of a society which had more or less held good even through the Samuel Doe years, however vulnerable, impacted attitudes and behaviour of young Liberians for a generation, if not permanently. Whereas ordinary Liberians were, and indeed are, friendly and respectful of elders in their communities, wartime experience blew apart much of the generation-based respect and upended gender-based roles for most. Although many young Liberians found useful roles in wartime which prepared them for a return to civilian life, whether in logistics, procurement, distribution and catering or as farmers, rubber tappers and hospital hands, much of the necessary infrastructure for reintegration into peacetime roles using these skills took many years to rebuild.

The new adults of Liberia, those who grew up through the war years, have little reason to feel a part of any structured society, because the one their parents lived in has been destroyed forever. Always having looked abroad to America, now many also turn their backs on what is left of the Liberia they never had a chance to grow up in. Remembering that their land was the wealthiest in West Africa in their parents' time, for many when exiled overseas this resignation can turn into resentment of their hosts, into disrespect for their culture and society, which still functions and offers a future to its youth.

The celebrated strength of a continent – its family cohesiveness, sense of community and belief in joint sacrifice above the interests of the individual – has largely disappeared for the new Liberian adults. What has been described as 'African communalism' went for centuries hand in hand with respect and maturity, granting status in society, which in turn could bring a steady accumulation of wealth with years. Those values have now been replaced by a generation for whom accumulation of material wealth at gunpoint in minutes was rife and whose leaders used and flagrantly abused their countries' resources and those of their neighbours, for personal enrichment above the interests of their community and their nation.

A Liberian writer on board the *Bulk Challenge* in 1996 has described the phenomenon of 'reverse adulthood syndrome' whereby adults, denied the authority and respect commensurate with their years, now cower in deference, leaving the vacuum to be filled by the war-hardened youth, the new orphaned, toughened Liberian young generation, whose values bear no resemblance to those that upheld past society. In the reverse adulthood world, advancement comes through chaos, not order, and community cohesion is an obstacle to the individual assertion of the strong and the ruthless.[9]

Another consequence of the descent of values of the young has been the increase in HIV/Aids infection in Liberia, now officially estimated at 6 per cent of the population in a region of Africa which had traditionally been less affected by the pandemic. In addition to the consequences of war rape, the influx of foreign forces, first

ECOMOG and then the United Nations, has further been associated with prostitution and infection in the country. Efforts to promote sex education and awareness have done little to affect behaviour, and negative examples such as the 2002 UN 'food for refugee sex' scandal have further weakened the authority of outside institutions ostensibly there to help.

Special post-conflict programmes aimed at educating former teenage fighters had to struggle against the wartime conditioning of attitudes. In particular, 'children associated with fighting forces', or CAFF, encountered extreme difficulty reintegrating and completing their education. According to one NGO education specialist in 2008, the UN disarmament, reintegration and resettlement programmes didn't fare too well, and young ex-fighters, now in their twenties, have tended to revert to a life of crime on the streets. Their experience has been made doubly difficult by the fact that they are often placed in classes with others eight or even ten years their junior, now studying at the same level as their war-affected fellow pupils.[10]

By mid-2003, one-third of Liberia's population of 3.5 million were homeless, 90 per cent were unemployed and half a million refugees were across the border in neighbouring countries. Others who had fled in the civil war of the 1990s had never returned. With half the population under 15 years old, there remained a massive educational challenge for the country in addition to all its other reconstruction difficulties. There were an estimated 2,000 teachers in the country, almost two-thirds of whom had no formal education; and when the war ended there were only 1,000 functioning schools, half of the pre-war total. In the following five years, progress was made, with more than 200 additional secondary schools opening and a total of over 4,000 primary schools now functioning again in the country. As ever, the time and – most of all – the cost of training teachers and re-establishing standards is enormous, when budgets remain constrained despite the improvement in overall conditions in the country.

Women and war

If the Liberian civil war was unusual for its high proportion of very young fighters, it was also characterized by the participation of women in fighting roles. Women were disproportionately represented among the victims, given the epidemic of rape and sexually based attacks during the fighting, as well as making up the greater proportion of civilian adults in a war which was waged mostly against non-combatants and not against rival fighting groups. But while most women were forced to adopt the roles of men as well as their own responsibilities during the civil war years – becoming breadwinners and educators as well as family raisers and housekeepers – a large number were also motivated to take up arms against the invaders of their territory – or against the government in Monrovia, whether that of Samuel Doe, Amos Sawyer or Charles Taylor, at each of the various stages of the fourteen-year conflict.

Women in the Liberian war often provided for extended families both at home or when in exile as refugees, where men had either become victims in the conflict or simply deserted the scene. Just as the generational crisis in the war may have created a 'reverse adulthood syndrome', so equally could it be said that the transformation of roles of women in filling the male vacuum created a 'reverse gender syndrome' in wartime Liberian society. A refugee single mother, one of four Liberian women living in two rooms in Accra trying to raise an infant, find work as well as train for a new occupation, described the new wartime Liberian woman simply and succinctly: 'The men are not there and so we have to do everything ... because in Liberia, the women are the men.'[11]

By late 2004, out of a total of 103,000 demobilized ex-combatants, some 22,000 women had been processed, together with 2,740 girls who had been disarmed and demobilized by UNMIL. They re-entered society with the double handicap of being known ex-fighters and, often, having the additional psychological problems associated with victims of sexually based wartime abuse.[12]

Indeed, for many women, entering the war as combatants was often the direct consequence of having been victimized in the first place. One leader of a group of women fighters supporting LURD in the June 2003 assault on Monrovia, who achieved fame for her looks as well as notoriety for her violence, said she joined up because a Liberian government soldier raped her. She began to fight and soon achieved military celebrity status under the name 'Black Diamond'. A supermodel of combat chic, she became leader of the LURD 'rebel women's military group' after joining at the age of 22, going into battle in earrings, painted nails and a fake leopard-skin jacket.[13]

Just as some women played the role of perpetrators of violence in the war, they also played an unusually strong part in ending the conflict, and in the rebuilding of Liberian society afterwards. The consistent track record of non-violent participation of Ruth Sando Perry in the Liberian political process, democratic or otherwise and no matter how flawed, made her a crucial figure in guiding the country back towards peace. Perry was the lone opposition voice in parliament after Samuel Doe's stolen election in 1985, remaining as a senator when others boycotted his government, fled the country or went into the bush to plot his violent overthrow. Her experience and stature earned her the key position of chair of the Council of State in the critical period between late 1996 and the elections of August 1997, after which she continued to be an advocate for peace both at home and in the wider West African region.

The efforts of the campaigner Leymah Gbowee, a Monrovia social worker who in 2003 began to lead singing groups of women, fasting and prayers for peace in the Monrovia fish market where she worked, were the genesis of a grassroots campaign that probably made the difference between the signing of the August 2003 Comprehensive Peace Agreement and a return to war. Gbowee attracted an ever-growing following for her movement, which became known as Women of Liberia Mass Action for Peace; amid the mounting violence of 2003 it attracted women supporters from both Christian and Muslim communities in the country. As their influence grew and as the violence worsened, Gbowee lobbied President Taylor to agree to sit down at peace talks and end the conflict that was torturing their people. He finally agreed, inviting the women's representative to the Executive Mansion on 23 April 2003 to deliver her statement to the president. In June, when peace talks finally began in Ghana, Gbowee led a band of her followers and camped for weeks outside the conference centre in Accra, continuing to negotiate with, and heckle, the faction leaders, whose sincerity she questioned.

Praying away the devil

Taylor fled the scene of the talks, returning to Monrovia after the botched delivery of his indictment by the Special Court for Sierra Leone, leaving an even less motivated band of warriors' deputies in charge. Realizing that peace was inevitable, their game became more one of jostling for position to see who would get the important and potentially lucrative portfolios in the government, not of bringing about an end to fighting and a start of reconstruction. The talks dragged on without progress for another six weeks.

Devoid of statesmanship and a sincere commitment peace as they were, the representatives of Liberia's merchants of death were cynical about it. At the talks, some even used their ability to destroy and kill for graphic emphasis in negotiations, in the way in which others might make a PowerPoint presentation on a conference room screen. At one of the talks a faction chief who was being denied a particular concession was noted withdrawing to his hotel room to make a call on his mobile phone to his commanders in Monrovia; minutes later, delegates could watch artillery under his control raining down shells on civilians in the capital, live on their television screens in the Ghanaian conference centre. Not long afterwards when the talks resumed, the concession he had argued for was granted.[14]

Through all this Ms Gbowee was unmoved; she and over 200 other women staged a sit-down protest on the floor outside the negotiating hall, even blocking one of the LURD war bosses, Brigadier General Joe Wylie, when he tried to leave the hall, still with no agreement signed. Attempting to use force to gain his exit, the war boss then kicked at the protesting women as he tried to get out, prompting a rebuke from Nigeria's former president and Accra talks mediator General Abubakar, who turned on Wylie and said: 'I dare you ... If you were a real man, you wouldn't be killing your people. But because you are not a real man, that is why these women will treat you like boys. I dare you to leave this hall until we have negotiated a peace with these women.'[15]

Ms Gbowee's efforts continued throughout the eight-week process and finally a peace agreement was signed, paving the way for Taylor's departure, disarmament of combatants, establishment of an interim government and a Truth and Reconciliation Commission to air grievances from the country's long and painful conflict years.[16]

Lastly and most recently, Liberia has elected a woman, also a long-time participant in the Liberian scene, President Ellen Johnson Sirleaf. Also an opponent of tyranny in Liberia since the Doe regime of the 1980s, she nevertheless was a significant financial backer of Charles Taylor and the NPFL at its outset, before leaving Liberia for almost two decades for the relative wilderness of global corporate banking and international development bureaucracy.

Disadvantaged by the timing, out of contact with the grassroots on the ground and organizationally ill prepared to take on the Taylor machine in 1997, she at least contested the democratic elections which brought the National Patriotic Party to power, marking her out as a serious contender for the future. Her time came after Taylor's departure, and she finally attained the highest office in the land after the second round of Liberia's controversial 2005 poll, in which she was defeated in the first round by international soccer star George Weah.

Truth, reconciliation and impunity

The Comprehensive Peace Agreement (CPA) that was signed in August 2003 to bring an end to Liberia's civil conflict also provided for the passage of a Truth and Reconciliation Act and the establishment of a Truth and Reconciliation Commission, as essential elements in the process of healing the deep wounds of Liberia's recent past and helping its badly battered society to feel its way more positively towards the future. The clear intention was that all actors would participate: protagonists, perpetrators, witnesses and victims alike. But from the outset of the process and given the identity of the most powerful signatories to the CPA, there was an implicit assumption of amnesty as a condition of participation on the part of the war's worst offenders.

In an environment where the victims were so numerous and the crimes against them so egregious, the need for retributive justice would clearly have been the preferred path in any world where accountability mattered more than survival and where morality was more than a footnote in the annals of the conduct of Liberia's warring leaders. But with fierce fighting still going on as the negotiations in Accra proceeded, the urgency for a peace deal at any reasonable cost prevailed. The power of the civilian actors was so diminished and the need to satisfy the demands of the respective heads of the warring factions so pressing that many provisions which could have satisfied the right to justice of ordinary Liberians were paid more lip service than real respect.

The Truth and Reconciliation Act was finally passed by Liberia's National Transitional Legislative Assembly on 12 May 2005, though with the process of establishing its structure and operations being delayed until well into President Ellen Johnson Sirleaf's administration. Lacking the necessary funds to attract high-quality legal personnel or to develop a strong investigative capacity in its operations, the TRC selected nine commissioners, to serve under chairman Jerome Verdier, an attorney and senior accountant who had been a leading human rights activist in the country and an active participant on the boards of numerous national advocacy groups. However, there were no commissioners with the stature required for the daunting task of taking on the powerful, lawless former armed commanders and their henchmen who had called the shots in Liberia for a decade and a half. Furthermore, lack of adherence to a rigorous methodology and strict legal criteria in reaching its conclusions proved to be significant drawbacks to the TRC's ultimate performance.[17]

It took several years for the TRC to get up and running and to complete its work. Nevertheless, during the course of its operations it was able to amass some 20,000 witness statements, many gleaned through outreach work across the Liberian countryside. Public hearings only began in January 2008 and participation was initially woefully inadequate. Many of those called to testify, particularly individuals bearing the greatest responsibility for the harrowing of Liberia, simply chose to ignore the TRC. The process only got properly under way in March 2008 with the release of a problematic statement from the commissioners that those coming to testify would be granted immunity.

This inducement worked, and soon all of Liberia's war chieftains, their deputies, as well as victims and witnesses, were queuing up to take the stand, or, as they saw it, the grandstand. Now with the declared guarantee of impunity, they could flout, they felt, the intended purpose of the TRC and discuss their ugly pasts in public and even brag about their murderous misdeeds. Some actually chose to enumerate the deaths and the suffering they had wrought, while at the same time showing contempt for the authority of the commission and a manifest disrespect for its officials. The commissioners themselves revealed their lack of gravitas in failing to rein in the bragging and bantering of some of the most notorious wartime offenders, displaying shyness and lack of engagement during cross-examinations.[18]

However, the problem was that the Act which created the TRC had clearly stated at the outset that those guilty of war crimes and international human rights violations would not be granted amnesty by the commission; thus the declarations of the commissioners with regard to immunity as well as the assumptions of the high-profile witnesses were at odds with the TRC's mandate. The sidelined and disrespected commissioners, whatever their shortcomings, had a serious job to do and they were empowered to deliver their findings, and to make recommendations of censure and prosecution, a fact which the grandstanding warlords and indeed the president herself may have taken too lightly during their testimonies.

In its preliminary findings, the TRC reported among other things that 'A form of both individual and community reparation is desirable to promote justice and genuine reconciliation' and that 'A prosecution mechanism is desirable to fight impunity and promote justice and genuine reconciliation.'[19] That was the faintly heard early warning shot of what was to come as a bombshell in the TRC's final report, which was released in June of the following year.

When the final report was issued, its general conclusions were wide-ranging and largely predictable: among a long list of recorded findings, it confirmed the universal use and abuse of child soldiers by warring factions; it recognized the widespread incidence of war crimes, sexual and gender-based violence and breach of international humanitarian law; and it documented the fact that no faction or armed party to the conflict had taken steps to control or mitigate the massive violations of human rights committed by its troops. It also contained an interesting reinterpretation of some of the historical received wisdom regarding Liberia's past which had bearing on its modern-day conflict.

However, it was the specific recommendations of the final report that contained the TRC's killer blow. It listed as recommended for prosecution a total of ninety-eight persons, including all the main faction leaders who had shown such disrespect for the commissioners during the prior year's proceedings. The list included high office holders in the government of the day as well as other former militia commanders who were by now holding prestigious positions in business, public administration and academia. Furthermore, it censured a further fifty persons, recommending their being banned from holding public office for thirty years 'for being associated with former warring factions'.[20] The list included numerous well-known names, among which was included none other than that of the sitting president of the Republic of Liberia, torch-carrier of women's rights and revered alumnus of the international community's blue-chip institutions, President Ellen Johnson Sirleaf.

The report recommended that Sirleaf be banned from holding public office after the end of her current term, which expires at the end of 2011. Furthermore, it recommended that a list of eight of the principal protagonists, the faction commanders-in-chief, which included Charles Taylor, be brought before a special tribunal to stand trial for their crimes.

At last, justice for the people of Liberia? Well, not quite. In fact events were soon to deeply disappoint many, including the domestic human rights organizations and other civil society activists, who continue to argue for the implementation of the Commission's recommendations.

Upon its release, the excitement that the TRC final report generated among ordinary Liberians was only matched in its intensity by the stunned silence of the country's elite, the international diplomatic community and many prominent international NGOs, including Amnesty International. All declined to comment on the TRC's recommendations. Amnesty, despite having lobbied strongly for a transitional justice process for Liberia in the early post-war years, apparently preferred not to break ranks with its international colleagues and endorse or even offer comment on the controversial TRC report. The embarrassment for the country's presidency was palpable. Even US Secretary of State Hillary Clinton, a former lawyer and vocal supporter of President Johnson Sirleaf, who visited Liberia weeks after the report's release, scrupulously avoided public comment on the detail of its findings.[21]

The former warlords were united, together with the president, in their condemnation of the TRC's report. The seven named for special tribunal trials joined forces to hold a press conference at which they committed themselves strongly to doing everything to prevent the TRC's recommendations from being carried out. Among these was former INPFL leader Prince Johnson, senator for Nimba County. Already known as the butcher of Samuel Doe and a leader with a volatile temper, Johnson now characterized himself and his fellow wartime killers, recycled as peacetime public servants, as being the victims of unjust accusations. 'Why are we being persecuted, and why have others been given amnesty?' complained Johnson, extending his arms as if he were still a military commander. 'Why was there no opportunity to confront the witnesses? Is that fair?'[22]

But in the streets of Monrovia, in towns around the countryside, in church meetings and in soccer clubs, there was excitement and eager anticipation at the prospect of the recommendations being implemented, and for the most part ordinary Liberians did not seriously challenge the TRC's findings. It is true there were those who agreed with the powerful who stood accused that going ahead with tribunals and banning leaders from office would only refuel the flames of war. For them, the whole process was better forgotten; the time, energy and money would be better spent on rebuilding the country and helping people to move away from the past.

Others on the list recommended for prosecution or censure went beyond verbal condemnation of the TRC's report. Commissioners received notes at their houses and calls on their mobile phones delivering death threats. A number went into hiding for a time after the findings were published.

A president repents

On 26 July 2009, President Sirleaf went before the country and made a public apology for having supported Charles Taylor in the early months of the war. She admitted that in early 1990 she had crossed the front lines into NPFL territory and given $10,000 to Taylor to equip his army and feed civilians trapped by the fighting. She then declared that she had actively opposed him from then onwards 'when his true intentions became clear'. Other than her visits to meet Taylor in the bush in early 1990 to give him funds, there is scant hard public evidence of a wider wartime role beyond those admitted early transgressions. However, Sirleaf was eager to minimize her involvement after the fact and there remain prominent doubters regarding the Johnson Sirleaf official version.

The NPFL defence spokesman, Tom Woewiyu, a close colleague of Sirleaf's in the United States during their period in pre-war activism in the ACDL, is also on the record regarding Sirleaf's deeper involvement as well as her commitment to violent change in Liberia during 1990. In an interview with the BBC in late June 1990, as the NPFL was poised to enter Monrovia, Sirleaf was asked how she felt about the impending death and destruction that seemed almost certain to engulf the capital. In a September 2005 open letter to Sirleaf, Woewiyu reminded the then presidential candidate that she had replied to the BBC: 'Level Monrovia, we will rebuild it.'[23] Sirleaf later apologized for the remark, which by the time of the publication of her autobiography had become the less belligerent-sounding 'If they burn the [Executive] Mansion down, we will rebuild it.'[24]

One of the TRC commissioners, journalist Massa Washington, who has known Sirleaf for decades and visited her in prison when she fell foul of Samuel Doe's security services, has said that the president's testimony before the TRC was 'at best, only 20 percent of the truth ... In fact, there was much, much more. And her support for Taylor lasted much longer than she told us.'[25] Washington has also said that in her capacity as commissioner she was shown CIA documents detailing a more extensive Sirleaf role in the NPFL, documents the exact content of which she was 'not at liberty to reveal'.[26]

Charles Taylor, in Special Court testimony in The Hague was more graphic in his exposé of Johnson Sirleaf's involvement with the NPFL, during one session producing an organizational chart of the NPFL's command structure which included the position of 'international coordinator' with by then President Sirleaf's name indicated as holder of the position. Giving the witness his marker pen, Presiding Judge Richard Lussick asked Taylor to confirm the name and indicate the dates of her involvement on the chart presented before the court – whereupon he wrote beside Ellen Johnson Sirleaf's name '1986–1994', after which he signed and dated the chart.[27]

In private interview response later, Taylor was more scathing still about his former backer and successor to the presidency of Liberia. With reference to the recognizably downplayed public versions of Sirleaf's NPFL involvement, he said:

> Everything Tom Woewiyu has said about our dealing with Ellen is true... At one point she denied any links to me or the NPFL. Then, after her being placed in the Presidency by her 'handlers' George Bush and Tony Blair, she changed the story to saying that I misled her. The Harvard-educated Ellen let the Bentley-educated Taylor mislead her?[28]

There was a stand-off between, on the one hand, the elite who had promoted and signed the TRC into law and who were now disowning its findings and, on the other, the survivors, the victims and the disempowered for whom the recommendations of the TRC were the only chance to see justice carried out in their land. Admittedly the TRC had been flawed in certain ways, its consistency and methodology had been criticized, and there were serious omissions from the list of guilty parties as well as the controversial inclusions.

Commentators have suggested that the work of the TRC would be unable to stand up to a process of judicial review.[29] But totally to ignore the outcome of a process which had just a few years before been deemed so central to Liberia's reconciliation seemed like one slap in the face too many for the tens of thousands of dead and hundreds of thousands more maimed, injured and bereaved from the fourteen years of war.

FOURTEEN

JUSTICE À LA CARTE

> Members of the jury, it is me sitting here with my black face and white wig, looking for all the world like a pint of Guinness. I have a good head too.
>
> Courtenay Griffiths, QC,
> Defence Counsel for Charles Taylor[1]

From Calabar to courtroom

The delivery of Charles Taylor into the custody of the Special Court for Sierra Leone (SCSL) on 3 April 2006 marked the end of a long period of stand-off and uncertainty for the international community in its dealings with the legacy of the Liberian civil war and its related conflicts. With the near disaster of an eleventh-hour Taylor escape from his Nigerian hosts averted, the forces of international justice could finally be brought to bear upon Charles Ghankay Taylor. Upon arrival in Freetown, Taylor was brought directly into a fortified United Nations compound by helicopter, just days after his recapture at the Cameroonian border while attempting a do-or-die escape from justice.

Waiting for him in Sierra Leone were chief prosecutor Desmond da Silva, officials of the court and the Samoan judge Richard

Lussick, nominated by the Sierra Leonean government to preside over Taylor's initial hearings. Upon arrival at the court, Taylor joined nine other indicted criminals, both RUF allies and pro-Sierra Leone government adversaries, also accused of perpetrating war crimes in Sierra Leone's eleven-year civil war.

Taylor was brought before the court to hear the charges against him, appearing confident as well as uncooperative with the protocol of the proceedings. Former President Taylor strode into the court wearing a blue double-breasted suit, white shirt and cufflinks, and a red tie. He smiled and blew a kiss to his family in the audience, and stared down Justice Lussick. He was defiant. At first, he pretended not to hear, or not to understand, the charges brought against him. When he finally confirmed that he understood the charges, he challenged the court's jurisdiction, claiming that it had none due to his immunity, being the twenty-second president of Liberia. He then responded, 'I did not and I could not have committed these acts against the sister republic of Sierra Leone.'[2]

Already beginning to smack of political correctness, the court had conveniently indicted three men from each of the Revolutionary United Front and the Armed Forces Revolutionary Council as well as the Civilian Defence Forces, the successor entity to the Kamajors, Sierra Leone's traditional fighters. Unlike the UN-run Arusha trials in the wake of the Rwandan genocide of 1994, the Sierra Leone court contained no provision for immunity of any side despite wide acceptance, by Sierra Leoneans at least, that the CDF, which had fought alongside Ahmed Tejan Kabbah's government army against the rebels, was a much less contemptible party altogether, and indeed had somehow served the interests of the population rather than being an instigator of war. It was at least widely agreed that the most brutal atrocities against civilians, such as amputations, were carried out exclusively by the RUF and AFRC, but the CDF nevertheless stood accused of war crimes against civilians.

There had originally been five indicted on the bench of the RUF accused. In addition to Issa Sesay, his deputy Morris Kallon and senior commander Augustine Gbao, Foday Sankoh had been indicted on seventeen counts of war crimes and had appeared before the court intermittently for months, with failing physical health and mental faculties impeding his ability to testify. Finally on 29 July 2003 Sankoh died of a stroke in detention. At the announcement of his death before the court, the chief prosecutor, David Crane, stated that he had been 'granted the peaceful death that he had denied to so many others'.[3]

The fifth member of the original RUF accused bench, Sam Bockarie, was killed on 5 May 2003 by Liberian security forces while attempting to evade detention. Bockarie, the former Foday Sankoh deputy who had fled Sierra Leone in 2000 and joined Taylor's ATU for a time, was trying to flee to Côte d'Ivoire after the SCSL pressured President Taylor to hand him over to its custody. Many believed that his testimony would have been damaging for the Liberian leader due to their former collaborative relationship in the prosecution of Sierra Leone's civil war.

Charges against Taylor

Charles Taylor's arrival at the court in April 2006 made him the first Liberian it had indicted and placed the spotlight back on a court whose proceedings had already been running for over three years. Having originally charged Taylor with seventeen counts of war crimes, the prosecution had pared these down to eleven by the time of his initial hearing on 3 April 2006. The charges were:

- Five counts of war crimes: terrorizing civilians, murder, outrages against personal dignity, cruel treatment and looting.
- Five counts of crimes against humanity: murder, rape, sexual slavery, mutilation and beating, and enslavement.
- Other serious violations of international humanitarian law: recruitment and use of child soldiers.

The Special Court, already mired in controversy as a result of the prior trials of Sierra Leonean accused, was thought likely to be in a particularly sensitive position as a result of Charles Taylor's appearance in Freetown. With a still tense political atmosphere in both Sierra Leone and Liberia, and with the departure of much of the UNAMSIL presence due by the end of 2006, the court believed that holding the Taylor trial in Sierra Leone could lead to renewed instability in the country. On 17 June 2006, a UN resolution provided for the transfer of Charles Taylor's trial to the International Criminal Court in The Hague, where it would be conducted under the SCSL's auspices. As of the end of 2010, the Special Court for Sierra Leone had tried a total of nine people in the eight years since President Ahmed Tejan Kabbah's peace declaration, at a cost of over $120 million.

As the Special Court's proceedings ambled on, and as the handful of convictions it secured were announced, many Sierra Leoneans felt that the funds used up by the body could have been better spent on helping the victims of the war. One such group was the Amputees and War Wounded Association, who declared that they forgave the perpetrators of the crimes against them and called on the UN to stop the trial, instead dedicating the resources thus saved to providing them with work and giving support to their most vulnerable members.

Charles Taylor alone among Liberian perpetrators of regional conflict stood trial for crimes allegedly committed in Sierra Leone; if there was never to be justice for the other architects of Liberia's war, could it be seen as logical and just that Charles Taylor alone should be punished? Or, to frame the question more broadly, what were the true objectives of the international community in pursuing Taylor to the end while many of his compatriot perpetrators of war once more sat in high office in Monrovia enjoying the trappings of power and privilege, just as they did a decade before when their forces were looting and murdering in the Liberian countryside?

If their motivations were not those of a personal vendetta against one man, as opposed to a desire for a more adequate administration of justice, then why try only Charles Taylor and not the others? And why so much expense of time, energy and money on Sierra Leone while Liberia was left with what outsiders regarded as an unsatisfactory and easily dismissed document, the Truth and Reconciliation Commission's final report? To those outsiders, the TRC was already rapidly becoming a forgotten forum, a lonely cry for a people's justice, muffled and ignored by those in the international community to whom its findings and recommendations should have been of the greatest concern.

Still mired in controversy two months after the release of its final report, on 28 August 2009, Liberia's TRC announced that it would delay implementation of its findings for a year to allow time for it to 'consult with its constituents'. But in the interim, those who had been named carried on with business as usual, as if the report had never been issued. Ellen Johnson Sirleaf even announced her intention to stand again as candidate for president in 2011, contrary to her own prior pronouncements and in the face of the recommendations of the TRC's final report barring her from public office for thirty years.

Since that time, the prospects for the implementation of the recommendations have worsened, rather than improved, with the issuance of perfunctory quarterly reports to update on status without any concrete action being taken. Unable officially to ignore the recommendations of a commission enshrined in an Act of Parliament, moves began to have Liberia's Supreme Court nullify its recommendations. If successful, such measures would come as a bitter conclusion to a long process whose results were widely accepted by ordinary Liberians, even if they were dismissed by others; the official burial of the TRC report would mark the end of the only serious attempt to date to deliver justice as well as promote reconciliation to a country where for over thirty years the only power to have been paid respect has been that of the gun.

Whatever the conclusion of the Charles Taylor trial, there will still be neither closure, nor healing nor justice for Liberians, and for many their period of trauma will continue.

Reflecting on the process of Liberian justice as served to date, TRC chairman Jerome Verdier lamented the state of affairs a year and a half after the completion of his commission's report, and at the same time issued a thinly disguised warning as to what official disregard for the TRC's findings means for the future. With few outside actors willing to intervene and so many of the same protagonist insiders still running the country, rewarded rather than rebuked or sanctioned for their acts, Verdier described it as nothing less than a 'recipe for renewed conflict' in Liberia.

With the exception of Human Rights Watch and a few other isolated voices, there seems no support from the international community to establish a tribunal for Liberia's perpetrators of war. Despite the presence of foreign observers during the TRC's hearings, the international community seems likely to ignore its findings and disregard its recommendations, just as many of those in power inside Liberia have already done. To date, the only 2011 presidential candidate who still supports proper follow-up of the TRC's findings is T.Q. Harris, who has called for their full implementation before the start of the campaign.

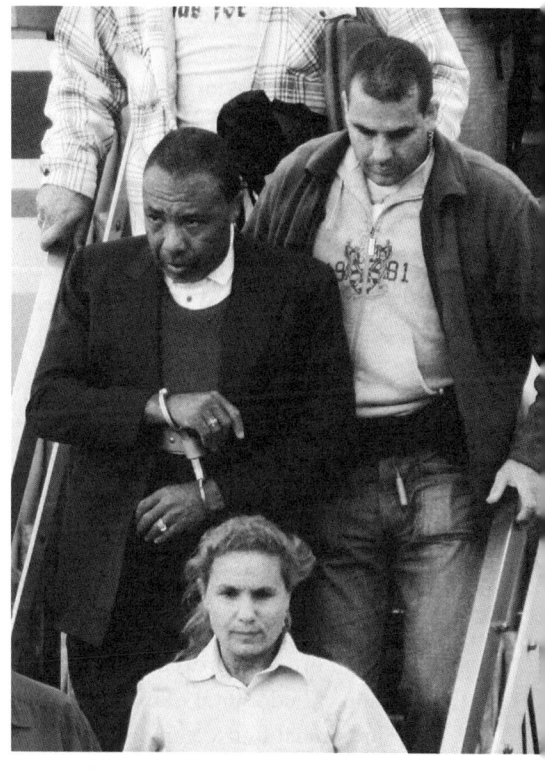

CHARLES TAYLOR COMING OFF THE PLANE IN THE NETHERLANDS TO STAND TRIAL, 20 JUNE 2006

Verdier challenged the critics of the TRC who said that the commissioners lacked stature and sufficient legal expertise to conduct hearings effectively and reach judicially sound conclusions. 'If we had included international commissioners', said Verdier, 'the results would have been diplomatic, they would have diluted the findings ... and the issue of sovereignty is very important to Liberians.' Defending the results of his enormous efforts but still with a note of bitterness, Verdier affirmed: 'we were successful ... people have not denounced the report, they have embraced it en masse ... but the [situation we are now in is] ... a temporary cessation of war'.[4]

Charles Taylor trial finally proceeds

At Charles Taylor's trial in The Hague, the chief prosecutor, Stephen Rapp, made his side's opening statement on 4 June 2007 outlining his intention to prove that Charles Taylor was guilty as charged of the crimes committed in Sierra Leone through his backing of the RUF and the AFRC and his control over those rebel groups' leaderships. The prosecution also set out to prove that Taylor was responsible for Liberian forces that fought alongside the RUF in Sierra Leone during the period of the court's jurisdiction, November 1996 to January 2002.

The prosecution further alleged that Taylor bears individual responsibility for the crimes by planning, instigating and ordering them as well as through his execution of a plan to take control of Sierra Leone, during which the alleged crimes were committed. In his capacity of commander and superior of the Sierra Leonean rebels, Taylor failed to prevent their crimes or discipline the perpetrators of those crimes, despite having full knowledge of them, it alleged.

In order to prove its case, starting on 7 January 2008 the prosecution called a total of ninety-one witnesses, whose testimonies lasted for almost fourteen months. Over half were victims of the war, while another third were 'insider' or 'linkage' witnesses, whose function was to prove the Taylor relationship with Sierra Leone's rebels. The remainder were expert witnesses called to testify on specific areas of interest to the judges in the case.

Some witnesses gave their testimony reluctantly, including the UK model Naomi Campbell, whom the prosecution interrogated about her apparent gift of 'conflict' diamonds from Charles Taylor following a dinner hosted by Nelson Mandela in South Africa in September 1997. Under threat of subpoena, Campbell appeared, giving testimony which was evasive regarding the diamond gift and later contradicted by the testimony of a fellow celebrity, Mia Farrow.[5]

Opening for the defence, UK barrister Courtenay Griffiths challenged the entire legitimacy of the proceedings on behalf of Taylor, calling his client's indictment a 'colonial witch hunt masquerading as justice'. He further took the opportunity to deplore the manner in which the indictment had been delivered by prosecutor David Crane, fully three months after its issuance in March 2003, with the attempt to arrest Taylor only being made in June of that year in Accra, at the opening of the Liberian peace talks.

Crane admitted that his purpose at the time had been a calculated move to put down Taylor on the international stage and strip him of his aura of power in public, a ploy which totally backfired as the Ghanaian authorities declined to carry out his arrest on behalf of the court and Taylor returned unhindered to Monrovia.

Referring to the incident, Courtenay Griffiths in his statement to the court quoted Bob Marley, attacking Crane's behaviour as 'iniquity to achieve vanity'.[6] In addition to its potentially delaying the onset of peace, the defence portrayed Crane's action as an inappropriate and inept use of procedure against the accused.

In front of the court, Griffith invoked the language of postcolonial accountability for the crimes of the white man in Africa. He posed the rhetorical but highly charged question: why should a black man from the world's poorest continent stand trial for crimes not unlike those so often committed by friends and allies of Washington in Latin America, for example, and who had never been brought to account before a court of law? Indeed, Griffiths argued, was it right that the superpower that had finally forced Taylor's capture and arrest did not even recognize the International Criminal Court (ICC), refusing to accept its jurisdiction over American citizens? What kind of trial and ultimate judgment could be expected from such a tribunal? How legitimate, in the view of a reasonable person, could its true purpose in international law be?

Although Charles Taylor could be held responsible for many more deaths and much greater destruction in his own country than he ever caused directly or indirectly in Sierra Leone, it was nevertheless his transgressions of international law in the latter country which finally brought about the issuance of an international warrant for his arrest, for the second time in twenty years. While his opponents at home now welcomed their tormentor's delivery into captivity, the paradox of this situation was not lost on Liberian civil society, and an unrequited yearning for accountability and reconciliation for crimes committed against them lingers on despite Taylor's departure from the scene.

Equally apparent, at least to Charles Taylor's defence counsel, were some other ironies of the unprecedented appearance of an elected African president before an international court of justice in the heart of Europe. This was, after all, the continent that had effectively conquered, if not enslaved, much of Africa and only relinquished its colonial grip on the majority of African territories some fifty years before.

Further issues of legitimacy plagued the Special Court from the outset of its proceedings. Under international law, a serving head of state, which Taylor was at the time of his arrest, cannot be compelled to testify. While he was no longer Liberia's president at the time when the international community finally apprehended him, it could be argued that he would have been had it not been for his arrest and detention under the indictment issued by the Special Court of Sierra Leone.

Interestingly, the same situation arose earlier in the same forum when it was still sitting in Freetown. Hinga Norman, former head of the CDF, ally of the government side in Sierra Leone's civil war and a popular figure in the country, claimed as part of his defence that, in ordering his forces to attack, he was acting on orders from the government. To complicate the situation, and to the enormous potential embarrassment of the president and the international community who had backed him, Norman called President Ahmed Tejan Kabbah as a witness. Kabbah, however, initially claimed that he was not obliged to testify due to his status as a sitting head of state.

Charles Taylor's guilt or innocence hangs on whether or not he continued to assist and direct the operations of the RUF from the end of November 1996, the date of the signing of the Abuja accords, until 18 January 2002, the date when President Kabbah officially declared the Sierra Leone civil War to be at an end.

While it is undisputed that the NPFL was strongly implicated in the early activities of the RUF from the start of the civil war in March 1991, its actions and those of its leader had no bearing on the deliberations of the court, since 30 November 1998 marked the legal beginning of its jurisdiction. Again, the court before which Taylor was brought could only try him for crimes committed in Sierra Leone after the ceasefire and the signing of the peace agreement in that country, and while doubtless of strong relevance and equally abhorrent in their nature, any war crimes or breaches of humanitarian law he may have committed in his own country were outside the legal remit of the court.

Thus, in seeking to prove Charles Taylor guilty, the prosecution was obliged to restrict itself to a relatively narrow period of time, during all but nine months of which Charles Taylor was president of Liberia. The efforts of the prosecution were therefore directed at showing that from the end of November 1998 on, Charles Taylor committed serious crimes in Sierra Leone; and one of Charles Taylor's strongest arguments in his defence was that he used his position as president of Sierra Leone's neighbour to help bring about peace in that country.

Taylor was able to exploit this issue of timing during his own testimony, which began on 13 July 2009. Freely admitting that he gave 'small amounts of arms and ammunition' to help the RUF in 1991 he in no way incriminated himself, while strongly denying that any such assistance was provided after late 1998, the period of interest to the judges.

Arms-for-diamonds allegations

The main thrust of the prosecution's case hinged on showing that, in addition to being present militarily in Sierra Leone, Taylor's army and government were responsible for either arming the RUF during that period or for directing it and its leadership in their actions and thereby being responsible and culpable for the war crimes and crimes against humanity which occurred. Thus it was necessary to show that he either arranged shipments of arms and ammunition to the RUF, or held meetings with the RUF and its leaders to direct their actions, or engaged in commerce which resulted in enhancing the resources available to the RUF, such as facilitating the trade in diamonds or illegal shipments of commodities through Liberian territory.

The arguments for the prosecution concluded in May 2009 and the defence began to present its case in the following month. Charles Taylor's own testimony started in July 2009 with testimony and cross-examination of witnesses continuing until November of 2010.

In his testimony, Taylor accused the UK and ECOMOG of being suppliers of arms to fuel the war in Sierra Leone and that he was used as their scapegoat. He made the argument that since ECOMOG had a military presence in Liberia and was charged with searching for arms in the country in the early part of the period, it was also in a much better position to pass weapons over the border, as it controlled the checkpoints across the countryside through which supplies had to pass. Furthermore, ECOMOG had a track record since the early 1990s in Liberia of dealing in arms with most of the warring factions in the country, as well as dealing in Liberia's mineral wealth; thus it could equally be argued that they were more likely to be the ones, rather than his government, who masterminded the supply of arms to Sierra Leone in exchange for diamonds through Liberia.

It was alleged in the Special Court that after the Lomé Peace Accord in July 1999, Foday Sankoh returned to Sierra Leone via Monrovia and met with Charles Taylor, together with other RUF commanders, who continued to meet the NPFL in Liberia regularly over the coming four years. It was also alleged that when Foday Sankoh was imprisoned, Charles Taylor directly or indirectly assumed control of the RUF, and that he had 'promoted' Sam 'Mosquito' Bockarie to the rank of brigadier general in the RUF. At one stage the prosecution produced photographs of Bockarie and senior NPFL generals wearing the same red-coloured generals' uniform caps, with the general's star similarly emblazoned on them, indicating that they must have been commanders of the same fighting force, namely the NPFL.

In response to these allegations, Issa Hassan Sesay, RUF leader from May 2000 onwards, denied that the NPFL generals and Bockarie were members of the same army, simply stating that they all wore caps that they had looted from ECOMOG in their respective territories, and so they would naturally have the same design.

What was undisputed was that Taylor offered to mediate in the UN hostage crisis in 2000 and spoke to Bockarie, Sesay and others in Monrovia in connection with the affair, ostensibly using his influence over his former comrades-in-arms to secure the release of the 500 detained peacekeepers. At the Special Court, the prosecution alleged additional meetings of a quite other nature, relating to the control and strategy of the RUF, allegations which Taylor and his defence team denied.

Throughout his cross-examination, Taylor stressed that his only meetings and contacts with the RUF during the period under scrutiny were aimed at furthering the Sierra Leone peace process, with which ECOWAS had asked him to assist and in connection with which he indeed attended various regional meetings at the time.

UN comes in for Taylor attacks

Taylor's testimony lasted a total of fourteen weeks, during which he was sometimes allowed to give long and often off-topic answers to relatively straightforward questions. Despite the protests of the prosecution on a number of occasions, the court largely gave the accused the benefit of the doubt when their challenges were issued. It has been suggested that the special nature of the trial as the first of its kind where the accused has been an African former head of state, on trial for the most serious of crimes in an international court of law, may have been a major factor in the court's leniency in this regard.[7]

One of the important exhibits in the prosecution's case was the UN Panel of Experts report of 2000, which cited Taylor's participation in the arms and diamonds dealings that fuelled Sierra Leone's civil war. The accused dismissed the UN report as biased and in particular referenced one of its panellists, Ian Smillie, who had already accused Taylor of criminal Sierra Leone involvement in previous reports, as being unsuitable for inclusion. Taylor had written to the UN secretary general to object to Smillie's inclusion at the time the panel was doing its work, to no avail.

Leaving no doubt about his views on the international body and its involvement in the region, Taylor took the opportunity at another juncture in his testimony to make a rambling presentation on the workings of the UN, stressing how it was a political rather than a legal institution, with all the shortcomings that implied for the validity of its reports in cases such as his. He went on to cite how the body acted with impunity and without accountability in, for example, freezing the assets of people and organizations as well as banning presidents and politicians from travel, without concrete proof of any wrongdoing.

Speaking after the close of the evidentiary stage of his trial, the prisoner in The Hague expounded further on his views of the international community and the dispensation of international justice of which he has become a prominent object. He asked:

> What is international justice? Or, for that matter, international customary law? These are an agreed set of rules acceptable by a majority of the members of the nations of the world (notice I did not say 'international community'). The international community in today's world, as most know, consists only of the US and the EU).
>
> Now let's look at the 'system of justice' part of the equation – every region of the world should be encouraged to set up a system of justice to investigate and discourage acts of violence anywhere within their borders and regions. In the present instances where the Security Council and its three vocal members (the US, Britain and France) are using their positions to conduct foreign policy from the UN; in my view, its improper!
>
> Both George Bush and Tony Blair have invaded countries, [where] hundreds of thousands were murdered, and Bush admitted to approving torture, and so-called targeted killings. When will they be brought to justice? This whole idea of justice internationally can only be proper if it is without borders.[8]

Challenges facing prosecution

The prosecution faced an uphill task in proving Taylor's guilt beyond reasonable doubt in the charges against him. One problem was finding evidence of arms shipments made to Sierra Leone during the time in question which were specifically traceable to Liberia and his government. While arms were clearly reaching the region in abundance from a variety of sources, and getting to Sierra Leone in considerable quantity as well, proving a direct link to Taylor as instigator and supplier was another matter altogether.

In addition, the issue of finding bank accounts traceable to Taylor proving the payments for all the arms and receipts for the diamonds allegedly being received by him was complicated. The prosecution contended that the money received by Taylor from the sale of Sierra Leone's diamonds as well as timber and other commodities, and used by him to buy arms, was deposited in various bank accounts in false names both inside and outside Liberia. The accused did not hesitate to remind the court that there was no financial record of all the wealth that he was supposed to have amassed from such criminal transactions. 'I challenge the prosecutor to bring any evidence of a bank account that I have. They know it's a lie but they keep repeating it', he declared. 'I ask anyone on this planet, if you know of any account that I opened or if you know anyone who was acting in my interest, you are obliged to come forward and say it.'[9] The efforts of the prosecutor, working together with the UN Sanctions Committee, have largely failed to obtain a foreign financial paper trail to evidence illegal Taylor dealings.

However, one domestic account with a very large balance was unearthed and its details put before the court in apparent contradiction of Taylor's contention that he had no accounts in his name used for concealing large sums. The prosecution produced evidence of an account opened at the Liberian Bank for Development and Investment (LBDI) in December 1999, in Charles Taylor's name, with the home address 'White Flower' – Charles Taylor's personal residence. The following year, a deposit of almost $2 million was made to the account by Gus Kouwenhoeven, a Dutch businessman who in 2006 was convicted of illegal arms dealing and 'complicity in war crimes in Liberia', although he was later acquitted on appeal. In March 2000, a further deposit of $3.5 million was made into the same account by 'The Embassy of the Republic of China' – the diplomatic representatives of the Taiwan government, which had backed Taylor's successful 1997 election bid.[10] Taylor did not deny opening the LBDI account, but explained that it was necessary to avoid UN scrutiny of the government's official accounts, which was being imposed at the time. He said that the account was authorized by the Liberian legislature and that it was 'a covert account ... it had to be opened in my name'.[11] Explaining the origin and purpose of these funds which Taylor said belonged to the Liberian government, he testified that the monies were used mostly for arms to fight the LURD rebellion, as well as for ATU and SSS salary payments and for discretionary presidential goodwill disbursements.

In addition to the UN and the prosecutors, various unofficial researchers and investigators have worked to trace the Taylor money trail, with varying degrees of success. Use of numerous accounts in names of businesses or business partners in a variety of locations where details are not always accessible points to a considerable surviving financial empire, probably controlled by long-time deputies and loyal associates.[12]

Those close to Taylor who remain in Liberia are certainly well looked after, and it seems his former deputies still look after him too. He was asked in court how it was that he continued to live in presidential fashion when in exile in Nigeria and how he continued to manage the upkeep of his White Flower residence in Monrovia. Taylor explained that he 'received subsistence from the Nigerian government', and that since then he still had 'friends who help him put food on the table'.[13]

Proceedings drag on and funds run short

The Taylor trial was characterized by delays of all kinds, from changes of counsel, to procedural objections, to large numbers of witnesses called and cross-examined by both sides and due to extensive testimonies and cross-examinations lasting far longer than anticipated at the outset. In June 2007, Charles Taylor sacked his entire defence team, which itself delayed the proceedings by around six months.

Taylor receives legal assistance of $100,000 per month, which, together with the location of the proceedings and the five-star calibre of the legal representation of both sides, makes the trial an enormously costly affair, estimated at some $30–$35 million per year. By the time of its conclusion, it may finally end up costing the international taxpayer (mostly in the United States) over $150 million. There have been rumours of the trial being terminated prematurely, something which the United States would be unlikely to tolerate, especially if it meant a Taylor acquittal by default. In November 2010, the USA approved an additional $4.5 million to continue to fund the court's proceedings, bringing the total US contribution to date to $81.2 million, some 70 per cent of the total.[14]

With the closing arguments under preparation and the verdict in the trial awaited, a bombshell hit the Special Court proceedings in January 2011, as a result of revelations made known via the WikiLeaks organization. Through US diplomatic communications obtained by the cyber-activists, it became known that the US government, on 10 March 2009, was considering other options to awaiting the long-delayed result of the trial, in order to ensure that Taylor 'cannot return to destabilize Liberia', according to Taylor's defence lawyers. The defence further alleged that in the text of another US diplomatic communication, on 15 April 2009, the Office of the Prosecutor (OTP) was leaking 'sensitive information about the trial' to the United States via its embassy in The Hague.[15]

The Taylor defence team immediately filed a motion before the judges seeking an investigation into the revelations, which they said were a cause of 'concern that the impartiality and the independence of the court may have been compromised'.[16]

Longer delays, shakier credibility, spiralling costs and above all a very impatient people of Sierra Leone, which has waited eight years for closure and the chance to move on, all threatened the survival of the trial in its final months. The very validity of the verdict will be placed into question if a legal resolution is seen to have in some way been elicited by pressure, whether of money, time or politics, rather than through an unbiased and acceptable process of international law.

While the seriousness of the charges against Charles Taylor as specified were grave, their scope in terms of temporal jurisdiction as well as geography allowed for much of what he did to remain unexamined. Legal innocence for his actions in the latter part of Sierra Leone's civil war leaves open the issue of accountability for his actions in its early stages; and innocence of or guilt for some or all of the charges relating to Sierra Leone leave entirely unanswered the even greater issue of his culpability in Liberia.

As Liberians go to the polls to elect a president for the second time in the post-Taylor era, with many of his contemporaries and erstwhile backers in the revolutionary struggle standing for election to some of the highest, if not the highest, offices in the land, voters can be forgiven for asking what their country has gained from the lengthy but nevertheless token justice that has been served in Liberia and the region. One Liberian held to account by a foreign court and scores censured or recommended for a prosecution which will not be realized, by an officially constituted Liberian commission, will not be a sufficient foundation for building a more just society with respect for human rights and the rule of law.

Charles Taylor's excesses were many and his country will take generations to rebuild after the suffering inflicted on it by his predecessors, by his peers and above all by himself. He is one of several Liberians who deserved to face true justice, but his conviction is more likely to serve as a case study for future students of international law than as an example to others that there can be 'no impunity' for war crimes in Africa, as the court's apologists have argued. Liberians know otherwise, and their fate, like that of others in small countries subject to the strategic interests of big ones, will remain as uncertain as the policies and future balance of power among those powerful nations themselves.

NOTES

INTRODUCTION

1. Colin M. Waugh, *Paul Kagame and Rwanda: Power, Genocide and the Rwandan Patriotic Front*, McFarland, Jefferson NC, 2003.

ONE

1. David Lamb, *The Africans*, Vintage, New York, 1987.
2. Nathaniel Richardson, *Liberia's Past and Present*, Diplomatic Press and Publishing, London, 1959.
3. Helene Cooper, *The House at Sugar Beach*, Simon & Schuster, London, 2008.
4. Ibid.
5. Richardson, *Liberia's Past and Present*.
6. Togba Nah Tipoteh, *Democracy: The Call of the Liberian People*, Susukuu, Monrovia, 1981.
7. www.liberiapastandpresent.org.
8. Truth and Reconciliation Commission of Liberia (TRC), *Consolidated Final Report*, Section V, Truth and Reconciliation Commission of Liberia, Monrovia, Liberia, June 2009.
9. Richardson, *Liberia's Past and Present*.
10. 'Liberia Makes Protest', *New York Times*, 2 June 1914, www.liberiapastandpresent.org.
11. Amos Sawyer, *The Emergence of Autocracy in Liberia*, Institute of Contemporary Studies, San Francisco, 1992.
12. Tipoteh, *Democracy*.
13. David Brown, 'Recollections of Early Liberia', *West Africa*, May 1981.
14. Ibid.
15. Ibid.
16. Mark Huband, *The Liberian Civil War*, Frank Cass, London, 1998.
17. Cooper, *The House at Sugar Beach*.
18. Ibid.

TWO

1. Special Court for Sierra Leone, *Taylor Trial Transcripts*, 14 July 2009, www.sc-sl.org/LinkClick.aspx?fileticket=DqhX5YnoIN4=&tabid=160.
2. Ibid.
3. Will Haywood, 'The Making of a Warlord', *Boston Globe*, 26 May 1996.
4. Testimony before the Special Court for Sierra Leone, 14 July 2009.
5. Stephen Ellis, 'Liberia 1989-94: A Study of Ethnic and Spiritual Violence', *African Affairs* 94, 1995.
6. Graham Greene, *Journey without Maps*, Heinemann, London, 1936.
7. Stephen Ellis, *The Mask of Anarchy*, C. Hurst, London, 2007, p. 240.
8. Greene, *Journey without Maps*.
9. Dorothy Mills, *Through Liberia*, Simon & Schuster, London, 1926.
10. In *The Mask of Anarchy*, Stephen Ellis describes in detail the importance of Liberia's spiritual world, past and present, as well as discussing its relevance to modern-day conflict.

THREE

1. A Liberian expression referring to ordinary people doing the work while those at the top reap the rewards.
2. Togba Nah Tipoteh, *Democracy: The Call of the Liberian People*, Susukuu, Monrovia, 1981.
3. Helene Cooper, *The House at Sugar Beach*, Simon & Schuster, London, 2008.
4. Tipoteh, *Democracy*.
5. Will Haygood, 'The Making of a Warlord', *Boston Globe*, 26 May 1996.
6. Ibid.
7. Johnny Dwyer, 'The All-American Warlord', *Observer*, 23 November 2008.
8. Haygood, 'The Making of a Warlord'.
9. Special Court for Sierra Leone, *Taylor Trial Transcripts*, 14 July 2009, www.sc-sl.org/LinkClick.aspx?fileticket=DqhX5YnoIN4=&tabid=160.
10. Author interview, November 2010.
11. Haygood, 'The Making of a Warlord'.
12. D. Adighibe, author interview, 2010.
13. Bai Gbala, author interview, June 2010.
14. Special Court for Sierra Leone, *Taylor Trial Transcripts*, 14 July 2009.
15. Haygood, 'The Making of a Warlord'.
16. Mark Huband, *The Liberian Civil War*, Frank Cass, London, 1998, p. 16.
17. Haygood, 'The Making of a Warlord'.
18. Bai M. Gbala, speech delivered at the General Assembly of 'ULAA', Minneapolis, Minnesota, 25 September 2010.
19. Victoria Tolbert, *Lifted Up: The Victoria Tolbert Story*, Macalester, Minneapolis, 1996.
20. Former justice minister Chea Cheapoo, testimony before the Truth and Reconciliation Commission hearings, Monrovia, 2008.
21. Tolbert, *Lifted Up*.
22. Stephen Ellis, *The Mask of Anarchy*, C. Hurst, London, 2007.
23. Cooper, *The House at Sugar Beach*.
24. Special Court for Sierra Leone, *Taylor Trial Transcripts*, 14 July 2009.
25. Special Court for Sierra Leone, *Taylor Trial Transcripts*, 15 July 2009.

FOUR

1. Special Court for Sierra Leone, *Taylor Trial Transcripts*, 15 July 2009.

2. Stephen Ellis, *The Mask of Anarchy*, C. Hurst, London, 2007.
3. Mark Huband, *The Liberian Civil War*, Frank Cass, London, 1998.
4. Special Court for Sierra Leone, The Hague, trial transcript, 15 July 2010.
5. União Nacional para a Independência Total de Angola.
6. William Berkeley, 'Between Repression and Slaughter', *Atlantic Monthly*, December 1992.
7. Herman J. Cohen, *Intervening in Africa: Superpower Peacemaking in a Troubled Continent*, Palgrave Macmillan, Basingstoke, 2000.
8. Huband. *The Liberian Civil War*.
9. Cohen, *Intervening in Africa*.
10. Martin Meredith, 'The State of Africa', Simon & Schuster, London, 2005, p. 551
11. Will Haygood, 'The Making of a Warlord', *Boston Globe*, 26 May 1996.
12. *New York Times*, 11 September 1990.
13. Haygood, 'The Making of a Warlord'.
14. Lynda Schuster, 'The Final Days of Doctor Doe', *Granta* 48, London, 1994.
15. Author interview, November 2010.
16. Letter to Samuel Doe, 10 January 1984, reproduced in Huband, *The Liberian Civil War*.
17. Huband, *The Liberian Civil War*.
18. Haygood, 'The Making of a Warlord'.
19. Ibid.
20. From Taylor 1983 affidavit, quoted in Matthew Brelis, 'A Rebel's Saga', *Boston Globe*, 31 July 1990.
21. Ibid.
22. *Patriot Ledger*, 17 July 2009.
23. Ellen Johnson Sirleaf, *This Child Will Be Great*, HarperCollins, London, 2009.

FIVE

1. Ellen Johnson Sirleaf, *This Child Will Be Great*, HarperCollins, London, 2009.
2. Mark Huband, *The Liberian Civil War*, Frank Cass, London, 1998.
3. William Berkeley, 'Doe our Dear', *New Republic*, 19 March 1990.
4. Ibid.
5. Lawyers' Committee for Human Rights, New York, 1986, quoted in Stephen Ellis, *The Mask of Anarchy*, C. Hurst, London, 2007.
6. Huband, *The Liberian Civil War*.
7. *Patriot Ledger*, 17 July 2009.
8. Ibid.
9. *Boston Globe*, 31 July 1990.
10. Author interview, November 2010.
11. Flynn conversations with author, August 2009 and November 2010.
12. Denis Johnson, *Harper's* magazine, October 2000.
13. Special Court for Sierra Leone, The Hague, trial transcript, July 2009.
14. Huband, *The Liberian Civil War*.
15. *Patriot Ledger*, 17 July 2009.
16. Agnes Taylor, author interview, March 2011.
17. Huband, *The Liberian Civil War*, p. 48.
18. B. Ankomah, interview, *Ghanaian Chronicle* (Accra), 12–18 October 1992.
19. Agnes Taylor, author interview, March 2011.
20. Alfred Cudjoe, *Who killed Sankara? Some hidden facts behind the tragic assassination of Capt. Thomas Sankara as revealed by the African Press: comments by an*

informed writer, Accra, 1988.
21. Radio France International, 27 October 2008.
22. Huband, *The Liberian Civil War*.
23. Sirleaf, *This Child Will Be Great*.

SIX

1. Dialogue between author and her sister in Helene Cooper, *The House at Sugar Beach*, Simon & Schuster, London, 2008. Liberian English 'fwenken' is an expression of hesitation or indecision, while 'foot help de body' expresses a decision to run from danger.
2. Mark Huband, *The Liberian Civil War*, Frank Cass, London, 1998.
3. Denis Johnson, *Harper's* magazine, October 2000.
4. Stephen Ellis, *The Mask of Anarchy*, C. Hurst, London, 2007.
5. Festus B. Aboagye, *ECOMOG: A Sub-regional Experience in Conflict Resolution, Management and Peacekeeping in Liberia*, Sedco Publishing, Accra, 1999.
6. Huband, *The Liberian Civil War*.
7. Bill Berkeley, 'Doe our Dear', *New Republic*, 19 March 1990.
8. Truth and Reconciliation Commission of Liberia (TRC), *Final Report*, Truth and Reconciliation Commission of Liberia, Monrovia, Liberia, June 2009.
9. Denis Johnson, *Harper's* magazine, October 2000.
10. Ellis, *The Mask of Anarchy*, p. 81.
11. J. Thomas Woewiyu, *An open letter to Madam Ellen Johnson-Sirleaf*, 15 September 2005, http://theliberiandialogue.org.
12. *West Africa*, 15 April 1991.
13. Woewiyu, *An open letter to Madam Ellen Johnson-Sirleaf*.
14. The role of the USA in negotiations is discussed in detail in Chapter 12.
15. Gabriel Williams, *Liberia: The Heart of Darkness*, Trafford Publishing, Victoria BC, 2002.
16. Arnold Quainoo, interview, *Daily Graphic* (Accra), 11 May 1981.
17. Ellis, *The Mask of Anarchy*.
18. Williams, *Liberia*.

SEVEN

1. Gabriel Williams, *Liberia: The Heart of Darkness*, Trafford Publishing, Victoria BC, 2002.
2. Ibid.
3. Ibid.
4. Stephen Ellis, *The Mask of Anarchy*, C. Hurst, London, 2007, p. 100.
5. E.g. in *Liberian Diaspora Magazine* (Monrovia), May 1992.
6. The OAU was disbanded in July 2002 and replaced by the African Union (AU).
7. Transcript of Statement by Tom Woewiyu, minister of labour, to LNTG, Monrovia, 19 July 1994, reproduced in Ellis, *The Mask of Anarchy*.
8. Special Court for Sierra Leone, *Taylor Trial Transcripts*, 4 February 2010, www.charlestaylortrial.org/2010/02/04/charles-taylor-executed-liberians-perceived-as-threats-to-his-political-ambition-prosecutors-say.
9. Tom Woewiyu, conversation with author, March 2011.
10. A patterned women's garment, normally worn as a wrap-around skirt.
11. John Lee Anderson. 'The Devil They Know', *The New Yorker*, July 1998.
12. Williams, *Liberia*.
13. Ibid.
14. Guilherme Mambo, author interview, 2010.

EIGHT

1. Hollis R. Lynch, *Edward Wilmot Blyden, Pan Negro Patriot*, Oxford University Press, Oxford, 1967.
2. Stephen Ellis, *The Mask of Anarchy*, C. Hurst, London, 2007.
3. Ibid.
4. Ellis, *The Mask of Anarchy*.
5. William Reno, 'Reinvention of an African Patrimonial State: Charles Taylor's Liberia', *Third World Quarterly*, vol. 16, no. 1, 1995.
6. Ibid.
7. Ellis, *The Mask of Anarchy*.
8. Testimony by Ambassador William Twaddle to the Africa Subcommittee, US House of Representatives, 1996, cited in Ellis, *Mask of Anarchy*.
9. Discussion of Taylor's State Department spy is contained in Chapter 12
10. Williams, *Liberia: The Heart of Darkness*, Trafford Publishing, Victoria BC, 2002.
11. PAE is a private California-based logistics company with close Pentagon ties.
12. Ellis, *Mask of Anarchy*.
13. Charles Taylor, interview with author, June 2011.
14. Ankomah Baffour, *New African*, London, March 2000.
15. Tom Kamara, *The Perspective*, 5 February 2001.
16. Ellis, *The Mask of Anarchy*.

NINE

1. J. Peter Pham, *Child Soldiers, Adult Interests: The Global Dimensions of the Sierra Leonean Tragedy*, Nova Science, New York, 2005.
2. Special Court for Sierra Leone, *Taylor Trial Transcripts*, 18 November 2009, www.sc-sl.org/LinkClick.aspx?fileticket=GeGxWgV55XA=&tabid=160.
3. Special Court for Sierra Leone, *Taylor Trial Transcripts*, 16 August 2010, www.sc-sl.org/LinkClick.aspx?fileticket=Jh2siGYxJCQ=&tabid=160.
4. *Africa Confidential* (London), April 1998.
5. *Africa Confidential* (London), Special Report, April 1998.
6. A graphic visual record of the events of January 1999 in Sierra Leone was produced in the 2000 documentary film *Cry Freetown*, directed by Sorious Samura, which has received international screening.
7. *Africa Confidential* (London), 6 March 1998.
8. 'Jesse Jackson in Sierra Leone Talks', BBC News online, 18 May 2000, http://news.bbc.co.uk/2/hi/africa/753728.stm.
9. UPI, 29 June 2000.
10. Douglas Farah, *Washington Post*, 15 May 2003.
11. Bryan Bender, 'Liberia's Taylor gives aid to Al-Qaeda, UN Probe Finds', *Boston Globe*, 4 August 2004.
12. Ibid.
13. Mambu James Kpargoi Jr, *New Liberian* (Monrovia), 22 February 2009.
14. Ibid.
15. Special Court for Sierra Leone, *Taylor Trial Transcripts*, 9 November 2009, www.sc-sl.org/LinkClick.aspx?fileticket=jV62eXBfZ4w=&tabid=160.
16. Ibid.

TEN

1. Akyaaba Addai-Sebo, commentary to author, March 2011.
2. Baffour Ankomah, interview, *New African*, December 1997.

3. David Harris, 'From "Warlord" to "Democratic" President: How Charles Taylor Won the 1997 Presidential Elections', *Journal of Modern African Studies*, vol. 37, no. 3, September, 1999, pp. 431–55.
4. Stephen Ellis, *The Mask of Anarchy*, C. Hurst, London, 2007.
5. *National Chronicle* (Monrovia), 17 July 1997, cited in Harris, 'From "Warlord" to "Democratic" President'.
6. 'Talking of Votes', *Africa Confidential* (London), 28 March 1997.
7. 'Not Charley's Aunt', *Africa Confidential* (London), 20 June 1997.
8. Charles Taylor, interview with author, June 2011.
9. Ankomah, interview, *New African*, December 1997.
10. Ambassador Diggs, author interview, July 2011.
11. John Lee Anderson, 'The Devil They Know', *The New Yorker*, 27 July 1998.
12. *Africa Confidential* (London), 19 December 1997.
13. Ellis, *The Mask of Anarchy*, p. 173.
14. Anderson, 'The Devil They Know'.
15. Reported in ibid.
16. Ibid.
17. BBC, 'Sierra Leone: Document One', BBC News online, 18 July 2000, http://news.bbc.co.uk/2/hi/africa/834252.stm.
18. Anderson, 'The Devil They Know'.
19. Charles Taylor, interview with author, June 2011.

ELEVEN

1. Kenneth R. Timmerman, *Insight*, 25 July 2003.
2. 'U.S., Britain say Liberia's Charles Taylor fuels war in Sierra Leone', CNN.com, 31 July 2000, http://archives.cnn.com/2000/WORLD/africa/07/31/leone.un.diamonds.reut.
3. Report of the Panel of Experts appointed pursuant to Security Council resolution 1306 (2000).
4. Lester Hyman, *US Policy Towards Liberia 1822–2003: Unintended Consequences*, African Homestead Legacy, Cherry Hill NJ, 2007.
5. Sebastian Junger, 'Atrocity: Liberia's Savage Harvest', *Vanity Fair*, October 2003.
6. Hyman, *US Policy Towards Liberia 1822–2003*.
7. BBC News online, 7 May 2002.
8. Hyman, *US Policy Towards Liberia 1822–2003*.
9. Baffour Ankomah, interview, *New African*, July–August 2002.
10. Ibid.
11. Junger, 'Atrocity'.
12. John Kufuor, 'We Are on Course', *New African*, March 2004.
13. www.irinews.org, UN Office for the Coordination of Humanitarian Affairs, 18 June 2003.
14. 'Liberia: Taylor, Stubborn since His Childhood', www.irinews.org, 25 April 2006.
15. www.irinews.org, 25 June 2003.
16. *The Economist*, 12 July 2003.
17. Loretta Nagbe, conversation with author, August 2010.
18. 'Text: Taylor's Farewell Speech', BBC News online, 10 August 2003, http://news.bbc.co.uk/2/hi/africa/3140211.stm.
19. 'Liberia leader defiant till the end', BBC News online, 11 August 2003, http://news.bbc.co.uk/2/hi/africa/3140417.stm.

20. Nnamde Azikiwe, *My Odyssey: An Autobiography*, C. Hurst, London, 1970.
21. www.irinews.org. Emyr Jones Parry, UN Security Council delegation, Monrovia, 24 June 2004.
22. www.irinews.org, 6 January 2006.
23. Jonathan Paye-Layleh, 'Liberia's Leader Seeks New Wives', BBC Monrovia, 21 October 2002, http://news.bbc.co.uk/2/hi/africa/2346021.stm.
24. *Boston Globe*, 4 August 2004.
25. Douglas Farah, *Blood from Stones: The Secret Financial Network of Terror*, Broadway Books, New York, 2004.
26. Akyaaba Addai-Sebo, phone conversation with Taylor, March 2006.
27. H. Nichols and L. Polgreen, 'Liberia Ex-leader Faces War Crimes Court', *New York Times*, 4 April 2006.
28. Sahara Reporters, 'Charles Taylor "Escape and Arrest" Staged', 29 March 2006, published online by Sahara Reporters, http://saharareporters.com/news-page/charles-taylor-escape-and-arrest-staged-saharareporters.
29. 'Taylor's Trajectories', *Africa Confidential* (London), 14 April 2006.
30. Special Court for Sierra Leone, *Taylor Trial Transcripts*, 10 November 2009, www.sc-sl.org/LinkClick.aspx?fileticket=vbrttapT6bs=&tabid=160.
31. Baffour Ankomah, author interview, December 2010.

TWELVE

1. Nathaniel Richardson, *Liberia's Past and Present*, Diplomatic Press and Publishing, London, 1959.
2. Baffour Ankomah, conversation with author, November 2010.
3. Ibid.
4. Herman J. Cohen, *Intervening in Africa: Superpower Peacemaking in a Troubled Continent*, Palgrave Macmillan, Basingstoke, 2000.
5. Ibid.
6. Ibid.
7. Herman J. Cohen, Testimony at the Diaspora Public Hearings of the Truth and Reconciliation Commission of Liberia, St Paul, Minnesota, 2008.
8. Stephen Ellis, *The Mask of Anarchy*, C. Hurst, London, 2007.
9. Speech at Emory University, Atlanta, Georgia, 1998, quoted in Gabriel I.H. Williams, *Liberia: The Heart of Darkness*, Trafford Publishing, Victoria BC, 2002.
10. Gregory W. Meeks, quoted in The Liberia Diaspora Truth And Reconciliation hearings, St Paul, Minnesota, 2008.
11. Gerald S. Rose, *Washington Post*, January 1995.
12. Mark Huband, *The Liberian Civil War*, Frank Cass, London, 1998.
13. Cohen, *Intervening in Africa*.
14. 'operating largely behind the scenes throughout the 1980s ... Reagan/Bush administrations permitted – and frequently encouraged – the flow of money, agricultural credits, dual-use technology, chemicals, and weapons to Iraq'. Ted Koppel, ABC *Nightline*, 1 July 1992.
15. Baffour Ankomah, author interview, November 2010.
16. *Washington Post*, 20 November 1992.
17. Ankomah, author interview.
18. Lester Hyman, *US Policy Towards Liberia 1822–2003: Unintended Consequences*, African Homestead Legacy, Cherry Hill NJ, 2007.
19. Ryan Lizza, *New Republic*, 19 November 2001.
20. *Boston Globe*, 22 July 1999.
21. Akyaaba Addai-Sebo, commentary to author, March 2011.

22. Ambassador Diggs, interview with author, July 2010.
23. John Lee Anderson, *The New Yorker*, July 1998.

THIRTEEN

1. UN Consolidated Interagency Appeal, November 1993.
2. Human Rights Watch/Africa, *Easy Prey, Child Soldiers in Liberia*, New York.
3. Ibid.
4. Gabriel I.H. Williams, *Liberia: The Heart of Darkness*, Trafford Publishing, Victoria BC, 2002.
5. Denis Johnson, 'The Small Boys Unit', *Harpers* magazine, October 2000.
6. Dick Shelly, *Liberians in Ghana*, Working Paper no. 57, Oxford University International Development Centre, Oxford, February 2002.
7. Moses K. Nagbe, *Bulk Challenge*, Cape Coast, Ghana, 1996.
8. Shelly, *Liberians in Ghana*.
9. Nagbe, *Bulk Challenge*.
10. 'Liberia's Big Challenge', *Africa Confidential* (London), Special Report, quoting Abraham Conneh, Oxfam.
11. Gladys Nettey, author conversation, Accra, 2000.
12. Karen Campbell-Nelson, *Liberia is not Just a Man Thing*, International Centre for Transitional Justice, New York, September 2008.
13. James Brabazon, 'Guns, Jeans and Jewels', *BBC Focus on Africa*, October 2003.
14. J. Steinberg, 'Liberia's Experiment with Transitional Justice', *African Affairs*, vol. 109, no. 434, January 2010.
15. Abigail Disney and Gini Reticker, *Pray the Devil Back to Hell*, Fork Films, Sydney, 2008.
16. Ibid.
17. Steinberg, 'Liberia's Experiment with Transitional Justice'.
18. Ibid.
19. Republic of Liberia, Truth and Reconciliation Commission of Liberia (TRC), *Preliminary Findings, Determinations and Recommendations*, December 2008, http://trcofliberia.org/resources/reports/final/volume-one_layout-1.pdf.
20. Truth and Reconciliation Commission, *Final Report*, Vol. 2, Monrovia, updated December 2009.
21. Steinberg, 'Liberia's Experiment with Transitional Justice'.
22. *Der Spiegel*, 7 August 2009.
23. J. Thomas Woewiyu, *An Open Letter to Madam Ellen Johnson-Sirleaf*, 15 September 2005, http://theliberiandialogue.org.
24. Ellen Johnson Sirleaf, *This Child Will Be Great*, HarperCollins, London, 2009.
25. Horand Knaup, 'A Recipe for Chaos', *Spiegel*, 8 July, 2009.
26. Steinberg, 'Liberia's Experiment with Transitional Justice'.
27. Special Court for Sierra Leone, *Taylor Trial Transcripts*, 22 July 2009, www.sc-sl.org/LinkClick.aspx?fileticket=h/TIEV4eH3g=&tabid=160.
28. Charles Taylor, interview with author, June 2011.
29. Steinberg, 'Liberia's Experiment with Transitional Justice'.

FOURTEEN

1. Alistair Foster, 'Forget Naomi Campbell', *London Evening Standard*, 12 August 2010.
2. *New York Times*, 4 April 2006.
3. 'Foday Sankoh: The Cruel Rebel', BBC News Africa online, 30 July 2003, http://news.bbc.co.uk/2/hi/africa/3110629.stm.

4. Author interview, 17 January 2011.
5. Lizzy Davies, *Guardian*, 9 August 2010.
6. Special Court for Sierra Leone, *Taylor Trial Transcripts*, 13 July 2009, www.sc-sl.org/LinkClick.aspx?fileticket=yvok6RPRgq0=&tabid=160.
7. University of California, Berkeley War Crimes Studies Center, *Charles Taylor on the Stand*, December 2009, http://socrates.berkeley.edu/~warcrime/SL-Reports/D08%20Charles%20Taylor_Monthly_Trial_Report_December_2009_final.pdf.
8. Charles Taylor, interview with author, June 2011.
9. Special Court for Sierra Leone, *Taylor Trial Transcripts*, 3 August 2009, www.sc-sl.org/LinkClick.aspx?fileticket=ouw2TzFKFHg=&tabid=160.
10. Special Court for Sierra Leone, *Taylor Trial Transcripts*, 7 December 2009, www.charlestaylortrial.org/2009/12/07.
11. Ibid.
12. Coalition for International Justice, *Following Taylor's Money*, Washington DC, 2005.
13. Special Court for Sierra Leone, *Taylor Trial Transcripts*, 12 January 2009, www.sc-sl.org/LinkClick.aspx?fileticket=IB%2bOVUNMy3A%3d&tabid=160.
14. US Department of State, Office of the Spokesman, 22 November 2010.
15. Special Court for Sierra Leone, *Taylor Trial Transcripts*, 20 January 2011, www.sc-sl.org/LinkClick.aspx?fileticket=1Sf6N9geD4E%3d&tabid=160.
16. Ibid.

BIBLIOGRAPHY

BOOKS AND REPORTS

Aboagye, Festus B. *ECOMOG, A Sub-Regional Experiment in Conflict Resolution, Management and Peacekeeping in Liberia*, Sedco Publishing, Accra (1999).
Advocates for Human Rights. *Final Report of the Truth and Reconciliation Commission of Liberia Diaspora Project*, DRI, St Paul, Minnesota (2009).
Azikiwe, Nnamde. *My Odyssey: An Autobiography*, C. Hurst, London (1970).
Banks, Russell. *The Darling*, HarperCollins, London (2004).
Berkeley, William. *A Promise Betrayed*, Lawyers Committee for Human Rights, New York (1986).
Cohen, Herman J. *Intervening in Africa: Superpower Peacemaking in a Troubled Continent*, Palgrave Macmillan, Basingstoke (2000).
Cooper, Helene. *The House at Sugar Beach*, Simon & Schuster, London (2008).
Cudjoe, Alfred. *Who Killed Sankara? Some hidden facts behind the tragic assassination of Capt. Thomas Sankara as revealed by the African Press: comments by an informed writer*, Accra (1988).
Daniels, Anthony. *Monrovia Mon Amour: A Visit to Liberia*, John Murray, London (1992).
Dick, Shelley. *Liberians in Ghana*, Working Paper no. 57, International Development Centre, Oxford University, Oxford (February 2002).
Ellis, Stephen, *The Mask of Anarchy*, C. Hurst, London (2007).
Ellis, Stephen, and G. Ter Haar. *Worlds of Power: Religious Thought and Political Practice in Africa*, C. Hurst, London (2004).
Farah, Douglas, *Blood from Stone: The Secret Financial Network of Terror,* Broadway Books, New York (2004).
Flint, John E. (ed.) *Cambridge History of Africa*, Vol. 5: *From 1790 to 1870*, Cambridge University Press, Cambridge (1977).
Fraser, Antonia. *The Gunpowder Plot: Terror and Faith in 1605*, Weidenfield & Nicolson, London (1996).
Greene, Graham. *Journey without Maps*, Heinemann, London (1936).
Huband, Mark. *The Liberian Civil War*, Frank Cass, London (1998).

Human Rights Watch/Africa. *Easy Prey: Child Soldiers in Liberia*, New York (1994).
Hyman, Lester. *US Policy Towards Liberia 1822–2003: Unintended Consequences*, African Homestead Legacy, Cherry Hill NJ (2007).
International Crisis Group. *Tackling Liberia: The Eye of the Regional Storm*, Africa Report no. 62 (30 April 2003).
Kourouma, Ahmadou. *Allah n'est pas Obligé*, Éditions du Seuil, Paris (2000).
Lamb, David. *The Africans*, Vintage, New York (1987).
Lynch, Hollis R. *Edward Wilmot Blyden, Pan Negro Patriot*, Oxford University Press, Oxford (1967).
Mayson, Dew Tuan-Wleh. *In the Cause of the People*, Mindex, Benin City, Nigeria (2010).
Meredith, Martin. *The State of Africa*, Simon & Schuster, London (2005).
Mills, Lady Dorothy. *Through Liberia*, Duckworth, London (1926).
Moore, Bai T. *Murder in the Cassava Patch*, Ducor Publishing House, Monrovia (1968).
Powers, William D. *Blue Clay People*, Bloomsbury, New York (2005).
Nagbe, K. Moses. *Bulk Challenge: The Story of 4,000 Liberians in Search of Refuge*, Champion Publications, Cape Coast, Ghana (1996).
Ogunleye, Bayo. *Behind Rebel Lines: An Anatomy of Charles Taylor's Hostage Camps*, Enugu, Delta, Nigeria (1995).
Open Society Justice Initiative. *Charles Taylor Trial Summaries*, Open Society Foundation, New York (2010).
Pham, John-Peter. *Liberia: Portrait of a Failed State*, Reed, New York (2004).
Pham, John-Peter. *Child Soldiers, Adult Interests: The Global Dimensions of the Sierra Leonean tragedy*, Nova Science, New York (2005).
Reno, William. *Corruption and State Politics in Sierra Leone*, Cambridge University Press, Cambridge (1995).
Reno, William. *Warlord Politics and African States*, Lynn Rienner, Boulder CO and London (1998).
Republic of Liberia. *Truth and Reconciliation Commission: Consolidated Final Report*, Monrovia (30 June 2009).
Richardson, Nathaniel R. *Liberia's Past and Present*, Diplomatic Press and Publishing, London (1959).
Sankawulo, Wilton. *The Marriage of Wisdom*, Heinemann, London (1974).
Sawyer, Amos. *Emergence of Autocracy in Liberia*, Institute of Contemporary Studies, San Francisco (1992).
Sawyer, Amos. *Beyond Plunder: Towards Democratic Governance*, Lynne Rienner, Boulder CO and London (2005).
Sirleaf, Ellen Johnson. *This Child Will Be Great,* HarperCollins, London (2009).
Tipoteh, Togba-Nah. *Democracy: The Call of the Liberian People*, Susukuu, Monrovia (1981).
Tolbert, Victoria. *Lifted Up: The Victoria Tolbert Story*, Macalester, Minneapolis (1996).
United Nations, *Report of the Panel of Experts appointed pursuant to Security Council Resolution 1306*, New York (2000)
Warner, Esther. *Trial by Sasswood*, Pergamon Press, Oxford (1970).
Waugh, Colin M. *Paul Kagame and Rwanda: Power, Genocide and the Rwandan Patriotic Front*, McFarland, Jefferson NC (2003).
Williams, Gabriel I.H. *Liberia: The Heart of Darkness*, Trafford Publishing, Victoria BC (2002).
Wreh, Tuan, *The Love of Liberty*, C. Hurst, London (1976).

NEWSPAPER, ONLINE AND JOURNAL ARTICLES

Africa Confidential. 'Blood under the Bridge', 1 August 1997.
Africa Confidential. 'Not Charlie's Aunt', 20 June 1997.
Africa Confidential. 'Pax Nigeriana, 21 November 1997.
Africa Confidential. 'Talking of Votes', 28 March 1997.
Africa Confidential. 'Taylor's Trajectories', 14 April 2006.
Africa Confidential. 'Threatening Good Order', 10 October 1997.
Anderson, Jon Lee. 'Letter from Liberia – The Devil they Know', *The New Yorker*, July 1998.
Ankomah, Baffour. Interview, *Ghanaian Chronicle* (Accra), 12–18 October 1992.
Ankomah, Baffour. Interview with Charles Taylor, *New African*, December 1997.
Ankomah, Baffour. 'Charles Taylor: Powerful Countries Want Me Out', *New African*, July 2002.
Bender, Bryan. 'Liberia's Taylor Gives Aid to Al-Qaeda, UN Probe Finds', *Boston Globe*, 4 August 2004.
Berkeley William. 'Doe our Dear', *New Republic*, 19 March 1990.
Berkeley, William. 'Between Repression and Slaughter', *Atlantic Monthly*, December 1992.
Brabazon, James. 'Guns, Jeans and Jewels', *BBC Focus on Africa* magazine, October–December 2003.
Brelis, Matthew. 'A Rebel's Saga', *Boston Globe*, 31 July 1990.
Brown, David. 'Recollections of Early Liberia', *West Africa*, May 1981.
Campbell-Nelson, Karen. *Liberia Is Not Just a Man Thing*, International Centre for Transitional Justice, New York, September 2008.
Coalition for International Justice. 'Following Taylor's Money', Washington DC, 2005.
Davies, Lizzy. 'Mia Farrow Contradicts Naomi Campbell in Charles Taylor Trial', 9 August 2010, www.guardian.co.uk/law/2010/aug/09/mia-farrow-contradicts-naomi-campbell.
Dwyer, Johnny. 'The All-American Warlord', *Observer*, 23 November 2008.
Ellis, Stephen. 'Liberia 1989–1994: A Study of Ethnic and Spiritual Violence', *African Affairs* 94 (London), 1995.
Foster, Alistair, 'Forget Naomi Campbell', *London Evening Standard*, 12 August 2010.
French, Howard. 'Liberia Waits: Which Charles Taylor Won? *New York Times*, 17 January 2008.
Gbala, Bai M. Speech delivered at the General Assembly of ULAA', Minneapolis, Minnesota 25 September 2010.
Harris, David. 'How Charles Taylor Won the 1997 Presidential Elections', *Journal of Modern African Studies*, September 2005.
Haygood, Will. 'The Making of a Warlord', *Boston Globe*, 26 May 1996.
Haygood, Will. 'The Rise and Fall of the Liberian Big Man', *Milwaukee Journal Sentinel*, July 2003.
Irinnews.org. Emyr Jones Parry, UN Security Council, Monrovia, 24 June 2004.
Irinnews.org. 'Taylor, stubborn since childhood', 25 April 2006.
Johnson, Denis. 'The Small Boys Unit – Searching for Charles Taylor in a Liberian Civil War', *Harper's* magazine, October 2000.
Junger, Sebastian. 'Atrocity, Liberia's Savage Harvest', *Vanity Fair*, October 2003.
Kamara, Tom. 'A Demon or Demonized?' *The Perspective*, 5 February, 2001, www.theperspective.org/demon.html.
Kamara, Tom. *New Democrat*, Monrovia, www.newdemocratnews.com.
Knaup, Horand: 'A Recipe for Chaos: Will Reconciliation Efforts Tear Liberia Apart Again?' *Spiegel*, 8 July, 2009, www.spiegel.de/international/world/0,1518,641102-2,00.html.

Kpargoi, Mambu James, Jr. *New Liberian*, Monrovia, 22 February 2009, http://newliberian.com/?p=717.
Kufuor, John. 'We are on Course', *New African*, March 2004.
The Liberian Dialogue, wwwtheliberiandialogue.org.
Liberiapastandpresent.org: www.liberiapastandpresent.org.
Lizza, Ryan. 'Double Take, Can Taylor's Apologists Explain His Ties to Al Qaeda?', *New Republic*, 19 November 2001.
Lizza, Ryan. 'Where Angels Fear to Tread', *New Republic*, 7 July 2000.
Mahtani, Dino. 'Taylor Seized at Nigeria border', *Financial Times*, London, 29 March 2006.
Nichols, H., and L. Polgreen. 'Liberia Ex-leader Faces War Crimes Court', *New York Times*, 4 April 2006.
Ogunleye, Bayo. 'Behind Rebel Lines: An Anatomy of Charles Taylor's Hostage Camps', *Delta*, 1995.
Ohene, Elizabeth. 'African View: Memories of Taylor', BBC News online, 28 July 2009, http://news.bbc.co.uk/2/hi/africa/8171244.stm.
Patriot Ledger. 'Accused War Criminal Charles Taylor Says He Had Help in Plymouth Jailbreak', 17 July 2009, http://www.patriotledger.com/news/cops_and_courts/ x1443001357/Accused-war-criminal-has-curious-local-past.
Paye-Layleh, Jonathan, 'Liberia's Leader Seeks New Wives', BBC Monrovia, 21 October 2002, http://news.bbc.co.uk/2/hi/africa/2346021.stm.
Polgreen, Lydia. 'Liberia Ex-leader Faces War Crimes Court', *New York Times*, 4 April 2006.
Quainoo, Arnold. 'Interview', *Daily Graphic*, Accra, 11 May 1981.
Reno, William. 'Reinvention of an African Patrimonial State: Charles Taylor's Liberia', *Third World Quarterly*, vol. 16, no. 1, 1995.
Rose, Gerald S. *Washington Post*, January 1995.
Sahara Reporters, 29 March 2006, www.saharareporters.com.
Schuster, Lynda. 'The Final Days of Doctor Doe', *Granta* 48, London, Autumn 1994.
Der Spiegel, 7 August 2009, www.spiegel.de/international.
Steinberg, Johnny. 'Liberia's Experiment with Transitional Justice', *African Affairs*, vol. 109, no. 434, January 2010.
Stern, Stefan. 'Lessons in the Bully Boy School of Management', *Financial Times*, 5 May 2009.
Timmerman, Kenneth R., 'Jesse, Liberia and Blood Diamonds', *Insight Magazine*, 25 July 2003. www.kentimmerman.com.
University of California Berkeley War Crimes Studies Center. 'Charles Taylor on the Stand', December 2009, http://socrates.berkeley.edu/~warcrime/SL-Reports/ D08%20Charles%20Taylor_Monthly_Trial_Report_December_2009_FINAL.pdf.
US Department of State, 'Statement of US Funding for Trial of Charles Taylor', Washington DC, 22 November 2010.
Van Der Kraaij, Fred, *Liberia Past and Present*, www.liberiapastandpresent.org.
Woewiyu, Thomas. An open letter to Madam Ellen Johnson-Sirleaf, *The Liberian Dialogue.org*, 15 September 2005, www.theliberiandialogue.org/articles/c091505tws. htm.

VIDEO

Bootle, Oliver. *This World: Diamonds and Justice*, BBC 2, 26 February 2008.
Disney, Abigail, and Gini Reticker. *Pray the Devil Back to Hell*, Fork Films, Sydney, 2008.
Sorious Samura. *Cry Freetown*, Insight News Television, London, 2000.

INDEX

Abacha, Sani, 168, 213, 218, 244–5; death of, 220
Aberdeen, Lord, 287
Abidjan, 121, 186; Ecobank, 187; peace deal 1996, 216
Abiola, Moshood, election victory, 168
Abubakar, Abdulsalami, 325
Abuja 2000 peace accords, 225
Accra: African-American Summit, 223; peace talks 2003, 307; Liberian refugees, 319
Addai-Sebo, Akyaaba, 284
Addison-Taylor, Victoria, 280
Adighibe, Delores, 66–8, 87, 94, 97, 111, 127
Adorers of the Blood of Christ, murdered nuns, 301
'African communalism', Liberia destroyed, 321
African protests, USA, 73
African Union, 275
Akainyah, Azanne Kofi, 199–200
Akosombo accords, 237
Al-Mathabh al Thauriya al-Alamiya, 120
al-Qaeda: Africa bombings, 225; September 11th attack, 226
Albright, Madeleine, 260
All Liberian Coalition party, 236
All-Liberia Conference 1991, 155
All People's Freedom Alliance, 58
All Student Alliance Party (ASAP), 59

Alley, Patrick, 227
American Colonization Society (ACS), 14–15, 18; white governors of, 19
American South, plantation style, 19
Americo-Liberians ('Congo'), 14, 18, 22, 24; child adoption, 27; fundamentalist Christian, 45; land appropriation/ownership 30, 44; light-skinned, 20; 1960s extravagance, 31–2; one-party autocracy, 43; supremacism of, 21
Amnesty International, TRC findings ignored, 330
amphetamines, child soldiers, 311
amputation, RUF practice, 214, 219
Amputees and War Wounded Association, 337
Angola, slaves from, 22
Animal societies, 53
Annan, Kofi, 223, 225, 269
April 1979 riots, 63
April 1980 coup, 75, 77
Armed Forces of Liberia (AFL), 7, 99, 123, 127, 130, 134, 136, 144, 148–50, 164, 311; Barclays Training Centre, 303; defections 1990, 126; Nimba County massacres, 124, 125, 128; remnants of, 158
Armed Forces Revolutionary Council (AFRC), Freetown, 218, 335, 340
Arthington, Montserrado County, 35–7, 42; Central School, 39, Montserrado

INDEX

County, 35
Ashmun, Jehudi, 18
assimilation, routes to, 27
Association for Constitutional
  Democracy in Liberia, 120
ATU ('Anti-Terrorist Unit'), 250–51, 253,
  348; off-budget funding, 252
Azikiwe, Nnamde, 9, 85, 277–8

Babangida, Ibrahim, 147, 168, 244
Banbatt, UN outpost, 41
Banjul, Gambia, 1990 Agreement/
  Ceasefire, 145–6, 153
Banks, Russell, 310
Baptist Ricks Institute, 39, 42 198
Barclay Training Centre (BTC),
  Monrovia, 77, 105, 108, 149; 1996
  massacre, 174
Barclay, Arthur, 259
Barclay, Edwin, 29, 52
Barlow, Eeben, 212–13
Bassa tribe, 16, 71
battle dresses, bizarre, 54
'Battles of Monrovia', 5
BBC Africa Service, 133, 190, 236, 269;
  Taylor use of, 125, 139
Bédié, Henri Conan, 214, 266
Bennett, George, 236
Benson, Steven Allen, 19, 32
Bentley College, Massachusetts, 65–9
Bentol (Bensonville), 32
Berlin Conference 1884, 195
Bethlehem Steel Corporation, 41
Biafra–Nigeria war, 147
Biddle, Keith, 224
Bishop, James, 93
'Black Diamond', LURD woman
  commander, 324
Black Panthers, USA, 58
Blah, Moses, 277
Blair, Tony, 220, 346
Blyden, Edward Wilmot, 181
Bo, Sierra Leone, 207–8
Bockarie, Sam, 217–18, 227, 344, 345;
  death of, 336
Boley, George, 166, 169, 171, 177, 235, 240
Bomi Hills, 41–2
Bomi, 239; mines, 164, 184
boom times, 1960s, 31
Booth, Donald, 284
Boutros-Ghali, Boutros, 164
'Boys Brigade', 121
Britain: Liberian recognition, 23; navy,
  17; Taylor accused, 344; troops in

Sierra Leone, 224; West African
  colonialism, 23
Brown, Kenneth, 298
Bryant, Gyude, 277, 280–81
Buchanan, Liberia, 130, 133, 140, 154,
  162, 182, 267; Associated Development
  Corporation, 187; ECOMOG capture,
  187, 193; refugees, 275
Bulk Challenge ship, 314–16;
  international indifference symbol, 317
Burkina Faso, 119, 124, 134, 208, 247;
  arms to NPFL, 182; interests of, 146;
  Liberian exiles, 118
bush devils, 49, 53; costumes, 50
Bush, George H.W., 131
Bush, George W., 247, 269, 274–5, 282,
  284, 299, 346
Bush School, 53
'Butt Naked' brigade, 173

Calabar, Taylor exile, 277–8
Camp Carter, massacre, 164
Camp Schefflin, 108; AFL forces, 177
Campbell, Naomi, 340
cane sugar, 37
cannibalism, allegations/rumours of, 52,
  198–201
Cape Montserrado, 16
Cape Mount, 16
Captan, Monie, 240, 262, 306
Carter, Jimmy, 61, 157, 170, 190, 198,
  229, 247, 295; Center, 229; support to
  Taylor, 159
Cassell, Shadrick, 39
Chad, 119, 285, 286
Chamberlayne Junior College, Boston,
  63–5
Charles E. Dewy School, Bomi County,
  40
Chase Manhattan Bank, 178
Chea, David, 273
checkpoint massacres, 138
Chesson, Joseph, 33
chiefs, patronage system/proxy, 44, 57,
  proxies, 44
child soldiers, 211, 310–11, 313, 322, 328;
  'shields', 312
China, 263; Taylor non-recognition, 248
Chissano, Joaquim, 275
Christianity, 50
CIA (US Central Intelligence Agency),
  247, 332; Tolbert abandoned, 61;
  Tolbert overthrow rumours, 76
Cisco, Martha Anne, 38

Citibank, 102, 187, 238
Citizen's Committee for Peace and Democracy, 143
Civilian Defence Forces (CDF), 335, 342
Clark, Ramsey, 101-4, 190, 244
Clark, Reid Page, 23
Clarke, Honerine, 42
Clinton, Bill, 221, 247, 260-61, 304, 306
CNN, 131, 269
Coalition of Progressive Liberians in the Americas, 261
Cohen, Herman J., 93, 289-94
Cold War, Liberian strategic position, 29
commodity prices 1970s fall impact, 34
Compaoré, Blaise, 115, 117-19, 124, 159, 266-7
Comprehensive Peace Agreement 2003, 324, 326
Congo, UN peacekeeping 1963, 203
Conkary, 185
Conneh, Sekou, 264-5
Conte, Lansana, 264
Cook, Robin, 221
Cooper, Helene, 31
corruption, Nigerian-Liberian, 283
Côte d'Ivoire, 121, 146, 186-7, 293; constitutional crisis 2002, 266; invasion from, 123; Liberian refugees, 2, 313, 319; 1991 negotiations, 156; Poro, 49
Cotonou Agreement, Benin, 164, 166
Crane, David, 226, 273, 336, 341
Crocker, Chester, 8, 107
Crown Hill, battle of, 18
Cuba, Tolbert diplomatic relations, 61
cullor speech, 288

Da Cintra, Pedro, 204
Da Silva, Richard, 334
Danane, 121
Davies, Phillip, 85, 277
Davis, Edward, 58
Davis, Elwood, 25
Dawson, Frank, 101
De Vos, Peter Jon, 133
Déby, Idriss, 285
Decree 88A, Doe regime, 105
DeGiacomo, Robert J., 104
Delafosse, Desiree 'Daisy', 89
demobilization, ex-combatants, 323
Dennis, Cecil, 33
development economics, 67
DeVoll, Thomas, 110, 112
Dewoin ethnic group, 35

Dey ethnic group, 16-17
Dhillon, B.S., 102-3
Diallo, Cellou, 281
diamonds, 213, 267; embargo on, 263; global terrorism link, 225-6; Taylor role, 212
Diggs, Rachel, 304, 306, 308; as Ambassador to USA, 242; resignation of, 307
Diouf, Abdou, 299
Doe, Jackson F., 106, 142, 167; death of rumours, 140, 199
Doe, Nancy, 94-5
Doe, Samuel Kanyon, 2, 7-8, 51, 77, 80, 87, 92, 98, 100, 102, 106, 115, 123, 126, 132, 142, 209, 229, 243, 260, 265, 290, 292, 296-7, 304, 320, 323, 326, 331; body of exhibited, 152; Côte d'Ivoire threats, 121; death squads of, 138; disembowelment of, 54; ECOMOG respite, 149; ethnic massacres, 4; Executive Mansion Guard, 129, 144; fantasy world of, 291; Gio marginalized, 97; interrogation/torture of, 151; Israeli commandos, 301; Krahn ascendancy, 81, 91, 95; ministers of, 88; murder of, 162, 298, 330; 1983 coup attempt, 116; 1983 coup revenge, 108; 1985 election, 105, 324; 1990 propaganda, 125; patronage system, 82; PRC chairman, 85; spies in Ghana, 116; Taylor extradition attempt, 103-4; True Whig purge, 89; USA relations/military aid from, 93, 96, 133, 288-9, 295; USA visit, 94
Dogonyoro, General, 154
Dokie, Samuel, 99, 167, 244; assassination of, 251
Doss, Alan, 284
Duopu, Moses, 70, 72, 120, 139; killing of, 167

Easter 1996 uprising, 5
ECOMOG (Economic Community of West African States Monitoring Group), 5, 146, 148, 150, 152-5, 162, 165-6, 173, 176-7, 186, 201, 209, 211, 213, 219-20, 234-5, 240, 244, 293, 298-300, 302, 304, 316, 345; anti-Taylor arming, 160; arms dealing, 344; Gbarnga attack, 168; invasion ('Nigerian') force labelled, 147, 154, 191; looting practices of, 232, 294; Monrovia atrocities, 161; Monrovia

positions, 312; Nigeria cost of, 245; NPFL dealings, 156–7; ostensible neutrality, 149; pro-government character, 157; prostitution link, 322; Sierra Leone presence, 182, 215, 223; support to ULIMO, 158; Taylor dealings, 281; transgressions of, 159; Tubmanburg evacuation, 172
ECOWAS (Economic Community of West African States), 145–6, 148–9, 153, 176, 178, 210, 219, 221, 239, 245, 264, 268, 272, 292, 300, 345; 'Committee of Nine', 235
education, 1970s impact, 56
elite(s): native populations absorption, 26; political, 7
Elizabeth ship, 15, 18
Ellis, Stephen, 199, 294; *Mask of Anarchy*, 198
ELWA (Eternal Love Winning Africa), 137; Taylor announcement, 145
Emmanuel, Burnice, 65–6, 189, 252
ethical boundaries, 195
European Union, 229
executions, Tolbert ministers, 78–9
Executive Mansion, Israeli-built, 144; Israeli-trained guard, 108, 150; ritual purification of, 243
Executive Outcomes, mercenaries, 212–13, 215, 217; cost of, 216
Eyadéma, Gnassingbé, 222, 290

Fahnbulleh Jr, Henry Boima, 80
Fahnbulleh, Boima, 113, 115, 117, 236
Farah, Douglas, 283
Farrow, Mia, 340
FBI, (US Federal Bureau of Investigation), 100
Federation of Liberian Youth (FLY), 59
Fernando Po, Spanish colony, 28
Firestone, Company, 45, 60–61, 302; Harbel rubber plantation, 14, 28, 137, 162, 187, 237; minimum wage, 193
Firestone, Harvey, 28
Firestone, Idabelle, 28
Flynn, Peter, 104, 110–11, 113
forced labour, 24, 28, 44
Forman, Peter, 110
former Yugoslavia, interventions, 295
France, 263; Liberian recognition, 23; Taylor support, 248
Freemasonry, 46–8, 51
Freeport, 149
Friends of Liberia, US, 229

Gaddafi, Muammar, 115, 119, 203, 207, 247
Gambia, 124, 146; MOJA branch, 58
Ganta, 129, 266
Gates, Robert, 292, 299
Gaughan, Joseph P., 305
Gayewea, McIntosh, 156
Gbagbo, Laurent, 266–7, 274
Gbala, Bai, 70–74
Gbandi ethnic people, 27
Gbao, Augustine, 335
Gbarnga, Bong County, 130, 156, 181, 189, 193, 197, 252, 276, 302; declared as capital, 154; NPFL retreat to, 153
Gbatala camp, 252
Gbawu, Dweh, 173
Gbowee, Leymah, 324–5
General Services Agency, 86, 97, 102
Ghailani, Ahmed Khalfan, 226
Ghana, 19, 124, 146, 148, 272–3, 315–16, 341; Liberian refugees, 1–2, 115, 313, 318, 320; MOJA branch, 58; UNHCR camp, 317–18
Gillen, Brian, 111
Gio ethnic group, 71, 96, 124–6; Doe massacres of, 109, 144; revenge of, 132; targeted, 99
Gola ethnic group, 37, 71, 196
Gono, Issa, 253; murder of, 254
Gow, Alvin (Alvin G. Jones), 27
Grand Bassa, 16
Grand Gedeh County, 80, 92; massacres, 132
Grand United Order of Odd Fellows, 197
Greaves, Harry, 261
Greene, Graham, 52–3
Greenstock, Jeremy, 262
Greenville, Liberia, 192
Griffiths, Courtenay, 201, 334, 340–41
Guinea, 5, 99, 124, 146, 160, 206, 238; Conkary, 208; Liberian refugees, 2, 313, 319; LURD support, 265; military, 205; USA military aid, 264

Harbel, rubber plantation, 28
Harper, Liberia, 154, 166, 267
Harris, Paul B., 123
Harris, T.Q., 339
heart eating: allegations of, 200; 'heartmen', 52
Holbrook, Richard, 262
Holder, Edwin, 64, 68
Hollis, Brenda, 167
Holmes Toweh, Lucia, 110, 113
Horton, Francis, 58

Horton, Romeo, 260
Houphouët-Boigny, Félix, 13, 89, 115, 118, 121, 147, 156-7, 222, 266
Howard-Taylor, Jewel, 239, 247, 261, 279-80, 306
Human Rights Watch, 339
Hurst & Co., 199
Hussein, Saddam, 300
Hut tax, 25, 44
Hutchinson, Maureen, 67, 68
Hyman, Lester, 246, 304-5

ICC (International Criminal Court), The Hague, 286; USA non-recognition, 341
Ikimi, Tom, 235
IMF (International Monetary Fund), 242, 249; IGNU suspended, 182
impunity, culture of, 245
Independent Electoral Commission, 239
Independent National Patriotic Front of Liberia (INPFL), 7, 129-30, 135, 138, 148-50, 155, 161-2, 298; Caldwell headquarters, 151; disarmed, 154; Freeport taken, 149; Monrovia presence, 143
indigenous Liberians, pantheist, 54
industrial action, 60
Inter-Faith Mediation Committee, 143
Interim Government of National Unity (IGNU), 5, 133, 146, 155, 164, 185, 188; Black Beret force, 160; official recognition, 182
interior, non-development of, 57
internally displaced people, numbers, 313
International Earthmoving Equipment Inc (IEE), 97-8, 100, 102-3
International Organization for Migration, 175, 230, 314, 319
International Red Cross compound, massacre, 144
International Registries Inc., 246
Internet access, 41
international justice, evolution of, 9
Interpol, 279
Iran, revolution in, 73
Iraq, 276; 1990 invasion of, 288, 300; second war on, 269
Islam, 51
Israel: Doe guard training, 108, 301; Liberia relations re-established, 91

Jackson, Jesse, 170, 198, 221-2, 244, 260-61
Jackson, Mahalia, 170
Jalloh, Agnes, 213
Janneh, Kabinah, 273
Jarbo, William, 76
Johnson, Donald, 140
Johnson, Elijah, 15, 17
Johnson, Elmer, 111, 127; death of, 136, 139
Johnson, Lyndon B., 101
Johnson, Prince, 112, 118-24, 127-8, 133, 142, 148-9, 151-2, 161, 208, 292, 298, 330; Lagos detention, 162; leverage loss, 160; Monrovia evacuation compliance, 293; NPFL defection, 139; parents killed, 129
Johnson, Roosevelt, 5, 160, 171-3, 235, 240, 302-3, 314
Jones, Geneva, 301
Joint Voluntary Association, 314, 319
juju, 243
Julu, Charles 'the Rock', 129
Jumbotown, 16
Juxton-Smith, Andrew, 205

Kabbah, Ahmed Tejan, 215, 217, 220-21, 225, 281, 337, 342; executions by, 219
Kagame, Paul, 6, 274
Kakata Rural Teachers Training Institute, 39
Kallon, Morris, 335
Kalomoh, Tuliameni, 245
Kamajors, fighting group, 215-16, 335
Kerr, John, 221
'Kimberly process', 307
King Jack Benn, 16
King, Charles, 28; impeachment of, 29
KISS-FM radio station, 236
Klay, town, 40
Kollie, Tamba, 27-8
Koroma, Johnny Paul, 218
Kouwenhoeven, Gus, 347
Kpelle ethnic group, 71
Kpolleh, Gabriel: disappearance, 139; killing of, 167
Kpormakor, David, 241
Krahn ethnic group, 27, 92, 96; Liberia Peace Council, 240; massacres of, 138; Nimba County reprisals, 99; revenge on, 132
Krio ethnic group, 23, 205; language, 4; Sierra Leone, 204
Krisan refugee settlement, Ghana, 317
Kromah, Alhaji G.V., 158, 160, 166, 169, 171, 176-7, 236

INDEX   369

Kru ethnic group, 58; 1915 insurrection, 25, 44; warriors, 76
Kufuor, John, 273, 275
Kuhn Loeb & Co, 1912 loan, 23
Kui, 48
Kupolati, Rufus, 154

La Salle Extension University, 42
LAMCO (Liberian American-Swedish Minerals Company), 60, 185
language(s), indigenous, 4, 44
League of Nations, 28
Lebanese Africans, Sierra Leone, 204-6
Leopard societies, 52; men, 53
Liberia: Action Party, 106, 142, 238, 261; administration of interior, 29; apartheid government approach, 34; arms embargo/sanctions, 265, 300, 306; Carter Center, 157; Central Bank, 307; Côte d'Ivoire-Burkina Faso axis, 148; Council of State, 235, 316, 324; diamond suppliers, 188; 1845 Constitution, 19; France support, 247; Frontier Force, 25, 28, 44, 194; General Receiver of Customs, 23; government monopolies, 250; HIV/AIDS, 321; languages, 4, 44; Mining Company strike, 59-60; Ministry of Finance, 97; National Bank of, 172; national debt, 249; National Transitional Legislative Assembly, 327; Nigerian presence, 186; 1997 elections, 229; 1985 coup failure, 109; 1985 elections, 106; non-colonized, 14; Presidential Banking Commission, 260; republic foundation, 1847, 21, 43; revisionist history, 21; sanctions on, 199, 267-9; Supreme Court, 338; Truth and Reconciliation Commission, *see below*; 2003 ceasefire, 266; UN peacekeepers, 284; Unification Party, 139, 238; USA Cold War ally, 288; USA non-interventions, 292-5; youth demographics, 322
Liberian Bank for Development and Investment (LBDI), 347
Liberian Broadcasting System (LBS), 108
Liberian Children's Assistance Programme, 312
Liberian Community Association of Massachusetts, 67
Liberian Council of Churches, 143
Liberian diaspora, USA, 69, 131

Liberian International Ship and Corporate Registry, 246
Liberian Maritime Agency, 237, 246, 268
Liberian Mining Corporation, 185
Liberian National Muslim Council, 143
Liberian National Students Union (LINSU), 143
Liberian National Transitional Government (LNTG), 164, 167, 171, 173
Liberian People's Party, 238
Liberian Truth and Reconciliation Commission, 112, 227
Liberian-American-Swedish Minerals Company (LAMCO), 184
Liberians for Reconciliation and Democracy (LURD), 5, 134, 264-5, 267, 270, 272-3, 277, 307, 323, 325
Liberian United Defence Force (LUDF), 158
Liberty Mutual Insurance Company, 68
'Liberty' dollar, 185
Libya: Tolbert diplomatic relations, 61; training camps, 115, 121, 203, 207
Libyan People's Bureau, Doe closure, 91
lightning societies, 52
Limba ethnic group, Sierra Leone, 205
Lincoln, Abraham, 22
local chiefs, Americo-Liberian dependent, 24-5, 27, 29
Lofa County, 27-8, 37, 265; Defence Council, 240; Defence Force, 166
Loma tribe, 71
Lomé Agreement 1991, 153
Lomé Peace Agreement 1999, 222-3
'looting rights', combatant groups, 7
Lumumba, Patrice, murder of, 203-4
Lungi Airport, Freetown, 157, 176, 209, 211
Lussick, Richard, 332, 335
Lutheran Overseas Mission to Liberia, 37

Maada-Bio, Julius, 213-15
Mahbubani, Kishore, 268
Mali, 263
Malu, Samuel Victor, 161-2, 201, 234-5
Mambe tribe, 16
Mambo, Guilherme, 175
Mandela, Nelson, 340
Mandingo, ethnic group, 215; NPFL massacres, 138; revenge on, 132
Mano ethnic group, 71, 96, 124-6; Doe massacres of, 109, 144; targeted, 99
Mano River Union, 260, 262, 281

Mao Tse-tung, 206
Maputo, 275
Margai, Albert, 205
Margai, Milton, 205
Marzah, Joseph 'Zigzag', 201
masks: civil war use, 54; coup soldiers use, 76
Massaquoi, Francois, 166, 240
Matthews, Gabriel Baccus, 58, 62-3, 80
Mbeki, Thabo, 275
McCarthy, Charles, 15
Mende ethnic group, Sierra Leone, 204
Milam, William, 302
Mills, Lady Dorothy, 53
Millsburg, 37
Mitterrand, Jean-Christophe, 187
Mohammed, Fazhl Abdullah, 226
Momoh, Joseph, 107, 157, 203, 208-9, 211; UK non-backing, 210
Momolu, Clarence, 89, 97-8
Moniba, Harry, 106, 108, 236, 291
Monroe, James, 18
Monrovia, 5, 18, 26, 43, 51, 58, 66; ECOMOG atrocities, 161; first battle of, 141; INPFL appearance, 143; interior resentment of, 44; international aid community, 174; Ivorian embassy, 89; low taxed, 25; ULIMO proximity, 159; US embassy, 176, 302
Morris, John L., 23
Movement for Democracy in Liberia (MODEL), 267, 273
Movement for the Redemption of Liberian Muslims, 158
Mozambique, slaves from, 22
Mugabe, Robert, 274-5
Mulbah, Joe, 190
Muslims, Mandingo, 160
Museveni, Yoweri, 6, 274

Nagbe, Loretta, 276
National Democratic Party of Liberia, (LPC), 162, 166, 169, 171, 174, 235, 276; 1997 election win, 228
National Patriotic Front of Liberia (NPFL), 4-6, 112, 118-22, 126-7, 129, 130-31, 133, 149, 155, 157, 165, 207, 234, 242, 249, 251, 290-91, 294, 296, 298-9, 301-2, 310, 312, 331, 342; anti-media, 190; arms to, 134; atrocities, 136; command structure, 332; composition change, 128; control tactics, 194; defections, 168; ECOWAS peace plan opposition, 145; Firestone revenues, 188; France support, 186; 'Greater Liberia' territory, 183; hard currency access, 181; hardwood exports, 187; Libyan training and arms, 115, 120, 182; massacres by, 132 1989 invasion, 123, 125; 1997 arms cache, 232; 'Operation Octopus, 161; 'Operation Pay Yourself' character, 173, 177; 'peace plan', 156; PR spin, 138; public support, 139; RUF allies, 158; 'right to loot', 195; Sirleaf backing, 326; Special Forces Commandos, 192; territory loss, 162; wartime rituals, 54
National Patriotic Party (NPP), 234, 239
National Patriotic Reconstruction Assembly Government (NPRAG), 145, 154, 186, 196; debt non-responsibility, 182; Gbarnga, 181; Greater Liberia, 19
Nautilus ship, 16
Nelson, Blamo, 72, 74, 87
New Democratic Party, 236
New York Times, 31
Newport, Matilda Day, story of, 17-18, 21
NGOs, looted, 174
Nigeria, 5, 148, 177, 211; *Bulk Challenge* to, 315; equipment to, 193; independence of, 278; interests of, 145-6; loot to, 189; 1993 political crisis, 168; NPFL attacks, 300; Taylor mistrust, 299
Nimba County, 4, 66, 123, 124, 140, 239, 290, 298, 330; AFL massacres, 126; Doe reprisals, 99, looting, 128
Nimba Mining Company (NIMCO), Yekepa, 184-5
Nimely, General Thomas, 150, 267
Nixon, Richard, 296
Norman, Hinga, 215, 342
Ntube, Dominic, 301

Ouagadougou, Burkina Faso, 117
Obasanjo, Olusegun, 223, 274, 281, 283-4; USA visit, 285
Odumegwu-Ojukwu, General, Côte d'Ivoire asylum, 147
oil crisis 1970s, consequences, 34
Olurin, General, 161
Omega navigational/transmission station, USA access, 30, 90
'Operation Octopus', 5, 161, 188, 301, 312
Organization of African Unity (OAU), 62, 165, 219, 221, 229, 264, 268; Durban summit, 2002, 306

Ouagadougou, 120
Outtara, Mamouna, 117

Paasewe, Sylvester, 284
Pacific Architects and Engineers (PAE), 177, 191
Pakbatt, UN outpost, 41
Palmer, Philip, 217
Pan-Africanist Movement for Justice in Africa (MOJA), 58-9, 81, 115-16, 146
Parker, Clarence, 33
Parrot's Beak region, Guinea, 264
The Patriot, 190
Paul, R.A., 284
Payne, Anne, 110, 114
Payne, Donald, 260, 308
Peace Corps, 288
Penfold, Peter, 221, 227
Pennue, Harrison, 77
People's Progressive Party, 58
People's Redemption Council (PRC), 77-8, 80, 85-6, 97; cabinet, 95; pro-USA policy, 81
Pepper Coast (Liberia), 19, 30
Perry, Ruth Sando, 178, 235, 324
Phillips, James T., 33
Pickering, Thomas, 261
pidgin English, 44
Pleebo, rubber plantation, 28
Plymouth correctional facility, 104
Plymouth House of Corrections, 102
Poro societies, 48-51, 196-7, 201; masks use, 50
Porte, Albert, 58
Press Union of Liberia (PUL), 143
Progressive Alliance of Liberia (PAL), 58, 62, 80-81
Providence Island, 16
Provisional National Defence Council, Ghana, 115-16

Quainoo, General Arnold, 146, 149-51, 154
Quiwonkpa, Thomas, 4, 75-8, 80-81, 85-6, 88-9, 96, 97-8, 103, 107; attempted coup, 116; dismemberment of, 108-9; escape to USA, 99-100

Radio Hirondelle, 236
Radio Liberia International, 236
rape, 321, 323
Rapid Deployment Force, USA, 61
Rapp, Stephen, 340
Rawlings, Jerry, 115-18, 121, 177, 248, 298, 315-16

Reagan, Ronald, 8, 93-4, 96, 107, 119, 247, 296; Liberia aid policy, 90
Redemption Hospital, killings at, 272
Reeves, Agnes, 101, 113-14, 117
Reffel, Victoria, 235
refugees: 'decadence' opportunity, 3; internal, 275; 1997 repatriation, 230
regional antagonisms, 197
religious assimilation, 26
remittances, for refugees, 318
'reverse adult syndrome', 321, 323
'reverse gender syndrome', 323
Revolutionary Patriotic Front, Rwanda, 6
Revolutionary United Front (RUF) Sierra Leone, 154, 157, 203, 207-8, 263, 269, 335, 340; AFRC alliance defeat, 218; amputation practice, 214; arming of, 343; Guinea border attack, 264; NPFL support, 209; Party, 225; resources control, 212; Taylor involvement, 225, 261, 267
rice: riots, 75; tax, 61; tax reversed, 63
Robertsfield Airport, 98, 134, 136, 154, 182, 277, 286; Taylor ousted from, 162; USA strategic base, 30, 90; USA access denied, 61
Roberts, Joseph Jenkins, 19-20
Robertson, Pat, 198
Robertsport, 208
Robinson Jr, Leonard H., 153
Roosevelt, Theodore, 23
Rostow, W.W., 67
Roye, Edward J., 20, 47
rubber: 1970s price fall, 61; plantations, 13-14, 28, 44
Romania, arms to Doe, 290
Russia, 263
Rwanda: civil war, 6; RPF, 7; UN Arusha trials, 335; UN retreat from, 293

Samuel Kanyon Doe sports stadium, refugees in, 272
San Pedro, 121, 186, 192, 315
Sande societies, 48, 51, 178
Sandline affair, 221, 227
Sankara, Thomas, 117; assassination of, 118-19, Thomas, 117
Sankawulo, Wilton, 169, 228
Sankoh, Foday, 115, 203, 207-8, 210, 213-16, 218, 221, 260, 335, 344; Commission for the Management of Strategic Resources, 222; death of,

336; diamond business, 223; Freetown imprisonment, 206; Nigeria detention, 217; NPFL support, 209; Sierra Leone imprisoned, 224
Savimbi, Jonas, 188
Sawyer, Amos, 23, 33, 58, 81, 92, 104-5, 120, 146, 153, 155, 159, 182, 185, 212, 241, 323
Schulz, George, 93
Scott, Eric, 113
Scott, Gloria, 199
secret societies, 45, 48, 51
Sekou Touré, Ahmed, 206
Senegal, 299
Sesay, Issa Hassan, 207, 225, 335, 344-5
SGBCI Bank, 187
Sherbro Island, 15
Sierra Leone, 15, 17, 22, 107, 124, 132, 148, 238, 344; All People's Congress (APC), 205; Army, 205, 215-16; civil war, 3, 202, 209; coastal elite, 203; corruption, 206; diamonds, 188; ECOMOG base, 182; Freetown, 15, 108, 143; January 1999 massacres, 220; Krio settlers, 23; Liberian Muslim groups, 158; Liberian refugees, 1-2; LURD support, 265; natural wealth of, 204; Nigerian intervention force, 211 1992 coup, 210; 1996 election, 214-15; 1997 coup, 218; People's party, 215; Police Special Branch, 252; Poro, 49; RUF, *see above*; Special Court for, *see below*; Taylor arms shipment link, 347; Truth and Reconciliation Commission, 223; UK intervention, 219; UN arms embargo, 221
Sinoe County, 25, 33
Sirleaf, Ellen Johnson, 106, 120, 140, 142, 146, 229, 237-8, 242, 249-50, 261, 281-4, 326, 327, 338; arrest of, 105; public apology, 331; Taylor support, 332; TRC condemned, 329; US funding of, 255
Slanger, Tia, 273
slavery, 9; Slave Trade Act 1807, 22
Smillie, Ian, 345
'Sobels', 212
Sollac corporation, NIMCO project, 186
Somalia, USA debacle, 293
Soussoudis, Michael, 116
South African Defence Force, mercenaries from, 212
Special Court for Sierra Leone, The Hague, 9, 76, 112, 114, 167, 200, 223, 225, 241, 255, 270, 273-4, 279, 334, 336, 342; costs of, 349
Special Security Services, 251-2
spiritual-religious life, native Liberians, 45, 48
Spriggs-Payne Airport, 144
St Peter's Lutheran Church, massacre, 144
Star Radio, 236
Stevens, Siaka Probyn, 107, 203, 205-6, 211
Strasser, Valentine, 210, 212-13; Nigeria appeal, 211
student protest 1984, 104
Student Unification Party for Free and Fair Elections, 59
Supuwood, Laveli, 167
Susu Kuu movement, 93
Swing, William L., 93

Taiwan, 348; Liberian recognition of, 239, 248
Tanzanian troops, 165
Tarnue secret society, 51
Taylor, Charles McArthur Ghankay ('Dakhpannah'), 1-2, 4-10, 32-7, 41, 55, 63, 65, 67, 72, 74, 79-81, 126, 176, 220; Abacha relationship, 168; admiration for USA, 296; adoption of, 38; Agnes Reeves marriage, 117; Allie Kabbah meeting, 208; assets freeze, 279; BBC use, 130, 134; Calabar exile and disappearance, 278, 284; cannibalism accusation, 201; child fighters, 313; Christian credentials, 198; CIA connection rumours, 298; clothes, 94; communications machine/PR, 131, 190; Council of State, 169; degree, 68; Delafosse rescuer, 90; diamonds export involvement, 212, 261-2; Doe adviser role, 77; 'dual-fiscal' system, 250; ECOMOG dealings, 281; ECOMOG invasion force label, 191; Elmer Johnson rumours, 136; ELWA announcement, 145; Gbarnga headquarters, 195; Ghana arrests, 116, 121; GSA procurement chief, 86-9; GSA demotion, 97; Heindi market massacre, 164; ICC court, 337-43; inauguration of, 244-5; international corporations deals, 185; international prosecution motives, 337; Jesse Jackson relations, 260; Jewel Howard

marriage, 239; Jimmy Carter support, 159; libel case, 199-200; Liberia escape 1983, 98-100; Libya training/visits, 120, 247; marriages, 66, 239, 280; minimum wage establishment, 193; Ministry of Finance job, 42; mistakes of, 300; mistrust of Nigeria, 299; Monrovia entry delays, 142; Monrovia evacuation compliance, 293; native society recognition need, 196; natural constituency lack, 71; Nigeria arrest of, 285-6; Nigeria asylum offer, 274; Nigerian hostility to, 316; 1997 election victory, 228, 230-40; NPFL-CRC expulsion, 167; peace deal refusals, 155; personal security force, 251; Poro society membership, 51; Prince Johnson relations, 129, 161; pseudonyms, 119; Quiwonkpa ally, 85; reconciliation rhetoric, 241; resignation, 276-7; Ricks Institute expulsion, 39; RUF links, 225, 342; Sierra Leone involvement, 3, 202, 209, 249; 'Small Boys Unit', 312; Special Court defence and defiance, 335, 349; Tapeta press conference 1990, 296; Teah threat to, 139; terrorist harbouring allegation, 226; travel ban on, 264; trial testimony, 76; ULAA opponents, 70; US allies, 114; USA arrest, 73, 101-2; USA extradition hearing, 103-4; USA part-time work, 64; USA prison escape, 109-13, 304-5; USA relations, 135, 255 , 259, 282, 289, 297, 301, 308; USA satellite technology, 131; USA spy rumour, 302
Taylor, Bob, 187
Taylor, Chuckie, 65, 189, 250, 252; torture by, 253; US imprisonment, 254
Taylor, Desiree, 284
Taylor, Louise Yassa Zoe, 37-8
Taylor, Nielsen Philip, 37-8, 144
Taylor, Tupee (*née* Enid Bokai), 98, 101, 110, 113, 117
Teah, Cooper, 139
Temne ethnic group, Sierra Leone, 204-5
Thomson, Sellee, 150
Times, The, 199
Tipoteh, Togba-Nah, 56, 58-9, 80, 92-3, 238
Toe, Nelson B., 77
Togo, 290
Tolbert, Adolphus Benedict, 89; execution of, 147
Tolbert, William, 13-14, 27, 32-4, 42, 48, 62, 60, 67, 69, 73, 75, 78-9, 82, 85, 87, 91-2, 105, 147, 184, 243, 248; disembowelment, 77; overthrow rumours, 76; personal wealth visibility, 57; Poro society role, 51; reform attempts, 56, 59, 74; UN address, 72
Tolbert, Frank, 78
Tolbert, Stephen, 33, 42, 58
Tolbert, Victoria, 58, 75-6
Townsend, Reginald, 33
'tribes', 47
True Whig Party, 4, 24, 27-8, 47, 57-8, 71, 109, 121, 236, 238; oligarchy, 14, 29, 33, oligarchy, hardliners, 33
Truth and Reconciliation Commission, Liberia, 112, 119, 127, 134, 326-7, 337; commissioners threatened, 331; elite disowned, 332; final report, 328; final report non-implemented, 330, 339; prosecution list, 329
Tsikata, Kojo, 116
Tubman, William Vancarat Shadrach, 14-15, 32-3, 57, 82, 184; death of, 13
Tubmanburg, 40, 265

Uganda: National Resistance Movement, 6; troops, 165
Union of Liberian Associations in the Americas (ULAA), 70-74, 80, 87, 101, 105, 120, 139; Liberia returnees, 81, 85; New York protest, 73
United Liberation Movement for Democracy in Liberia (ULIMO), 69, 158-9, 162, 165, 207, 310, 312; ULIMO-J, 171-2, 174, 235, 240, 303; ULIMO-K, 166, 169, 171
UN (United Nations), 186, 264; Chapter VII, 282; Development Programme, 238; 'food for refugee sex', 322; Freetown compound, 334; Gio/Mano compound massacre, 135; High Commission for Refugees, 230, 313-14, 317-19; hostage crisis 2000, 345; IGNU suspended, 182; illegal diamonds export, 262; Liberia exported diamonds embargo, 263; Mission in Liberia (UNIMIL, ex-UNOMIL), 41, 165, 323; Mission in Sierra Leone (UNAMSIL), 222-4, 268, 337; Observer Mission (UNOMIL), 165; Panel of Experts 200 report, 345;

Sanctions Committee, 347; Security Council invasion of Kuwait votes, 293; Security Council resolution 1408, 268; Special Court, *see above*; Taylor courtroom attack on, 346; UNICEF, 310, 312
UNITA, Angola, 90, 188
Unity Party, 229, 236, 239
University of Liberia, 33-4, 58, 81, 104, 243; April 1979 demonstration, 62-3
USA (United States of America), 4; Cold War foreign policy, 7; Congressional Black Caucus, 260; Congress, 308; Doe military aid/backing, 82, 109; Doe temporary military aid suspension, 105, 290; dollar currency, 14, 30, 183; 1819 Congressional Act, 15; US embassy, 72-3, 175; US embassy shooting incident 1998, 304; General Services Administration, 86; Ghana 'spyswap', 116; ICC non-recognition, 341; Liberia non-intervention 1990s, 8, 142; Liberia 1985 election approved, 107; Liberia military aid, 29, 92; Liberia original non-recognition, 22; Liberian admiration for, 288; Liberian exiles in, 313; Liberian military stations, 30; Liberian policy, 69, 191; Liberian view of, 287; National Security Council, 93, 262, 292, 299; Obasanjo visit, 285; post-Cold War policy, 297; PRC military aid, 91; pressure on Nigeria, 284; refugee resettlement, 314, 320; Roosevelt Johnson support, 177; Sirleaf favouring, 237; Special Court funding, 349; State Department, 131, 289, 293, 301, 305, 314; Taylor admiration for, 296; Taylor relations, 248, 255, 259; Tolbert alienated, 61
USS *Kearsarge*, 274

Varney, Samuel, 161
Verdier, Jerome, 327, 338-9
Voice of America: Liberian transmitter, 30; Taylor use of, 133
voting eligibility, 33

warlords, modern-day, 55
Washington, Massa, 331-2
Weah, George, 326
West Africa: francophone influence, 23, 247; peacekeeping forces, 5; pidgin Liberian, 4
West Africa magazine, 302
West Side Boys, 224
WikiLeaks, 349
Woewiyu, Tom, 72, 120, 142, 147, 156, 167, 240-41, 290-91, 331
women: fighting roles, 323; rights, 32
Women of Liberia Mass Action for Peace, 324
World Bank, 105, 238, 242, 249
World Baptist Alliance, 51
'World War Three', 5
Wylie, Joe, 325

Yamoussoukro agreements, 153, 156, 159, 214, 299
Yeaten, Benjamin, 244, 251
Yekepa raid, 99
Yonbon, Tailey, 144
Youlo, General Armah, 172-3
Yuen, Harry, 120

Zigita town, 52
Zimbabwe, 275
Zowolo, Poro degree, 35